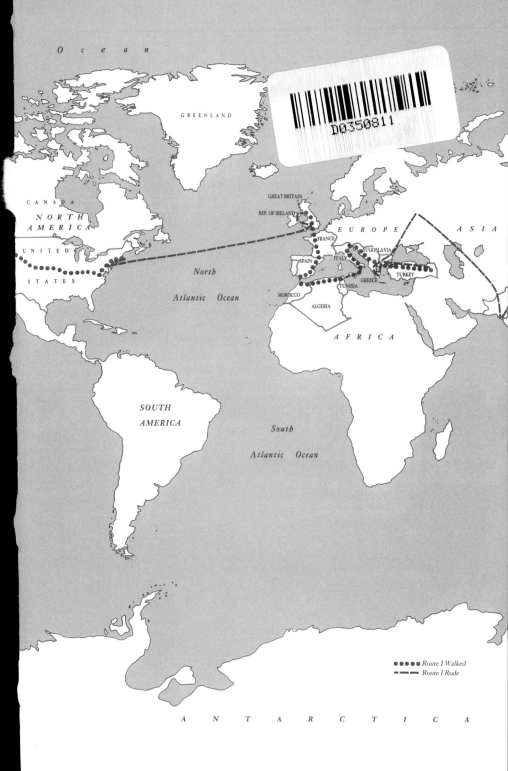

O c e a n

GREENLAND

D0350811

CANADA
NORTH
AMERICA
UNITED
STATES

GREAT BRITAIN
REP. OF IRELAND
EUROPE   ASIA
FRANCE
YUGOSLAVIA
SPAIN   ITALY
GREECE   TURKEY
TUNISIA
MOROCCO
ALGERIA

North

Atlantic   Ocean

AFRICA

SOUTH
AMERICA

South

Atlantic   Ocean

●●●●● Route I Walked
― ― ― Route I Rode

A   N   T   A   R   C   T   I   C   A

WORLDWALK

STEVEN M. NEWMAN

WORLDWALK

William Morrow and Company, Inc.
New York

To Mom and Dad,
who sent me on my journey with their blessings,
and
To all who saw me safely back to home

Acknowledgments

To all those individuals and families who shared their homes, their food, their warmth, and their dreams with me, I owe my everlasting gratitude. I wish there were room to list each and every one of these people, whom I shall never forget.

Also occupying a very special place in my heart is an extremely talented lady in New York City named Jeanne Bernkopf. She is truly a delightful editor. It is because of her patience, her expertise, and her great love for exploring the world that this book is so much fun to read. She was the perfect companion and guide as I mentally relived the worldwalk.

Deserving of credit, too, are the newspaper editors at *Capper's* and the *Columbus* (Ohio) *Dispatch*, especially Dorothy Harvey, Gary Kiefer, Frank Hinchey, and T. R. Fitchko. They had enough foresight from the very start to believe that in the ordinary people of the world I would find a story their readers would look forward to knowing more about each week.

Finally, there were those whose moral support was so crucial during the year it took me to write this book. They included: my mom, Mary, and her reminders that I had to eat to stay alive; my sister Sandy, who transcribed enough taped conversations to drive anyone insane; my brother Elliot, who jotted down innumerable phone messages; my friends Bob Hollenbaugh in Poway, California, and Mike Brooks in Nelsonville, Ohio, who were always willing to listen to my concerns despite their own heavy workloads; Rebecca Neu, who let me retreat with my word processor to her big old house in Georgetown, Ohio, when things became too hectic in Bethel. And, the dearest of all, Suzi, the beautiful young schoolteacher whom I was able to see so few times that year that I still marvel she said *yes* when I asked her to marry me.

WORLDWALK

1

The door stood at the end of the hall-way like a tall and powerful black sentinel. *Open me, step through to the other side, and you shall never know peace again,* it seemed to be saying.

Still . . . I knew I had no choice.

I pursed my lips, brushed a jacket sleeve across my eyes, and prayed. *Lord, please, don't let this be our last good-bye. Please, watch over him and let him still be here when I return. . . . He's so weak, and I love him so much.*

My father's heart and lungs were failing, my mother had revealed to me only hours before, in the curtained dawn of my bedroom. She had begged me to assure him I was not going off to perish.

Very slowly on this gray and bitterly cold April Fool's morning, I coaxed my lungs into tasting a full breath, as I prepared to say good-bye. Would my father give me his blessing, or ask me at this last minute not to go?

Except for one son who had died in infancy, all six of my father's children had grown up as his treasures. And now that he had been bedridden for two years with a weak heart and emphysema, we and our mother, always in her rocking chair in a corner of his room, had become his whole world. But the nest was breaking up; his twenty-eight-year-old son was going off to possible tragedy in a desert or jungle.

I had told him of my plans four months ago—had returned home from the snow-covered peaks of Wyoming to confess to a journey that I knew would only make his heart weaker. Behind that same door he had sat up in his bed, and Mom in her chair, as I pointed to a large map of the world I'd pinned to the closet door and revealed the meaning of the thick dotted line drawn across its colorful seas and continents. Trying to disguise my nervousness, I had revealed for the first time to my family what I had found hard to say even to myself:

"On the first of April, 1983, I will step out the front door to start a journey never before made by anyone. I've spent many years preparing. I won't fail. And"—I looked at my father's sad eyes—"I won't die. Please believe in me. What I am going to try to do is walk around the world . . . alone."

My mother had gasped, slammed her hands down upon her chair's spindly armrests, and glared at me. "Oh, no, you won't! You'll never live! There're too many bad people out there who'll try to rob and murder you. You *can't* be serious."

Dad had simply lowered his head and shaken it slowly back and forth. In his silence I thought I heard the one implication I dreaded more than anything: that I was a fool.

Determinedly, I had said, "This walk is something I *must* do if I am ever to get a true sense of what the world and its peoples are like.

"I want to do this not just as a learning experience, to find out what all those other people's dreams and hopes and fears are, but also as a test to see if the world is still a place where love and compassion prevail. And a place where romance and adventure abound as much as they did in the days of Marco Polo and Sir Francis Drake.

"I want to do it alone, without sponsors, so that I can have total freedom to do anything and go anywhere I want to, when I want to. Except for a librarian or two who've helped me find the right maps, I've done everything alone on this project. I've done it because I want to show others, particularly the young, that an individual *can* realize his or her dreams without outside resources.

"I will have only a backpack to carry my supplies, so that I will have to depend upon the generosity of others to help feed and shelter me. Hopefully, that will get me into many homes, so I can see what their everyday life is like."

"And you think that people will come running out to the road to invite a total stranger into their house?" Mom had asked.

"Well, that's what I'm hoping. Because if they don't, I'll probably never last. You see, I've set two conditions for myself: never to pay for any accommodations, except if my health is in jeopardy or I am way behind on my writing and need privacy, and never to eat in any restaurants fancier than a sidewalk café or a teahouse."

"But you've never been outside of America, Steve. What do you know about these other places?" Dad had asked.

The truth was that I knew very little about most of the countries I planned to visit; only what I'd read in my schoolbooks, or seen on television and in newspapers, or found in the travel booklets sent to me by their embassies. And that was exactly what I had planned.

"As much as possible, I want what I encounter in each country to be a surprise—from, say, what they eat to even what language they speak. Then, every day there will be something new for me to learn, and my mind will remain curious."

I sat on the edge of Dad's bed.

"How long will all this take?" Dad had asked with his eyes averted.

I fidgeted and rose to the map, as if I needed that space between us to be able to answer.

"Three to five years . . . I figure I have fifteen thousand to twenty thousand miles to walk."

I started tracing with my finger the dotted line I'd drawn across the map.

"My plan is to walk from here to Washington, D.C., then north along the Atlantic Coast through the major cities such as Philadelphia, Baltimore, and New York, to Boston."

The slap of a palm against the rocking chair behind me made me cringe; Mom had grown up in the New York City area and had told me over the years about its high crime rate and violence.

"From there I will fly to Ireland and walk north from Dublin to Belfast, where I will take a ferryboat east to southwestern Scotland. There I will go only far enough to cross into England. Which I will then walk the whole length of, from just north of Carlisle to Portsmouth."

I started to glance back at Mom, hoping that she had softened somewhat at the mention of Ireland. But my eye got only as far as the front tips of her chair's rockers, which were going up and down as rapidly as if in an earthquake.

Almost timidly I threw in, "I thought it might be nice to start the foreign part of my journey in the countries where our families came from . . . and where it's supposed to be very safe."

Then, after a deep breath:

"I will cross the English Channel by ship to the north coast of France and then continue south to Spain, where I will use the Spanish I learned in high school and college. I am curious to see if Spaniards are as moody and passionate as they are portrayed in novels."

I took a deeper breath still, painfully aware that what I had to say next would sound suicidal to my parents—especially to Mom, who thought Islam was practically the same as Satanism.

"Because there is so much in the news nowadays about the violent anti-Americanism in the Arab countries, I plan to go from Spain to North Africa, to find out why so many Moslems feel antagonistic to us."

Creak-creak creak-creak creak-creak . . . Mom's chair sounded as if it would fly out the window. Quickly—very quickly—I continued:

"I'm hoping I will be permitted to walk east at least across Morocco, Algeria, and Tunisia. Since I probably will not be allowed to go into Libya —I'll find out for sure in March, when I go to Washington, D.C.—my idea is to go directly north from Tunisia by boat to Sicily, to walk north through all of Italy, then south through Yugoslavia to Greece.

"In Greece, I have two options: head south to Athens, where I can board a boat to Egypt, to walk across it and Saudi Arabia; or head east to Turkey. Either way, I am sure I will have to travel by plane or boat around the wars in Iran and Afghanistan."

My finger had jumped to the far right side of the map.

"At any rate, the second half of the journey will take me through Pakistan and India and Southeast Asia, because I want to see if those areas are as impoverished as they seem on television. And to Thailand and Malaysia to meet the Buddhist monks and pirates I've heard so much about.

"Of course I will go to Australia. I hope to cross the outback through its most sparsely populated region—the vast, rugged deserts between the north and south coasts.

"Finally, I will return, most likely by plane, to North America, probably to San Francisco, and then cross the heartland of my own country. And back to you."

There were several seconds of silence. At last Dad asked softly, "Wouldn't it be quicker, and safer, if you went in a straight line across Europe and Asia, rather than swinging down through places like Africa and Thailand?"

"Yes," I conceded, "but this may be the only chance I have to see the world so completely and closely. I want to touch base with as many cultures as I can. And"—I glanced at my mother—"that means exploring both the safe and the supposedly dangerous countries, because otherwise I won't come away with an accurate picture of mankind."

I sat on a corner of the bed and faced both my parents. "Please try to understand. I'm tired of all the pessimism from the media and the ministers and even my friends about the future and condition of the world. I have to go out to see once and for all, while I'm young and able to, if all those who are condemning this world are right.

"Maybe I'm crazy, but I truly believe this is a far better place than we give it credit for. But how can I know for sure?"

Dad had nodded, as if he was beginning to understand. Mom continued to frown, and fire still flashed in her eyes. I knew better than to argue with her; she could be extremely stubborn at times. But then, so could I. It was a trait I had inherited from Mom and her Irish grandparents.

I had put off telling my parents about the worldwalk out of fear that Mom would think I was just chasing my dreams.

My independence had always meant more to me than anything. Exploration and adventure had been paramount in my life. In my last two summers in high school, I had hitchhiked on my own all over the United States. That my worried parents had forbidden me to do such a thing had not deterred me in the least.

Graduation in 1972 from Bethel-Tate High School had meant I had less time than ever to spend with my parents and siblings. For the next five years I was away studying journalism at Ohio University and prospecting for uranium in Wyoming. Then, in 1977, I had taken a reporter's job with the *Casper Star-Tribune* in Casper, Wyoming. And in Casper I had remained, with no more trips home until this past December, when I had returned to reveal in this bedroom plans for one more lengthy adventure —one that could mean good-bye forever.

I had spent every evening possible since my December return with Dad in his bedroom. He had listened, fascinated, to my stories about the four-and-a-half years I'd spent preparing for the worldwalk. With such a large family to raise, neither Dad nor Mom had ever had the luxury of freedom to travel. Besides, all his life Dad had had a bad heart. But he had reveled in my descriptions of the rugged scenery and men I had worked with for three-and-a-half years on the oil rigs in the West to save the twenty thousand dollars I figured the worldwalk would cost me. And of how I spent another year toughening myself physically and mentally by camping, hiking, and running alone in the snows of Montana's mountain peaks and the enormous dunes of Wyoming's harsh and empty Red Desert.

Dad's enthusiasm for my journey had seemed to grow with each visit I made to his bedside. He had ideas about how to get my money and mail to me. And suggestions about the routes I was planning to take.

He liked my plan to follow the quieter, less-populated secondary roads. But he worried that such roads might not be as well marked as they were on my maps. Wouldn't that slow me down, or even get me lost?

I almost let slip that I did not want to hurry through this journey, that I planned to be flexible enough to depend upon the locals to tell me the most interesting way to the next province or country. And that even though I had a general idea of which roads I was going to take across each country, I was actually willing to start over from scratch upon crossing a border, so as not to miss out on those little lanes and paths that might be more scenic and adventurous than the lines on my map.

But I knew that was not what Dad wanted to hear. Not when time was so precious to him, and not to be taken for granted. So, instead, I had pretended that I knew exactly where I was going to walk in each place. And that each route was the quickest and safest one possible.

To my surprise, Dad's health had seemed to improve along with his interest. Sitting there on his bed reading aloud the brochures sent to me by the embassies, or discussing the pros and cons of the advanced hiking gear I had ordered at cost from Jan-Sport in Washington State and the William Brooks Shoe Company in Ohio, he had hardly needed the tall oxygen tank beside his headboard.

Just three weeks earlier, when I had returned from the trip to Washington, D.C., he had hung onto my account of my experiences there as if I had gone to see the president.

Though he was unable to leave his bedroom, Dad's interest in the outside world had not dimmed any. He still ran the family's nursing home on the other side of town by telephone, read thoroughly each of the Cincinnati dailies, and, every evening, right at six-thirty when the CBS evening news came on, paused from his paperwork to listen to all the major news stories of that day—stories about wars in the Middle East, Central America, and the Falkland Islands; huge antinuclear protests all over Europe; Americans being kidnapped and killed in Lebanon by Arab terrorists. I had enjoyed watching the news with him, as well as discussing the major stories from abroad. I had never told him how concerned I was that I might not make it unharmed through those dangers.

Now, I forced my hand to turn the door handle.

He was seated on the far side of the big old double bed, his bent back facing me. I quietly closed the door behind me. In a tall dresser mirror on my right, I met his light green eyes with my own blue ones.

He was the first to try to speak. "All ready to go?"

I shrugged. "I suppose . . . so . . ."

Since I am over 6'2" and had strapped to my back an enormous expedition pack that had a sleeping bag and a tent lashed to its top frame, I easily dwarfed everything inside the room. Yet my reflection in the mirror did not seem very large to me at all that morning.

Dad gave the mattress a good push with his thin arms, stood unsteadily, and looked at me—still through the mirror. Outside, the barren branches of the giant sycamore in the side yard slapped together briefly in another gust from the dying winter. Wordlessly, our images—one tall, the other bent—moved from the looking glass. We met at the end of the bed, beside the curtained windows overlooking the property Dad had finally come to own in his last years.

With a hand that looked almost translucent in the morning glow, he held out to me a small, flat card. I took it and read slowly to myself the long row of numbers written on it. It was an international telephone credit-card number of some sort. I looked up, surprised, since no one in our family had ever been outside of the United States.

"I thought you could use this," he said softly. "I had to get it in my name, but I wanted to make sure you could reach your mother and me whenever you needed our help—or just wanted to talk."

He squeezed my shoulder. "Please never hesitate to call home. We are here to help you. Your mother and I want so much to know how you are. We want to hear from you. After all, you—"

Almost before I knew what was happening, he was reaching for me with both of his arms. I had to grab him to steady him. At my touch, he sagged into my arms weeping like a boy of six, instead of a man of over sixty. I held him to my chest, scared.

"Promise me one thing, Steve. Promise me you'll place a red rose on my grave when you come home," he sobbed. "I want to know you're home and safe."

I nodded. It was all I could do. Try as it might, my throat couldn't squeeze out even so much as a whisper.

At the bottom of the stairs, crowded around the front door, were Mom and all my brothers and sisters—Gary, Mary Ann, Edwin, Elliot, and Sandra. They seemed more nervous than I, yet very proud. Mom was still trying her best to make sure I was well prepared for just about every emergency possible. Some of the things in my pack, like mouthwash and laundry detergent, I probably wouldn't have thought essential to conquer the world had she not elbowed my common sense a bit. Descending the long, straight stairway, I tried my best to look happy and eager. I knew my brothers and sisters expected that. They had all been excited about my walk, even though apparently none of them had ever been bitten by the travel bug.

I hugged Mom more tightly than I had done since I was a child. She hugged me every bit as strongly, her face buried in my heavy jacket. Then, as one, we squeezed through the front door and out onto the porch of our seventy-year-old brick home. From the street below there rose what had to be some very frozen cheers. Around two dozen of the local villagers were waiting to see me off. I guess I should have known that to a community as small and close-knit as Bethel, it just wouldn't have seemed proper to let someone go walking around the world without a ceremony of sorts.

Some of the faces were as familiar as school memories: Debi from the Midway cinema and Rick from the little clapboard Canter Insurance office building on the village's only main street. But some were known to me more by the way they said hello and good day than by name. Some of those cheering me on had been alerted by a telephone call from Dad, while others had undoubtedly heard about my trip from one of the clerks at the Ben Franklin five-and-ten, where I'd purchased the wall map of the world.

However, one face was missing. One whose big smile and long blond curls could have eased so much my fear of loneliness. She was the girl-friend I'd had to leave behind in Wyoming when I returned here to pursue my dream. My long love letters to Charlene from isolated oil rigs and camps in the deserts and mountains had helped me to keep going emotion-ally in that period of my preparations. And I knew she would have been proud of me right now.

When Charlene had first learned of my plan two years ago, she had exhibited so much excitement and pride that I had had no hesitation about acting on my dream. Yet as the day for my return to Ohio grew nearer, our mutual sadness had several times exploded into tears. More than once I had thought of abandoning my plans. And on that freezing gray windy day last December when we'd parted for good, we'd buried our heads in each other's shoulders on the edge of Casper and cried like children, totally oblivious to the passing traffic and howling wind.

Yet what could I do? I could hardly expect her to wait another three to five years for my return.

I waved numbly at my friends, thinking of the big bouquet of white daisies that had been delivered to our house from Charlene yesterday. Was this walk so important that it was worth the loss of the only woman I'd ever really loved? For my heart's sake, I hoped so.

And so my back was slapped, I smiled for Instamatics, and I was comforted by hearty promises of prayers. I made room in my jacket for a little flashlight that would shine when its sides were squeezed, and for yet another present of several stamped generic postcards to be mailed, as the excited lady put it, "home to your mother every so often, young man!"

Naturally, in a place like Bethel no crowd could be without a police chief and a mayor. So everyone stood around as P.D., the mayor, wrote into the school composition notebook I was using for my Witness Book: *4-1-83, 9:56* A.M., *Bethel, P. D. Brittain, Mayor.* And then he surprised me with a letter on village stationery that read:

April 1, 1983

To Whom it may concern:
Subject: Mr. Steven M. Newman
Objective: "Walk Around the World"

This letter of recommendation for Steven M. Newman comes to you with a great sense of pleasure.

I have personally known Steven since he was thirteen years of age. He is a trustworthy gentleman.

He is a person that our community is proud of. I recommend him to you, without any apprehension. I feel that Steve represents the fine young people throughout the world.

We hope that in his passing, through your country's villages and towns, he will leave you with a ray of hope, in the fulfillment of your own dreams and aspirations.

Any assistance you may afford this young man, I am sure will be remembered by him and the citizens of the village of Bethel, Ohio.

Our best wishes, our thoughts, and God's will are being extended to Steve, as he endeavors to fulfill an ambition he has had since he was a very young man.

In closing we wish to invite you to extend to Steve the courtesy he deserves, and in return, I am sure he will extend to you and your citizens the same favor.

Upon his return home we will welcome him, and only then will we be able to understand his undertaking, and realize that a life-long dream has finally come true.

Cordially yours,
Parks D. Brittain, Mayor

And then everyone looked all the more proud, if a bit colder also, when Chief Fambry entrusted me with an honorary police badge from Manchester, England, which he said he prized, and pulled out a typed letter, too, that read:

April 1, 1983

To All Law Enforcement Officers:

I would like to introduce to you Mr. Steven M. Newman, who will be fulfilling a life-long dream to walk around the world.

As we all know in Law Enforcement, our existence is mandatory. I would like to say to you, at this time, if all the people in the world had the character and honesty of this young man, law enforcement would not have to exist.

I have given to Steven a badge, from a very dear friend of mine, from the country of England. He will be carrying this, not as a law enforcement officer, but for the ideal of justice it represents.

Steven understands the dangers connected with an undertaking of this nature. Our good wishes go forward with him, and we look forward to be able to greet him in our village of Bethel, Ohio, upon his return.

Very respectfully yours,
Charles Fambry, Chief of Police

When at last it was decent for me to start saying my own share of good-byes, I turned to the east, to the Williamsburg-Bethel road, and smiling bravely took the very first of what I figured would be about 40 million steps.

No one who watched me leave 450 North Charity Street that bittersweet April Fool's Day knew of the horrible pain and sadness gripping my insides. No one, that is, except for the gaunt little man whose crying eyes peered down at me from an upstairs bedroom window.

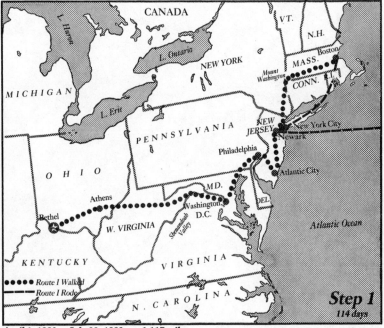

CANADA

L. Huron

MICHIGAN

L. Ontario

NEW YORK

VT.

N.H.

Boston

MASS.

Mount
Washington

CONN.

L. Erie

PENNSYLVANIA

NEW
JERSEY

New York City

Newark

Philadelphia

Atlantic City

OHIO

MD.

DEL.

Athens

Washington,
D.C.

Bethel

W. VIRGINIA

Shenandoah Valley

Atlantic Ocean

KENTUCKY

VIRGINIA

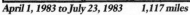

Route I Walked
Route I Rode

N. CAROLINA

Step 1

114 days

April 1, 1983 to July 23, 1983   1,117 miles

2

During all those years of planning, I had determined never to let the backpack I would be wearing on the journey get any heavier than fifty pounds. And yet, at the last minute, like so many travelers going off on a long journey, I'd foolishly ignored my common sense. For some reason, I was overcome by a tremendous surge of affection for all the books and fishing gear and whatever else I had said "No!" to countless times before. So from a trim forty pounds, my backpack, "Clinger," grew quickly to an obese seventy pounds! Which was enough to make my ankles and knees—to say nothing of my spine— wonder after just the first three miles why I was tromping around with something akin to an elephant on my shoulders.

Fortunately, Mom's big yellow Ford station wagon pulled alongside after about an hour. With her were my oldest brother, Gary, my oldest sister, Mary Ann, and Bo, Gary's Alaskan malamute husky. Mom was waving something round and black in her hand. It was a cap from one of my camera lenses.

"I found it beside the bed. I figured you had forgotten it," she said, after parking the car in the gateway to a barn.

I slumped against the car and admitted I'd forgotten something else, too. Water. I was so thirsty, my tongue was sticking to the roof of my mouth. In all the commotion of this morning, I'd forgotten to fill the goatskin wine bag I was using for a canteen. Beneath my sweater and coat and long johns, it felt like the middle of July.

Mom drove off to the house to get some water. The others stayed behind. Gary, who lifted weights for exercise every day and was as stocky as a professional football player, helped me out of Clinger.

"What's in here?" he groaned as the bulky pack thumped onto the ground.

I sagged against a fence post. The pain of overstretched muscles shot through my back and neck like long, hot needles. If Gary thought something was heavy, then it *was* heavy. He and Mary Ann looked at me with expressions that asked how it was I could be so miserable after such a short distance.

There was no way they could have known that my aches were due not only to Clinger's weight, but also to a terrible car accident I had survived only hours ago, around midnight. Greg Abell, my best friend, had been rushing me home from a quick visit to some friends, when suddenly, on a hairpin curve, his little Fiat sports car went airborne. Crashing back to the asphalt on its driver side, the wedge-shaped car had rolled twice, careened off the road upside down, clipped a telephone pole on my side, and had finally come to a stop—still upside down—in a woods, with gasoline and battery acid spilling out.

Luckily, neither of us suffered anything worse than bruises and some strained muscles. The car, however, was totaled.

That auto accident was something I did not want to reveal to anyone. Mom and Dad had enough heartaches and worries as it was. This was no time to be saying I had nearly been killed already.

I had meant to pare down Clinger's weight this morning, but instead had overslept because of the accident. If only now I could wish myself back to yesterday, to when I'd last packed Clinger. Suddenly, a lot of the things I was carrying didn't seem so indispensable.

Into Clinger's upper-right-side pouch, which I referred to as the "closet," had gone a large bone-handled hunting knife I'd traded four books of S&H Green Stamps for, a Berlitz foreign-language phrase book I'd bought for a quarter at a garage sale, a road map of the eastern United States I'd gotten for free at Duckworth's Sunoco Service Station, a large bottle each of shampoo and rinse, one pair of aviator sunglasses given to me by the local optometrist, a pair of mittens, two pedometers, spare shoelaces, a snakebite kit, several fishing lures, bobbers and sinkers, and hooks, and a large can of shaving lotion.

Into the smaller lower-right pouch, or the "bathroom," had gone my toothbrush, as well as a spare, plus bottles of mouthwash and after shave and cologne, a large tube of toothpaste, a dozen disposable razors, a large bar of Ivory soap, a comb and brush set, one of Mom's old, half-rusted nail clippers, a roll of toilet paper snitched from the bathroom, sunscreen, suntan lotion, sunblock cream, skin lotion, and a three-inch-square camp mirror for shaving.

Into the lower-left pouch, the "photo lab," I had stuffed my only extra camera lens, a forty-dollar clearance-sale Vivitar 28mm wide-angle lens that sometimes worked if I shook it hard enough, two sun filters, a camera lens-cleaning kit and fluid, and three rolls of Kodak color-slide film and one of Plus-X black-and-white film. Which then had led me to the upper-left-hand pouch of Clinger, known to me as the "pantry." Into its dual fist-sized cavities I had put my entire medical kit—a small free sample pouch of half a dozen aspirin, a little vial of antiseptic Mom had scavenged from the nursing home throwaways, a sewing needle for breaking blisters, and nine or ten bandages—and my kitchen facilities, a P-45 military can opener about the size of a postage stamp that I'd kept from my university ROTC C-rations, a butter knife and fork and spoon from the kitchen drawer, some waterproof matches, and one of Mom's plastic drinking cups.

Next had been the two large main pockets between those side pouches. Into the top one, the "office/kitchen," I had chosen to place my food staples of peanut butter, jam, bread, powdered milk, dry cereal, sugar, salt, pepper, a half-dozen eggs in a shatterproof plastic holder, hot dogs, Carnation Instant Breakfast mixes and bars, a small tub of margarine, dry spaghetti, and lots of Snickers candy bars, as well as a Boy Scout mess kit, a roll of paper towels, a pot scrubber, dishwashing lotion, the laundry detergent, a dog-eared paperback Webster's dictionary, a similarly ancient Roget's thesaurus, a book of synonyms, a large address book, a blank diary that was a gift from Charlene, a couple of Bic pens, some lined school-notebook paper for composing the stories that the *Columbus Dispatch* newspaper in the state's capital and *Capper's Weekly,* a nationally circulated family newspaper from Topeka, Kansas, had asked me to send them, a box of envelopes, a book of stamps, Scotch tape, my library: a paperback anthology of Ernest Hemingway short stories and paperback copies of Mark Twain's *Tom Sawyer* and *Huckleberry Finn* and John Steinbeck's *Travels with Charlie* (all of which I had rescued from a garage sale), two notebooks—the Witness Book and the Daily Log Book—for recording the peoples and the miles of my journey, the highway maps and several of the travel booklets from the embassies, a retractable fishing rod and its spinning reel, and a pipe and pouch of tobacco.

All that was left was the lower large pocket, appropriately known as my "trunk," and the map pocket on the front of the lower pocket's flap. Into the trunk I had dropped my complete wardrobe of a rain poncho, an extra wool sweater, four cotton socks and two wool socks, four extra pairs of underwear, swimming trunks, three extra T-shirts, a bath towel, a hand towel, sweats for pajamas, extra jeans, a wool shirt, extra long johns, and my dress-up clothes—a pair of khaki slacks from K Mart and one long-sleeved plaid shirt from the Salvation Army thrift store. Into the map pocket had gone my "international briefcase"—a Roman Meal bread-wrapper bag containing my United States passport, five hundred dollars in American Express traveler's checks, a pocket-sized laminated birth-certificate card, my free-lance journalist business card, my Ohio driver's license for additional identification, and visa information about other countries from the State Department.

The final compartment had been the "bedroom," an enormous sleeping bag lashed to the pack's top area, along with a large plastic ground cloth and the heaviest item of all—a two-man dome tent that folded into a drawstring bag as long as my arm, and every bit as heavy.

All that had remained to be tied to the sides of my backpack or worn on me were the wine bag, a ten-year-old banged-up Minolta 35mm camera and the 50-mm lens that had come with it, a fifteen-year-old Timex watch I'd retrieved from a garbage can while a reporter, and my walking ward-robe: a straw scarecrow hat, a pair of straight-legged Levi's jeans, a fifty-cent cotton office dress shirt I'd picked up at a Catholic thrift store, a T-shirt, my main long johns, a thickly insulated nylon jacket, and, most important and most dressy of all, my lightweight nylon-topped *Rocky* "Scrambler" hiking boots.

I rubbed the back of my neck harder. Several more days—let alone years—of torturing my vertebrae with such a load, and surely I'd return home stooped over like a crippled old man. What was I thinking, training this past year without any weight on my back? The weight pressing down on my joints was making a mockery of all that jogging and lifting weights.

And what could I have been thinking, too, when I packed at the same time gear for *every* season and country? Suntan oil and swimming trunks in April? Maps of Africa and India and Australia, when they were still months or years away? Survival gear in *Ohio*?

Mom returned with a quart jar of water and half an apple pie. To-gether they must have weighed five pounds. I smiled kindly: Sometimes mothers could be too nice.

While I stood with my back to him, Gary took a deep breath, gripped the long gray pack with all its loose straps, and hefted it up onto my unsteady backside. As I turned and said good-bye again, I swore that in more than one face I saw the words *Better* you *than me*.

Still, that first day wasn't all bad. There was the elderly man who handed me ten dollars to buy my next pair of boots with, a farm housewife who came out to the road to offer me such long-tested painkillers as brownies and hot chocolate, and a young lady who hopped from her car to kiss me on the chin. They helped me to forget the gargoyle twisting my back muscles and the trolls grinding my knee ligaments. And even better, just as night came, there was Sandy Barker waiting for me at the lone traffic light in Mount Orab. A laid-off Ford auto-plant worker, she had searched me down to invite me to her house for a big steak dinner and a dry place to rest overnight. Her twenty-year-old daughter, Ella, had been at a going-away party at McIntosh's Winery thrown for me by several of my former high-school classmates, and Sandy had heard about me from Ella.

"I've been looking all afternoon for you clear out on U.S. fifty. Why, I thought you'd have been clear near Hillsboro by now," Sandy said on the drive through the dark and rain to her home near Fayetteville.

I sighed. *So had I.* How embarrassing that I had barely made it to the county line. Based on my long training walks, which had always gone so easily and quickly, and my background as a marathon runner, I had been confident I would average around forty miles a day with hardly any effort. Yet here I was with barely fifteen miles to show for all the aches racking my shoulders.

But luck was still with me even with all of my miscalculations and bumbling. On the second evening, I put up my tent in a pouring rain, in a marsh full of gossipy frogs, only to be rescued by a county worker who had me come into his house just east of Fayetteville and sleep on the living-room floor. Dennis Kiley had planned to go to a movie that night with his girlfriend, but instead opted to order up the three of us a pizza and some beers and put the fireplace to good use.

"We decided the movie could wait. It's not too often you get to meet someone walking around the world," he jested.

Then, on the third evening, on the eastern edge of a don't-blink-or-you'll-miss-it place called Hoagland, again alongside the same nearly deserted Route 50 that would hopefully lead me clear to Washington, D.C., I came across a Tastee Freeze shack still miraculously in business that Easter Sunday. To the girl on the other side of its sliding order window, I pushed through an order for a Big T Burger and a cup of water.

Soon after, she pushed back to me through that same window the sack with my dinner and a very nice surprise: It was on the house, er, shack. Either I looked as wretched as I felt, or my ordering the cup of water, while shivering in a downpour, had been too much for her. At any rate, her kindness helped me to walk another mile along the flooded road, where I found an old barn with a packed-dirt floor and a corrugated roof that didn't leak . . . much.

I discovered that along with the burger she had given me a surprise order of what I call truck-stop fries—those extra-stubby fries. To me that night they were the best food in all the universe. And certainly better than the cold hot dogs and chips in Clinger that I would have had to eat if the Tastee Freeze had not been open. For with everything so soaked from the rains, a campfire was out of the question.

To the groans of a body so stiff it made me cry, I peeled off many pounds of soggy smelliness and eased my body into my sleeping bag. Once warm, I forced myself to reach back out of the bag and feel inside Clinger for a candle, the yellow spiral-ringed notebook that was my Daily Log Book, my diary, and the Ohio road map. In the weak glow of the little candle's flame, I studied the map and found the little tick mark I had made last night marking the location of Dennis Kiley's house near Fayetteville. Moving my eyes further along U.S. Route 50, I found Hoagland and made a similar tick mark just to the east of it, to mark my present stopping point. Then, with my ruler I measured the distance between the two ticks—six-eighths of an inch. I measured the same distance on the map's mile scale. Eleven miles.

After turning to the first page in my Daily Log notebook, I wrote into the six columns labeled *Date, Time Start, Time Stop, Location, Mileage,* and *Total Miles:* 4-3-83, 12:45 P.M., 7:30 P.M., abandoned barn on east edge of Hoagland, Ohio, 11 miles, and 40 miles.

Three days of walking, and I'd gone only forty miles from Bethel. My shoulders slumped, and I crawled back into the bag's depths, too tired to add the day's high and low points to the diary. That, I decided, could be done later, when I came across a library or café where there was a table and a chair and some semblance of comfort.

How am I ever going to make the remaining 19,960 miles? I wondered. I couldn't even straighten out my legs in the sleeping bag, because of the damage to my ligaments. I was going through the worst pain of my life. Lumps, bumps, blisters, and festers—in places where I didn't know such things could even grow!

And as each day the aches grew crankier and the pack heavier, I began to seriously wonder if the walk was worth it.

Yet . . . again, and again, and again, examples of warm hospitality kept encouraging me to push further toward the other side of Ohio:

On the morning of the fourth day, in the Quaker town of Hillsboro, Winona and Melissa Storer, a half-Indian mother and her daughter, turned their perfumed bathtub over to my reeking mess of aches and then helped me send back to Bethel, via UPS, at least twenty-five pounds of the dead weight I'd been carrying. Also in Hillsboro, on that same day, a goateed puppeteer, Daniel Llords, and his live-in manager, "Jones," gave me a place in Llords' old Victorian-style mansion to peck away undisturbed on an old Remington typewriter at the first of the "Letter from Steven" columns due for *Capper's Weekly.* Near the "World Famous Seven Caves," a very poor former coal miner named George had reached from his squat black 1949 Plymouth to hand me a Pepsi Cola and a hot fish sandwich he'd bought at a carry-out in nearby Bainbridge, as well as to insist I accept ten dollars from the Social Security check he'd just cashed. Wilona Laessle, the plump and matronly middle-aged driver of a school bus for retarded children, pulled over just as I was leaving tiny Bourneville to crumple a five-dollar bill into my palm rather shyly and say, "Mind you, I've never pulled over before for any strangers. But I wanted so much to be a part of what you're doing."

". . . to be a part of what you're doing." Surely I had heard that one hundred times in my first five days of walking. When I looked at the love in the eyes of so many of those strangers who helped me each day, I couldn't shake the feeling that they saw something of themselves in my solitary wandering figure.

I knew there really was something mystical about the lone traveler with a pack on his back. It was as old as history. In the Middle Ages, monks and people of the Church used to go on long pilgrimages alone. For thousands of miles they would walk, and people always took care of them. The magic those monks had known was still alive. Even in this sophisticated age of technology, there was still compassion for the lone traveler seeking nothing more than knowledge and friendship.

3

I was grungy from the mud puddles I'd splashed through that first week away from Bethel. By the time I reached Bainbridge, I was desperate for any shower other than that which had been falling from the sky nearly nonstop since the day I'd left home.

Yet everywhere I'd asked where I might find a hot shower, I'd been greeted only with shrugs and glances of suspicion. Even at the "police station" in the waterworks building, the droopy-eyed officer had stared out the dripping windows until I knew I wasn't welcome there either.

But then I had knocked on the door of a dilapidated church on an alley and been welcomed by a woman who was straight out of the Middle Ages. Her black hair was in complete disarray; her eyes poked out of her face; and from a body too used to being hungry, there hung at the total mercy of gravity a tattered dress that could have been borrowed from a scarecrow.

The inside of the church looked as though it came from a John Steinbeck novel. The walls were cheerless planks, and except for a ragged Jesus ripped from an old calendar, they were as bare as the floorboards. Clinging to the ceiling were the shards of a plaster with more stain than paint. For furnishings, there were a couple of rickety pews, a smoky wood stove, and for a pulpit, an orange crate on a folding metal chair. No carpeting, no lights except for one bare bulb in the ceiling, and not even a discarded songbook.

Probably the poorest of all the churches in Ohio, it still shone like a cathedral to me when the woman said I could have a shower at her family's farm off "in the hills." So, in the midst of a downpour, she and I and two of her small boys climbed into a mufflerless deathtrap of an old Ford, to *chug-chunka chug-chunka* our way through miles of snaky ruts to a farm that consisted of coon dogs, pigs, cats, mud, and leaning buildings.

Even in such poverty, the children were a joyful bunch. They showed off their pets and ran about playing games with all the laughter and energy of children everywhere. The boys, I noticed, wore their school track jerseys. Their sneakers, however, were so full of holes that I wondered how they stayed on.

After I was clean, we had supper: several cups of black coffee, a cup of milk, and three hot dogs with white bread. And then the little girl ran off to another part of the house to retrieve her only toys, a small pile of seashells in a shoebox—and I showed her she could hold the large ones to her ears and hear inside them the ocean itself. I was amazed that no one had ever bothered to tell her such a simple thing before. Or that those shells had once been homes . . .

My legs, particularly my knees and ankles, seemed on the very edge of disintegration. My knees were no longer just knobby, but as huge as overripe grapefruits. And my neck was racked with sharp bolts of pain if I even thought of trying to turn it.

As I limped whimpering into some woods along the Scioto River and collapsed into a heap, the pain in my body was worse than ever. I seriously doubted I could make the fifty miles still remaining to Athens, Ohio, where I planned to take my first long rest stop of the walk.

All I felt like eating was a handful of M&Ms, and I spent that night curled in pain beneath a crude tarp shelter.

The next day I was convinced that something terrible was happening to my insides. My right foot and knee were hurting so badly I couldn't go more than a mile or two at a time. I was hobbling like some of those old patients my mother, a registered nurse, cared for at my father's nursing home.

"Need a ride, guy?" a tobacco-chewing "feller" wearing a Southern Ohio Hog Feeders cap and driving a Dodge calamity asked toward dusk, just past Londonderry.

"Thanks, but I'm walking," I said for the umpteenth time that miserable rainy day.

"Huh?"

"You know. Hiking!"

"Oh, I see. Where to?"

"Arou—er, across America."

"REALLY!"

"Yep."

"Man, have you got guts. No way I'd even try to walk to the next town. Just too many crazies out there. Need to get you one o' these jobbies, like I got here on my belt. Hah! Ain't nobody gonna mess with this sucker."

"Yeah. That's pretty nice. I always did want to have a folding hunting knife like that."

"Here! It's yours."

"Wha? Ah, no—shoot, that's too expensive."

"Hey, no matter. I respect what you've done, man. Takes guts to walk across America like that. More 'n I got, fer sure."

"Gee . . . thanks for this. I'll wear it all around . . . around the rest of the trip."

"Say, you ain't goin' through Vinton County, are you?"

"Well, yeah. I'm pretty sure that's the county line right there. Ain't it?"

"There's no way I'd walk through there. They like to bash in your brains in those hills. You'll never live if you go across there all by yourself." He rubbed his jaws, as if he'd been ambushed many times in that county. "The people there are mean, ignorant, real poor. Got the highest unemployment in the state."

He shook his head and drove off, convinced, I'm sure, that I'd never make it alive across Ohio's poorest and ruggedest county.

And what I saw as I progressed deeper into the hills of Vinton County did not exactly help to dispel the fear the stranger had instilled.

All along Route 50 there had been an incredible amount of litter along the shoulders of the highway—cans, bottles, paper. But in Vinton County the garbage grew even more prolific, as did the abandoned and shuttered buildings. Activity in the towns was virtually nil, as if they were there mostly for the sake of the map makers.

The roads were in an advanced state of decay. The creeks and ditches were gorged from the excessive rainfall, and the bridges seemed to be rotting right before my eyes. Even the earth itself was turning into water, I thought.

So it wasn't in the best of moods that I realized I was going to have to sleep that stormy night inside an abandoned church surrounded by an overgrown cemetery in the dead center of that area I had been warned relished brain-bashing. Aware that vampires and resurrected chain-saw murderers liked to vacation in such settings, I tried to pretend I didn't know my mummy bag and I were surrounded by four invisible corners filled with all sorts of you-know-whos. With the wind howling, dead tree limbs scratching, and rain hissing, I could only think about how I would look when my body was found someday.

Eventually, as I surrendered to the side of me that thought sleep was more important than seeing a ghost, the last thing I heard in my head was, *Come and get me, Satan. I'm pooped. . . .*

Had a young lady not pulled her car over and offered to haul Clinger the last ten miles, I might never have made it to Athens. After I told her I had walked all the way from near Cincinnati, she couldn't seem to do enough to try to help ease my pain.

Though she drove away with everything I had, I was sure she could be trusted. Perhaps it was the Bible on the seat beside her. Or maybe it was the way she had gently scolded me for even thinking of walking in the rain.

"You'll be a lump of grumbling arthritis someday, if you don't get a car," she'd said, pulling away with a look that said men had to be about one step above jackasses in the brain department—worldwalkers included!

Trudging onward through the darkness, misery dripping from my hat, I cried out loud in frustration at how my fantasy had turned out. But the worst of my anguish I held inside, until I saw looming ahead of me the bald dome of Ohio University's basketball arena and I knew I was at the outer limits of Athens.

Then, in the middle of the Richland Avenue Bridge, over a Hocking River straining to contain its guts, and in a blackness pierced only by an occasional lightning bolt, I flung back my arms and my head, and screamed with every ounce of vengeance I had:

"I made it! You *hear* me? Every! . . . Single! . . . STEP!"

So much pain, and struggle. And yet I had gone only one hundredth of the worldwalk's probable distance. If I was this exhausted and discouraged simply from walking to Athens, what would I be like the rest of the way? I was too scared to face that thought for more than a few seconds.

4

"**O**hhhh, STEVE! Why, you're all wet!"

Mary Stalder was pushing eighty, but no one would have known it, given the energy and enthusiasm she unfailingly showed. As stinking and soaked and godawfully late as I was, she was thrilled to see me again, as she proved with a big hug, her slender arms reaching halfway to the sky, her nose dangerously close to my armpits. It had been six years since I'd left her home on North College Street to drive off to Wyoming in my fire-red 1963 Falcon sports coupe to become another Ernest Hemingway, and in all that time we'd had to be content with memories and Christmas cards.

Son of a gun, was it ever nice to be back. If ever there was a place where memories did stay still, this was the place for sure. Aside from Wyoming, Mary's enormous two-story home next to the "townies" ' Catholic church was the only place outside of Bethel in which I had invested any sizable chunks of my short manhood.

We had become acquainted in the spring quarter of my sophomore year at the university. I'd knocked on that same front door to tell the sweet-voiced little old lady who answered that my curiosity about her house was killing me. Every day that I walked past it, with its high, narrow chimneys and drawn windows that gave it an air of the setting of an Agatha Christie mystery, I wondered what it looked like on the inside. Was it possible to see? It was.

And was it possible, she in turn had wondered, that I'd be willing to clean chandeliers some weekend? Of course!

In the fall, I'd returned again to her shuttered drawing room to share

with her my adventures of another summer spent prospecting for uranium
in the Red Desert of Wyoming. And she in turn shared her idea that
boarding in her house and tending after her yard—with pay, naturally—
might be better than wasting money on some noisy apartment. Of course!

So for the next two years, the pages of life during the rigors of "Harvard on the Hocking" included fat red tomcats stalking white pigeons on
church eaves, paint swirling onto canvas in a sunny studio, the occasional
secret lover *ticking* my upstairs bedroom windows with pebbles in the
middle of the night, notes rising from the ivory of a baby grand, and bells
ding-a-linging for biscuits and tea on glass tabletops beside honeysuckled
hedges.

But on our soaked reunion of April 9-going-on-April 10, it was asparagus and tuna on toast, which we were too excited to eat; a bathrobe
substituting for clothes too wet to be healthy; hours spent chatting in the
library till even the paintings' eyes were turning red; and, thankfully, a
much-needed passing out in my old haunts upstairs, in the company of
fireplaces and poster beds . . . and Clinger.

Tired and full of aches was I in the nine days that I stayed in that
house Mary's rich, coal-mining father had built. But also full of hot meals,
bubbly baths, and thick-quilted beds.

In a way, Mary was the perfect person to have at such a crucial point
in my journey, because she was forever spilling over with humor and
optimism and support. I was sure that not a negative bone could be found
in all her body. Because she was practically deaf, she was especially animated in her speaking, and yet she was wonderfully attentive when listening. In short, she was both a marvelous audience and a lively cheerleader.

I had missed Mary in those years away from school, and I knew she
had missed me. She had always done what she could to build up my
confidence as a writer—requesting autographed copies of all the magazine
pieces I'd done while in school, making sure the house was quiet when I
was working on a story, volunteering to go get me a submarine sandwich
at the nearest deli or maybe some more writing supplies when I was trying
to beat a fast-approaching deadline. And now I couldn't help but feel that
she was once again bolstering that writer side of me by believing in this
walk as much as I did.

Still, when April 18 came and I was saying good-bye to Mary once
again, I knew that I was in serious trouble emotionally. There was a large

and powerful dark force seething and slithering deep inside me. It was something even more devastating than pain. Doubt. What difference would all this make? Was I crazy to be doing this?

As the weather went from cloudy-cold to a full-fledged snowstorm only two hours later, I knew the walk's gremlins hadn't been fooled by my sojourn in Mary's house. The survival of the walk was truly hanging in the balance these next few miles.

Belpre was what many liked to call a river-rat town. Set on the banks of the Ohio River, with as many belfries as bars along its main drag, it looked every bit as rough as it really was. When I reached it on the afternoon of the second day out of Athens, it was the perfect place for how I was feeling. The night before, I had slept in a barn loft over a ton of cow flesh that didn't have the slightest idea of the meaning of constipation. Then, in the morning, I'd nearly frozen to death just trying to get my cement-hard boots back on my swollen feet.

Sullen as a snapping turtle, I'd walked all that day in silence, contemplating how I could bring an end to my seemingly infinite parade of miseries. It would have been easy to take two quick steps to my right as the logging trucks came smoking past. But with the luck I was having, I couldn't be sure even that would suffice. I was in such a foul mood that I'd managed to kick myself out of the Beehive pizza parlor in Coolville when the waitress dared to serve me without a smile pasted on her makeup. Stomping out the door, I'd fumed, "I've been walking all morning in the snow and cold, and if you can't serve me with a smile, I'll go down the road!"

Which I did. Right to Belpre and the bridge connecting it to *the* place I'd decided, when a tree limb dumped its snow on me, would be where the epitaph of the worldwalk was written: Parkersburg, West Virginia.

No sooner did I reach the bridge and what I honestly—fervently!—hoped were the last strides of this accursed walk when from nowhere a voice boomed out a command for me to ignore my inner demons.

"STEVEN! STOP!"

I whirled around to face a large pair of green eyes haloed in a wildly whipping bush of red incandescence. Hobbling inches from the rushing traffic, a long camera lens poking from her freckled face and her red hair billowing in the cold wind of the river, was Tammy Mobley, a photojournalism student from Ohio University who had walked with me out of Athens the day before.

"Tammy! What-are-you-doing-here-and-how's-that-leg?" I asked without a pause in my determination to get across that bridge.

She fired back her reply without moving her eye an inch from the camera's viewfinder:

"The doctor at the click! health center said I probably fractured click! click! click! one of the little bones in the ankle."

I glanced at the leg she'd twisted in the snow while trying to keep her stubby gait from falling too far behind my own yard-long steps. The way her jeans were straining to keep their seams together on that leg told me she had a cast on. Watching her trying to keep her balance on the ice and potholes of that bridge, thinking about the pain she had to be in, made me wince.

Yesterday she had come to me weighted down with her own backpack full of camera lens and camping gear, hoping to accompany me for a couple of weeks on the road. She wanted something different for her photojournalism class project. And more than that, a good excuse to get out of the classroom. At the age of twenty, she was already a pro who knew the art of photography inside-out (her father was photo editor for the *National Geographic*). And she was—plain and simple—a tomboy who'd jump at the chance for adventure the way a hungry lion would a zebra.

I wanted to keep marching right on across the crowded two-lane bridge's span. But if there was one thing I admired in a person more than anything else, it was the love of adventure. Especially in a woman. I stopped my advance and looked up at the red-haired Nikon.

Click!

"Steven . . . I phoned the Parkersburg newspaper. They're waiting to interview you, and take some pictures of you at the mayor's office in Belpre. You have to turn around and go back, or they'll miss you," said her camera.

HONK!

There was a long line of cars and pickups nearly crashing into each other, because of her.

"Let's go!" shouted Tammy, as if we were stuntmen on a movie set. Parkersburg could wait a few minutes more, I decided, limping for all I was worth after her. Why couldn't things ever go the way I planned them?

In front of the dull brick façade of the Belpre town hall, two men strode up to me to shake hands. One was the photographer from the *Parkersburg News;* the other was Dan Surber, the reporter. We went directly to the unsuspecting mayor's office, just inside the entrance and to the right. Quite naturally, he was surprised to have his office invaded by someone stinking of *essence de cow* and caked in windburn and chapped skin.

With cameras clicking and pens pecking, I awkwardly pulled my straw hat off and shuffled over to his desk to explain. I used pretty much the same lines I always did when I approached someone to persuade him that he should trust his name and address to a tattered notebook with the ominous title Witness Book penciled across its cover.

"G'day, sir. My name is Steven Newman. I'm a journalist from near Cincinnati who's walking around the world to learn about people.

"Whenever I pass through any city or town or village, I try to get someone official, like the mayor or the police chief, to sign this Witness Book I'm keeping. It's proof that I really did walk through here."

Then, before he could let what I had said sink in too deeply, I slipped Clinger off, dug out the notebook from its trash-bag covering, and placed it on his desk, opened to the other signatures. Being sure, too, that I said at the same time:

"I'm not on any kind of crusade or peace march, or anything of that sort. I just want to see the world up real close while I'm still young. And as long as I'm doing it on foot, I figure I might as well get credit for it."

"Yeah. Sort of like a memento of all the places you've traveled to, and the people you met. Right?" he said with a grin at the cameras.

"Yes, sir."

Plucking a long, tapered pen from its holder, the mayor wrote down: *April 19, 3:13 p.m., City Hall, Belpre, Ohio, Ivan C. Smith,* then handed it to me with his chest puffed out another inch or so.

That completed, I thanked him several times, packed away the book, slipped Clinger back on, and turned to go back to Parkersburg and the end of my walk. I was already out the door when the mayor's voice caused me to pause, then turn around.

"You know, I just thought of something, Steven. Something real special." Humming and hawing and scratching his head, he ransacked his desk's drawers. "Ha! Here it is," he said finally.

"I'd like to give you something more than just my name for a memento of Belpre. I'd like to present you with this key to the city, to remember us by," he said in a manner fit to make me stand and salute.

It was a brass skeleton key as long as my hand. Long, thick, and shiny, just like the kind mayors in the big cities presented to movie stars and astronauts.

I handled the red-velvet-lined box the key was cradled in and felt goose bumps punching up all over. An honest-to-goodness true "key to the city." It even said so through the clear lid of the box. In big, proud, authoritative letters perfectly engraved along the middle of the key's round stem were the words CITY OF BELPRE.

I hardly knew what to say. Never in all my life did I think I'd be special enough to receive a key to a *city*. No matter that only seven thousand souls called this corner of the Buckeye State their home; Belpre was still officially a city in the books . . . and on that key.

Walking back across that bridge to Parkersburg, my eyes on the big brass key still in the box, my insides were about as mooshy as the river water below.

I was mighty proud. Yet I was also in quite a fix, too. Tammy and the newspaper reporters had made it hard enough for me to go through with my secret plans to quit the walk. How could I now, with a key to the city?

If news of my quitting got back to these parts, I'd be making all seven thousand residents of Belpre laughingstocks. I could always tolerate being the fool myself; that I had a lot of practice at. But there was no way I could ever be low enough to make an entire city one!

And so, that night, after much turning and tossing on my bed in the attic of the Salvation Army Transient House in Parkersburg, where I also had a much-appreciated dinner of red beans and potato gumbo, I decided that the worldwalk must continue—at least to Washington, D.C., at which point I could at least say to my future grandkids, "Well . . . at least I tried."

Maybe it was the gumbo, or maybe credit should go to the mysterious power I thought I could feel in that big key. Whatever the cause, that next day saw my still-aching body break the thirty-mile barrier for the first time. That was double my average. And then, like a marathon runner who has finally caught his second wind, my body began to relax, to the point where in the following days I was feeling almost as healthy as before the walk. Apparently, now that my mind had peace, so had my body.

"Yoo-hoo . . . Yoo-hoo . . ."

I cocked an ear into the thick white fog swirling past. What was going on? It was six-thirty in the morning, barely five minutes since I'd crawled from the hayloft I'd awakened in, and I was on a stretch of road in the middle of the Virginia countryside; yet I kept hearing someone calling. Maybe it was only some type of birdcall I'd never heard before.

"Yoo-hoo! Yoo-hoo!"

There it was again! And real close.

"Young man! Have you had any breakfast?"

I jumped a good inch off the wet road's pavement, which wasn't all that easy to do with a sixty-pound pack on my back. A few yards to my left was a teeny old lady who looked to be suspended in a bank of clouds as light as cotton candy. Where had *she* materialized from? I could have sworn there was no one on that cabin's high veranda two seconds before.

She waved the frailest of arms at me and stamped her foot, as if I were being scolded.

"Well, young man . . . have you eaten any breakfast, or not?"

"Why, no, I haven't," I confessed. In fact, I hadn't eaten in almost a day, because I'd spent most of yesterday in the loft of the neighbor's barn catching up on my diary entries.

"Well you get up here *right now* and eat something! You're not going any further, young man, till you do. You hear?"

From the tone of her voice I knew she wouldn't take an argument. So I did as the strange little old lady wished. Besides, it was awfully chilly, Winchester was still a good twelve miles farther, and I *was* pretty darn hungry.

I walked over to the porch, then kind of eased my way up the steps.

She was so tiny she could've told me if my belly button needed to be washed. If she weighed even as much as a lamb, I would have been surprised. Unquestionably, she didn't seem the type to be hustling giants off foggy country lanes for mealtime company. She was the sweetest, most harmless-looking person I'd seen since visiting my own grandmother back in our family's nursing home. Her full head of white hair could easily have doubled for a cloud on a Colorado summer day, and her smile would have made any elf jealous.

"My name is Estaline," she said in a voice as tiny as a field mouse's and as pure and sweet as the tinkling of crystal glasses.

"I'm Steve. I'm walking around the world to—"

Her gorgeous blue eyes got so big, I thought she had felt a spider scamper up her leg.

"I . . . thought . . . so. Yes!" she said, as if in a trance. "Then you must *really* be hungry, you poor thing. Oh, dear, that's *so* far to have to walk. I do hope you're not the only one. Come! Come!"

She shooshed me past the screen door, through an old-fashioned living room with its pictures of the grandkids on the television set and a throw rug on the floor, and straight to the kitchen with its linoleum-topped table. There, beside a refrigerator too ancient to qualify for second-hand, she paused only long enough to ask in an increasingly thrilled voice:

"Would you like a big breakfast, or just a light one?"

I was setting Clinger on the floor, under some shelves of upright plates with things like the Lord's Prayer, Niagara Falls, and the bleeding heart of Jesus on them. I must have taken just a little too long to reply, because she answered herself with:

"Of course you'll want a big breakfast! My, how could I think you wouldn't be starving after walking all that way to here?" She pulled out a chair for me to sit on. "You must be so tired. You'd think someone would have stopped to give you a ride by now.

"The Apple Blossom Festival starts today in Winchester, so there'll be plenty of people I'm sure that'll be driving past you. But just in case you have to walk all the way to town for lunch, I'm going to make sure you have plenty in your stomach. Like pancakes? Eggs? Bacon? Biscuits? Oh, my, grits too!"

Soon she was stirring and frying and baking and toasting and flipping —all the while praising the Lord and leaving no doubt that she'd read the Bible every way but backward.

Mmmmmmm . . . could she cook! And she heaped the butter on the pancakes as if there were a dairy factory just the other side of the back door.

It seemed she could not feed me enough food to satisfy herself. While I was eating, she would sit as quiet as a butterfly across from me on the other side of the table, her pretty face cupped in her hands, and gaze at me as if I reminded her of a mountain meadow carpeted in buttercups.

Someone else might have been a little embarrassed by all Estaline's fussing, particularly because she was obviously a poor widow who probably couldn't afford to be handing out so much of her groceries to a stranger. But I was too grateful for her hospitality to be embarrassed; I'd been on the road now for 417 wretchedly painful miles, and there was a world war going on inside my every muscle and joint.

Estaline and I, with Clinger once again high on my back, finally found our way back out onto the porch. But before I could let myself start off again, I had to ask my dear Good Samaritan:

"Estaline, why *did* you invite me in for that wonderful breakfast? Why did you trust me—someone you've never laid eyes on before? You live all alone, have practically no neighbors, and you're so little, compared to me. Couldn't I have been a bad man, who would rob you or even kill you? Why did you trust me immediately?"

She lowered her eyes and looked over the still-misty pastures and bare maple trees of her part of this Virginia paradise; she seemed to be trying to collect her thoughts. After a few minutes, she looked back up at me and said ever so gently:

"When I was a little girl, my mother used to read to me from the Bible every evening. Her favorite passage was one that says God sometimes sends angels to us disguised as men to test our charitableness. Well"—redness flushed through a pair of cheeks that were like mother of pearl—"I'm eighty-eight years old, and my eyesight is not so good anymore.

"And when I awoke this morning and looked out the screen door into the forest and saw this tall, pale figure coming through the fog, I felt my heart suddenly beating faster. For, you see, no one ever walks down this road so early in the morning. And as I watched you coming closer, and closer, my heart nearly stopped completely.

"Why, there was something very big and long on your back!"

Her right hand shot up to her face, as if she might giggle. Instead, she nervously gripped her chin and continued with both frustration and relief in her voice:

"I thought I was seeing *wings* on your shoulders. Surely, after all those years, this was one of those angels being sent to finally test me. And there was just no way I was going to let you go by without feeding you.

"For I've been so good all my life since I was a little girl, and—darn it!—I'm just too old now to be blowing my chance of getting into heaven.

"Why, I might never have another chance to feed an angel!"

Come the morning of May 5, my fingers were rapping against the highly polished oak entrance to a Chevy Chase, Maryland, home belonging to a cousin of Mary Stalder's.

For five days in that suburb of Washington, D.C., I was blessed with a hostess every bit as much a bolt of energy, talk, and smiles as Mary had been. Jodie Evans and her Churchill look-alike husband not only gave me a chance to see the inside of life in an exclusive neighborhood, but also made me feel as welcome as a son.

In their two-story brick home set amid tall oaks, flower gardens of azaleas and roses, pink or white dogwoods, and hedges and ivy, my imagination was rejuvenated. Spring was at its zenith, and so was my eagerness to push onward along the Eastern Seaboard, and then to fly across the Atlantic Ocean from Boston to Ireland to experience firsthand those exotic settings I'd so often dreamed about.

But first I had to reduce the weight of Clinger once again. There were at least 650 miles to go to Boston, with many of them along the hot and crowded concrete sidewalks of Baltimore, Philadelphia, Atlantic City, and New York City, and common sense dictated that I become more mobile and comfortable. Furthermore, should I meet any of those muggers and gangs that the movies and television kept indicating were common fixtures of the East's big cities, I'd best be prepared to move quickly.

So, to the silent stares of Chinese vases and the *tick-tock* of a grandmother clock on the third afternoon with the Evanses, I reduced Clinger to the trim backpack that he should have been all along. Onto the deep blue Persian carpet of the living room went all of my friend's innards. I picked for shipment back home all but the very necessities of my gear. With five hundred miles and one month of walking now under my belt, I was much more confident of what was, and wasn't, necessary.

Into the right side of a large cardboard box addressed to Bethel went items that would have been necessary on a hike through the wilds of nature but were only luxuries in the jungles of the city: the mess kit I never used, the fishing rod and reel and lures, the tent and ground cloth, the jacket and long johns and all other cold-weather or bulky clothing, the spare shoelaces, and the snakebite kit. Into the other side of the same box went all those things I had used too infrequently to be important: the cologne, the after shave, the pedometers (which were too inaccurate anyhow), the mouthwash, the dishwashing detergent, the camera lens-cleaner solution, the paper towels, the mirror, and the most ridiculous things of all since I didn't even smoke—the pipe and the tobacco.

And finally, on top of everything else, went the gifts from all those beautiful people who had treated me as if I were a son or brother. Carefully, reflecting on the memories those gifts stirred, I packed each with a smile, and usually a chuckle, too. There were many, ranging from a little LIFE BEGINS WITH JESUS button with a picture of a hairy puppet in a floppy straw hat, which was from the poor girl in Ohio with the seashells, to a flat, cellophane-wrapped Moon Pie cupcake that had been one of four given to me by Cecil, a bartender, and his Alcoholics Anonymous girlfriend, Sam, at Whitie's Bar just east of Aurora, West Virginia. ("You can have these only if you promise not to meet with that President Reagan when you get to Washington," he'd joked.)

What remained looked so sparse as to be ludicrous, especially when you considered it had to get me around an entire planet's worth of jungles, deserts, mountains, farms, and roadways. I looked at each item carefully as to whether it would be impossible to travel or to do my journalist work without it. Neatly and with purpose, I stored all those that passed the test back into the waiting Clinger.

Recruited to accompany me further into the worldwalk were the bone-handled hunting knife, a small jar of peanut butter, some crackers, a candy bar, the road map from Duckworth's Sunoco, a two-inch sliver of auto-mirror glass I had picked out of a ditch, one toothbrush, a free miniature sample tube of toothpaste, the rusty nail clippers, only a couple of the disposable razors, the bar of Ivory soap that would now have to double as my shaving "cream," a film canister filled with salt and pepper, another one filled with baby shampoo, a twenty-five-cent comb, the same broken Vivitar wide-angle lens, one roll each of Kodak color-slide film and black-and-white negative film, the same homemade medical kit of half a dozen aspirin and sewing needle and pilfered Band-Aids, the tiny P-45 can opener, a teaspoon, my torn paperback Webster's dictionary, the Witness Book and Daily Log, the almost-filled diary, one Bic pen, the address book that was already running out of empty pages, the Huck Finn paperback, and for clothes just one extra pair of cotton socks, one extra pair of underwear, a T-shirt that could also be my bath towel, the K Mart khaki slacks, the Salvation Army plaid shirt, and a plastic trash bag for an emergency rain jacket.

The only things left were my camera, which I now always carried hanging from my left hand, the Roman Meal bread-wrapper containing my passport and travel documents and traveler's checks, and a professional Sony Walkman cassette recorder I had bought yesterday for $250— an amount that was nearly ten times what the walk had cost me so far, due to all the hospitality. I had cringed at spending so much money, but I had realized that all the wisdom and clever anecdotes being shared with me should not be entrusted just to my memory.

Since I was a writer, I looked at the walk as a living book. I knew that should it someday evolve into an actual one, I would then need 'all help possible to accurately reconstruct it. My resources were already quite extensive: the ten to twenty photographs I averaged each day, the diary, the names and dates and places in the Witness Book, the concise logistical information in the Daily Log Book, the scribbled notes on the maps with each day's progress marked as precisely as possible, the gifts given to me by those I'd stayed with, the scribbled notes on the backs of others' calling cards, and, very important, the stories sent to the newspapers. Still, in regard to conversations, the tape recorder was a must. I didn't plan to use it every time I met someone, but certainly I would if that person had a particularly poignant or interesting story to share.

How much lighter the weight of my gear would be if I were not a working journalist as well as a worldwalker. But I was not one ever to do something without a purpose, and for me this walk was as much my work as it was my childhood fantasy.

My office . . . my home . . . my life, for the next four to five years of my life, I thought, looking at the gaunt Clinger. Except for what was in my wallet—two five-dollar bills—all I'd be carrying in Clinger were the core elements of what I figured was surely the most Spartan and inexpensive of world expeditions.

Due to the frequency with which I was now passing through neighborhoods and towns, I saw no reason to carry food and water. As many times as people had invited me off the street into their homes for a meal or a soda pop during the walk to here, I was confident I would be well fed by others all the way to Boston. And even if I wasn't, there would always be a water faucet or a convenience store somewhere just ahead.

So there. Now . . . what to do about the key to the city from Belpre? Send it home? Or keep it for the good luck and power it seemed to possess?

With more than a touch of reverence, I lifted it from its box for the first time. Its smooth and beautifully molded brass form was just as solid and heavy as I thought such a special key would be. I turned it over and was delighted to find additional letters engraved along the long stem's other side: MAYOR IVAN C. SMITH.

To carry it or not? It was heavy and bulky, yes. But it was also very special to me. Why did life have to be filled with difficult questions? If only . . .

A piece of white paper just barely poking out from beneath a corner of the velvet in the box caught my eye. I pulled it out and read it—and nearly dropped the key to the floor. I looked at the pretty heart-shaped ring at the end of its handle, then reread that slip of paper once more:

PLEASE ENJOY YOUR NOVELTY KEY BOTTLE OPENER

A *bottle opener*? My magic key! My greatest honor!

"Jodie!"

I rushed into the kitchen, where she was putting the icing on a chocolate cake, and asked if she had any bottled soda pop.

"I don't like the tinny taste of canned pop," I lied, bending into the refrigerator for a bottle of Mountain Dew.

"There's an opener in the little drawer by the sink," she said.

"That's okay. I've got an opener I had in my pack," I said, keeping my body between her and the key I was hooking over the bottle cap's serrated edge.

I eased the key upward to an angle.

Phsssst!

"Well, I'll—"

"Oh, I see you have that magic key," Jodie said, catching me by surprise. "Are you going to keep that with you all the way around the world?"

I chuckled. "Well, now, I'd be a fool if I didn't. It's magical, right?"

I sauntered out the kitchen door, sucking on the bottle. At the cardboard box to be sent home, I paused long enough to let something big and bright and bronze drop heavily from my hand.

The key to the city would be going home all right . . . but not the long way.

5

Ten days and 130 miles farther along, I awoke to one of the most beautiful bedrooms yet on my walk. It was very much like a corner of Paradise.

Just inches from my head was a minty, clean stream. Standing guard over my sleeping bag were large, full maple and chestnut trees. For once, in a state that had seemed the epitome of sogginess, everything in Pennsylvania that morning was dry and firm.

Behind a large boulder in the stream I took a quick bath in a pool as cold as ice, then let the sun be my towel. By ten-thirty, I was off and away, feeling as free as freedom is. Four hours later, I crossed over the Philadelphia city limit, my lips still bouncing happy whistles off lush stands of maple, oak, and crab apples.

When I arrived at the pretty and leafy St. Joseph's University on the southwestern edge of the city, I started asking whether I was anywhere near St. Joseph's Prep School. June Railey, the mayor's secretary at the Chevy Chase Town Hall, had told me that her son was a teacher at St. Joseph's Prep School, as well as a Jesuit seminarian.

When I found out that classes at St. Joe's would be letting out for the day in only another hour, and that the school was clear over on the city's north side, I decided to go directly to the Jesuit house at Forty-sixth and Chester Avenue. I accepted a ride to the house with one of the university's administrators when it became obvious I'd never find my own way there through the maze of old neighborhoods that surrounded the campus. I figured I could always return to the same spot to restart my journey.

The drive to the Jesuit seminarians' three-story old house was quite an eye-opener for a country boy like me. We passed block after long, dark block of crumbling, rotted structures that, incredibly, people were living in. And so much graffiti. EVERYWHERE! I couldn't believe my eyes. Surely not a single brick or wall or building or tree or parked car had escaped the stroke of a paintbrush or the streak of a spray can. Oddly, most of the marks were peculiar-shaped streaks of white, yellow, red, and black, the words making absolutely no sense to me: REX, RAZZ, KAROT . . . And more often than not, the graffiti was slashed on in a vertical fashion, as if the strange denizens that came in the night to leave these marks could walk over everything like flies.

There were people everywhere I looked. All shapes and sizes, but mostly black. Darting from shop to shop, house to house, across the streets, and between the autos parked along the curbs. Man, *so many* blacks. As thick as the graffiti! It all looked so exciting, so different from anything I'd ever experienced before.

And streetcars. Well, almost. Sort of electric trolley buses. They reminded me of something from another era—say, the 1920's. In fact, the whole bustling, noisy street scene had my mind rocking back to bygone eras.

The only person at the seminary to greet me was the cook, Ruby, a kindly looking black lady of probably sixty or so. She offered me a slice of her homemade apple pie and a glass of lemonade while I waited for Mr. Railey at the building officially known as Farmer House. (I later learned it was named for Ferdinand Farmer, a contemporary of Ben Franklin. Farmer was one of the first board members of the University of Pennsylvania, and had been "the most active itinerant missionary of the Revolutionary War years.")

I took up some space on the front-porch swing, and gobbled pie, swilled lemonade, sucked on ice cubes, and fanned myself with straw, while all around the hedged island of the Jesuit house there swirled a maelstrom of black skin and "Hey, how's it going?"

At last Railey arrived. And a nice man he was.

He was tall (probably 6'3"), a year younger than I, with a graceful build and a very friendly smiling face set under thick curly hair of a gray-flecked brown. In a calm, deep voice he insisted I make the Jesuit house my house for as long as I needed, and that I, please, simply call him Clay.

Dinner consisted of salad, spinach pie, butterscotch pudding, Schlitz beer, and prayer. Afterward, it was everyone to the drawing room for a strange mix of politics, Philly baseball on TV, philosophy, and the evening Eucharist. I felt as welcome as if they were truly my own family. I would have been as content as a saint—except for one disturbing fact.

Earlier, when I'd been about to shower, I'd stepped on the scale in the bathroom and nearly jumped out of my ribs. My weight was a pathetic 136 pounds. I'd lost thirty pounds! How could that be?

And yet there it was, in black and white. And I knew deep inside that I looked it, too. So skinny and tired-looking. For me, losing thirty pounds was nothing less than a catastrophe. At that rate, I wouldn't even be a skeleton by the time I reached Ireland!

When I settled into bed in the guest room on the second floor, where Clay and two others had their own personal studies and bedrooms, I decided to make myself at home at the Farmer House for a while: My body needed a few pounds. But, most important, my spirit sensed that from these men of the cloth I would receive some important insights into life.

That spring was labeled the wettest in Philadelphia history, and the next morning did little to challenge that description. Through the rain and mist, Clay steered the "house car," a 1978 Dodge Dart, into a part of America I could barely believe existed. It was North Philadelphia, he explained to me. The black slums. The poorest of all those poor who called the City of Brotherly Love their home.

The stripped cars rusting in the streets, the torn curtains hanging out broken windows, the trash spilling from every gutter and sidewalk, the blank stares of the jobless watching from beside the missing doors of one burnt shell after another, the sunless puddles, the cold-soaked bums and winos trying to find sleep beneath posters and barbed wire. And that screaming graffiti.

Squiggly lines here, squiggly lines there. An odd bold-faced word here . . . then again . . . then again. None of it made an iota of sense. Why the same strange words (were they words?) again and again?

"Those are the territorial markings of the rival street gangs," Clay explained, as calmly as if he were a tour guide in a museum of natural history. "That's why the same word will keep appearing on everything for blocks on end."

"And the words themselves? What, for example, is a ZAK?"

He laughed. "You got me. It is usually the name of the gang's leader, or his nickname."

It was evident by the way every square foot was marked that the people had given up entirely any thoughts of getting rid of the eyesores.

The campus of the all-boy high school covered an entire city block, except for a large cathedral that appeared to have been gutted by fire and abandoned for many years. I was told over eight hundred students poured into the aging buildings each school day.

Clay and I walked through a pair of large glass doors, passed beneath a giant seal of the school, and came into a front atrium that was at least three stories high. I found it spectacular, especially when compared to Bethel-Tate High School's little entrance hallway. There was so much noise and roughhousing and yelling and boys and priests rushing all about that there looked to be absolutely no order to anything!

Each class of Clay's that I spoke to that morning seemed at first hopelessly riotous. But no sooner would I step to the podium than they would become perfectly attentive. It seemed to me that to God above, the St. Joe's campus must have looked, and sounded, like a carousel set in the middle of a massive crumbling shantytown. And come lunchtime, I had to admit to Clay that it seemed rather dangerous and surely unattractive for the mostly white parents to have to send their children into the middle of a giant slum each morning, especially one notorious for crime and violence.

"There was talk of moving out of the slum, of building a new school in a nice area outside the city," answered Clay. "But then we realized that the boys are getting the best education they can with the school right here. How many of these boys do you think would ever get to see up close what poverty is really like if they didn't have to come through it every morning to get to school, then go right back through it again in the afternoon, when they go home?" He shook his head and continued, "Many of these boys come from very well-to-do families, and for them life is set. But at least for a few years, we make them see just how the other side lives.

"And you know what?" He sat straighter, and his voice grew excited. "The parents think it's a good idea, too. They keep sending their boys back, and even though it's expensive, we have a list of other parents who would love to send their boys here."

Still, I was skeptical. What I had seen that morning through the rain streaks on the car windows had frightened me. I just couldn't imagine any of those boys walking down those streets filled with drug dealers, or drunks, or worse.

Clay looked as if he might laugh. Instead, he dared me to spend the afternoon walking those same streets myself. Go to the city hall building downtown, he said, then return to the school before he left for Farmer House. And let him know what I felt about the boys being in danger.

Leaving my backpack in the trunk of the Farmer House car, I borrowed an umbrella (for the sky was very heavy-looking) and took off briskly toward the direction of City Hall. Clay told me it was easy to spot, even from afar, because it was a large, tower-style building with a huge statue of William Penn on top. The hat-topped Mr. Penn was supposedly at least eighty feet tall, and the old tower around fifty-four stories high. And if that wasn't impressive enough, he said that before the statue of William Penn was put atop the building in the 1800's, a horse-drawn carriage was driven around on the brim of his hat!

Much of the way was rundown and filthy. Poor blacks standing or milling about greeted me from nearly every block. Muscular young men, looking as if they were the "coolest" dudes alive, leaned against the outside of loud bars with dark interiors. Loud soul music filled the air.

I was the only white person I saw, except for a couple of filthy winos, and yet the entire length of my walk I did not feel unwelcome or mistrusted. Many of the people waved and wished me a fine day. I became much too intrigued and entertained by all the friendliness and the natural street "performers" to worry. It was like walking through a mile-long circus in some ways. Each block was a new ring, filled with wild and strange performers, clowns, and even ringmasters, while in the background was the loud, funky music.

Now, I knew why Clay had not seemed overly worried about the schoolboys who passed this way each day. Those living around St. Joe's were just a neighborhood of moms and dads and sisters and brothers and aunts and uncles and cousins and neighbor folk making the best of their circumstances—like the rest of us.

When I awoke on Sunday morning, all I wanted to do was rush back into the streets for more exploring. Everyone else was still asleep, and through the beveled-glass windows of my beautiful little alcove I could see it was still raining, so I decided to tiptoe down to the kitchen and try out a bowl of corn flakes for company. Along the way, I made a detour to pick the *Inquirer* out of a puddle on the front walk. On the porch I pulled the newspaper from its plastic husk and scanned three news stories on the front page. One said it had now rained during eleven of the last twelve weekends in Philadelphia. Another said Britain had had rain for forty-five consecutive days. And the third went on about yet another kind of rain, a very dangerous kind, in an area I planned to soon be passing through— Northern Ireland.

"The rioting in Belfast yesterday was the worst in several years," read a caption beneath a photograph of a wrecked neighborhood that could have been a sister to North Philadelphia. "Over 500 firebombs were thrown at British troops, with several injuries resulting."

Some of the Jesuits had warned me to be careful in Ireland. I would ask that they pray for me when I was there. Then I went back inside, enjoyed some breakfast, and idled away yet more of the dawn by roaming the house, imagining what it would be like to have such a place as my home for years and years, as most of the Jesuits had.

With its very high ceilings, there was a lot of emptiness in the house. And, I had little doubt, a lot of loneliness, too, at times. I returned to my room and settled down at the desk in the alcove to work on the diary I kept each day in addition to the Witness and Daily Log books. But the restlessness inside me refused to go away.

Staring out the window to the front street below, I was struck by how quiet the neighborhood had become overnight. It hardly seemed possible that that wide street was normally choked with humanity and noisy energy. The large, leafy dark oak and maple trees surrounding the house seemed to have drawn in closer around the house's dark sides.

A dog I'd seen before slinking about the yard limped up the broad front steps and sniffed in the bushes below my window. The bones of its small skeleton showed through its skin as it raised its head every few minutes to let out a howl. It was dying of something, but of what? Hunger? Sickness? An injury? Whatever, the floppy-eared animal seemed to accentuate the junglelike atmosphere of the inner city. It was at times like this that having a family around oneself had to be the most important thing in this world. But what about those like Clay and the other Jesuit brothers and priests at Farmer House? Why didn't they find it lonely, even heartbreaking, to be celibate and separated from their home place and family? Or did they?

A sharp rap on the door made me jump out of my concentration. It was Clay, wearing the black uniform and white collar of his vocation. He asked if I was interested in accompanying him to the ten-thirty mass at the nearby St. Francis de Sales Cathedral. I was, but I asked him if he had a few minutes first for some questions of mine. And, of course, he did. He dragged over an old stuffed easy chair; I opened a window to the cool spring fragrances outside.

"Clay, how long have you been studying to be a Jesuit priest?"

His answer came back as quickly as if he had been counting the days. "Six years. I have four still to go, before I am ordained."

"That's such a long time to wait for something that you want. Don't you ever miss your family so much that you want to give up and just be like everyone else? I mean, it must be so lonely at times, watching other young men having families and going out each night to have fun. And here you are, nowhere near your parents and all alone."

He folded the fingers of both hands together and rested his chin on them.

"Naturally, I miss my family, but this desire to be a priest is something I can't deny myself. I want it more than anything else, and so I don't mind the sacrifices.

"The priesthood always fascinated me as a kid. Going to mass on Sunday mornings was oftentimes a tension-filled thing because everybody would always be late, and I would always want to get there on time. I loved the ritual of the mass and the mystery that it speaks.

"My favorite was the early-morning mass on Christmas Eve. Because I knew that I would be back in the church for midnight mass. I just loved that whole day. Overall, there has been very little question that this is exactly what I think I should be doing. Everything in my mind just seems to have been toward this end, toward God and God in this particular way, in serving Him as His priest."

"What makes a good priest?" I wondered.

"He has to be able to listen. There is this story in the Old Testament about . . . Isaac, I think. He was told to go up to this mountain, and he was going to talk to God. And a great hurricane came, and God was not in the hurricane; and a great fire came, and God was not in the fire; and a great earthquake came, and God was not in the earthquake. And then a gentle breeze blew by, and God was in the gentle breeze. I think it is that sensitivity and listening that a priest needs not only for his own life, to hear God in his own life as anybody does, but to hear God in other people's lives so as to help them hear Him in themselves.

"We live in a fragmented world, and it is very hard to find the unity within all the fragmentation. And yet in the mass it all comes together. Of course, it is oftentimes very hard to see that. But that is where a lot of faith comes in, in a sense a blindness of faith. But it is there. That's what you are dealing with, a mystery."

He leaned nearer to my ear and said softly, "Weren't you telling all those boys in class Friday that your walk began as a dream and then grew into an obsession? Sort of like my wanting so much to celebrate the mass?"

I nodded, and with my eyes looking past Clay, thought back to when it had all begun for me.

"I was nine years old. I loved to learn, and to laugh, and with every freckle in my face I truly believed I had been blessed with so much magic. Maybe that's because my three brothers and two sisters and parents and I lived in a tiny village whose name meant "house of God," in a part of

America that still waved at strangers and thought *Tom Sawyer* and *Huck-leberry Finn* were the best stories ever written. Anyway, I had been up-stairs in our tall, old, peeling house on South Charity Street, ignoring yet another rainy Ohio afternoon, my imagination caught in the pages of a big stack of old *National Geographic* magazines, when the seed was planted. The covers of those magazines were faded and worn, but the glossy photo-graphs inside were still very beautiful. 'What a fantastic world we live in!' those paper windows to our planet seemed to say to me."

"I knew then and there that someday I would visit all of those exotic lands, meet all of those smiling faces. And that night, when my mother came in to say good night, I looked up at her and said, 'Mom, when I grow up, I know exactly what I'm going to do. I'm going to become a writer and I'm gonna walk around the world!' "

"She laughed and said, 'Oh, you mean you'll be like a soldier of fortune?' And I simply replied, 'Yeah.' I wasn't sure what she meant, but it sounded awfully exciting.'

I took a deep breath. Clay asked if my dream remained strong all through the rest of my growing up.

"Well, I did become the writer I had envisioned. Right after gradua-tion from the university, I became a newspaper reporter in Casper, Wyo-ming. But the idea of walking around the world had gotten lost. It wasn't until one night in the winter of 1977, when I was driving back to my newspaper office in Casper to write about a triple family murder I'd been investigating, that my dream of walking around the world began to haunt me again. Until, at last, I *had* to stop and park the car to think about it there beneath all those millions of bright stars. I mean, it seemed so crazy at the time, now that I was all grown up and supposedly more rational. Walk around an entire planet—*alone!*"

"Why did it seem crazy to you?"

"Why, because it was utterly and completely impossible! Anyone but a Don Quixote could see that. There were at least a million trillion things out there waiting to rob or kill or hurt someone stupid enough to try such a trip on foot. All you had to do was look at the newspapers and the television news on any night to see how dangerous the world is. But once that dream had returned, it just didn't seem to want to go away again."

Clay rose and stood silently before the window. I followed his gaze just in time to catch a dog's skinny tail disappearing around the front hedge. At last he spoke.

"Obviously, you wanted this so badly that you were willing to risk your life, even before you took that first step." He gestured to my right hand.

I turned the hand palm side up and studied the jagged scars running across it. After I had decided to do the walk, I had quit the newspaper to find a higher-paying job that would enable me to save the twenty thousand dollars I figured it would cost to prepare for and make the walk.

I didn't want help with the expenses. It was important to me to prove that I could live my dreams on my own. But after a year of slaving at a computer terminal, I had only fifty dollars in the bank. So I had gone to work for three-and-a-half years on the oil-drilling rigs in Wyoming as a roughneck. For fourteen hours a day, every day of every week, in 100 degrees below and 120 degrees above, somehow my number had kept from coming up. Until right near the end, when an explosion on the rig floor turned my hand into hamburger meat.

Two hours I'd ridden in a bouncing pickup, faint from shock, the useless hand wrapped in a towel. And for almost six months afterward, it was still as useless and shrunken as the claw of a dead chicken, until the doctors had no choice but to declare my writing hand permanently crippled.

Only to marvel one day, when an unseen strand of nerve still alive in there sent a message to the fingers to get back to work.

I flexed the healthy hand now, as I gave a silent thanks to God once more. "Obviously, I did," I said to Clay with all the pride of a combat veteran.

He smiled strangely, the sparkle in his big, soft eyes hinting that he had been building up all this time to something.

"So how long was it, from the beginning to the end of your preparation for the walk?"

"Almost six years." The same amount of time he had spent studying so far in the seminary.

"And how long do you think it will be before you get back home?"

"Probably four years . . ." A total of ten years to realize one dream. Just like Clay. He'd be a priest at the altar at just about the same time I'd be coming home.

"And you thought *I* was the one who was sacrificing so much, for such a long period. Turned out neither one of us has it easy. But don't give up on the mystery, Steve. Go for it. There're a lot of wonderful gifts of God out there, waiting for you. Get them and bring them back for the rest of us to see. We need them, more than ever."

He looked at me and added, "God will be with you, too. Every step."

When it came time for me to leave the following afternoon, Philadelphia was looking pretty darn nice for a change. The sky was clear and the ground dry, and I discovered that the city of Philadelphia is actually very beautiful, at least downtown: wide boulevards, large water fountains, beautiful old buildings like the library and the Ss. Peter and Paul Cathedral, and tall modern skyscrapers.

The air was just the right temperature to give me "energy," and I strolled on in the direction of Atlantic City for a good two hours before I realized, too late, that I had not taken any photo of Clay or Farmer House. In fact, the only things I had to remind me of that pause in my trek were a bagged lunch of bologna sandwiches and pumpkin pie from Ruby, a letter of introduction from one of the Jesuits, Brother Dean Ludwig, to a friend of his in the Vatican, and a black pen. Oh, yes . . . and a tape recording of a conversation with Clay. He had been the latest in a growing chain of interviews I'd done with the recorder.

When I thought of some of the other interviews I'd done just between Washington and Philadelphia—Carol Beck, a volunteer at the Our Daily Bread soup line, where I ate my lunch both days in Baltimore; Sister Mary, at a convent I stayed in one night; a tearful poor drunk in posh Bel Air, Maryland, who presented me with five dollars for my next meal; and dear teeny Eddie Bernard, a seventy-eight-year-old black hermit in the middle of Pennsylvania's mushroom country, who lived in a windowless shack in a junkyard with a rooster named Billy—I realized more than ever how rich and vibrant this country was in human resources.

What a good thing, indeed, that I had the recorder. Because with persons like Clay and the others, it was their words, rather than their faces, that were their greatest treasure.

The Ben Franklin Bridge to New Jersey was open to foot traffic. So I walked across the muddy Delaware, with its oil slicks and floating plastics, and thought of the poverty and decay I had left behind me—and of the human energy and love and beauty I had found even there.

Before I reached the end of the mile-long span, it was evident I'd have only cars for company the whole way. Emboldened, I reached for the pen given to me by the Farmer House Jesuits, whipped off its cap, and gleefully scribbled STEVEN M. NEWMAN, MAY 24, 1983, "THE WORLDWALKER" onto the railing.

There! Now I had *my* territory marked, too. And at least I knew the identity of *one* of the ink-and-paint demons!

6

vil. Whatever it was that had just caused me to snap from the deep, dreamless sleep I was immersed in was deathly evil. My mind sensed that clearly. I didn't dare open my eyes, even though my head was buried with the rest of me deep inside a sleeping bag with the drawstring pulled tight. What was it every cell in my body was fearing so terribly all of a sudden? I was so frightened I couldn't even shake.

There!

From near to my head it sounded, the low and thick growling of something powerful, something large, something ready to cut across my throat like a jagged saw.

As I lay there, the deep sounds grew louder. And closer.

I was like a giant larva frozen with fear, in a cocoon that blinded me to all except the horror about to tear through my thin cover.

I could hear the creature creeping closer and closer. In the chill of my fright, its advancing wickedness seemed to have an ally even in the rain pounding on the motel's tin roof. I wanted so much to release the screams clawing at the inside of my throat, but I didn't dare. For that could be all the monster might need to plunge its fury into my bowels.

I inched a trembling hand to the only hope I had of escaping with my life: my hunting knife. It seemed an eternity before my fingers crawled to the bone handle nestled against my ribs. I dragged the knife's long blade slowly up to my lips. I breathed silence and sweat. I slitted an eye. I was ready to fight.

My mind plotted: *Breathe deeply . . . pull the drawstring slack . . .*

count to three and spring screaming from the open end of the bag . . .
slash the creature with the knife . . .

"One, two . . . THREE!"

With the fury of a madness that only one eye-to-eye with the devil can know of, my upper body exploded into the room. I screamed death and revenge at everything vile and wicked in that cold tomb of rot and stench. My knife cut angrily into the bodiless nothingness that should have been a killer.

Silence. Horrible, mysterious silence.

Something wet dripped onto the hand that held the knife outstretched. It pricked the skin like wet ice. Rainwater. A leak in the roof!

Grrrrrrrrr.

The black hunchbacked son of the devil materialized from behind a pile of moss-covered tiles to my right. Like something born of the night itself, the pit bull's body became a glistening silhouette, waiting for a reason to kill.

I stared wide-eyed at the messenger of death.

If I screamed, would someone come before it was too late? I doubted it. The nearest house was much too far away, its inhabitants probably sound asleep at such an early hour in the morning.

No, it was just the pit bull and me. I was on my own.

My free hand worked the zipper down along the side of the bag; my legs drew up into a crouching position.

Never before on this walk had I slept with my knife at my side. Yet somehow I had sensed strongly before going to sleep that something very dangerous would soon be upon me. It was almost as if I could now *feel* whether a place I was passing through was evil or good.

As I crouched naked, never blinking, never taking my eyes off the side of the room with the dog, I felt beside the bag for a boot. I found one, tensed every cell in my body for action, and heaved both myself and the boot at the animal. The animal veered and bolted into plyboard and tile, barking and tearing at the air with at least as much confusion, fear, and anger as I had. Then, just as suddenly, even more frighteningly . . . the silence returned.

I crouched again, grabbed the other boot, sprang upright shouting, and flung it at the far shadowed corner the dog had dashed into. More silence.

Nothing was making any sense. And yet I was not about to venture into the black to feel for the thing. It had to be somewhere in there; I'd watched it leap into the blank space.

I stood motionless for what seemed an eternity and listened more intently than ever. But all I heard were raindrops splashing into puddles.

I had watched the doorway the entire time, and I was positive nothing bigger than a rat had darted through it.

Tired and cold, and nearly as frightened as ever, I eased myself back into the bag until I was once again enclosed tightly within its fabric.

Fear. How greatly I hated that emotion, especially when I found myself exhibiting it. If there was one thing that perplexed me in my adult life, it was the fear I was seeing among my fellow Americans, friends and strangers alike.

Maybe, I told myself now, I had never known how fearful I actually should be. Over the years, there'd been plenty who had joked that I was too nice and naive to know about such things. And maybe they were right.

Anyway, if the creature I had just confronted in this motel room was a visitor from hell, it seemed appropriate. For the closer I had come to Atlantic City this day, the more I had felt that I was nearing a place of wasted and broken souls.

On my way across south New Jersey, the Garden State, it was a rare moment for me when anyone said hello. For the most part I was treated as if I were distrusted and disliked.

I had passed boarded-up motels and refreshment stands, and what were once fancy restaurants now decaying into wrecks. On this strip into A.C., as the locals referred to their tiny state's most famous city, those few motels still running looked to be nearly dead. And yet this was the first big holiday of the summer season—Memorial Day weekend.

At one shuttered former restaurant and nightclub, I had stopped to wolf down the last of a package of Oscar Mayer frankfurters I'd purchased at a tiny general store in the morning. (You do not know the taste of monotony until you have eaten twelve old franks in one day.) In the back of the building, I saw old mattresses rotting with hints that hoboes or other transients had slept on them lately.

Several of the shop owners I'd talked with said there had been a large influx of unemployed and unskilled transients looking for work in the booming "casino row" of A.C. So, south New Jersey, which had built the casinos in the hope of easing the high unemployment, now found itself with more unemployment and crime than ever before.

"We who've lived here all our lives are scared," said the owner of a bar halfway between Camden and Atlantic City. "It ain't like twenty years ago, when people waved and stopped to talk. It's a rougher bunch now; we can't trust no one.

"Business along the pike stinks. No need for any of the tourists rushing to the casinos to stop. Besides, the casinos bus them in anyhow, to make sure they ain't going to find no way to spend any of their money on the way to the gambling tables. Everything they'd ever need—even a haircut!—they can get right inside the casino they're at. Most people here have to go forty or fifty miles every day to work. But nobody's leaving, because they ain't got the money to move anyhow. Most are just surviving."

When I fell asleep, I was still clutching the knife as tightly as a soldier might his rifle . . . or an exorcist his crucifix. The dog's disappearance would remain a mystery until dawn, when I found a hole in the wall of the bathroom the dog must have escaped through . . . maybe.

On one of the low-railed bridges crossing from the "offshore" (mainland) to the "shore" (Atlantic City Island), I had my second brush with death in less than ten hours.

A speeding pickup truck towing an empty horse trailer whipped drunkenly across a huge pothole on the narrow and curved bridge, causing the trailer behind it to careen toward the thigh-high railing and myself.

Not about to leap into the swirling brackish tidal waters just to my left, I held my breath and waited for the impact. But it never came. Instead, the trailer whacked into the railing inches before me and bounced back onto the roadway.

The shoulder of the bridge was only a foot and a half wide, so why the trailer didn't at least graze my body was a miracle of sorts. If it had knocked me off into the deep, strong currents below, the weight of Clinger would have dragged me quickly to the bottom.

Still, once in the fabled old resort town itself, I sensed a new surge of energy within me. As I stood across from the circular "monument" in the center of Albany Avenue and gazed at all the traffic and the towering casinos, I knew I'd ventured into something very different from anywhere I'd ever been in my whole life.

"IN APRIL OUR SLOT PLAYERS WON $64,627,358. DID YOU GET YOUR SHARE?" taunted one casino billboard.

Like a child in a big, crazy department store, I roamed the main drags along the casinos and then the actual boardwalk itself. At last, here I was on the great Atlantic City Boardwalk, the actual raised walkway along the Atlantic Ocean that I had seen in so many movies, read of in so many novels and short stories.

Yet as I walked over its tightly fitted boards and stopped occasionally to lean against its silver-painted metal tube rail, I found that the most romantic and intriguing side of the boardwalk was not the side with the numerous souvenir shops, casinos, and pizza/frozen custard/salt-water taffy eateries, but the side with the ocean and deserted beach. As I gazed out over the enormous expanse of green-gray water, its cool, salty breath caressing my sunburnt face, a deep sense of awe washed over me. Soon, very soon, I would be crossing that endless restless horizon to the strange lands that existed "just" on the other side. How close, yet how distant. To think that even as I was being mesmerized by the waves before me, other waves from the same ocean were captivating someone else in another part of the world, thousands of miles away.

I headed through the dusky light to the city's interior, hoping to track down charity in the form of a hot shower and soft bed, both of which I hadn't known for many days now. Down one litter-choked street after another I wandered, looking for the Salvation Army's overnight house. By the time I found it, it was well after dark—and to my dismay, the Army had no overnight accommodations.

The kindly old man behind the front desk, however, told me of a place that did have free beds and a shower. And he fished a map out of his filing cabinets and traced the route to the Rescue Mission.

It was about ten blocks away, in one of the city's poorest and supposedly most dangerous sections. But figuring there couldn't be anything worse-looking than North Philly, I didn't worry. For me, slums had long ago ceased to be a novelty. Ever since Washington, D.C., they had seemed to be the rule. Continuing south on Atlantic Avenue, I passed one loud and sleazy bar after another. Yet it was not the bums that held my attention but rather the long, sleek, shiny limousines that kept appearing every few minutes from the side streets leading to the casinos along Pacific Avenue.

The chauffeured cars were so filthy-rich-looking, with their elongated bodies and black-tinted windows. Whoever rode in the backseats of those cars must have been multimillionaires many times over, I figured with envy. Why, in Bethel, one could stand on Main Street for a hundred years and never see such a vehicle go through. The closest thing to it would be the funeral home's hearse.

Could those be the personal cars of the Mafia? They certainly looked sinister enough. And hadn't I heard about the mob's roaming in this city of money?

Hard as I tried, I could not catch a glimpse of the car's elegant riders, and so I did not know that in reality, those cars were glorified taxis shuttling businessmen from the airports to their reserved rooms in the hotels.

As I made my way down the dark side street of Ohio, the air was filled with the loud sounds of African-style music, and large groups of black men and boys slowly passed me. Many eyed me suspiciously, as if wondering what I was doing in that area so late. Once, when the music was its loudest and the men the most numerous, I thought for a moment of turning and fleeing. Some of the men were beginning to mutter as I passed them, and it was so dark I could become easy prey.

I knew better than to be so afraid, but still I breathed a big sigh when at last I stood before the fairly new and surprisingly small mission building. Inside, the Reverend Mohr barked like an army sergeant at each of us transients, lining us up before dinner to ask loudly of each, as we looked up at him on his high pulpit, if we believed everything he had preached of the Devil and the Gospels that evening. No one dared to say no. But I hardly minded. I'd survived.

Even a fistfight in the sleeping room later that night hardly interested me. Nor the knowledge that my gigantic-armed, small-headed, furry-browed, crater-faced bunkmate was a confessed murderer of redheads.

I was just plain too tired . . . and anxious to see the ocean again.

7

As I stepped from the graffiti-covered subway train at exactly 9:00 A.M., the sweat was already trickling over my ribs. On my back was a Clinger at his lightest yet, and under my left arm a cardboard box addressed to my home and stuffed with my sleeping bag. With it now the middle of June and the nights almost as hot as the days, the thick bag had become more of a burden than a necessity. And I was glad to replace its bulkiness and weight with a secondhand cotton blanket that I'd purchased for two dollars from an admiring street bum on Staten Island.

After nine days of wandering all over New York City, I was anxious to end my stay there and head for the countryside north of it, before the summer grew any more oppressive.

From the moment I had left the Staten Island ferry and ventured into the deep canyons of Manhattan's skyscraper forest, I had felt myself caught up in an atmosphere of "sink or swim." As I walked the eighty blocks from lower Manhattan's Wall Street district to Central Park, I was swept along in a tide of three-piece suits, briefcases, shopping bags, and loud tape players hanging from the shoulders of gyrating teenage boys. I felt I was in another dimension, one where time and imagination never rested.

For me, Cincinnati with its million residents had always been the Big City, and so when I knew I was about to enter a city thirteen times *larger,* I could hardly keep my nerves still. And the day I arrived, I was sure that every single one of those millions of New Yorkers had picked that same sunny, hot afternoon to be downtown with me. Clinger and I were engulfed.

As I walked from First Avenue to Eighth Avenue, I passed a Puerto Rican street carnival, the banks of six nations, the airline offices of ten countries, restaurants offering every cuisine from French to Indian, and street vendors hawking everything from Italian ices to Greek newspapers. It was as though at this one point on the earth modern civilization had produced a collage of every race and face in the world.

Before I had even begun my worldwalk, I had been told by almost every person I knew who had ever visited New York City how they'd had their pockets picked or their purses snatched. And my mother, who had been an operating-room nurse in New York City, had told me about the many knifing and shooting victims she'd seen on the operating table. And then there were those interminable statistics in newspapers and magazines to the effect that New York had a mugging about every twenty seconds and a murder every thirty.

And along with the crime, I had been warned to expect dirt. It seemed that if a bullet or a hypodermic needle didn't finish me off, there would be plenty of air pollutants and giant rats or cockroaches around to do the job. By the time I had reached Staten Island (by walking illegally over a long and narrow highway bridge whose name I could never remember), I had figured that if I survived the jungle of New York, I could survive anything the world might throw at me.

But it had taken no more than that first day on Staten Island to show me that, once again, the purveyors of fear were going to be wrong. Late in the evening I stopped at a Sunoco service station for a drink of water, and met seventeen-year-old Kevin Lopes and nineteen-year-old Neal Britton, the two friendliest young strangers I had yet encountered on the walk. They were both gas-pump attendants, but when they found out what I was doing, they wouldn't let me leave their neck of the woods before they had presented me with twenty dollars apiece, two soda pops, a beer, *and* a large, rich, luscious extra-cheesy Domino's pizza! And all I'd asked for was a sip at their water fountain!

And the next day in Manhattan—on East Forty-ninth Street, to be exact—the hospitality that was New York was every bit as great as out on the fringes. There, in an apartment that back home we would have used as a closet, lived a struggling free-lance writer the same age as I, who told me I could stay with him for as long as I wished at no charge whatsoever. Kevin McDermott and I had never met, but that didn't stop him.

So I was able to use Kevin's place as my latest "camp," while I explored the city day and night, walking to places close by, like Times Square and the United Nations, and taking the "notorious" subways to the farther places, like Queens. And except for a few passes from some streetwalkers along Forty-second Street, I experienced none of New York City's crime life. As a matter of fact, I felt safer walking alone in Manhattan at two in the morning than I did in any of the other large metropolitan areas I'd explored, especially Washington and Baltimore. With so many people up and about in New York at all hours, I felt the truth of "safety in numbers." And there was something wonderful about going to an outdoor opera in Central Park with over seventy-two thousand others, with their wine and French bread and blankets, or having to stand in line at three in the morning to pay for a melon at a corner fruit stall.

"Don't believe it!" a wild-eyed Yugoslavian cab driver laughed, when I asked him about the dangers of living in New York. "I dare you to walk anywhere in Manhattan—yes, even Central Park—at any time of the day or the night, and see if anything happens to you." He loved his new home, wouldn't trade it for the world.

And so now, on my last day in the city, as I walked east along Twenty-third Street to the address on the scrap of paper in my hand, I knew better than to let this particularly nasty-looking part of the city scare me. I had come to this impoverished area to locate the *Daily World,* a newspaper I knew nothing about and had been unable to find at any of the newsstands. Kevin had told me someone named Rodriguez had telephoned and requested an interview with me, and I had figured that with a name like the *Daily World,* it had to be a fairly large and prestigious publication.

Still . . . why weren't its editorial offices closer to midtown Manhattan? And how could it be that Kevin, who'd lived in New York for over four-and-a-half years, hadn't heard of the newspaper either? Something was not right; but I was not about to miss the chance to visit a huge daily in the media capital of the world. For me as a journalist, this was like a priest visiting the Vatican. Or so I was hoping.

At the street number I'd been given, I found only an office building that had seen better days—probably in about World War I. There was no proud display of the newspaper's name over the front doors, merely some half-inch-tall white plastic words—DAILY WORLD OFFICES—sloppily stuck onto a cheap black message board just inside the grime-coated entryway.

Uneasily, I stepped into an unlit and cluttered hallway and was immediately face-to-face with a large black man in a blue T-shirt and faded jeans. The way he rose from behind the low metal office desk blocking the hall made me swallow involuntarily. His expression was not friendly, and his right hand was suspiciously concealed beneath the desktop.

"Who do you want?" he asked almost threateningly, eyeing the box under my left arm.

"The *Daily World,*" I answered.

"Why?" he growled, the thick lumps of muscles on that right arm tensing noticeably.

"They want to interview me," I said irritably.

He moved suddenly from the desk, and I flinched, as if expecting a punch in the face.

Instead, he went to an empty elevator stall that reminded me of those found in old warehouses, threw aside the metal gate, and screamed up the shaft for someone to send the elevator down. When there was no response, he cursed and rammed a buzzer button. This went on for a good five minutes, during which I inched my way carefully over to a bulletin board and, just beneath it, a crude wooden table weighted down with piles of newspapers. Almost as soon as I looked at a copy of the *Daily World,* my heart sank.

It was none other than the old *Daily Worker,* only with a slicker layout and, of course, the new name. The *Worker* I remembered from my college days, when it was the official newspaper of the Communist party.

I wanted to leave right then. The last thing I wanted in my worldwalk was any kind of politics—capitalist or communist. But especially not this kind.

The hateful headlines running across the front page I was reading, and the photo of a grossly deformed embryo child tacked to the bulletin board with the words "The Last Picture" beneath it, told me I'd stepped into something I didn't want to be a part of.

Just as I started for the door, the rickety elevator clanged to the ground floor.

"You going up or not?" the security man asked crossly.

"Yes," my voice surprised me.

As always, my curiosity had overruled my common sense. I told myself there would be no interview, but I had to see what the editorial offices looked like. Would they be as seedy and dusty and depressing as everything else in this part of New York?

The gray-walled elevator shuddered to a stop a good foot above the third-floor hallway. I pushed the cage door open and hopped down onto yellowed and scuffed linoleum tiles.

Opposite me was a long window similar to those in police stations, made of scratched bullet-proof glass and with only a tiny metal vent to talk through.

Glaring out at me from behind a cluttered desk on the other side was a woman in her twenties who looked capable of taking on any street gang.

"Who are you looking for?" she shouted impatiently.

"Rodriguez."

She threw up her hands. "Hey, look, we got two of 'em. Which is it, mister?"

I didn't know.

She turned her head to scream at someone in another room to answer the damned telephone. Then her dark and baggy eyes glared back at me. "Is it a guy or a woman?" she demanded.

"Guy," I guessed.

She marched off past a maze of shelves stacked with back issues of the *Daily World*. A few seconds later, the sound of her screaming for Rodriguez filtered back through the vent. Wearily, I sat down on the only piece of furniture in the hallway, an old church pew.

Bullet-proof glass, husky security men, screaming voices, buzzers . . . How could anyone work in such an environment of fear and hate?

For that matter, was it really necessary for me to see more? I decided it wasn't and climbed back into the elevator.

It was a relief to step back out onto the hot pavement of Twenty-third Street. I felt like a man leaving prison as I heard the door behind me clunk shut. Gladly, I let the sidewalk crowd sweep me toward the subway.

But at the entrance to the underground trains, I heard a frantic voice calling my name from behind. It was Rodriguez.

He had run the entire way from the *Daily World*. His thin, drawn face was coated with sweat, and his breath was labored.

"I was in the cafeteria when you came. Is it still possible to talk to you?" he gasped.

Around his neck was a thin silver chain with the wooden letters FALN dangling from it.

"I'm sorry. I've got to race to another appointment," I lied.

His shoulders slumped, as if receiving denials was all too common in his life. I knew writing for a regular daily was frustrating enough; it must have been doubly bad working for one as controversial as the *Daily World*.

I ran down the steps and through the turnstile, before he had a chance to recover and ask me again.

Maybe it was my imagination, but as the train jerked away from the platform, I thought I caught a fleeting glimpse of Rodriguez standing by the token booth, his dark eyes still hoping.

8

"D
o you have any draft?" I asked desperately. The heat was still strong, even though the concrete of New York City was fifty miles behind me.

The tall, graying, stoop-shouldered bartender took his eyes from his *New York Times* and looked with a raised brow at me and the huge backpack I'd leaned against the far wall by the door. The way he studied the small American flag I'd added to Clinger's backside that morning made me tighten slightly inside. I hoped he didn't recognize it as being from the public cemetery at nearby North Tarrytown. I had "borrowed" it from a soggy Memorial Day wreath still lying on a veteran's grave that I had waked beside in the dewy dawn.

"No, sir, I'm sorry to say we don't. What we do have is in that cooler against the wall."

I settled on a bottle of Miller. He lifted one from the unlighted shelves of the glass-fronted cooler, opened it quietly, and poured it slowly and carefully into a glass, which he then set upon a white napkin before me.

I felt as if I were at the Hyatt Regency, not in a tiny one-room country bar near Cold Spring, New York, in the Hudson River valley.

"This has to be one of the cleanest bars I've ever been in," I remarked after looking more closely at the spotless area behind the bar counter.

"Thank you," he said. "Would you care to buy it?"

I laughed. "Why do you want to sell such a nice place?"

He folded his long fingers together on the shiny bar top and looked at me. "How old would you guess me to be?"

I studied him carefully. His hair wasn't too gray, most of it was still there, and he looked quite strong.

"Fifty-five."

"You are a very kind young man. I'm seventy-two."

I could hardly believe it.

He pointed behind me. I turned, and in the shadow of a far corner saw an old lady with one leg in a cast. She was knitting, but her only light was the little that came in through a window.

I hesitated when he asked me what her age was. With her frail frame and white hair, she could be either his mother or his wife.

"I'm eighty-four going on eighty-five," she said without waiting for my guess. Her eyes hadn't left the needles in her tiny hands.

"Now do you see why the place is for sale?" he asked.

I nodded.

"We're just too old to be bothering with all the headaches anymore," he went on.

"What sort of headaches?" I asked.

He tucked his chin in and rolled his eyes in an expression of disbelief. "Why, taxes, for one thing. Twenty years ago, we paid something like three hundred dollars a year in taxes on this building; now it's over three thousand dollars. There's no way we can make a profit when we pay that sort of taxes and all the other expenses like heat and electricity."

That explained why there were no lights on in the bar, except for one tiny lamp on the wall behind it. And also why the jukebox was silent and the liquor bottles few.

"How long have you owned the Dew Drop Inn?"

"Ask the little lady."

I turned to her. She looked up only long enough to say she'd owned it for forty-three years.

The shadows in the empty bar grew longer, but our conversation became warmer, and within seventy minutes we were seated around one of the old metal-legged dining tables chatting about everything from the walk to growing old. The old woman continued her knitting in the dim light, while I savored a second beer—a free one.

Her name was Anna Olley Engelhardt, his Elmer Eaton. Anna's husband had passed away in 1962, a few years after Elmer had started bartending at the Dew Drop Inn, so they'd decided ever since to live together and watch out for each other. Their deep affection showed in the courteous and gentle way they spoke to, and of, each other.

For a while, Anna and I talked, while Elmer tinkered about in a back kitchen fixing dinner. He spread a red-and-white checkered cloth over the table's well-preserved linoleum top and brought out sardines, white bread, a lettuce-and-tomato salad, and three small bowls of clam chowder.

He offered me another Miller, but I insisted on paying for it.

Only once during the evening did any customers come in. Two middle-aged men and a slightly younger blonde, all workers at a nearby atomic plant, bought one round of beers, played a couple of games of pool, listened to Frank Sinatra for a while on the jukebox, then left laughing at something the man had said about blondes.

"We have a number of young people who come in here, and I always try to tell them that they should be nice to people," Anna told me. "I tell them they should never hold grudges, because as you get older, you need friends.

"Cooking and meeting people are two of the nicest things in life," she went on. "And with this place, I've gotten to meet so many nice people. See, Steve, I don't have to go looking for them; they come looking for *me*.

"Some people say I'm too nice to be running a bar, that I care too much. And maybe they're right in some ways. Lord knows I don't like people who come in just to get drunk. I get to worrying about them too much. I don't like to think of them going out and getting into any trouble, or getting hurt. And that is when I ask them to go home and have the drink in their homes."

"You really say that?" I asked incredulously. "Isn't that bad business? I mean, you'll lose their business if they think you're calling them drunks."

"I know lots of bars that wouldn't do that," she said. "I know—I have seen them take the last nickel from someone and didn't care. I couldn't sleep at night if I was that way."

Anna reminded me of the only grandparent I had really known while I was growing up—Grandma Roos, my father's mother. Grandma Roos had started a small nursing home in her own home and with her own savings, and had spent many decades caring in a personal sort of way for all those old people who came to know the Morris Nursing Home as their last refuge. She had lived for a while upstairs in the same big old house on South Charity Street as the elderly "residents," then moved into a trailer in the backyard, and then finally had become a patient herself in that same home.

While I was growing up, I had frequently gone to her tidy little trailer to seek out her advice and stories, just as I had been drawn countless times to the old folks in the home. I was fascinated that there at one address were so many lifetimes' worth of lessons to be learned, simply for the asking. Those wrinkled, kind people who never lacked for time to chat were, in a sense, talking crystal balls that could tell me what lay ahead in my own life. Even as a youngster, I felt strongly that if I learned what mistakes they had made in their lives, I could avoid those mistakes myself and have a happier existence.

And one of my most valuable lessons had come one night when Grandma Roos had placed a small, thin hand on mine and said, "Whatever your dreams are, Steve, do them *now,* while you're young. Because when you get older, your body won't feel anymore like doing those dreams. Even though your heart still does."

That advice had returned to my thoughts when I was deciding whether to do the worldwalk or not. And when I had visited her in the old nursing home just before this past Christmas to tell her about my walk, she alone had believed right away that I could actually succeed. She had said she'd be there cheering me on to the house at the finish.

She was about the same age as Anna, and similarly short, thin, and sharp in the mind. It would have been nice to imagine Anna as my grandma, except that the idea made me feel too lonely. A month or so ago, I'd learned during a telephone call to home from New Jersey that Grandma Roos had passed away in her sleep while I was in Philadelphia at Farmer House. It hurt to think she wouldn't be there when—if—I made it back home. And it frightened me to think of how different the home I left would become in the many years still remaining in the journey.

"Do you have any favorite kind of customer?" I asked.

"Somebody who doesn't give you a hard time," she answered straight away.

Elmer joined in. "If you are going to discuss something, okay, but don't argue about it. There are too many people who don't know the difference between an argument and a discussion. That is the whole trouble. We shut off arguments. Quick as we can."

"How do you do that?"

Anna spoke up again. "Well, if I see two boys starting to push one another, I go right over to them and I say, 'You don't do that in here. If you don't like the way things are, just go home for a while, and we will see you again sometime.' Forty-three years and I've never had to call the state trooper on account of any trouble in here. I handle people gently but firmly. How come you can't do that, Elmer?" she kidded.

He chuckled and ribbed her back with, "Because, my dear Anna, I am a man. You can look at some guy who is six foot four and say to him, 'You really didn't mean that, did you?' And he looks down at you, and he melts and says, 'No, sweetheart, I didn't mean it.'

"I go to the same person who is six foot four, and I'll look at him and say, 'Knock it off.' And that's exactly what he'll try to do—knock my head off!"

He put an arm around her and gave her a big hug.

Anna gave me a wink. "I like people," she said, handing Elmer a mass of yarn to hold while she rolled it into a ball for the sweater she was knitting for one of her two great-grandchildren. "Yes, I really like people."

And so passed that lovely summer evening in what might have been the most caring bar in the world.

9

The lush dairy-farm meadows and thickly wooded hills lulled me into a sort of easy, lazy stroll. Several times I stopped for no reason other than to stretch my long bones in the grass beneath a shady oak. This was the famous Rip Van Winkle country of old, and it was easy to envy anyone who lived in such restfulness, even if it did put you to sleep for twenty years sometimes. Like a little boy, I stared imaginatively at the big fluffy clouds floating across the blue heavens.

The air was as moist and hot as ever, but now I didn't mind so much, for I'd purchased some shorts to wear. The red of my skin was beginning to take the color of a tan, and I relished the way my slightly burned pores tingled in the slight breeze.

I took my time walking, and found around every tight bend in this lightly traveled section of Route 82 one surprise after another. Sometimes it was as small as a strange-sounding Dutch name on a mailbox. Other times it was a clear, noisy brook spilling through dense brush and over rainbow-colored boulders.

That clear, clean water running free was not only aesthetically beautiful, but also represented a way for me to wash off all the grit and smell of the city. And do my laundry, too.

And what a bathtub I had on that second afternoon after leaving the Dew Drop Inn: cold as ice but clear as glass, and to the skin like pure oxygen would be to the lungs. I had it all to myself—just me, the trees, and a loud waterfall as high as my shoulders. The water in the secluded pool beneath the falls was to my thighs, but its chill was so sharp, I felt as if I were in it up to my hairline.

I had not felt so clean and alive since perhaps northern Virginia. I splashed diamond droplets all about me, and shouted with delight as several of the droplets stung my torso.

Then I scrambled up into the jaws of the waterfall and stood unsteadily while the stream tried to wash me back into the foamy pool. I let loose with a Tarzan yell that sent a curious squirrel leaping further into the maples and oaks.

I might have splashed and splished in my little paradise for most of the day if my right foot had not made a discovery. As I eased myself back into the pool, my foot brushed against something that *felt* as smooth as a stream boulder, but not rocklike. Rather, it felt long, and worse, it slithered.

Glancing down at my red toes, I saw the one thing I hate to no end— a snake! Or, was it an *eel*? I swore the long, grayish, writhing, disgusting creature had a flat tail. Instantaneously, I thought of something from the sea. Something with fangs and forked tongues and whatever. After all, there'd been sharks spotted this far north in the Hudson River (which was still salty at this point), so why not eels, too? Eels that somehow came up the stream to eat innocent people like me.

Before the thing could fade into the churning water directly beneath the fall, I was out, yanking my drying clothes off the crab-apple-tree branches and ready to be back on the road.

My several layers of goose bumps had barely had time to recede when, about a mile up the road, I came upon some sort of large outdoor family gathering. There were at least twenty people, middle-aged on down, in the side yard of a big old wooden farmhouse. One of the older men invited me to join them to eat, and I promptly scampered over to their gathering. It was a birthday party for two of the family's sons. One brother was twenty, the other twenty-one, and they were as dark-haired, strongly built, and handsome as movie stars.

The family was named Strong. Although they probably didn't have all that much financially, as evidenced by the general rundown condition of their house, it seemed they didn't know hunger. Spread out on the lawn were three long picnic tables laden with meats, salads, snacks and breads, and cookies. A nearby brick grill was buried in sizzling hot dogs and fist-thick hamburger patties, and just six feet away stood a metal tub at least three feet in diameter and two feet deep, stuffed with bottles and cans of beer and soda pop.

"Come on, people, let's finish off these hot dogs and burgers!" Mrs. Strong yelled, fanning the delicious-smelling smoke from the grill.

The others ignored her, or groaned about how full they already were. But I looked hopefully toward her dark eyes.

"Well, I guess you'll have to finish them off," she said to me.

It was too good to be true! I felt as if it were *my* birthday party!

I grabbed a paper plate, slapped a heap of potato salad on one side, and strode to the grill. I hadn't seen so much food for the taking since I didn't know when. Four times I went back to the grill, and each time I came back with more meat to add to my potato salad, beans, chips, and soda pop. Uhh-Uhmmmmm!

After I'd cleared a sizable patch in the meat, an enormous vanilla-and-chocolate ice-cream cake was brought out and put on one of the picnic tables. The cake measured a good three feet long, two feet wide, and four inches deep. On it, in large candy frosting, was HAPPY BIRTHDAY SONS.

The cake brought all the kids back to the group from a game of basketball they'd been playing behind the farmhouse. So the eating started all over again. And about the time I was into my second piece of cake, a sunburned, wrinkled, and thin neighbor lady of around fifty named Flo dropped in on the gathering. She was, it turned out, Irish. And despite having lived in the United States for forty years, she still had a very Irish brogue to her voice.

"Does me heart good to see a young man eat so," she directed my way with a touch of jest. "From what the young ones been telling me, you'll be needing a few more pounds on you," she added warmly.

Since my stomach was beginning to hurt slightly at that point, I slowed down my fork enough to discuss the walk with this intelligent-looking farm woman.

Of Ireland, she said excitedly, "The Irish love to talk. You'll find you always have an audience to listen to your stories—especially with the children."

Her green eyes glanced at the small crowd of little ones who'd formed a semicircle about us. They jostled to get nearer. Obviously, she was a favorite storyteller of theirs.

Flo placed a small but strong hand on my shoulder and continued, "What you be doing is something the little ones *everywhere* will enjoy hearing about. You'll not be forgetting them, will you?"

I shook my head, and she leaned back with a contented, motherly smile.

"Good," she said, motioning to the others that she still had more to say. She continued, ever so seriously, "You see, Steven, in Ireland the little things count as much as the big things. The people there haven't as much as others in richer places, and so they do their best to make the most of everything that comes their way. And as long as you remember to look upon the small with the same importance as the big things, you'll never be wanting for food or shelter, or friends. Not in Ireland, you won't."

Then, with ever so subtle a smile, she signaled to the children that it was okay for them to speak now. Immediately, a little boy stepped up to me and asked how I was going to walk across the ocean.

I'd already answered that one in that gathering at least three different times, but very patiently I explained that once I got to Boston, which was still two hundred miles away from where we were in Pine Plains, I would fly across the water on one of the commercial jets.

Soon the grown-ups joined our discussion, and they moved their lawn chairs and picnic benches closer to Flo and me. Although their bodies were work-weary, their eyes were as sparkling with curiosity and life as the children's.

And Flo told us her own dream. "Building with stone is what I'd do all the days of me life, if it were possible," she said calmly. "It's so mindless, mind you." Laughter at her little pun, and from one of the men, "Flo, you'd tear down a stone wall just so you could rebuild it, you would." She chuckled, and replied with her eyes half-closed, "Just me and the stones and the sun, and the wind blowin' through me hair . . ."

I looked about me. Everyone else had eyes half-closed now, and heads leaning back as if in a daydream.

Flo continued in her even, low voice, "You lift the stones and carry their solid weight, and then place them ever so carefully together. Stone after stone after stone . . . all day long. And then, all of a sudden, a wee little voice somewhere deep inside you reminds you you're tired and hungry. And without any hesitation, you just put everythin' away and simply call it quits. Ah, now that's when you know you're living: when you feel like you've done something, and you can actually stand back and look at what it is you've done, and say to yourself, 'My! I did all that?' "

Eventually, others of the grown-ups and little ones had a chance to entertain with a story, too. By the time dusk crept up on our bug-bitten flesh and the melted remains of the cake, a good dozen stories had passed my ears.

Finally, the coolness of the evening reminded everyone, particularly the mothers, that another day had run its course.

"Would you like to stay overnight with us?" Mrs. Strong offered. "You'd have to sleep on the floor, but it'd be better than the ground, wouldn't it?"

I was very tempted, for the sun and food and stories had put me into the most relaxed mood I'd been in for weeks. But I told myself I should push on for a few more miles, at least. This was good farm country, and I knew there'd be plenty of barns just up the road for me to sneak into, as soon as I felt like sleeping.

"I could fix you a big breakfast in the morning," Mrs. Strong said.

Her husband looked at her with amazement. "Man's got a long ways to go, Ann. Let him go," he said.

I assured her I'd be all right. "You watch, I'll get five miles down the road, and there'll be a big comfortable hayloft waiting for me," I said confidently.

"Well, could you please drop a line sometime to us, and let us know you're all right, then?"

I took her address and, much to Flo's delight, promised a postcard from Ireland. It was the same promise I'd made to everyone on the journey to date who had helped me. I slipped into some long pants, and then shook the hands of each of the children.

The strongest handshake, however, came from Mrs. Strong. Something told me she saw in my leaving the inevitable departure of two young men she could not bear the thought of ever losing—her own sons. In me, perhaps she saw the future. And she wasn't quite ready for it.

About an hour later, as I sat in the hayloft window of a big red Dutch-style dairy barn, I stared at the rising night mist and the occasional phosphorous wash of a passing auto below, and at last admitted to myself the real reason I'd declined Mrs. Strong's offer of shelter.

Quite simply, she and those grown children had reminded me too much of my own family. To have spent the evening with them in their big old rambling house would have made me too homesick.

And that was the last thing I needed right now. Not with several years of walking yet to go.

10

Two equally sunny and beautiful days later, I was just north of Anacramdale. I'd been told of a little road that went from New York State into Massachusetts through an area in the mountains called the Taconic State Park.

At first I decided against taking it, for it was much more winding and uphill than the way I had planned. But finally I decided it'd be worth the extra effort and time.

At the tiny village of Copake, I found the road (Route 344) and followed it east about three miles and into Massachusetts. As I wound higher and higher, it soon became obvious why this road had been suggested.

Golden buttercups, white-petaled daisies, and yellow Indian paintbrush flowers were in full blossom along the shoulders of the road. For many of the six miles I walked to the park's north boundary, tall oaks, maples, and white-trunked aspens shaded my overheated body. Since it was a weekday, the park was empty of people, and I again took the opportunity to bathe nude in a cold, clear mountain stream that rushed along the road.

The streams in the park were some of the most scenic and crystal-clear I'd seen anywhere. This couldn't be Massachusetts, I kept telling myself. I'd never been in the state before, but because I knew it was one of the first in America to be settled, I had fully expected another New Jersey —lots of congested shopping malls, strips of fast-food restaurants and convenience stores, frequent liquor vendors, and endless car lots.

But no. This was more like a piece of the Rocky Mountains. And there I was, for the first time since West Virginia, drinking directly from the streams.

As I dipped my red-nosed face into the shimmering waters again and again, I felt as if I were drinking from some magical energy flow.

Surely this was not real. There was no way such a pure place could exist so close to places like New York City, Hartford, and Boston. I knew the whole scene would burst apart any second: that just around the next curve would be a big, bright trailer-park billboard, and behind it a dusty, littered lot, packed with hundreds of mobile homes and junky cars.

I couldn't have been more wrong. There was only more trees, more wildflowers, more quietness—and more mosquitoes.

As the shadows lengthened, then joined together to form dusk, I found myself fighting a losing battle with what seemed a universe-sized army of bloodthirsty mosquitoes. They were as bad as their cousins on Staten Island!

By the time I reached an area of the park named Mount Washington, the mosquitoes were so overwhelming I was seriously considering throwing off Clinger and running for my life.

Those bloodsuckers weren't just hungry: They were downright evil! It was as if each and every one of the dozens of little humming winged needles was determined to inflict on me with as much pain as possible.

For at least a mile and a half I was forced to slap myself nearly senseless. Finally, I had no choice but to surrender and beat a frantic retreat to a nearby house.

Desperately, I banged on the screen door.

A bespectacled gray-haired woman came to the door.

"Yes?" she asked.

"Ma'am, I—I know this is going—going to sound silly"—I could hardly talk for all the mosquitoes biting me—"but do you please have any bug spray?"

I'm sure I looked as desperate as a man on the verge of death.

"I just can't *bear* the mosquitoes any longer," I pleaded.

"Oh, my. Dear me, young man. Come in," she uttered.

I could have cried. I rushed past her, as did several of the mosquitoes. While I stood in the tiny front foyer with my remaining winged foes, she rushed off for some repellent.

I attacked each of the mosquitoes with a vengeance.

One by one, I slapped them between my palms so loudly that it sounded like rifle shots. And each victim brought a shout of victory to my lips.

At last there was only one. But he wasn't about to be as foolish as the others, and he fled into the living room. I lumbered after him through the open doorway with the pack on my back.

As I stepped through the doorway, I caught sight of an old, balding man sitting in an easy chair against the far wall. He was looking at me over the top of a newspaper he had been reading, but I decided he must have just returned from work: He was wearing gray dress slacks, gray dress socks, a conservative blue dress shirt. A plain dark tie hung a little loosely about his neck. Placed neatly beside his chair was a pair of polished black leather shoes.

Embarrassed, I realized he must have been watching my theatrics and listening to my little war whoops. And by the way his thin eyebrows were furrowed, it didn't look as if he held my sanity in very high opinion at the moment.

Reluctantly, I let the last of the bloodsuckers go into hiding.

"Hello, sir," I said, ever so politely.

There was an awkward moment of silence as he studied me a bit more, then he slowly set the paper down onto his lap.

"The mosquitoes are really bad. . . . I couldn't believe how many followed me right into your house," I half muttered. "I thought I ought to kill them, so I—"

"I take it you don't particularly care for them," he said, ever so seriously.

"No, I don't. Next to flies and snakes, they're about the worst things around."

His lips remained as straight as ever, and his pale eyes looked right through me, as though he were a principal disciplining an unruly student.

"Don't you have any repellent? You should, if you're going camping in this area," he said sternly.

"I'm walking to Boston, and I thought I'd be through the park by now," I said with a shrug. Behind me, on a color television, an announcer was giving the play-by-play of a Yankees baseball game.

"You like baseball?" I asked, hoping to change the subject. He looked as if he might be a bank vice-president or some other very conservative executive type, and I didn't feel comfortable with the idea of telling him I was doing something as "zany" as walking around the world, particularly after my circus performance with the mosquitoes.

"Are you doing it for world peace?" he asked gravely.

I took a deep breath. "Believe it or not, I'm actually walking around the world." His expression didn't change one bit. Was that good or bad? "I'm a journalist, and I'm not the type to belong to any sort of group. But I do hope to explore very closely the common people in all the countries I cross."

The lady returned with a huge can of Cutter's insect repellent. "My, my. Around the world!"

The man folded the paper and set it on a small table next to his chair. I sprayed myself and immediately realized I'd stunk up the whole room.

"I'm sorry. I wasn't thinking." Why did I have to be such a klutz before the impeccably dressed man who sat so still before me?

I handed back the can, thanked the woman, and started to turn to leave.

"Oh, no, you can't go out there without any repellent," she said. "Take this can with you."

"But this is worth several dollars," I protested.

"That's not important," she pshawed. "What is important is that you have some protection."

She was right. It was insane to go back out there into the dark with the mosquitoes. I doubted a *tank* of Cutter's could have scared those killers off, let alone some twelve-ounce can of the suffocating stuff. I took off Clinger, slipped the can into a side compartment, and had started to lift him back up to my shoulders, when suddenly the man spoke.

"Would you like some tea and cake?" he asked gently.

I set the pack back onto the carpet, scarcely believing the sudden concern coming from the man of the stern stare.

"Please sit down," he offered, pointing to another easy chair.

"The smell of the spray will get into the fabric," I said. At last I was beginning to show some manners.

He said it didn't matter. So I sat beside him, all the more aware of the strong aura of power about his presence.

He was, he said, the Reverend James Chase, and the woman his wife of forty-one years, Helen. He was sixty-six; she was four years younger.

Actually, he had very recently retired from the ministry, he admitted. But he still remained active visiting those in need from day to day, and that was why he was dressed so formally. He had spent much of the day visiting his former doctor, who was now himself bedridden with cancer at a nearby hospital.

"He took care of me all these years. Now, it is my turn to return the favor," he said softly.

"But enough of me," he went on a bit uncomfortably. "Let's hear more of your walk. Where did you start from?"

Mrs. Chase returned from the kitchen with a small tray of angel-food cake and a ceramic pot of hot tea and a cup and sugar. She sat the tray on the table between the reverend and me. Then she sat down opposite us on a hardwood chair and knitted a child's sock, while the minister and I discussed my walk.

As we talked, I realized that the power I sensed in him—and in Mrs. Chase, too—was that of a man and woman who have acquired great wisdom. And with it, great peacefulness.

These two people were so happy and sure of themselves that they were personal bastions of peace. Their home was small, simply furnished. But they had the bearing of two very secure people.

Almost shyly, Mrs. Chase talked of the five children she had raised, and of the joy she'd found in being a mother, not only to her own, but also to the many preschool children for whom she'd been a nursery-school teacher for twenty-five years.

Reverend Chase, meanwhile, spoke of another family—the community and surrounding families on the mountain. He told me of the affiliation he'd developed with his congregants at the Baptist Church in North Egremont and the First Congregational Church in South Egremont—two tiny villages that were little more than post offices and antique shops set into the thick forest of the park.

When he began to speak of his philosophy that being good to others begets many, many rewards, I asked him if he would mind my recording him and his wife. He smiled, as if to hint that my placing any importance on his thoughts was a bit absurd. But they both agreed.

"First, however," he said, "I'd like to show you something you'll probably never see in another house during your walk." He leaped from the chair eagerly and waved me to follow him into the dining room.

He switched on a simple ceiling lamp over the dining-room table and pointed to the wall by the narrow open doorway to the kitchen. I looked at a dark painting in a wide wooden frame hanging on the wall and could hardly believe my eyes. I'd have recognized the signature in its lower right corner a mile away.

It was an original Norman Rockwell. And of Reverend Chase himself, no less. I ran my hand lightly over the paint on the canvas, as if to assure myself the painting—which was very large—was for real.

I'd seen Norman Rockwell's work countless times on the covers of *The Saturday Evening Post.* But never had I actually seen the real McCoy, so to speak. Not until now.

"This was given to me," the reverend said lovingly.

"You were a personal friend of his?" I asked with awe.

"No. I hardly knew him," he said. "We met a few times, to be sure, but we didn't actually know each other all that much." Then, with a tone of sadness: "He was a very gentle man."

He switched off the light, and we returned to our seats. On the way out, I reached over and touched the canvas lightly once more.

"How did you ever get him to do a painting of you, if you hardly knew each other?" I inquired.

The minister leaned back in his chair, took off his eyeglasses, and slipped them into his shirt pocket. I glanced over at Mrs. Chase. She was setting her yarn and needles on the coffee table and folding her hands in her lap.

With his eyes half-closed, Reverend Chase looked toward the far wall and said, "Not only was that painting given to us, but also this house and many of the things you see here. Why? It wasn't because of what or whom we knew, but because of the kindness we've always made a point of sharing with others."

He looked me in the eyes. "If you remember anything on this walk, Steven, let it be this: Always keep looking for the good in people and places, not the bad. If you do that—as I believe you have so far—you will have mostly kindness come your way.

"But as soon as you start to look at things in a bad way, a bitter or angry way, then so you will be treated, too.

"I'm a firm believer—and our home is perhaps proof—that if one does only kind things, he will be likewise inevitably rewarded, without his even having to ask for any rewards."

He then told the story of the painting. The famous painter had on occasion come to one of the churches where Mr. Chase was a minister, and so the reverend had regarded the artist as no less a member of his "family" than he would have anyone else who came on Sunday. And when Rockwell had become sick once and was in the local hospital, the reverend had gone every day, for weeks, to talk to the painter and make sure he was comfortable and not in need of anything the reverend might be able to get him. It was just ordinary courtesy, the reverend said.

Well, the painter recovered, and when he returned home, he asked that the reverend come and visit him there. It turned out that Rockwell's way of thanking people all his life had been to do portraits of them. Beautifully detailed paintings. And for no cost.

And so, simply by being a nice man who treated others as lovingly as he would have others treat him, this simple country minister had acquired one of the world's material treasures. Being nice, the reverend believed, was one of the surest ways to assure that God would look after you over the years.

Ten o'clock rolled around, and I thought it was probably their bedtime. I rose to leave. Mrs. Chase insisted I sleep in one of their spare bedrooms, but I declined.

I did, however, accept her offer of a breakfast. And after a night of sleeping in the nearby forest wrapped in my blanket, I returned the next morning to delight once again in their peacefulness.

Breakfast was a large helping of scrambled eggs with cheese, half an orange, milk, coffee, and orange marmalade and toast.

And a lot of sunlight and warm smiles.

The Mount Washington forest was one of the quietest and most beautiful areas I had seen to date on the walk. I therefore decided to hide away in the depths of its maples, oaks, beeches, white birches, pines, and hemlocks for a few days to catch up on my journals. As always, I was behind on my daily notes. In a place like this, however, it was actually a welcome burden.

I probably had gone no farther than two miles from the Chases' home, when I decided to hike into the thick forest. I cut through a small meadow on the east side of the road and walked deep into the forest until I found a secluded knoll that overlooked a clear, fast-moving little stream.

Against a background of birdsong and small waterfalls, I was able to concentrate on my memories of the past several days. I stayed there nearly all afternoon, and might have been tempted to stay longer but for the fact that I ran out of peanut butter and cookies, and thus had no more food.

It was early evening when I ventured back onto the open road. Although I knew night was coming, I could not help but take my time, for there was so much beauty and peace here. I didn't want to return to the "ordinary" outside world.

At one wide spot, where the mountain road cut through a thick stand of pine trees, I came upon several white-tailed deer, who let me get within fifty feet before they bounded off into the trees.

So this was the fairyland called New England that I'd heard so much about all my life. Even after so few miles, I knew I loved it! And obviously, by the look of things, so did the gods.

Magic. Magic everywhere. I could see it, smell it, taste it, hear it with every step. Even with the pack, I felt as if I could just take a deep breath and float away, away, away . . . right to the stars.

Surely I was bewitched. For why the sudden laughter that broke from my chest, and the tears in my eyes, and the goose bumps? Why the sensation of being a leaf caught in a friendly breeze?

I told myself even Genghis Khan would have been a Reverend Chase if he'd lived here.

In my many years of living in the West, I'd seen mountains that were awesome, others that were evil, and still others that commanded respect, but none that seemed to pour forth such gentle love as this little one.

Near the bottom of the mountain was a broad, grassy meadow, the texture and color of black velvet. Sprinkled over it were glowing fireflies, and far above them, like diamonds on yet another cloth of black velvet, twinkling stars.

Call it a spell or just plain foolishness, but I had to go out into that panorama of black and light to try to capture one of those fireflies. It was something I'd spent countless hours doing as a pajama-clad boy long, long ago. Perhaps—just perhaps—I could recapture a little of that magic now, if I could just wrap my finger around one of those glows.

I set my pack against a telephone pole and took off, my eyes darting quickly from one tiny exploding pinlight to another. The first one I lunged for eluded my grasp as easily as if it had never been there. But then another flashed inches from my left shoulder, and he was mine.

Funny, I thought, as I stared at him breathing light across my open palm, I could have sworn it was much harder to catch them. This had been too easy, too quick. Not at all as when I was a boy and I'd chased for what seemed miles—my one hand holding up my pajama bottoms, the other trying not to shake too hard the jar of fireflies I had already captured.

Ah, but of course. That had been the secret of the fireflies—the chase! The fun had been the pursuit of something, not the capture itself. Only I'd been too young then to realize that. All I'd known was that when I crawled into bed with the jar of crawling lanterns, I had felt so contented, so alive.

Now, I blew on the insect balanced on my fingertip. It rejoined the other stars.

Standing there with the universe revolving around me, I thought of the profusion of life I'd seen so far on my walk across eastern America. Even where man had spread his liquid stone and sticky tar, there had still been plants trying to live in the cracks.

More and more, I was convinced man would never wipe life off this planet. He might kill himself, but there would always be something born somewhere.

I put the pack back on and continued on to the main highway, State Route 23, north of the park. It suddenly occurred to me that I was hungry. I'd fed the mind, now it was the body's turn.

In Great Barrington, I barely made it in time to a little supermarket. There I purchased some more bread and peanut butter and jelly, and a pint of milk. I ate dinner around eleven-thirty on the steps of a big church across the street. I was back in civilization . . . like it or not.

11

Sometime after midnight I climbed a farm fence and slept wrapped in my blanket beneath a tree. Not much later the rustling of the tree's leaves told me a storm was approaching. I gathered my gear, crept in my underwear to a dark farmhouse's back porch, and quickly returned to my dreams, too tired to worry about being discovered.

At dawn I woke feeling like flypaper. The porch roof had leaked, and I was not only soaked from the rain, but still sticky and smelly from yesterday's humidity. I ambled out to Route 23 and turned toward Boston with only one thing on my mind: I needed a bath—badly.

With the late June heat and thick humidity constant companions once again, I was continually looking for ways to bathe and wash my damp, smelly clothes. Because Clinger rode close to my backside, very little air was able to circulate over that part of me. So I was usually overheated and as rank as a plow horse well before noon.

But now that I was walking where towns and cities were closer together than ever, taking a bath was not an easy thing to do. Each day there were fewer and fewer clean streams and rivers to take a swim in.

I wanted to bathe so badly this morning, but the only stream I crossed had on its bottom a sediment that smelled vaguely of sewage. No plants were growing in it, and the only living things in the whole creek were some ugly black worms. If I didn't see any minnows in a stream, I would not bathe in it, figuring that there had to be poisons or harmful bacteria in the water.

By nightfall I still hadn't washed. I crawled under a rotting bridge to sleep, feeling every bit as grungy as a postman's dirty socks. When I woke the next morning with a slug sliming its way across my face, I had to wonder about my sanity.

All that hot, bright day the road seemed as hilly as the ocean is wavy. On the soles of my stewing feet there appeared blisters, as a result of sliding up and down on the insoles of my boots. And beneath my straw hat, my head was but a degree or two from boiling over.

But then, around three o'clock, I came to a forest thick with shade. The only lane going into it was made of dirt and marked simply by a red-and-white hand-painted sign that said PHOME. Having no idea what the strange word meant, I decided to use it as an excuse to venture into that refuge from the sun.

For half a mile I walked down the lane, seeing no homes or people. Only more thickly leafed oaks and maples, and taller ferns.

Finally, I came to a wooden bridge over a sparkling, fast-flowing stream with water as clear as glass. And with many minnows.

Happily, I scampered downstream out of view of the bridge. When after several minutes I broke through the brush, I was standing at the top of a beautiful waterfall. And directly beneath it was a waist-deep pool that glimmered like crystal.

In no time at all I was scrubbing myself and my clothes as merrily as the water was cascading over the six-foot high fall. When my bar of Ivory soap was reduced to a sliver, I draped my clothes over some of the larger rocks to dry, and then myself along a bare ledge. Like a long lizard, I stretched out fully, giving every muscle a good twist and turn. Within minutes I was napping soundly, basking away in the sun as contently as were the many long-winged dragonflies clinging to the cliffs about me.

When after an hour cool shadows fell across me, I tried copying the dragonflies—moving from one sunny rock to another. Eventually, I retired to my blanket on a patch of grass in the trees near the top of the waterfall. I folded half the blanket over my naked body, put an arm behind my head for a pillow, and read further into *The Adventures of Huckleberry Finn*. The last I remembered before sleep caught up with me again was that Huck and Tom Sawyer were hiding an awful lot of garter snakes under Aunt Sally's bed.

The next morning I opened my eyes wide and quickly. I knew it had to be my imagination, but I swore there were several stark-naked bodies jumping up and down just a few yards from me, their owners screaming and flailing their arms as if they had been thrown into boiling oil.

I squeezed my eyes shut, swallowed hard enough to make my ears pop, and looked again. I wasn't dreaming!

I was afraid to move—because those naked women I was practically lying beside could see me as plainly as I saw them. Holding my breath, I reached very slowly to my underwear hanging on a nearby bush, wriggled it loose, and then rolled ever so agonizingly lightly into the forest, my blanket wrapped tightly about my body.

Once at the lane, I paced back and forth like a cornered criminal. *Phome* had to be the name of a nudist colony, I decided. Why else would there be all those naked women frolicking together in a waterfall this early in the morning?

I stubbed my toe, bit down on my hand to stifle my yell, and limped further along the lane into the forest. I would give them half an hour to finish whatever it was they were doing, then return for my gear, I decided.

Less than a hundred yards along, a female voice from the trees to my right caused me to jump. It belonged to an attractive blond-haired woman in shorts and a white blouse. She was sitting on a picnic table, with a newspaper in her hands. A friendly brown Airedale rushed from her side to mine.

"Delila! Don't be so rude," she said, laughing.

I gripped my blanket more tightly as the large dog playfully tried to pull it off me.

"How was the water?" the woman asked as calmly as if she had been expecting me.

I looked at her pleasant face. She didn't seem the least bit suspicious of this blanket-wrapped stranger with puffy eyes and mussy hair hobbling around in her forest.

"I'm hiking across Massachusetts, and I camped beside the waterfall last night. Believe it or not, I woke ten minutes ago to find a bunch of naked women only a few feet away in the creek," I explained sheepishly.

She slapped her hands together and laughed. "Those are the phome dancers! They're camping nearby for the weekend, and that's where they take their baths."

"Dancers?" I repeated.

"Yes. Phome is a very old kind of English folk dance." She rubbed the dog's head. "They're performing outside in Russell today. Perhaps you'd like to go watch?"

She stood and introduced herself as Patricia Wise. "Care to come up to the house for some coffee?" She pointed to a large wooden house only a little distance behind her.

"Uh—I wouldn't want to wake your husband."

"Oh, Gerald's in New York showing his paintings. There's just me and one of my daughters at home."

"Well, I don't really think so. Thanks anyhow."

"I can fix you some tea or hot cocoa, if you prefer," she persisted. "You look so cold."

I swallowed my pride. "My clothes are down by the waterfall. I'm . . . only wearing underwear."

She couldn't keep from laughing at my extreme embarrassment, but she offered to help me retrieve my clothes.

I followed her and Delila back to the bridge. But once there I paused, much too shy to face the bathing women.

Patricia said I was being silly; the others wouldn't be embarrassed at all to have a stranger seeing them nude. I wasn't so sure. I followed from a distance of twenty steps, so she could tell the others I was nearby. From the trees I watched Patricia scramble to the waterfall, say a few words to the others, then turn and wave to me to advance. I stepped out into the clearing gripping my blanket as if my life depended on it.

There were seven women, mostly around age thirty. To my amazement, they acted as if nothing were out of the ordinary.

"So these are *your* clothes," said the oldest with a sly glance at the others, then added, with much flair, "Why didn't you join us, for goodness' sake?"

So they had seen me sleeping nearby after all, I realized with a red face. It was all I could do to shrug my shoulders, quickly gather my things together, and dress behind a tree. I was such a clumsy fool around women —especially ones as uninhibited as these New Englanders!

As Patricia was leading me back to her house, I revealed that actually I had much farther to go than Boston on my hike. She was very excited by the news that I was walking around the world, but also curious as to why I had not said so earlier.

It was my habit, I said, to tell many people that I was just hiking to the next town, because I feared someone might consider me weird or crazy for attempting such a journey.

"But why do you think that?" said Patricia, placing a kettle of water on the stove. "Don't you realize that you're living out so many people's fantasies? All of us would love to do something like what you're doing, at some time in our life. But we can't, because we don't have the courage, or we get too caught up in things like paying bills and raising families. So *you* are doing it for us, Steve. We live our own dreams through people like yourself."

Though Patricia was making good money as an executive director of a human-services program for preschoolers, she revealed that her deepest dream was to someday write stories for children. "I've tried to do some, but I never seem to finish them," she confessed with much frustration.

The kettle whistled her back to the stove, where she poured its hot water over instant coffee in two ceramic mugs. Those and a bowl of fresh strawberries she set before me, then sat back down across from me.

"Are you still going to keep trying to be a writer?" I wondered.

She shrugged her shoulders. "I worry sometimes that maybe it's getting too late for me to do that." She froze her gaze for a second on the steam rising from her coffee. "The house does get so big and quiet at times. It's really perfect for writing . . . if only I could get the hang of it. For I have a lot of stories in my head."

I tried to encourage her not to give up on her dream. I told her of a fiction story of mine that was published in a little magazine called *Sunshine.* It had started out being about a schoolteacher and evolved after many rewrites into a story about a teenage girl.

"The secret of being a writer is to just write and write and write, until eventually the story goes ahead and writes itself," I said firmly.

But she didn't look convinced.

I wanted to gnash my teeth. Couldn't she see that all the tools she'd ever needed to be a writer were right here at her fingertips? That all that was keeping her from being what she wanted was *believing* in herself?

When Patricia offered me the use of one of their spare bedrooms for as long as I needed to catch up on my writing, I accepted, eager to update my notebooks, and to begin preparing for the hop across the ocean.

She ran up the stairs and woke her fifteen-year-old daughter, Brooke. Together they moved a desk, a chair, and a lamp into an empty upstairs bedroom.

Gerald returned that evening and was just as enthusiastic about helping me. For three days, I stayed with the Wise family, bringing my journals completely up to date and making sure everything I would need for the trek through the British Isles and Europe would be waiting in Boston. I called my parents and had my tent, a raincoat, ten rolls of color-slide film, and a dozen blank recording cassette tapes sent to the General Delivery at the main Boston post office. To the American Express Office in

Cambridge (where I was planning to visit Harvard University for a day or two) my folks wired a thousand dollars in additional expense money.

About all that remained was getting a plane ticket, and that I decided to take care of when I reached Boston.

12

B ut when I finally arrived in Boston, after much more hospitality along the way, I found myself traveling not to Ireland next, but right back to New York City!

A note in my mail at the post office said to call CBS Network News in New York City. When I did so, I was told to catch a shuttle flight to New York, to be their guest on the next morning's show. Their White House correspondent had read a full-page interview done with me by the *Washington Post,* said the program's director, and she had thought it interesting enough for the CBS morning-news television talk show.

So from canned baked beans and peanut-butter sandwiches and sleeping on the bare ground in a ragged blanket that rightfully belonged in a back-alley dumpster, I was whisked away—still grimy and sweaty from the day's walking—in twenty minutes from Boston to New York over the same countryside I had taken a month to cross on foot.

Since it was already late afternoon and there was only one more shuttle flight to New York, I had no time to go to Cambridge to pick up the money sent by my parents. When I landed at Kennedy Airport in New York, I had less than five dollars in my pocket. Yet what followed for the next twenty hours was chauffeured limousines, a two-hundred-dollar room at the Parker Meridien Hotel in Manhattan, and room service on spiffy trays—all at CBS's expense. I couldn't eat at the restaurant at the hotel because I had no tie and jacket.

It was the closest I had ever been to feeling like a celebrity or a millionaire, and on the ride to the airport after the show I couldn't resist

poking my excited face from the limo's huge backseats, with their color
television and bar, to the front and asking the chauffeur:

"Who's the most famous person you ever had ride in your car?"

He answered immediately. "Rocky!"

My eyes widened. "You mean the actor Sylvester Stallone?"

"Yeah. They was premiering one of them Rocky movies here, and I
drove him to the movie house."

"What was he like?"

"Oh, I thought he was a nice man. He certainly is rich, for sure. He
had eighty limos, I think, that he rented that day to bring his friends to
the movie."

"Wow . . ."

I leaned back beside Clinger and looked out at the barred shop windows and littered sidewalks of Queens rushing past. There probably
weren't that many limousines in all of Ohio, I thought.

That night in Boston it rained. Still, I slept wrapped in my rain
poncho on the back alleyway step of an abandoned factory. It was okay if
CBS wanted to foot the bill for a hotel, but I was still as determined as
ever not to pay out of my pocket for any sleeping accommodations.

When the next afternoon I arrived at Harvard Square in Cambridge
on a subway train, I was hardly prepared for what I found. I had visual-
ized a prim-and-proper college scene, with a lot of rich, stiff-lipped young
people dressed in khaki slacks and white polo shirts standing about in
small groups discussing money and tennis. Instead, what I found were
noisy milling crowds that looked closer to the flower children of the sixties
than the debutante-ball set.

Even the campus was not that different from many of those in Ohio.
Where were the crew cuts, the dark-rimmed glasses, the leafy peaceful-
ness, and the ivy-covered red brick buildings I thought epitomized the Ivy
League?

It wasn't until several hours later that I found, inside a huge and very
old hall, the deep sense of traditionalism and perfectionism I had always
associated with Harvard. There, in an interior of dark polished wood walls
that rose at least fifty feet to meet arched ceilings, the sounds of singing
reached my ear from down a long hallway. I searched out the pleasant
sounds, passing along the way several tall massive wood doors set into
walls bearing the names of every Harvard graduate killed in the Civil War.
When I arrived at the double doors from behind which the sounds were
coming, I pulled on their handles slowly, almost reverently.

What I found was a large and very high auditorium of rows and rows
of dark wooden seats and wide, sweeping balconies set into a great semi-

circle around an enormous stage. On the stage were thirty or forty choir singers and an instructor.

For several minutes the singers' voices flooded the air with what sounded to me like perfect harmony. But the teacher thought not, for he loudly commanded them to a halt.

They practiced again, and again, and again. Until there was no doubt in my mind that what was expected of them was nothing less than perfection.

Nine days later, I stepped into the taxi that was to bring me to the airport. On the way there, my plan to go directly from Boston to Dublin was discarded at the very last minute, for the cab driver told me that he knew a much cheaper way than the five hundred dollars the airline wanted.

"In fact, how does only a hundred seventy-five strike you?" he asked.

I was all ears as he told me to take the $23 shuttle flight from Boston to Newark, New Jersey, then from there fly on the $149 flight to London on the new economy airline called People Express.

I didn't want to waste a minute getting to Newark. Common sense told me that the costs of a train or bus from London to the Irish Sea, and then a ferry boat over to Dublin, added to the People Express fare wouldn't bring my costs anywhere near five hundred dollars.

There was, however, one big risk he warned. He had read that the economy airline's once-daily flights to London were booked solid until October. Which meant I'd have to wait on standby at the Newark terminal until someone canceled a flight and made room for me. And with London being such an extremely popular vacation spot for Americans, that could mean, depending on the number of other standby passengers there before me, a wait of several days, he said gravely.

How did he know all this? I wondered, fascinated.

He pushed his chewing gum to the other side of his mouth and said matter-of-factly, "I read *The Wall Street Journal.*"

He must have seen through his rearview mirror my eyebrows rise just then, however, because a minute later he added with a laugh, "Of course, they ain't *my Wall Street Journals.* I get them out of the trash at the garage."

Fortunately, Lady Luck was with me when I touched down in Newark.

No sooner did I walk up to the People Express London flight ticket counter, which was closed since it was well past midnight, and place my backpack beside all the other luggage piled there, than a sunburned middle-aged man in shorts and sneakers approached me. "Would you be wanting a reservation, chap?" he asked in a voice heavy with a British accent.

"Why, yes," I answered eagerly.

With a smile as long as the counter itself, he said, "Me son Michael and me daughter Laraine and I come to try standby, too, and found out at one of their other counters that they's 'ad four cancellations to London. If ya 'urry, per'aps ya can grab the last one!"

I glanced at the many other standby hopefuls, dozing in chairs or on the floor, waiting for the ticket counter to open in four hours. Surely someone else had had the sense to ask at one of the other People Express ticket counters.

"Come, come, you'd best 'urry!"

It was his beautiful daughter now tugging at my arm. I followed her to the airline's Newark-Florida ticket counter, the only one open at that hour. Skeptically, I inquired of the clerk if they had any empty seats on the London flight.

"Yes, sir, we do," he responded triumphantly after a check on the computer. "One, to be exact."

"I'll take it!"

Laraine smiled. Her father laughed. Even the ticket clerk seemed to take delight in my reaction. With a flourish, he handed me my boarding pass and said, "Your flight attendant will collect the fare after you take off. You can pay cash, with a personal check, or with traveler's checks. Have a nice flight!"

Twelve hours later, as our 747 cruised above the Atlantic at thirty-five thousand feet, I asked Laraine why she and her father, who had been there at the Newark terminal for many hours, had picked me out of all the other standby people to tell about the remaining cancellation.

She pushed her long blond hair to one side and said with what I took to be a bit of English humor, "Why, you were the only one awake."

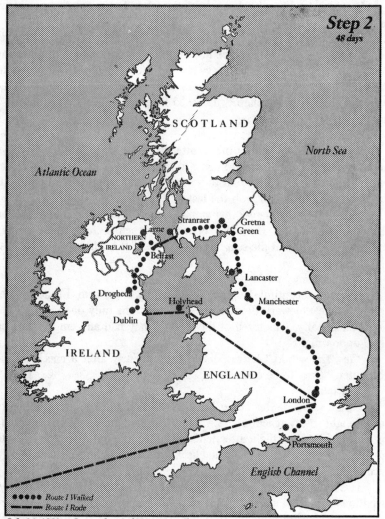

Step 2
48 days

SCOTLAND

North Sea

Atlantic Ocean

Stranraer   Gretna
Larne   Green
NORTHERN
IRELAND
Belfast
                      Lancaster
Drogheda
            Holyhead   Manchester

Dublin

IRELAND

ENGLAND

London

Portsmouth

English Channel

●●●●● Route I Walked
━ ━ ━ Route I Rode

July 24, 1983 to September 9, 1983   633 miles

13

So it was that my first glimpse of the British Isles was not of the jagged coastline of Ireland, as I had planned, but of hedgerow meadows in south England. And when viewed through gaps in the early morning mist beneath the 747, it all seemed almost a picture postcard—the fog, the hedges, the green pastures . . . And yet, there they were, only a few thousand feet below and coming closer every second.

Strangely enough, I was certainly one of the calmest—if not *the* calmest—passengers. All the other 390 passengers were buzzing with excitement as the giant jumbo jet thundered to a landing on the gray-green countryside. Yet there I sat, as calm as a statue. You'd have thought I'd been overseas a hundred times before, had seen Gatwick, with its round terminal building and rows of jets, as many times as I'd seen the main street of Bethel. Strange.

Perhaps it was because I was so tired from getting only two hours of sleep in the Newark terminal and one hour's sleep on the six-hour flight over. All I knew was that whatever my body was showing, I was as filled with excitement as when, as a boy, I'd originally dreamed of the walk. After all those years, I was actually about to take my first steps on another country's soil.

"How long do you plan on visiting?" wondered the passport inspector.

"Five weeks," I replied without hesitation.

"You say on your card you'll be in Dublin, Belfast, and London."

"Yes. I plan on walking from Dublin to the others."

"Walk! Why?"

"I'm a writer. I want to learn about the people in a special manner."

He stamped the passport and handed it back. "Well, the best to you. I expect to be reading about you," he said in such a cheery voice that I couldn't help but grin from ear to ear.

I glanced at the rectangular stamp mark. It was good for six months.

The door to my American past had just clicked shut; I had "officially" entered into the foreign phase of the walk. From here on out, I was on my own to a degree I had never really experienced in America. Home was no longer here, but over *there,* as far away in time and distance as once the rest of the world had been. And it was only going to get further and further away, at least for a while.

But it was not until Clinger was secured, and I had bid Mr. Moorhead and Michael and Laraine good-bye, that I really began to realize what an undertaking I was stepping into.

First there was the exchanging of money.

At a little window I signed over a twenty-dollar traveler's check and received back twelve English pound notes and various coins. I felt excited, but also a little cheated. Surely the dollar was the strongest currency anywhere, wasn't it? And yet I had just exchanged twenty of them for twelve of the other.

Next there was the problem of getting to Dublin, Ireland, the real starting point of the walk's foreign phase.

On the flight over, I had made up my mind to hitchhike west toward Ireland right from the airport. But upon landing, I realized I was too weary and unfamiliar with the country to leap into it in such a raw fashion. It would be wiser, I decided, to get a shower, a decent meal, and a bit of sleep before setting out to conquer the British Isles.

London, which was probably thirty miles to the east of the airport, was the best bet to supply me with all three necessities for the cheapest prices, but how was I going to get there?

It was Tom, a fellow American from Norristown, Pennsylvania, who came to the rescue.

"Do you need to be rushing right off?" he asked me in the customs line.

"No, not really."

"What do you say that you come to London then, and we'll share the cost of a room for the night? I can show you where the cheapest places to stay are."

I accepted right off. I told myself I might be able to find a decently priced bus or train to the west coast from the city.

I resolved to let Tom be my guide, and I strapped my pack onto my back and followed him, letting him ask the directions to the London train. He hadn't been to England since 1979, and he had to ask quite a few people for help, but at least he knew of someplace to go to in London. As for myself, I might as well have been in the middle of China.

On the train platform I was again aware that I was no longer in America. The silver train that pulled alongside us barely made a sound. No roaring and screeching of brakes, no doors slammed open. It came to a slow and gradual stop, and conductors in neat, trim dark suits and caps stepped out to open the doors.

Everything was so orderly I couldn't believe my eyes. Was it like this all the time? Or was it just because this was early morning Sunday?

The interior of the train was plush and comfortable. The air outside the train window was veiled with fog, but as I peered through the hedges lining the tracks, I saw very little sign of life. Quite obviously, the English were not early risers on a Sunday. But then, who was?

At Victoria Station in London, the incredible politeness of the whole morning was summed up when, as the train was easing into its stop, the voice of the train conductor came over a loudspeaker: "Please assist the elderly, and any others who need help, on and off the train. Thank you and have a nice day."

From Victoria Station, Tom and I rode one more train to the Earl's Court Station on the western edge of the city. There we would find many "bed and breakfast" hotels: cheap lodging in simple rooms with some sort of breakfast the next morning. But we were both worried that with it being the height of the travel season, there might not be any empty rooms.

When the train halted at our stop, we stepped from it with what seemed hundreds of other weary-looking hotel-room seekers. Looking at all of the backpacks rushing past us, I could feel my bed and shower slipping away.

We followed the throng up toward daylight and the sounds of traffic. Suddenly, two young Indian boys darted toward us, as if they'd been expecting us.

"We take you to where you can stay tonight for four pounds!" the smaller one shouted.

Tom looked skeptical. And with good reason. At Victoria Station's tourist-information counter, the harried clerks had said there were no more rooms in the city under twelve pounds a night. And while we had declined to make a reservation at that price, opting to try to luck into something, most of the others in the long lines at the counter had played it safe and asked for whatever was available.

"It's less if you stay for a week," the boy added in a voice that said we must decide quickly.

We went for it.

The boys led us as fast as their legs could carry them to a white building several blocks away marked with a small sign that said VICTORIA HOTEL. Inside, their rotund father smiled at the boys.

"They get paid by commission, you know," he said through a mouthful of gold teeth. "Today, they make their father happy, for they filled the whole hotel."

My watch said it was only 10:00 A.M.

Tom asked to see our room, and the man motioned to a heavyset redhaired girl to show us. We followed her down some narrow stairs to the basement.

The rooms in the dim lower level were what would be expected for four pounds: tiny, peeling paint, musty, and with little more than cots. There was only one toilet and shower for the entire floor. But we decided to stay, for we were too tired to care.

Tom was put in a room with two other men; I shared mine with a tall, balding young man with blond hair named Ed. Tom went right to bed, while I went and washed clothes at a coin laundry.

When I returned, I slept until nearly 8:00 P.M., at which time Rosie, the red-haired girl, woke me as I had instructed her to do.

Dinner was at a Chinese restaurant nearby. During the meal, Tom hardly touched his food. Something was wrong, but I brushed away my inner anxiety and asked if I could finish his food. He was glad to have it not go to waste and handed it right over. He had hardly touched it, especially the pork.

"I forgot this dish has pork in it," he said, as he pushed the noodles and meat onto my plate.

"You're Jewish?" I asked, perplexed.

"No, no. It's just that I have trouble digesting pork." He hesitated, then added mysteriously, "I-I have stomach trouble, and pork irritates it."

I took his explanation to mean he had an ulcer, and let it go at that. Still, it disturbed me to see how he slumped over the table, as if from some great internal pain.

At a pub around the corner we met one of Tom's roommates, a short fellow from Australia, who bought us a round. I had my first taste of English draught: a warm, sudsy concoction that smelled like stale wine and tasted like day-old dishwater.

I ordered a second round later, but Tom declined, even though his pint glass was empty. I was sure something was amiss; he certainly didn't strike me as a one-beer man.

There was a fairly heavy mixture of internationals in the pub. Indeed, I met no one there who was a native of England. I was very eager to stay up for several more hours and chat, but, alas, English custom prevented that. The pub closed at ten-thirty, as required by law.

Perhaps it was a good thing. Tom was looking progressively worse. We headed back to the hotel and our beds.

I woke around 8:00 A.M., showered, and had the hotel's complimentary breakfast of five cups of heavily sugared tea and several slices of toast.

Breakfast ended at 9:00, and since Tom planned to stay another night at that hotel, I moved my gear into his room. I planned to be on my way to Ireland that evening, but first I wanted to see more of London, since I had someone like Tom to direct me to the sights.

I went to the coach station to see about getting a bus to the west coast of England, and encountered a throng of tourists as thick as in Times Square on New Year's Eve.

After standing in line for a good hour, I finally had my turn at the ticket window, only to be told that the express buses to Dublin were full. Would I like to reserve a seat for tomorrow? No, thank you! So much for my notion that the English transportation system was efficient.

In the afternoon Tom and I returned to Earl's Court, after making the rounds of Westminster Abbey, Parliament, Fleet Street, the Tower of London (which was actually the original fortified city of London), and the adjoining Tower Bridge, which I had always thought was "London Bridge."

On the whole, what struck me the most about the city was the overbearing grayness of it. The gray sky, soot-coated buildings, black taxis, businessmen in dark blue or gray suits (especially in Fleet Street), and the smoggy air all combined to make London neutral. Sad to say, the most colorful feature of the city was the Thames River. Not its parks and boats, mind you, but the unbroken stream of trash that was floating down it to some doubtlessly growing mound beneath the Atlantic.

More and more as the day wore on, I grew anxious to be in Ireland with its green countryside. Quite frankly, one day of stone and overcast skies was all I cared for.

Even Tom, who kept repeating how glad he was to be back in London, grew quieter and quieter. His shoulders were drooping badly, and from three o'clock on, we had to stop every half hour so he could rest or use a toilet.

I was burning to ask him what was really ailing him, but I refrained. At long last, at the Tower Bridge, he raised his head weakly from the park bench he had been lying on, and told me the truth.

"Remember my telling you about my friend who caught all those intestinal diseases in India and Africa? The one who got careless?"

I nodded, recognizing immediately the confessional tone of his low voice. The "friend" had actually been himself.

He stared in silence at a gray royal naval ship moored on the far shore, then continued in a voice I had to strain to hear. "I didn't think I'd ever get well again. Actually, I'm not, when you come down to the truth. The pork, the headache, my tiredness, they're all reminders of how sick I still am, even after all these years."

"Why did you say it happened to a friend?" I asked, watching a seagull pass overhead.

"I tell everyone that. You're one of the only ones I've ever shared the truth with. Most people just can't relate to it. It's one of those things you had to be there to understand. Kind of like being in a war, in some ways."

He rose, and we walked along the river. "You'll be okay," he said. "I was searching for something, and left myself open." He stopped and nodded approvingly at me. "You, though, are doing it the right way."

"Just being an observer?"

"Yes. You're not searching. You want to learn. That's the best way." He breathed deeply. "I envy you. You know where you're heading, what you're looking for."

I shrugged. "Maybe I'm just lucky."

"I think there's more to it than luck in your case," he replied softly. "Shall we head back? . . . I'm feeling very tired right now."

From Earl's Court I traveled by train to Uxbridge on the western edge of the Greater London area. Then from Uxbridge to Oxford by bus. All the way, my thoughts were on Tom. I wondered if he was an omen of what my own future held, should I ever reach the African and Asian continents. Back in early March, before the walk began, when I had gone to Washington, D.C., to visit the embassies, I had visited one of the doctors for the Peace Corps workers, to find out about immunization shots against all the terrible diseases I had heard were rampant in some parts of Africa and Asia. I hate needles, and so I had been more than a little pleased when the doctor had advised me not to get the shots I thought I needed. His reasoning was that sometimes the shots themselves were as deadly as the diseases, and he felt I shouldn't risk them when in all likelihood their protectiveness would be weak by the time I reached those parts of the world.

But now . . . now I wasn't so sure that had been good advice.

Surely Tom had been properly immunized by army doctors before he had been shipped off to Vietnam, and still he had come back a dying shell of his former self. And now here I was: completely without protective shots or medicines of any kind, heading into an intimacy with millions of the world's impoverished. I was vulnerable to the trillions of deadly germs and microscopic parasites quivering out there. There were all kinds of invisible executioners that could visit me on things as innocent as a drop of water or a piece of food. And since I was determined to survive off the food and water of the people I was walking among, my chances of ingesting the world's diseases were as numerous as the atoms in my body. There were only two chances I had of surviving intact in my present unguarded state: a miracle, or else the discovery that those dangers had been as exaggerated as the two-legged kind.

Since no more buses were going westward from Oxford after eleven, I slept that night in the center of the town—in some bushes beside a large parking lot. Twice during the night patrolling bobbies with cackling walkie-talkies strapped to their belts woke me as they approached.

Each time, however, their flashlight beams passed over or around me, and I escaped their detection.

From the college town of Oxford I continued the next morning by bus to Worcester, Leominster, Shrewsbury, and Holyhead, a total of about twelve hours.

The roads the buses followed were major routes, and yet I could see from their narrowness and lack of shoulders that when I walked through England later I would have difficulty. Time and time again, the side of the bus swiped against the hedges alongside the roadways, and I shuddered at the thought of walking between those hedges and the thick traffic.

I took a map of the British Isles from my pack and studied Scotland and England for possible side roads that wouldn't be so well traveled. Scotland looked promising; England, however, looked as if it had a terminal case of varicose highways.

On our way from Shrewsbury to Holyhead on the Irish Sea, we did pass, however, through a region that looked as empty and rugged as many places on the American continent. With its low, moody sky, sparse vegetation, and rocky mountains, the area reminded me of parts of Wyoming and Montana. In the highlands of this mysterious-looking region, the air was cool, cold even. I had to put on a wool sweater to keep from shivering badly.

Even though it was only around five in the afternoon, the light outside was dim and shrouded by a fairly thick fog. The air smelled of coal and water. Farms and villages were farther apart than I'd seen in England. Adults and children alike reflected the darkness of the land, most of them dressed in clothes of black or a dark gray. They looked as if life was a little tougher perhaps in these parts.

During the entire three hours it took the bus to groan and whine its way across that rugged scenery, I didn't take my eyes from the window, even after the day had been swallowed by the earth's blackness. I told myself I had to return to this area someday to explore it and its people.

To me, Wales—the homeland of my father's ancestors—made the rest of England look hopelessly tame and ordinary.

The giant, multidecked ferry ship didn't leave for Ireland until 3:00 A.M.—after it had unloaded what seemed to be the entire population of Ireland. Sleeping in the noisy, packed waiting room at the docks was out of the question, so I entrusted my pack to a young Swedish couple and took to roaming the streets of Holyhead.

As in any coastal fishing town, the smell of rot and fish was as heavy as the fog.

Down the middle of a street running along the docks, I spied the flashing neon sign of a fish-and-chips shop. I made for it not so much because I was hungry, but because it looked warm and free of suspicious shadows in that dead of night.

I took my order of fish and chips (french fries) and sat on the outside step of the closet-sized shop to eat them. They were the first true fish and chips I'd ever had, and they were almost too delicious.

In America, the fish was always small and previously frozen. The piece I had now, however, was a long, wide one and as fresh as the water slapping against the dock pilings. The fries were thick and crisp—and so hot I had to wait five minutes before my tongue could tolerate them.

At least half a dozen times while I was eating, locals walked past, smiled amusedly, and asked, "Enjoyin' yer fish and chips, are ya?"

How in the world could they tell I was an American eating my first English fish and chips? I must be doing something out of the ordinary. I tried crossing my legs, eating with my left hand, not blowing on the fries, but they kept on smiling and asking. Finally, I just concentrated on enjoying my meal and only answered with a grunt each time the question was put to me.

On my return to the ferry station, a teenage boy with thick muscles and unkempt black hair stepped from a doorway to block my path. He stood perhaps only to my chin, but acted as if he were the bigger man.

"Wha' be yer name?" he asked me in a voice only his mother would've thought friendly.

"Steve," I answered, all the while watching his hands.

"Would ya be takin' the boat to Dun Laoghaire tonight?"

I nodded.

"Steve, do ya 'ave a quid to gi' me fer a box?"

"A box?"

"Smokes."

I'd forgotten that here many of the brands of cigarettes were packaged in cardboard.

"Well . . ." I started to shake my head no.

"Are ya on 'olidays?" he pressed.

"You could say that."

"Why Ireland?"

"Never been there."

"Better ya take yer 'oliday in this country."

"Why?"

He edged closer and spoke with a tone of disgust. "The Irish are a lot of dumb trash. There's nothin' over there worth seein' or speakin' to."

"I take it you don't care for the Irish too awful much."

He laughed harshly. " 'Tis aren't no secret that there's not much love lost between the Irish and the British." His voice grew louder, more serious. "Ever' time they kill another of our men, I'd like to see the whole of their murderin' lot pushed into the sea! Is it any wonder we look down on them? When all's they's good fer is makin' babies and murderin'?"

I decided I'd better move on while his thoughts were occupied with the Irish and not quids.

He grabbed my shoulder. "What of me quid, Steve? It's two miles to me house, and I got no money on me."

I gently pulled away. "Maybe the walk'll cool you down. Besides"—I smiled ever so slightly—"my mother's family was from—"

"Ireland?" He backed off as if I were diseased, then spun about and skulked off, uttering profanities.

He hadn't been the first Englishman I'd heard call the Irish lowly, dumb, and no good. But he'd certainly been the most vehement.

Several hours later, I was asleep on the ferry while it plowed its way across the calm Irish Sea toward Dun Laoghaire, about fifteen miles south of Dublin.

When I stepped ashore in the dawn, the weather was cold, blustery, and spitting rain. Hardly the greeting my tired soul needed. I added a little excitement, though, to the bland setting by riding a double-decker bus to the center of Dublin.

Dublin struck me as a "small big city." There was a heavy mixture of old structures with new ones, none of which were very tall—say, over twenty stories. With the usual bumper-to-bumper traffic and crowded buildings, it hardly struck me as a very quaint place. And yet it had something that set it apart from any other town or city I'd seen so far in the British Isles.

It had color. The drab conformity of the British was absent. Everyone I saw heading to work was dressed in whatever color and style and degree of orderliness he or she felt comfortable with.

Dublin was by all appearances a city of individuals, not an institution, like London.

But were the Irish as friendly as I'd always heard other Americans say they were? I fished into my pack for the letter from the Jesuit, Brother Ludwig, in Philadelphia. It was time to put the Irish to the test.

Back on the streets again, I combed my greasy hair, stepped into an alley and changed into a white shirt, and tried as best as I could not to look as if I'd just finished a six-month ocean voyage through hurricanes.

Two nuns strolled past just as I was putting my comb away. They directed me to the Jesuits' residence, three blocks from there.

The letter worked beautifully. Or nearly so.

"You realize this letter isn't addressed to us, but to Father O'Keefe in

Rome?" the white-haired head priest at their Leeson Street row house said to me.

I shifted the pack on my back as if to hint at its heaviness, and nodded.

He looked over his glasses and smiled. He was tall and thin and seemed fragile as he stood in front of a massive dark Dutch-style painting that showed Christ being kissed by Judas in the Garden of Sorrows.

"Normally, we only put up students studying at one of the universities. But I think we can find room for someone walking around the world."

"Thank you." I smiled. Ireland had passed its first test. And with flying colors, at that.

"We could easily double our number of rooms and still have to turn away hundreds of applicants," the male servant who led me to my room on the fifth floor said.

"Busy, busy, busy all the time, I be," he continued with a wave of his elderly arms. "The hostels and cheap hotels aren't profitable any longer and are shutting down. We get so many letters from students wantin' to rent a room for the school year. And yet we have space for only a hundred."

My room was very large, very old, and very humble. But it was the best kind—free. It was seven long strides wide, with the ceiling another six feet above my head. Its only furnishings were a faded rug, a small rectangular wall mirror, a single cot, a well-used portable closet, and two wooden desks with one stiff-backed wood chair. In the wall above the bed was a fist-sized hole in the plaster. The ceiling was breaking out all over.

Below the two narrow vertical windows was a courtyard of perhaps one hundred square feet, with a small garden in the center in which were rosebushes as tall as a man, with flowers of white, yellow, and red.

And directly across from me below was a ten-foot-high wall of thick brick, with a rounded top edge studded with jagged stone and glass.

The wall seemed absurd. Why was such a peaceful place fortified with gates of spiked iron and walls topped with broken glass? All against mere burglars?

"Maybe they're to keep people in, not out," the servant answered my inquiry.

I gave him a startled glance. He chuckled to let me know he wasn't serious.

"After all, it's 'ard to keep a man in the cloth anymore, ya know," he jested. "This used to be the visitin' quarters for a lot of priests and brothers."

I made plans to shower, shave, lunch, and then nap till dinnertime at five. But somewhere between taking off my shoes and my shirt, I fell victim to the sandman, and everything else remained plans.

When I did stumble into the cafeteria hoping to grab a morsel, it was after seven—teatime, no longer dinnertime. Sadly, I sat, teacup in hand, at a table with two other young men. I needed the energy of a good solid meal in me, after all the junk food I'd eaten on the trip from London. Tea, no matter how much milk and sugar I added, was just not enough.

"Miss your dinner, did you?" asked a voice behind me.

I turned to face a lad of about eighteen with thick, curly black hair and a big smile.

"Yes, I overslept."

"Are you from Canada?"

"No. America. Cincinnati, about six hundred miles inland from the Atlantic Ocean," I explained carefully. "In the state of Ohio."

"Oh, yes, I have a sister who lives in Ohio. Cleveland, is it?"

It occurred to me that everyone I'd met in Dublin and on the ferry, too, had relatives of some sort or other in America.

"I can still get you some dinner if you like," he offered. He motioned for me to follow him into the kitchen.

In the huge, ancient room he went to a large cast-iron oven. From it he produced a plate heaped with chicken covered in barbecued sauce, peas, thick fries, and bread. The food was still steaming as he handed the plate to me with a towel under it to keep me from burning myself.

A kindly-looking elderly lady entered the kitchen just as he was handing over the plate. She stopped and smiled at us.

"Givin' up your meal again?" she asked the lad.

"This is yours?" I asked, offering it back.

"No, no. Take it," he said firmly. "I cook the meals and get plenty to nibble on while I'm cookin'. Also, it's kind of a waste, since my mommy always has somethin' cooked for me when I get home." Then, turning his attention back to the old lady, he said, "He overslept and missed dinner hour."

"Oh, my," she said, like a worried mother. "Are you feelin' sick?"

She shuffled over to stare up at my face, which was a good two feet above hers. I looked down at her expression of concern and shook my head.

"He's come from the States," the lad said.

"America?" she said with such eagerness I had to laugh. "I've three sisters and a brother who went there to live."

She led me back to my seat, and like a doting mother made sure I had plenty of silverware, margarine, and tea. The other two men at the table watched in amazement as she pampered me.

After she made sure I was completely settled in, the woman left, only to return a minute later with another plate of food.

"Oh, no. I can't be taking your dinner, too," I protested. "This is plenty. Honestly."

"Nonsense." She set the new plate of food beside the other.

She made it clear it'd be useless to refuse any further, so I gave in and set about stuffing myself nearly to the point of sickness.

That night, around nine-thirty, I talked with the two men who had been seated at my table. One, a dark-skinned fellow of medium height and build, was a thirty-three-year-old doctoral student from Jordan. He called himself Sam and was majoring in math.

The other man was from Dublin, and also a graduate student majoring in math. Good-looking, muscular, and only in his early twenties, he had an Irish name that refused to stick in my head for more than two seconds.

Like most foreigners I had talked with, they questioned me for a long time on America, wanting to know how big it was, if wages were high, how the job situation was, and what were the costs of rent and food.

Already it was becoming obvious to me that a great many young people abroad were interested in working in the States.

After dinner we went to a local pub, where I had my first taste of Guinness, which was brewed right there in Dublin. Like all draught in the Isles, it was served at room temperature. In other words, quite warm. I took mine in a pint glass, or "jar," and sipped it for at least a half hour. Very dark colored—almost black, with a brown head—and bitter, it took me a while to get used to its taste. Over the course of the next two hours— the pubs closed at eleven-thirty in Ireland—I had three of the pint ales. But in spite of all I'd heard of the potency of Irish beer, I never felt much of a buzz.

Back in my room, I switched on the bare, unfrosted bulb hanging from the ceiling's middle and sat on the bed's stiff sheets. The realization that tomorrow I would actually be walking alone on a road I had never seen before and through towns whose names I could not even pronounce had me literally shaking with excitement. No way could I go to sleep right away.

Taking the Rand McNally auto-touring map off the table, I reclined against the pillow and studied, again, the ways I might find my way back to southern England. Unfortunately, there weren't many choices, because of the relative narrowness of the isles. Only one road connected Dublin to Belfast, almost 125 miles to the north, and it missed entirely those parts of Ireland—counties like Cork, Kerry, Donegal, Galway—that others said were the best parts of this country. I thought seriously of taking a bus to the south, to Cork, and starting my walk there, but something inside me cautioned that it was more important to make the walk through the first couple of countries, Ireland and Scotland, as simple as I could. There would be plenty of time later for sightseeing; right now, it was more important to build my confidence and be comfortable with being in a foreign culture.

A few hours later, when dawn's gray light snuck over the courtyard walls to color my windows' panes, I pulled Clinger's straps tightly against my body and took a deep breath. I was every bit as nervous as if I were stepping up to the starting line of a marathon race. Only I wasn't worried about winning or losing. Only finishing.

15

The walk north out of Dublin was anything but easy. The traffic as far as the airport was as thick as any in America. And faster, much faster. The four lanes of compact Fiats, VWs, Fords, Renaults, Toyotas, Datsuns, Volvos, Citroëns, and Peugeots screeched past me like race cars, only an arm's length away. The noise was constant, and the fumes heavy. I was very disappointed; I thought I'd left that all behind on the other side of the Atlantic.

Then, as if the Devil himself had heard my desire last night to get through this first foreign country without any complications, a bright orange Volkswagen Beetle sputtered just fifty yards ahead of me and rolled to a stop in the *middle* of the lane next to me. I glared at the old lady behind the steering wheel, fully expecting a massive pile-up any second that would send all sorts of cars tumbling into me.

Much to my amazement, however, every other car zipped around the tight curve and *somehow* missed her. The way they blended so skillfully into the inside lane without even slowing made me think of Grand Prix drivers.

I knew someone should shove her car up on the sidewalk. But with no driveways or even a shoulder along that stretch of road to park on, none of the other drivers had any way of pulling over to assist her.

"Don't fail me now," I prayed anxiously, as I took off Clinger and stepped, terrified, into the river of metal and noise. I tapped on the left front window, the passenger side in Ireland, and she smiled and waved across the car's interior as sweetly as if she had stopped to admire a flower garden.

"*Please* open the window," I begged with one eye on her and the other on the charging traffic. She smiled more widely and pointed for me to come to her side of the car. On the other side, the passing cars were only inches away, at best!

I eased my way to her window feeling like a man sinking in quicksand. I didn't dare turn my back to the ribbons of metal nearly grazing my moustache. I spoke from the side of my mouth.

"Ma'am, please put the car in neutral, and I'll push you up onto the sidewalk."

"Thank you so much, young man. You're—"

I didn't care to hear the rest, for just then a semitrailer belching black smoke like a steam locomotive roared around the curve straight at us. There was no way it was going to blend gracefully into the other lane. I high-jumped the car and dived onto the sidewalk in one second flat, my eyes pressed shut and my ears trying to do likewise.

Brakes screamed and horns howled. But no crunching of metal against metal.

I took a cautious look. The truck driver was shaking his fist at me, obviously thinking it was *my* car in the road—while the old lady, invisible to him, sat there smiling, looking gently backward at the massive truck bumper only inches from her own. She should have been a general.

I rushed to her car and pushed it as easily as if it were a shopping cart. The truck was an effective barrier between her rear end and the other traffic. Still, the cars sped past us in the other lane as if the checkered flag were just ahead. We were going faster and faster, and yet she seemed to have no intention of turning onto the sidewalk. What was she thinking? That I'd offered to push her all six miles to the next town?

"On the sidewalk! On the sidewalk!" I screamed.

Finally, the nose of the car angled to the side.

I'd lived. But at what cost to my nerves? I strode back to Clinger just in time to catch a German shepherd raising his leg over the blanket roll.

That was it! Somewhere out there had to be the Ireland of the storybooks, I fumed. I stomped past the wagging dog tail, a head-scratching truck driver, and a *still*-smiling grandmother, my face as red as my hair.

By late afternoon, near the small town of Swords, the scenery began to turn noticeably greener and less crowded. And I finally began to feel some of the natural beauty and ancient history of Ireland.

That night, on a rock beside a stream, I finished off a corned-beef sandwich and some angel-food cake that had been placed outside my bedroom door last night by some unseen saint at the Jesuit boarding house. Then, soon afterward, I fell into a deep sleep inside a very old stone church building that had been converted into a hay-storage barn. I didn't bother to ask permission, for there was no house in sight. I just crawled into its massive pile of hay and dropped off to sleep.

Sometime after midnight, a bitterly cold wind swept through the building's Gothic-style windows and woke me. I was covered with goose bumps, and the squeaks of what sounded like bats in the rafters high overhead didn't exactly help any.

I was too tired, though, to consider doing battle with Dracula, and only snuggled deeper into the hay with my two-dollar blanket, and was sound asleep again in less than a snore.

The morning air was chilly, and the straw soft and warm, so I stayed snuggled in its depths like a fieldmouse until after nine. I remembered the Irishwoman, Flo Warren, I'd met at the birthday party outside New York, and her advice: "If ever you see an empty barn in Ireland, go and sleep in it without askin' for permission. No one will bother you; that's how friendly they are."

I hoped she was right, because I knew there was lots more hay outside waiting to be brought inside. And the farmer wasn't likely to be much more patient. Not with such an overcast sky above.

Around ten o'clock, the farmer and his helpers caught me. Not in the barn, but outside at a spring-fed watering trough, where I was in the middle of shaving.

As he and the tanned, whiskered men rumbled through the gate and then drove by in their old Mercedes truck, the farmer cocked his chin to the left and flashed me a look that seemed to say, "Ah, life can be tough, can't it?"

I waved, and they all waved back cheerfully. Darned if Flo hadn't been right, I chuckled.

Just north of a tightly packed village named Gormanstown, I passed dozens of dilapidated trailer homes parked on the shoulders of the highway. The trailers were little ones, no longer than twenty feet. The tires were still on the wheels, so it looked as if their occupants planned on living beside the highway only temporarily.

Piled outside of the cheap trailers were carpet rolls and auto junk parts for sale. The whole scene was one of a mini-ghetto—clothes hanging from bushes and rickety lines, small children running about in soiled clothing, litter and garbage of all sorts strewn about.

Some of the children charged toward me, asking arrogantly for

money, usually a two-pence. They were a rough-looking people, and I
knew it must be awfully trying to cram an entire family into one of those
trailers at dinnertime, or bedtime. And since there were no water hookups
or toilet buildings anywhere, they must have had to depend upon the
hedges and tall weeds of the farms nearby.

In some of these nomadic camps, however, the people looked quite
well off. Their trailers were later models, cleaner, and parked alongside
them were new and quite expensive vans and autos. These "upper class"
trailers kept in their own little separate groups, away from the other,
"common class" ones.

Later on, I was to learn that the people I had passed alongside the
highway were the "caravan people," or "gypsies," as they were once
known. They were a by-product of the Great Potato Famine of the last
century.

During the potato-crop failure of the 1800's, millions of farmers were
forced to give up everything and move on.

For many years, around one hundred thousand Irish a year emi-
grated.

As one retired farmer I talked with, Tom Mills, put it, "The families
were big, the land small."

Some of this new class of nomads chose to stay in Ireland but to
remain rootless. They became the gypsies, the forerunners of today's caravan people. They were named after the trailers they lived out of.

At first, I didn't know what to think when gypsy children came up to
me to beg for money. They looked so poor, but I couldn't help them. And
they came so frequently—frequently enough to be a real nuisance. I was
glad when I reached the outskirts of the ancient port city of Drogheda,
and had no more of their camps to walk through.

I stopped at a small grocery store, then sat outside on the curb to
drink a pint of milk and eat some peanut-butter sandwiches. No sooner
had I taken a bite than yet another beggar approached from an adjoining
low-income housing complex. This one, however, was not a child, but a
short, dark-haired woman of about my age. Tailing her were two little
girls, one about eleven pushing a stroller with an infant.

She came right for me with absolutely no hesitation, like a bee to a
flower.

"Good day, dear kind sir. May the dear Virgin Mary bless ya," she
said softly. "Have ya a couple of pounds to give me so's I can feed the
young children? They've nothing to eat all day, and there's nothing in the
house. God bless ya for helping us."

Standing over me in her long black dress with stains of all sorts on it, and thick white stockings on her thick legs, she knew she had me trapped. When I didn't reply immediately, she pressed harder.

"Just two pounds, sir. God and the Virgin Mary will bless you, and I'll pray for ya."

"Hold it!" I shouted angrily. What upset me the most was that she was practically demanding three dollars' worth of my money. Whatever happened to "Have you a quarter or a dime to spare, please?"

"Where's your husband at? Isn't he working?" I demanded.

"He left us several months ago. I don't make any money myself, 'cause there's no work. Just a couple of pounds, and I'll pray for ya, dear kind man."

I looked the children over. They didn't look the least bit deprived, and yet how could I be sure they weren't actually hungry? Out of the corner of my eye, I noticed the shopkeeper looking disgustedly at the beggar woman.

"I tell you what; I'll buy some food for them," I said with resignation.

She looked a bit disappointed. But only for an instant. "Yes . . . yes. May Holy Mary bless ya."

I had to gather everything back into my pack, and carry the whole load back into the store. I purchased a quart of milk and a loaf of bread, and brought them out to her.

She took them without so much as a thank you, and walked away. I went back in to get something to eat in place of the sandwiches that had become dried out in the hot sun.

While I was standing in the line at the counter, I looked outside and saw the beggar woman talking to a carload of caravan people who had just pulled up.

They all laughed heartily at something she said, and then one of the women in the front seat of the Ford Capri stuck a pound note out the window. The beggar woman handed over the food and took the note. She waved them good-bye, put the note in her pocket, and shooed her children further along the street.

Right then I made up my mind I'd not give in to any more beggars, except perhaps for those who were crippled and obviously unable to work.

But I was disturbed. If only a handful of beggars in Ireland could make me so upset, what would I be like in countries like Pakistan or India?

Drogheda struck me as a place still trapped in another century. And not even the last one.

The three- or four-story flat brick façades and stone buildings were packed against one another like the stones of a wall. Many of the fronts were painted, but the paint could not disguise the age of the structures.

As with many of the older settlements in this part of the world, the doorways of the buildings opened right onto the street. And the roadways themselves were very narrow and clogged with autos and jaywalkers. I decided to hurry through the town as quickly as I could. Tight spaces, crowds, and my large pack never seemed to agree with one another.

Suddenly, a gray sedan whipped to the curve, and a young man in his early twenties dressed in white sneakers, blue jeans, and a Grateful Dead T-shirt came rushing at me from the passenger side.

"Are you the American walking around the world?" he asked, running his fingers through his black hair.

"Yes, I am."

"I saw your picture in the paper this morning. Do you have a place to stay tonight?"

"No. I was just going to walk on through Drogheda."

"That's Dro'heda. We don't say the g."

"Sorry. I have a rotten time with the Irish names."

"My mum sent me out this morning to look for you, but I didn't find you. I was just returning from the beach, when I saw you walking up the side of the road. Would you like to come and have some dinner at least? My mum wants to meet you."

"Sure."

"I'll walk the rest of the way with you and show you where we live. It's just a little ways." He turned to the young red-haired lady driving the car. "Roseanne, drive the car home. We'll meet you there."

She slid the car into gear and squealed it away, her hair whipping about in the open window.

I followed him toward the center of town.

"Your sister, or girlfriend?"

"Sister. She went swimming with me."

"What was her name? Roseanne?"

"Roshin. R-o-i-s-i-n. It's an Irish name. Mine, by the way, is Fiacre. Fiacre O. Caribre."

"Do you mind if I just call you Phil?" I asked desperately.

He laughed. "Why not?"

The center of the town seemed even older-looking, with cats and snippets of smoke and people everywhere. And the cobblestone streets were so crowded and narrow. We passed beneath a massive and ancient gray fortress gate of stone into a part of the town that looked so decrepit and abandoned it could have been a setting for the Black Plague pictures in my school history books. We turned down a narrow street running parallel to a river a block to the east, and every building on it seemed deserted, including one rotting old factory with the word OATMEAL on its crumbling walls.

Before long, I began to wonder if I was being led into some sort of robbery trap. We had been walking for at least an hour, and it seemed I was being led to one street corner after another. And deeper and deeper into an area that seemed shunned by the rest of the people.

I scrutinized my guide more closely, and did not like what I saw: His faded jeans had holes in the knees; the sneakers were more frazzled than I'd have liked; I wondered when was the last time the T-shirt had been washed; his dark pupils were crowned by dark hairy brows that looked older than the twenty-two he had told me he was; and the stubble on his angular face and the dirt under the nails of his long fingers made me even warier.

"What do you do for work?" I asked nervously.

"Oh, sorry, I should have told you." He laughed in an odd pitch. "I thought you might know from the way I'm dressed. I'm a college student, but now it's the summer break. I'm a math student at Berkeley University in California. I live there with an older brother, and I'm on a scholarship. Otherwise, I couldn't afford it."

Suddenly, the world didn't look quite so dark and empty.

"I'm an honors student, and I want to work in your country after I graduate. Hopefully in computers." With a frustrated shrug of his shoulders, he added, "No jobs for me in Ireland."

Halfway down the short street we were following, we came to a noisy little pub with a funny-looking black car parked in front. The car looked to me like a giant sea-tortoise shell with two buggy eyed headlamps. A Citroën, it said. The pub's name above its dusty panes was Ni Caribre. From the dark and smoky interior there came a lot of noise. Fiacre motioned for me to follow him through a narrow doorway.

To my surprise, it was not the pub we entered, but a stone drive that had a little open ditch running beside it, with water running through the ditch out to the street. I soon realized the ditch was a drainage for urinals in an open outhouse. Behind the pub was a wide courtyard with leaves all over its stone floor, and two or three picnic tables made of little more than stumps, with rickety chairs set about them.

A woman with fiery red hair waved at us through a window. His mother, Fiacre explained. Hers was a friendly smile and wave.

We walked onto a small porch, past an old washing machine, stacks of beer bottles, broken crates, hanging laundry, various bits of wrecked furniture, and God only knew what else. I could hardly squeeze through. And then, along with what seemed a thousand flies, we stumbled through another narrow old door to the living quarters.

The room in back of the pub was perhaps twenty feet long and ten feet wide, but it should have been as large as a warehouse to contain all the things stuffed into it. To the left was the sink with its tons of dirty dishes, an old gas range that would have looked modern only in previous centuries, and across from a boarded-up fireplace a kitchen table with enough scraps of food on it to feed me for weeks. A long bar piano immediately to my right didn't help my feelings of claustrophobia any, nor did the piles of yet more laundry, the family knickknacks and photos on everything even remotely flat, children's toys, cases and kegs of beer, statues of places visited and of the Virgin Mary, cigar boxes for holding the pub's receipts, kids and adults around my age pushing everything hither and thither to make room for me and a cramped Clinger. Absolute mayhem.

"Ah, Steven! Welcome to the last *true* pub in all of Ireland!"

It was Fiacre's short little mom, Caitlin. And from the way she charged me from the doorway to the pub, I could have been one of her own sons. She squeezed me so hard I couldn't answer her.

Immediately, she ordered a beer be fetched for her American guest. I looked at her with disbelief—it wasn't even midmorning. And then onto the table went a breakfast of tomatoes, eggs, bacon, and lots of homemade bread with jam and butter. Along with a big bowl of custard pudding buried in milk, sugar, and cinnamon.

Suddenly, it was as if I didn't exist at all. Everyone above the age of six rushed past without speaking. It was, Caitlin explained as she hurried on her way, the height of the day for the pub's business. The night shift for the dock workers had ended a little while ago.

Five minutes later, there slunk in beside me a wild-looking young lady with heavily painted black eyes, skintight black leather pants over a pair of legs almost as long as mine, fire-red lips, and a leopard-skin blouse that knew no modesty. Her hair was done in punk style, a dishwater-blond color and frazzed in every direction like the mane of a creature born with the genes of a lion and a punk rocker. I felt I should hide the butter knife.

She turned out to be a disc jockey at a local "pirate" FM radio station. And another of Caitlin's daughters. Between clouds of cigarette smoke, she told me her name was Aine, she was thirty-two and had never married.

"Let's go somewhere private, what do you say?" she suggested in a voice that made me choke. Her reason, she said, was that she wanted an interview for the station.

Into Aine's black little Spitfire sports car I went, to be whipped down snakelike back streets, past row after row of medieval-looking buildings, and finally spun around at a sinister black pier. All for the sake of privacy! From the floor of the car Aine brought up a large tape recorder.

By the time we returned to the pub, everything was finally quiet. Caitlin and her family were taking a breather in the back room.

With the height of the day's business already over, Caitlin swung back and forth in the rickety rocker in her living room/kitchen/dining room/pub storage room, and talked for hours about her family, her dear Ireland, the pub, and local history. With sparkle in her green eyes, she told of St. Patrick's stay in their valley along the river Boyne. And how here was where the present "troubles" in Northern Ireland started, where the Battle of the Boyne was fought, in which the English King William III of Orange defeated in 1690 the Irish Army led by the rebel James II, and hence came the bitter division of Ireland that has persisted.

The more I listened to her recount the area's history, from the "Gaelies" of the ninth and tenth centuries to the martyrdom of a local archbishop whose four-hundred-year-old head was still on public display in the town's Catholic church, the more I wondered if everything in this valley was steeped in legend. She knew of so many colorful and mysterious links to a long, long-ago past.

Her fine frizzy hair, which refused to stay close to her very pale face, seemed charged from the electricity she generated in her storytelling. It stuck out wildly in every direction in the pale light of the overhead bulb.

She warned me not to bring up religion or politics during a discussion with Irish people, or that would be all they would talk about. The trouble in the North she seemed to blame on religion. Yet it was obvious from her tone and choice of words that she had little love for the Protestants. She believed they had no place on her beloved, magical island.

Two other daughters of Caitlin's stopped by during our talk, along with their husbands and their many children. I even caught a glimpse of Caitlin's husband. He was a taxi driver, when he wasn't helping run the pub.

That night Caitlin and Fiacre brought me to an apartment they rented to teachers during the school year. Since it was the end of July, the flat was empty. I slept on a mattress in the front bedroom, while Fiacre stayed in the back bedroom. I couldn't blame him for sleeping in the empty apartment, where there was at least room.

For the next two days Caitlin and her children treated me to more locally caught salmon, potatoes, oxen tongue, home-grown peas and to-matoes, freshly baked bread, gooseberry and custard desserts, and gallons upon gallons of hot tea with milk and sugar.

And Caitlin spent those two days teaching me some of the Gaelic she and her family spoke so fluently, showing me the green humps of the Cooley and Mourne mountains, and delighting my senses with the fishing fleets of the Irish Sea and such historic ruins as ninth-century Celtic crosses, an abbey built in 1142, the tower where St. Patrick defiantly lit the Pascal fire in A.D. 432, and even a twelfth-century cemetery still in use.

But best of all were my final hours with the O Caribre clan. First, in the early afternoon, there was the weekly sing-along in Caitlin's pub. From every part of the city's lower quarters, there streamed in happy locals bearing mandolins, guitars, and flutes. And for hours in the crowded little pub, reality and hardship took a backseat to fables and sonnets. To me, in the middle of all that sawdust and foam, it was a scene from an Irish *Zorba the Greek:* the smells of smoke and the docks, dim light filtering through dust and cracks, crooked-nosed children climbing and dashing everywhere, mothers balancing babies in laps and mugs in hands, and a crazy choir of everyone from dock workers to gypsies to shoppers to old men with their old women.

My God, *this* was what life was truly all about. This was what being friends and neighbors and a community *really* meant. Oh, how I wished everyone back in America who thought man was a doomed and pathetic creature could have known but five minutes of Caitlin's lair that afternoon. How could they possibly go away not believing God and love and magic were still as alive in our veins?

Individual men broke out into song. Some of the songs were very funny, some sad and mournful. Most of them made fun of an Irishman stuck in a bad job or marriage.

A group of men who called themselves the Hugh Sands Folk Group asked me to sing an American folk song. Surprised and embarrassed, for my singing voice has always been one of the worst imaginable, I wanted to hide. But so much did they egg me on that I finally tried "She'll Be Coming Around the Mountain"—with predictably disastrous results.

I eventually had to give up, because I couldn't remember the words. Still, they slapped my back and made me feel I was now one of them.

I'd tried. And something told me that in Ireland that was all that counted. Caitlin treated me to yet another large pint of lager; the others cheered; the kids crawled onto my lap. And the band broke into a vigorous rendition of the song I'd attempted, as if to let me know that this wretched crooner, who didn't know a note from a key, was still a hero.

Late in the afternoon, when the shadows were beginning to stalk the streets, Caitlin took me to the large Catholic church in the center of town to see the head of the martyred archbishop who had just recently been made a saint by the Vatican.

She led me to a small altar along the left side of the enormous cathedral's stone and Gothic interior. Atop the altar sat a small glass box framed by two candles flickering weakly on either side. A railing kept us and the other curious from getting any closer than fifteen feet. The area was so dark my eyes needed several minutes to adjust. But when they did, I beheld a shrunken head no bigger than my fist and as black as a lump of coal, resting, its eyes closed, on a cushion darkened with age.

A small group of elderly women, dressed from wrinkled faces to swollen ankles in black, knelt to pray at the railing, then crossed themselves, whipped out opera glasses, and enjoyed the dismembered archbishop up close.

They seemed to me like natives going to an ancient temple to be bedazzled by the spirits.

I fell asleep that night feeling restless in my soul, as if too many spirits had passed through it that day.

By nine in the morning the pub was as crowded as ever, and to the clatter of pint glasses in the sink, I ate my last breakfast in Drogheda.

Caitlin looked sad, as if she did not like to lose any of her young ones, even a visitor of sorts. The last image I had of her was as she stood with the rest of her wild angels in front of the pub, waving at me.

"Zo N-eiri an bozair leaz!" she shouted.

I smiled. *And may the road rise with you, too,* I prayed.

16

I resumed my journey to Belfast along Route N1, the same road on which I'd entered Drogheda. I traveled slowly, enjoying the hay fields, pastures, low hills, and unbroken hedges of ripening blackberries. About four miles north of Drogheda, I paused briefly to test my imagination on the large open field on my right where Pope John Paul II had held an open-air mass a couple of years before, tried to visualize what it must have looked like covered with half a million people. To my left, on a distant hilltop, was the ancient stone tower I'd climbed the day before to see the wide meadows and thick, stubby Celtic stone crosses of St. Patrick's domain. I wondered if that craggy old saint would have approved of the fifteen-foot-high, forty-foot-long stone monument the locals had left in the meadow, with its eloquent prayer: "Let peace, not violence, decide the course of the world's history."

That night, fourteen miles nearer to the border of Northern Ireland, I learned the hard way that not all Irish pastoral scenes were as peaceful as they appeared. I wanted to bed down for the night in a nearby meadow. I thought it would be a simple matter to step through the blackberry hedge beside me to reach that meadow's soft grass. After all, I'd climbed over many a barbed-wire fence in the States to claim a barn loft or a clump of trees as my bedroom, and so I didn't see how any simple hedge might be stopping me. To be honest, I was filled with admiration for the Irish farmers for trusting each other so much that they saw no need for barbed wire.

Surprise! My first step into the hedge sent me plunging five feet into a hidden trench. The shock of plummeting toward hell without warning was bad enough, but—ouch!—to be buried in mature blackberry vines, bristling with thorns, was nothing short of heart-attack material.

Those picturesque hedges were surely some of the meanest traps anywhere. As I hung suspended in midtrench, a living pincushion at the mercy of Nature at her worst, my only solace was that Clinger was keeping my back free of the pain the rest of me was going through.

For the longest time I was at a loss as to how to escape. If I moved even an eyelash, some sadistic thorn would take its turn at giving me a good sharp poke. I was sure I was doomed to spend the entire night in that hole of thorns.

I finally escaped by slipping ever so carefully out of Clinger and using him as a shield for my face. As thousands of thorns tore at my pants and sweater, I painfully inched my way to the top of the ditch. Once out, I noticed with what little sanity I had left that I was no closer to the meadow than I had been before. I headed down the road to the next town's lights with a tremendous new respect for the mind of the Irish.

The first day of August in Ireland wasn't feeling any less unbearable than it did in the Ohio Valley. And from the way I was walking unsteadily at times and Clinger was feeling ever heavier on my spine, I feared that I had a mild case of sunstroke.

What I saw in the town of Dundalk didn't do much for my spirits either. Much smaller in size than I had anticipated, it was an ugly and cramped town that seemed half-empty and economically stagnant. Again I was seeing a people who were mostly used to low wages, hard work (if any), and the downing of a lot of their misfortunes in the pubs. Alcoholism seemed to me to be a very large problem in Ireland, with many drunken older men in particular stumbling about on the towns' side streets. From what I could see, I figured there had to be a lot of wives and children who never saw the man of the household, except when he returned home in the evening drunk from the pub.

In a way, thinking about all those drunks scared me every minute as I walked along the roadway. Surely, many of the drivers speeding past me had no business being behind the wheel of a car or truck. And surely someday, somewhere, I would be walking right where one of them ran his vehicle off the road. I just hated it on days like this, when there was virtually no shoulder to walk on.

In the short time I had been in Ireland, I had realized I was with a highly individualistic and volatile people, and I could see why there would be a natural conflict between their kind and the more somber English. So many Irish I had met favored driving the British out by violence if necessary. Caution and following rules were just not in the Irishman's blood. Or shyness and liking bosses, either. I suspected that the reason many a man could be found in the pubs for most of the day was that the wife was the boss of the house, and he was not about to trade his boss at work for another one in his free time.

But if anything struck me as being most representative of Irish emotionalism, it was the way they talked to each other. Both the men and women frequently did so in loud, argumentative tones. So many times I had looked at a nearby conversation thinking a bloody battle was about to erupt, never to see even so much as a fist raised the whole time.

Still, I found myself liking very much their fierce independence. I decided I had more of the blood of my Irish ancestors in me than of my Welsh ones, who I thought had looked almost *too* quiet and moody on my bus ride to Holyhead. Though the Irish, too, could have used a little less moodiness.

At the border that evening the guard in the booth looked at me for several long seconds, then motioned me past.

I was in Northern Ireland, and after dark at that. I had been warned I would not be as well treated in the North as I had in the Republic of Ireland. Those in the North had learned to be suspicious of any strangers. Americans, especially, were not liked, because they were considered the chief arms suppliers to the IRA guerrillas. Would there be British soldiers coming to me now, ready to search me for weapons? Would some terrorist squad, waiting to ambush a British patrol, mistake my backpacked figure for that of a soldier and open fire? Might I step on a booby trap, or stumble onto some hideout, in my search for a place to sleep?

No longer did the land seem quiet and friendly. It was darker, rougher. My imagination or not, I sensed something uneasy in the air. Actually, I had been sensing that something was wrong even before I'd crossed the border. For one thing, there'd been the elaborate security around the bigger homes. And twice that day vicious dogs had rushed out of open gates at me, as if they had been trained to kill.

The first time had been about ten miles from the border. A large German shepherd, fangs showing, had rushed at me, only to be commanded back by the owner, who—thank God—had been close by. For only the second time on my walk, I took out my knife and stuck it in my belt.

The second incident was two miles from the border. Two fully grown Dobermans had rushed out full force from an open gate and stopped, growling deeply, just outside of my knife's range. Obviously sensing I was not an intruder, they had turned on their own and returned to their yard, but they had followed me the length of the property on the other side of the wall.

From what had been almost flat fields, there now rose low, dark forest-covered mountains. I wondered if there were terrorists holed up in those mountain forests—or if all the talk of violence in this part of the world was as exaggerated as it was for New York.

Then, almost as if on cue, two black silhouettes that were unmistakably military helicopters materialized above the mountain ridges to my left. The *thump-thump-thump* of their long blades sounded so startling in the quiet I felt my skin crawling in fear.

From the sides of the copters, beams of searchlights scanned the sides of the mountains, like long white arms feeling for something in a dark pool of water. Then, almost as suddenly as they'd appeared, they were gone, back over the ridge and to the west. All that remained of the helicopters, to assure me I hadn't imagined them, was the distant pulse of their blades.

So there were, indeed, men of death in those mountains. No longer was I in a land of only peace and fanciful legends.

17

It was a cold, damp, dark, and musty valley that Newry, my first city in Northern Ireland, had been dumped into those many centuries before. Too much darkness dwelt along each street for my comfort, and the air that hung limply between its long rows of chimneys smelled strongly of rot and coal.

From the weak glow of the dull yellow streetlights and the lights of many smoky factory yards rose a thick, foglike cloud of smoke that hung over the entire area.

Every few blocks I passed small groups of young, leather-jacketed men and women, who eyed me carefully as I passed. By the time I reached the northern edge of the city around an hour before midnight, I felt lucky to have made it that far without any hassle.

I was tired, hungry, and in no mood to be bothered by any ugly-faced thugs.

I ordered a fish and chips in a greasy little shop on one of the narrow twisting streets, and sat down to eat it on the steps of a trashed building that reeked of urine. Across the street stood a court building surrounded by a barbed-wire fence at least thirty feet high, with a thick steel gate topped with more coiled barbed wire. On the windows of the spotlighted building were iron bars a good inch thick. Such a small building, yet fortified with enough material to surround a medium-sized penitentiary. The tallness of the fence, I finally figured out, was to make it difficult to throw any bombs over into the yard. At the gate was a booth for guards.

The longer I sat there studying the city, the more it resembled something from hell: grotesquely shaped buildings that looked more suitable for rats than human beings, smoke and soot everywhere, trash lying all about, screaming voices, barbed wire, pungent and unpleasant odors, the roar of factories, and roughly dressed people slinking by with hard eyes.

I fished my map of the British Isles from Clinger. I'd had all I could take of the main highway to Belfast. There had to be a better route.

I squinted in the ugly yellow light of the overhead street lamp and found what I was looking for. Going out of Newry, toward the northeast, was a small secondary road. Number B25. It looked perfect. I could follow it to a little place called Rathfriland, then turn north to Belfast on an even smaller road, B7. To my satisfaction, the two roads passed through what looked to be pure countryside, with no towns larger than a couple of thousand people.

I struck out up a steep and winding narrow road and paused at the top of the hill just long enough to take one last glance at the mass of ugliness below. Newry seemed something out of *David Copperfield*, not 1983.

Was this an example of what the rest of Northern Ireland had in store for me? Maybe even Scotland and England?

Too scared to continue walking in the dark, (a habit I had gotten into, so that I could spend more of the daylight hours exploring and talking with the locals), I made up my mind to sleep in the first likely place I came to, which turned out to be only a few hundred yards away—a newly plowed farm field across from an all-night truck stop. Crouching behind some weeds, I spread out my blanket on the already dewy ground, on a piece of cardboard I scavenged from the roadside ditch, and practically collapsed into a sweaty lump. Dirt clods the size of shoe boxes kept me as restless as ever that night, and it was with a feeling of pessimism that I awaited the sun.

Before entering Rathfriland the next afternoon, I knocked on the door of a farmhouse for a glass of water. Joan Lawson, a lady of about sixty, answered, and immediately asked me to come inside to join her and her gardener, Joe, for a Coca-Cola and a lunch of roast ox tongue, potatoes, bread, and fresh gooseberries topped with lots of sugar and custard.

When I asked about the troubles in Northern Ireland, she said she had seen no evidence of it and thought it was really quite insignificant. She sent me on my way with my first nice smile in Northern Ireland, and my goatskin wine bag plump with spring water.

About two miles after I left her house, two armored troop carrier vehicles sped by me, their open backs revealing interiors filled with soldiers in battle dress and holding automatic rifles. They had sped by, I learned later, to foil any possible ambushes.

In Rathfriland, I had to go up a steep street to reach the center of the town. Fluttering from the ends of many flagpoles sticking out from upper stories was the British Union Jack, its bright red, white, and blue colors contrasting sharply with the plain white or gray of many of the buildings. There could be little doubt I was on British soil. It was almost as if the flags were being flown so thickly and openly to dare anyone to think otherwise.

But as much as the Irish side of my heart ached at the sight of those flags, my feet were my main concern at the moment. I was still wearing the same pair of boots and innersoles that I'd left home twelve-hundred miles ago with. And the innersoles were looking like remnants of an atomic war—to say nothing of how they smelled!

So into a drugstore in the center of town I went. However, there were no insoles on the shelves close to my size 12, so I left after only a couple of minutes. Waiting for me outside was a fat poorly dressed woman with a dirt-smeared but very cute small girl by her side. Holding out her hand, the woman begged for some money to buy milk for the child. As much as I hated to, I forced myself to say a firm no.

I rushed away feeling terribly upset with myself, wondering if I shouldn't have given her something. God, how much poverty I was finding everywhere I went.

"Hey, lad. Come 'ere," said a baker from his door. He gave me a jelly roll and said simply, with a nod at the beggar woman, "Them kind are quite well cared for by the guvment. No need for you to ever give 'em money. Eh?"

I smiled and went away feeling a little better.

Thankfully, all the emotions boiling away inside me cooled considerably over the rest of that afternoon, as I became more distracted by the scenery than my thoughts. The mostly Protestant farms were larger in size than in the Republic of Ireland and certainly much richer-looking, with nice two-story stone homes and spacious barns made of the same gray stone. The hills also were larger—sometimes steep but always calm and populated with fat sheep or dairy cows.

Now, at last, I was seeing the scenic Ireland that had been in my head when I'd left America. For the first time since crossing into this region, I sensed peace.

When I came upon an abandoned farmhouse just before five-thirty, I decided to rest and collect my thoughts together for a while. Dinner was a couple of peanut-butter sandwiches, a can of cold Campbell's bean soup, and water. My nose was badly sunburned, and I fell asleep in that house at dark feeling very achy inside, too.

It was called homesickness.

My next meal was lunch at a tiny fish-and-chips shop in the farm village of Dromara the next day. While in the snack bar, I noticed it had milkshakes listed on the wall menu board. I eagerly ordered the large size that cost twenty-five pence. I loved milkshakes. They, along with hot dogs and Cincinnati Reds baseball, were a part of America that I was missing so much lately.

Instead, I became even more homesick when the "milkshake" was set on the counter before me. It was bad enough that it had only one table-spoon of ice cream in its milk, but then it was served to me in a teacup! My first desire was to cry. I wanted the fabled "monster-sized" malts of my youth—malts so huge and thick and cold that they used to make me wonderfully sick for days.

Still grumbling from the milkshake that wasn't, I stopped a short while later at the Dromara Police Station and photographed a policeman coming out the front gate of its heavily fortified yard. Hardly a minute later, a police car was blocking my path, and a tall, thickly moustached, red-haired policeman was demanding to see my identification. On his hip was something I had not seen anywhere in the Republic of Ireland—a gun.

"You could be taking photos for an IRA hit squad," he said gravely. "They use the photos to identify the policemen that later they may kill. Don't make such a mistake again. Next time could be fatal." He checked through my gear.

From windows behind hanging Union Jack flags, faces stared out at me and the police. I was in the middle of the village, but I felt I was in the middle of a prison yard.

Slowly, the beauty of the land and of the people who relied on it for their livelihood gentled my own spirit back into a good mood again.

That afternoon I stopped to photograph a man who was training two young border collies to herd sheep on the slope of a beautiful hill. The small black-and-white dogs moved quickly, expertly, and eagerly at the slightest command he issued, and from the large smile their actions elicited from him, I could tell even from afar that he enjoyed being with those dogs. Having grown up with a big old collie named Laddie, I felt very drawn to the scene in my viewfinder.

Obligingly, the man had the collies move the sheep closer to the stone wall I was beside. Doffing his wool cap, the stout white-haired trainer introduced himself as John McAdam. The farm, he said, belonged to a Scottish-Irish man of the name of Samuel Campbell. As did the flock of about thirty sheep.

He invited me to follow him and the dogs to the farmhouse on the hill, to meet the Campbells and take a bit of a meal. I followed, listening to Mr. McAdam sing the praises of the dogs he had spent a lifetime breeding and training. He was training nineteen other such collies, he said. And they were jolly good dogs, too, sometimes fetchin' up to two thousand dollars apiece.

In the small stone farmhouse I was met with a warm handshake by Samuel Johnson Campbell, and with lots of additional handshakes from his gray-haired wife of over fifty years, Mildred, their two grandsons, a granddaughter, two neighbor boys, and a brother of John McAdam. It was a relaxed and happy group, who said they loved their part of Ireland. To a person, they believed there was no prettier area on the island. Nor any quieter.

Mrs. Campbell hustled up a tray of cookies (biscuits), breads of several types, blackberry jam, and the customary tea. And all of us sat at a table by the kitchen window.

Many of the families in the area were also originally of Scottish descent, Mr. Campbell explained, as well as nearly all Protestant. What many Americans probably don't realize, he said, was that the histories of Scotland and Ireland were very closely related. In fact, the original settlers of Scotland were from Ireland. Yet, as he put it firmly, "We are British, not Irish."

"This is Ulster, or Northern Ireland, here. Very rich, beautiful countryside," he related. "I have lived here sixty-five years. And I have loved every minute of it."

"Is there a lot of violence in Northern Ireland, as I read in the American newspapers?" I wondered aloud.

His large brows shot up. "Oh, definitely not."

"Have you seen any of the violence I am talking about?" I persisted.

"No, I haven't seen any." And the others backed him up, with John

McAdam observing politely, "You have more in your country than we have in ours."

"What about the future of Ulster, especially for your grandsons? Do you think it is going to remain a calm, peaceful place to live?"

Mr. Campbell chuckled, as if he'd heard that question a hundred times before. "I think it will, definitely. The worst thing that happened here was we had a local government in the town below several years back. But they done away with it."

"So you don't even have your own local form of government?"

"No. And better for it, believe me. We can run our own lives quite well enough, without others telling us how it should be done."

"I'm curious. Do you consider yourself Irish or Scottish? Or a combination of both?"

"We would claim to be British. Ours is a British passport."

All my way to the city limits of Belfast itself, people of the North kept emphasizing to me that violence in their province is overplayed by the press.

"To just walk down the street, you'd not know it even existed," I was told by several well-meaning people. But they were wrong. Very wrong.

Just two days after meeting John McAdam, I was camping in a wheat field on the edge of Belfast the night before I entered its gray mix of poverty and old businesses, when I again saw the helicopters with the probing searchlights. Only this time it was not some mountain flank the lights were feeling out, but the Catholic slums of the city's east side. Being from a small town where four policemen took turns sharing one car, I found the sight of those helicopters very frightening.

In the south of Ireland, I hadn't seen a single firearm. In the Belfast I entered at midmorning, I saw firearms in the hands of hundreds of policemen and British soldiers, many more helicopters patrolling overhead, and dozens of heavily armored troop carriers darting from street to street. The scene in Belfast during the two days I was there was like that of a war zone.

How could anyone claim with a straight face that there were hardly any "troubles," when no one could go shopping in the downtown area without first passing through a police check station and being frisked for weapons and bombs? Yet, so used to this had the people of Northern

Ireland become, that they were able to live as normally in their turmoil as anyone else might in a peaceful everyday setting.

My first stop upon entering the city limits on the fifth of August, now four months into my journey, was a little public library in Mount Oriel, next door to the Newtownheda Day Centre and Mount Oriel Clinic. I needed to catch up on my notes, as usual, and do another *Capper's* column. So I was sitting outside eating a breakfast of doughnuts and waiting for the library to open, when to my surprise (considering how grungy I looked), one of the senior citizen ladies from the clinic stopped to chat.

She, too, told me that the violence of the North was being "wrongly" emphasized in the press. And while she spoke contemptuously of the Irish, calling them "poor trash," "emotional," "unstable," and "murderers," she had high praise for the British soldiers and the queen. She was grateful that she did not have to live under the Irish, who, she said, could never take care of her like the British government did. Irish rule would mean higher taxes, higher prices, fewer benefits, and even fewer jobs in a country where unemployment was already at a staggering 25 percent.

Yet she saw the day when Ulster would again be under Irish rule, because the Catholics were growing faster in number than the Protestants.

At noon, as I was leaving the library to get some lunch, the same well-dressed elderly lady met me out on the front steps. She had been sent over by the nurses and administrator of the clinic and senior-citizen center to ask if I would give the residents a short talk. I thought that was a pleasant enough idea, especially when I was told it included a lunch.

I was nervous about how my first foreign "speech" would go over with that Protestant audience of around fifty people. But I needn't have been, for they were as enthusiastic and receptive as Father Clay's boys back in Philadelphia. And as I was about to leave, I was stopped in my tracks by the sound of their voices breaking into a song, as if it had been their secret plan all along.

"When Irish eyes are smiling, sure 'tis like a morn in spring. . . ." rang out those voices in perfect harmony.

Those old, old voices were as sweet and every bit as delicate as those of children. I had to leave the room. I was crying. The irony was almost too much. These same people who hated to be called Irish, who dreaded the thought of ever living under the Irish, were singing that most special of all Irish songs as if they had been born with it in their very hearts. How was it possible that voices so heavenly could exist among so much hatred and death?

And there was a more painful reason for my bolting from their applause and voices: The smiles and sparkling eyes of the men had reminded me so much of Dad.

A tall old lady with white hair rushed out to stop me. She was hopeful that I might spend the night in her nearby cottage. All of the emotions Ireland and Northern Ireland had put me through the past two weeks suddenly had me feeling older than anyone back in that room. I gave her the answer she was wanting: I told her I'd be proud to be her guest.

Mrs. Connie Heasley was her name, and she was seventy-eight. Every bit as tall, straight, and spry as most ladies fifty years her junior, she was a widow but still a doting mother. All that afternoon she spoiled me rotten with soda bread, sausage, eggs, pancakes, tea, milk, ham, potatoes, corn, and maple syrup. I looked much too thin and sunburned, she fretted. And certainly my own dear mum must be fretting herself gray with worry about if I was eating and safe. She insisted that if I was any sort of loving son, I would call home, and gave me her own telephone to do so.

The call home helped tremendously to bring my spirits back up—as did Connie Heasley's love—and as if to make sure I had no relapses in the meantime, she insisted on washing my clothes herself and making sure I had no shortage of down quilts and hot water bottles for my sleep. She even took me on a tour of her rose garden, to meet her best friend, Mr. Gnome, a chubby little stone leprechaun with a mischievous smile.

Her home was in a quiet, modest neighborhood of many other backyard flower gardens and lots of maples. Called Breda Park, it was as pleasant to the untrained eye as any neighborhood in the States. But in a voice that betrayed no panic or anger, Mrs. Heasley told me of two trucks filled with dynamite that had been found just two blocks away the day before. The trucks were wired to explode. And still she insisted as all the others had that the violence was being overplayed by the media. To walk down the street, you'd never know it existed, she stressed. She admitted, though, that she hardly went out of the yard anymore, for fear of what *might* happen.

"The worst thing is not when those terrible bombs go off," she said, "but the waiting." It took a lot out of people her age, she added, worrying that the next bomb might be where *they* chose to walk.

Larne, an ancient port twenty miles northeast of Belfast, was where I took my final steps in Ireland. And what happened there could only have happened on an isle of scholars, poets, and saints.

When I visited the town hall of that city of around twenty thousand, I was told the lord mayor, the Honorable Thomas Robinson, wished to have a private chat with me in the elegant second-story meeting chamber. He was aware, explained his secretary, that I was a journalist from the States. His Honor wished to discuss the types of stories I might be doing of my trip through Ulster.

I thought the chat a good idea, scheduled it for that afternoon, and then rushed away to seek a laundromat. All of my clothes that Mrs. Heasley had washed three days ago were already smelly with perspiration and as wrinkled as prunes. But not a coin laundry could I find, and I ran back to the simple brick building sweating and panting in the fierce humidity. It was all I could do to set down my laundry sack outside the entrance and run a quick comb through my matted hair.

Inside the front foyer, the white-haired doorman greeted me and led me as he would a member of the aristocracy up the grand staircase and through a massive double doorway of dark oak until at last I was face to face with the lord mayor himself in a room filled with chandeliers and wood panel walls rich in art.

Graciously, he seated me on a claw-footed sofa and offered me a drink from a closet bristling with crystal and labels. We settled on scotch whisky and water, and he made himself comfortable on a nearby lounge. Then, for the next half hour, the young and highly energetic leader of what some said was the oldest town in Ireland tried his best to persuade me, again, that the media unfairly overplayed the amount of violence in the region. It was just not true, he said, while serving me another scotch. And furthermore, it was causing him and the other leaders in Ulster much trouble in attracting new industry.

Could I not help to make their job of trying to attract American industry easier by writing something nice about Northern Ireland? Would I let people in the States know that it really was not so dangerous at all in his homeland, that I, in all my walking, had not seen any of this so-called bombing and killing that others were saying was commonplace?

So it went, masterfully and enjoyably, until at last I was ready to concur that Northern Ireland—Ulster—was really quite a safe haven after all. I admired a man who could believe so strongly in his own home and people. And who had such good taste in whisky.

I had leaned a bit unsteadily toward the mayor, ready to give a rousing endorsement and a promise of support, when suddenly there burst through the heavy doors the old doorman. From the heavy blush in his wide cheeks and the way he was gasping for breath, it was obvious he had just run up the stairs.

His eyes were as wide as half dollars. "Lord mayor, there's a *boomb* downstairs!" he gasped.

At the mention of a bomb, I was up and off the sofa in a flash. The

doorman was still jabbering away with the mayor, but I was already looking for an escape route away from the direction the doorman had come.
Just that morning a local resident had told me of the central police station
nearby being totally destroyed by a bomb around ten years before. I had
images of me hurtling headfirst out the windows to the street below, with
the building collapsing into smoke and fire beside me.

"It's been planted by the front windows, and has a white wire poking
from the package. I've telephoned the police, sir."

The mayor motioned for me to be calm. "I'll be right back. I'd best
give it a look," he said, rushing off after the old man.

I, however, was anything but calm. Nervously, I hurried to the corner of the room farthest from the windows. I'd learned as a child during
the Cuban Missile Crisis to stay away from windows, because the glass
shattered by an explosion could be as dangerous as anything. Like some
helpless fool, I squatted, whisky still in hand, and waited for the BOOM.

Slowly, though, a strange thought came to my sobered mind. What
had I done with the white plastic sack that I had my dirty laundry in?
And didn't it have a *white* plastic drawstring? The windowsill . . . comb
my hair . . .

Suddenly not feeling at all good inside, I peered over at and around
Clinger. Just as I feared: no white laundry sack. Oh, no!

I darted down the stairs, just in time to see from the landing some
policemen cautiously reaching toward the sack of dirty laundry on the
windowsill. What was I to do? Should I slink back up the stairs and
pretend I knew nothing of this terrible embarrassment? Or go downstairs
and save my underwear from being blown all over the city? How could I
have allowed such a disaster to happen while I was with the mayor of the
city? Such a disgrace to him, too. I could have jumped off a cliff.

"Stop! Hold it! That's no bomb!" I shouted, leaping three steps at a
time and bolting past the startled mayor and doorman to the policemen.
Somehow, somewhere inside me, I found enough courage to look the
grim-faced officers in the eyes and confess humbly, "Uhmm, that's my
dirty laundry. Sir."

You could tell it was Ireland: Everyone had a good laugh.

And the mayor treated me to another whisky, whether I needed it or
not.

Oh, yes, the story of Northern Ireland I promised to write for the
newspapers in the States? I did it. In fact, I sent it off to *Capper's* that
week. However, I wasn't so sure Lord Mayor Robinson would have approved of the title: "The Laundry Bomb."

18

Scotland rose to enchant me from the eastern horizon of the North Atlantic the evening of the bomb scare in the lord mayor's fort. I was on a ferryboat to the port of Stranraer. Low, shrouded in the red mist of a melting sun, its gold-tinted humps of grass lolled on the waves in such a playful manner as to make me think of whales.

With the white plume of a lighthouse spouting from its most forward ridge, a particularly lonely peninsula captured my attention. I was fascinated by how the chilly sea breezes swept across its unpopulated hills and dells with total freedom. I sensed a pocket of time and space where the past still weighed heavily on the second hand of the present. Where, instead of being trampled under, history was allowed to crumble away at its own pace.

My passage overland on foot the following week was steeped in quiet contemplation. Life in the farmlands of southern Scotland struck me as so uneventful that even the devil of the Irish, if he would pardon me for saying so, would have been hard-pressed to cause much of a commotion there.

My days across Scotland might have passed completely without incident if not for the peculiar incident that happened on the twelfth of August in the rolling pasture lands near the village of Castle Douglas. That day, the halfway point of my walk in Scotland, started off like a page out of the novel *Watership Down,* and ended like a scene from Alfred Hitchcock's movie *The Birds.*

I awakened early that morning, having slept in my blanket on a plastic groundsheet in the middle of a soft, grassy field covered with thick dew. Still somewhat groggy, I opened my eyes to what at first I thought were dozens of rounded clumps of grayish weeds. I was about to close my eyes again for a few more minutes of snooze, when I blinked and stared harder at those lumps I certainly didn't remember from last night. Sure enough, they were moving—slowly but surely, an inch every few minutes.

They were HUGE rabbits, nibbling everywhere on clover and dandelions. They were all around me, and some only inches away. My mind tried to make sense of what I had awakened to, but came up a blank. Was it possible they grazed rabbits in Scotland, as we did cattle in the States? They sure looked big enough to be corralled and branded.

I remained as still as a fallen tree for many moments, fascinated by what I was seeing. Then I tried ever so slowly to rise, but the nervous creatures sensed my return to life, and with all the quickness of phantoms in a children's fairy tale, they scampered with a zig here, and a zag there, to the giant field's surrounding hedges. I could actually hear their long heavy paws *thump-thump-thump* over and into the otherwise quiet earth.

Every hippity-hop sounded as clear as the footsteps of a human on a porch floor. With so many big rabbits running every which way for their lives, it was as though a cross-country race had just commenced. I laughed out loud before I could even stop myself, and clapped with sheer delight. What a nice way to start the day!

I had an easy, level roadway, with wide shoulders to walk on, for most of the day, which made for excellent mileage. I saw few towns or people, and many abandoned stone farms and barns, as well as wide sun-swept fields and an occasional low mountain. I marveled at how lush and bountiful this country was—birds, livestock, rabbits, pheasants, salmon-filled rivers, streams, thick fields of grain. Such a rich land, and so blessed with the space and solitude needed for everything to thrive. I told myself I would love to buy one of those abandoned farms and spend my summers hidden in its peacefulness, with but a dog and a typewriter. Yet in almost the same thought, I shuddered at how cold this must be in the winter, with such wide-open spaces, and the sea only a handful of miles away.

Toward dusk the ocean came into view again on my right. I passed occasional small forests that, as it grew darker, looked thicker and sounded noisy in the sea's breezes. It was nice to see such thick forests again, after all the open rockiness of Ireland. There, it had seemed that every foot of land had been put to some farming use. Here, the residents—what few there were—were evidently content to leave the land be. Even the animals seemed unperturbed by my approach.

As night came on, gusts of strong wind started to knock me about a bit. Near midnight, I decided I'd had enough of such games, and snuck up to some woods at the top of a hill to pitch my tent. I hid myself deep in a stand of tall and thick hardwoods. It was very dark and very, very quiet in such thick cover. Just the way I liked it.

Just as I was falling into a nice sleep, I realized that the swaying trees just outside my tent's thin blue dome were making *very* spooky sounds. Goose bumps pimpled my arms. The fine little hairs along my nape stood to attention. I didn't want to, but I made myself slip out from under the blanket, unzip the tent door's flap, and peer outside into the creaking, groaning blackness.

Straining my eyes to the point where they hurt, I thought I could make out the shapes of something other than leaves on the tree limbs high overhead. Whatever those things were, they were large, nearly as numerous as the leaves, and seemed as sour-tempered as seasick rats. Each time the trees bent in the winds, first far to one side then far to the other, there was long and mournful groaning from what sounded like a million suffering ghosts. Or else a headachy sick hen the size of the Empire State Building, I thought.

No, sir. Those weren't big leaves up there fluttering in the wind. Those were long black wings. Thousands of them!

I slowly rose to my feet. The wind howled, screeched! Dead, dry leaves the size of my hands whipped and swirled and danced about me as if I was suspended in the eye of a furious evil twister. Behind me, the tent struggled violently to keep its tenacious grip onto an earth that seemed about to be torn apart. Any second, the whole of the universe might explode. Meanwhile, every griffin from hell was slapping and poking at my body.

I was convinced I had become entangled with some kind of enormous ravens, not unlike those in an Edgar Allan Poe nightmare, and my muscles shuddered at the realization of just how alone and helpless I was.

I retreated into my tent and tried sleeping with my head under the blanket to diminish the noise. But it only grew louder, with each sweep of the approaching storm.

It was getting to be too much for that part of me that still believed in spirits and spooks. More vividly than I cared for, whispers from my soul's darkest catacombs taunted more and more that there was something more to those birds than feathers and mocking eyes of ebony.

If the birds had been there all along, why hadn't they made any sounds while I was walking through the woods earlier? How could I not have heard such a huge flock descending onto the branches? Why that horrible moaning? It was almost as if they were acting on the command of some demented voice that only they could hear.

Increasingly, I scared myself senseless, until finally it was all my poor trembling fingers could do to fumble my clothes back over my clumsy limbs and grab the blanket. Like a man who has just met the wrong sort of thing in a graveyard, I beat a hasty retreat to the road, leaving the tent and Clinger behind. Those things in the trees could have everything else, but I wasn't quite ready to give up my body or soul.

I emerged from the tangle of woods into the smoky grayness of an open field. Wrapping the light-colored blanket around me like a poncho to ward off the chilly wind, I stumbled down a long, steep hillside to the road I was following to the English border near Carlisle. I tossed myself painfully over a fence of grabbing wire and leaped onto the blankness of an empty road from the weeds of a ditch. The blanket flared about me like giant wings, just as something larger than I ripped through the air, shrieked wretchedly, and then crumpled into the weeds I'd just sprung from.

A loud voice screamed out more in fright than in anger, "What the bloody 'ell?"

I couldn't find my own voice. Whatever or whoever it was that I had scared had scared me far more terribly.

It turned out to be a passing lone bicyclist I had scared into crashing. His name was Peter, and he was a touring Australian about my age, who was going to Stranraer to catch the ferry to Northern Ireland. Luckily, neither he nor his ten-speed suffered any lasting damage through our accidental meeting on that haunted stretch of road.

"You nearly stopped me heart," he gasped.

I knew so much what he was feeling that I couldn't help but laugh. So much so, that the tears poured from my eyes. After all that tension in the woods, it was such a good feeling to have something to laugh about. And even better, what turned out to be some great company.

I needed company now. I had found Scotland beautiful and big, but too quiet. The people in the villages were nice, but offered little more than the necessary number of pleasantries.

They were, in short, as reserved and cautious as they were reputed by so many writers to be, and perhaps even a bit suspicious of this odd American roving their yards and streets. None had been as open and trusting as the Americans or the Irish, and I was finding myself with too much time to my dreams.

Peter, thank goodness, was a typical, friendly Australian, who was spending his holiday bicycling the entire British Isles. For perhaps twenty minutes we hunkered down beside the sleepy road to swap tales of travel, eat some of his biscuits, and brew tea in his compact butane camp stove.

We used a hedge to break the wind, and between us he set, in a sitting position, his good-luck traveling companion, Ted, a stuffed teddy bear of gruffish tan fur and loose, lumpy stuffing.

"Me charming travel companion," Peter laughed, with a fond nod at the well-mannered friend. "Without 'im, I'd a been a lot lonelier this past fortnight. Oh, man, never I seen such a snobby, say-nothing mob like these pommies on this dink of a rock they's got the notion to be callin' their sweet and deary England. Believe me, mate, I wish this wind could push me toward Ireland a sight faster. I hear over there they still know how to laugh."

I hoped he was wrong about the English, or "pommies" (prisoners of Mother England), as he liked to call them. My trek down the entire length of England was bound to be many times longer than my walk in Ireland and Scotland combined, and I certainly didn't fancy the prospect of spending most of my time there staring out at the countryside, as I'd had to do here.

Peter loved to poke fun at things, and when I told him why I had jumped out of the weeds at him in the middle of the night, he couldn't stop laughing.

"You let a bunch of bloody birds scare you down 'ere to sleep in the weeds?" he roared. "And *you're* expectin' to tramp around the world?"

He made it all sound so absurd, I had to laugh with him. "But you would never have believed the sound those birds made. And it was so dark in those trees," I remonstrated.

He pushed away the stove and biscuits.

"I've got to see what it is that could 'ave been so bloody scary," he said.

We climbed over a gate and walked briskly up through the wind toward the trees. When we entered the woods, there was no sound of any sort to hint of the birds in the interior's trees. Again it was as dark as sin, though. And I had such a difficult time finding the tent that I worried for a while that it and Clinger had been carried away by the trees' spirits.

Back within reach of the tent, I suggested Peter stare up into the tangles of the forest, to see if he, too, saw what I had. Sure enough, there the birds were. To my disappointment, though, they weren't making the moaning noises anymore. Just an occasional squawk, a flutter of wings. The wind wasn't swaying the trees so much either. I assured Peter that this was nothing at all like what I'd experienced only half an hour ago.

" 'ave you a torch, mate?" he asked.

Torch? What could he be talking about? Wasn't the night spooky enough, without waving flames in a cursed forest like vigilantes out to find Frankenstein? Oh, well . . . I squirmed into the tent, groped for some matches and paper, and reemerged to hand them to him. He looked at the matches and the rolled-up newspaper as though he'd never seen such things before. I felt more foolish than ever.

"What are those fer, mate?" he asked.

"You said you wanted a torch. So I—"

He placed a hand on my shoulder and said with a slow shake of his head, "Sorry, I forgot you Yanks call 'em flashlights. 'ave you one of 'em?"

I didn't. I felt like an idiot admitting it, but I hadn't carried any sort of night light since Ohio. Normally, my night vision was impeccable. And though I would never have admitted it, I was training my eyes and senses not to depend upon such things. For I felt that in the future, in places like Africa and Asia, where there might be bandits prowling in the dark, I did not want to have to chance any of them spotting my campsite through my use of flashlights or lanterns. My life could depend on how well I learned to discern shapes of the night.

"You're either a fool or have bloody good eyes," Peter murmured, turning his own back to the darkness above our heads. Rolling the newspaper tightly, he took a lighter from his pocket and set the paper wick afire. Carefully, he raised it high over his head. The flame flickered and hardly surrendered enough light to illuminate the top of Peter's head. But then suddenly it flamed much brighter, casting a red, spooky glow that reached well up into the trees.

And what we saw made both of us gasp.

There were even more birds than I'd thought. They did indeed seem thicker than the leaves. But it was not their numbers that made me catch my breath; it was their size. They were enormous!

Surely as the rabbits I had seen that morning had been the size of small dogs (they could've snacked on our little Ohio cottontails!), these long-beaked ravens (crows?) were like small vultures.

Peter was the quietest I'd heard him since our meeting. He looked intense, his eyes not leaving the birds. They, in turn, were growing more restless by the second. Peter tipped the roll of newspaper a bit to one side. Again it flared several inches higher.

The birds disliked the extra light, and from somewhere in that nearly solid ceiling of thick, curved beaks and long, talonlike claws, there came a loud rasping cry that nearly made Peter drop the torch.

"Blimey!" he shouted.

Then all the flock took up the sharp, angered cries.

The cacophony was that of a million hags laughing, crying, and screaming at the same time. And the rippling of those restless feathers made it clear we were about to pay dearly for our intrusion into their leafy hideout.

"Aaaaah!" Peter shouted. The torch tumbled from his hand to the ground. He had been so mesmerized by the birds, he'd not seen the torch's flame clawing for the tips of his fingers.

The torchlight flared for a few seconds as the paper uncurled, but then it was gone. Once more we were in darkness—a darkness all the more suffocating because our eyes had adjusted to the torch's light. And strangely enough, with the descent of the darkness there rose an even greater commotion in the trees.

Something big swooshed so close to my head, I could have reached out and touched it. Whatever it was, I knew it wasn't any bicyclist this time.

Peter cursed aloud and ran into my side as several more of the invisible attackers brushed us. I suddenly had a frightful memory of the time my best friend, Greg Abell, and I had gone on one of our youthful night fishing trips and had walked into a swarm of bats.

The din was too much to stand. It was as if the whole lot of them had gone totally berserk. Movement everywhere—flapping, screeching, cursing, gusting, snapping. Help! We dived into the tent. I zipped the door shut behind us.

We had to shout to hear each other, even though we were but inches away in the darkness.

"They're treatin' me like I's about to be their tucker," Peter shouted.

"Tucker?"

"Food!"

"Oh, yes!" I'd definitely felt that any second those birds would begin pecking at my face.

For several minutes more, we were forced to sit there in that tent and wonder what was happening.

Then . . . dead silence.

Were the birds gone? Were we free? Or was this just the silence before the real storm broke loose?

Inch by inch, I unzipped the door flap. Timidly, I gazed out. Above us, I saw much fluttering, but only of leaves speckled occasionally with stars.

They were gone. Just like that. As if they had acted in unison on one command. Scotland and the Devil were once again back in their respective places.

Peter and I returned to his waiting bicycle. "My ten-speed Mercedes," he said. Then to the teddy bear, Ted, "Ah, my dear, you should have seen it: The gods were screaming for your sacrifice. But I wouldn't give in. For you're the only true friend I have."

I hated to see them leave. But I sent them away down the road with the encouragement that Ireland would give them all the laughter and dreamers they'd ever wish for.

And I offered a couple of handshakes—one for Peter and one for Ted, who sat latched to the handlebars.

And then silence again.

Peter told me his last name as he was peddling off. I promised not to forget it, and to visit him if I made it to Melbourne.

But sometime during the silent night his name stole away, too, as I slept in the weeds.

19

As I stepped into England, I came upon a brown-and-white Jersey cow that had just given birth to a handsome calf, and with her nose was trying her best to get it to stand upon its wobbly legs. I watched the scene with my elbows propped on a wooden gate and told myself I was seeing Mother Nature in her best and proudest mood.

The charm of the countryside increased with each mile I walked further south. Miles of thick, meticulously laid stone walls, bordering grassy and treeless meadows, formed a backdrop all the way into the city of Carlisle, where a huge stern statue of Queen Victoria waited to scold me for feeling devil-may-care. Even the gray little one-factory village of Shap, where I stopped to eat a lunch of baked beans and to drink a pint of milk on the steps of a rain-soaked schoolhouse, seemed true to form. I was finding every bit of England just as I'd imagined it from my reading. This was especially true in the northwestern corner, the refuge of such great poets as Wordsworth and Coleridge. Known as the Lake District, it had a stark simplicity and sense of solitude that left me in awe every step across it.

Here there were oftentimes no sounds other than those of the wind torturing the stones in the walls or the rainy mist dripping from my cap's bill to my poncho. As I moved up and down along the curling roadway I followed over the bald mountains, I could not resist resting on a stone wall and staring dreamily at the mysterious huge swells of the earth that knew no movements except for those of an occasional sheep or a cloud across a crest.

The farms I passed were old and massive, their square stone buildings as brown as centuries of rain and unfettered winds could paint them. Their occasional dark slate roofs accentuated the emptiness of that land. As though the reflection of a poet's soul, the sloping pastures seemed to turn into mist amid the clouds. It was, quite simply, beautiful.

The people who lived in that stretch (and there were very, very few), looked to be prosperous sheep farmers and dairy-cow farmers who could trace their families back to the days of sandals and Norse ships resting on rocky beaches. I had the sensation that those hardy people had found what the poets from London and Liverpool had come there in search of: peace of mind and soul.

Although the rain and gray skies never ceased, I actually enjoyed the weather there. For those tears and sighs of Nature served to make the land more mystical.

Very rarely did the little narrow lane that I followed for two days introduce me to any lorries (trucks) or autos, let alone any other walkers of less than four legs. So I had as much time to my thoughts as I did to the area's dales and vales. At the top of the highest pass, the sky's heavy clouds rolled overhead at what seemed only an arm's length away. I thought of myself as back on the plains of America's West. But for some quivering clumps of weeds and, oddly enough, a lonesome red pay-telephone booth, it was easy on that pass to forget there were another 4.5 billion persons like myself carrying on with their dreams and follies.

As I wound down the other side of the Lake District's slopes, I saw even fewer people. Just bigger sheep pastures, taller cows with noisier bells about their necks, and even more of those amazing old stone walls.

Nearly all the walls were around five feet high (and some were higher), and usually at least eighteen inches thick, of unmortared gray flat stones neatly stacked and fitted together. Each farm must have had at least a dozen miles of them enclosing the many small pastures that made up their property. No matter how steep the slope of a pasture, there were still those walls around it. How, I wondered, awestruck, could human beings have the patience to lay seemingly millions of thick, heavy stones with such precision? Surely, all the sons and fathers in those long-ago generations had spent their lives out there lugging, cutting, and placing those stones. Was it *really* possible that there were humans with such perseverance? Surely, even today there were not enough able-bodied men in the whole region from Penrith to Lancaster to build walls for even one of the larger properties. So how had they been built? And by whom?

On the south side of the Cumbria Mountain range, I learned from a farmer who stopped me to give me a couple of fresh peaches from his garden that the walls had been constructed by serfs. Centuries ago, those properties had been part of feudal fiefdoms worked by hundreds of serf households, and each serf had marked his little individual plot of land by building a wall around it. Joined to all the other walls built by the other serfs, it looked as if it was all the same network.

To think that the walls I loved to rest upon were built before America was even known! It was the ease with which one could reach out and touch the ancient in the British Isles that I loved so much. I, for one, believe deeply that a people who forget their past will not have much of a future.

By the time I reached the bustle and congestion of the city of Lancaster the afternoon of the seventeenth of August, it was a scorching day, and I was just about ready to sell my soul for a drink of water. One of the most unpleasant aspects of English cities and towns for someone like me was the lack of public drinking fountains. It was as if every traveler was expected to bring his own supply of water—or else drink the dark warm beer of the pubs.

I stopped at what looked to be the rectory of a large church of some kind. Whether it was Protestant or Catholic I could not tell, because many of the old Church of England churches looked so similar to Roman Catholic churches—since indeed they were once all Roman Catholic—that, more than once, I went up to the black-suited minister and addressed him as "Father."

The rectory was an immense old mansion three floors high and built of brick and dark wood. I knocked on the door a bit hesitantly, feeling insignificant against the richness of the architecture. A thin man answered my knock. He opened the door only a few inches, as if afraid of me, and from his action and appearance I decided he had to be the housekeeper. He was dressed in wrinkled slacks and a stained white T-shirt.

A scroungy yellow tomcat that had been purring at my feet made a mad dash for the door. The man's voice boomed out:

"Oh, no, you damned thing! Get!"

Whereupon the cat spun about immediately and leaped back in the direction of the front steps, just barely escaping a swift kick from the housekeeper's tennis shoes. Adjusting his glasses, the man glared over my shoulders and turned livid at the sight of two young teenage boys straddling the neighbor's high wooden fence. The boys quickly fled when they realized they'd been spotted by the man.

"The idiots," he mumbled darkly.

I was by then sorry I'd ever knocked on that door. He was evidently not the type to be expecting any kindness from.

"What can I do for you?" he demanded.

I just wanted to say, "Forget it, you grouch!" But I was way too thirsty and tired from the heat. When I asked him for a glass of water, he had me follow him around to the side of the house, and I figured he was probably going to have me drink from an outside faucet or the garden hose. To my surprise, he told me to take off my backpack and come into the kitchen.

"How about a milk instead?" he asked nicely.

"Okay."

"You hungry, too?"

From a huge old white cabinet set above some massive deep ceramic sinks, he produced a can of Argentine corned beef. He brought it and a bottle of milk into the dining room, set them beside a wide silver tray of cheeses, and together we sat at a polished wood table long and heavy enough to be from a king's castle. On the walls were two photos of popes, one of the current Pope John Paul II and the other of a mean-looking, hawk-nosed Pope whose name I could not remember. And around me were heavy large chandeliers of brass and cut glass, thick carpeting, long window drapes, fancy dark wood bureaus, and silver serving trays.

"I'm sorry, it's not much," my host apologized, looking at the food.

"A feast, compared to my usual fare," I said happily.

We divided the food and ate it. He was as hungry as I, as if he had been waiting for someone to come and give him an excuse to sit down to eat. I asked his name. He replied in a friendly manner that I should call him simply Bryan.

"How long have you worked here, Bryan?" I asked.

He looked up at me strangely. "You mean, how long have I been a priest?"

I nearly choked. A priest!

He laughed. "I hope my language didn't offend you. But that cat has something wrong with it, and it's been trying for days to get inside the house." He pushed some bread my way. "And as for those boys on the fence, they have been climbing all over the trees and breaking the limbs. There isn't much for them to do, and so they come around here to see what they can wreck with their grubby little hands."

How times had changed, I thought, chuckling. I was in the area with the largest concentration of Roman Catholics in England, where once priests and bishops had been hunted like criminals and oftentimes imprisoned or executed. Now the "enemy," at least for one priest, was no longer men on foamy-mouthed horses but merely conniving kids and cats.

"Oh, no, I wasn't offended," I said. "I've known some priests, particularly one I was an altar boy for in my hometown, who could cuss the arm off a drunken Irishman."

"I wouldn't mind the boys, except that those two go out of their way to wreck the church building and property," he explained.

"Don't the other priests give you a hand?"

He chuckled loudly. "Other priests? You're looking at the only one."

He had to be kidding. The house alone could have taken care of a whole diocese. And there was the cathedral to be kept up, too.

"A very wealthy old lady had this house built for herself, and then decided to have the church built, so she'd have a nice place to worship," he explained as calmly as if that were the normal thing to do in Lancaster. "When she died, she left everything to the Church."

"And you take care of all this by yourself?"

He nodded, a smile of satisfaction on his lips.

The parish had around five hundred people in it, and maybe two hundred showed up on any given Sunday, he told me. To me, that didn't seem very many parishioners for a city the size of Lancaster. I wondered if religion in England and Scotland was very strong anymore. In Scotland, I'd seen several former churches being used as stores and houses. And not many of the church grounds were in good condition.

But the priest assured me the local participation in religion was still quite high.

The more I listened to Father Bryan talk, the more I decided there was something different about him. Most priests whom I'd met were too busy to do any idle talking, but Father Bryan acted as if he had all the time in the world. Talking with him was like being with someone in a park on a lazy day.

"Surely, it must cost the Vatican a lot of money to run such a large place as this. Yet with only two hundred people coming to mass on Sunday, that seems so inefficient."

He sat straight. "Rome pay? We pay *them*. They don't send us a bit of money. Only ask for more and more."

"But how can you pay for all the expenses for the church, the house, and yourself?"

He held up both hands, palms up. "On an average Sunday I receive maybe seventy-five pounds. That wouldn't begin to cover even the upkeep. But the money and properties left to us by the deceased make it possible for us to keep going. That and the other properties we get income from, our rental flats and our investments in the bank." He sighed. "And who

do you think must oversee all the bookwork, and plan the budgets, and
schedule events, and figure out what goes where?"

"You?"

Again he nodded, but this time with a look of exasperation.

"There are those in the parish who volunteer their skills and time to
help," he pointed out. "But ultimately I am responsible for making this
parish self-supporting. Which isn't easy anymore, with costs always going
up."

He threw a glance over his right shoulder at the photo of Pope John
Paul. "And then there's the Church in Rome. Sometimes I have to send
them less than they expect of this parish, along with a note saying, 'You'll
get the rest when I've got it to give.' After all, if I don't keep this parish
self-supporting, it won't be around very much longer."

He gave a harsh laugh. "He [the Pope] may be very appealing to the
masses, but who do you think pays for all his trips and especially the
security."

"The parish churches?"

"You bet," he replied. "Take the trip to Lourdes, in France, he just
finished. Three thousand policemen! Just for one man! Plus who knows
how many other personnel, vehicles, helicopters, and communication. It's
crazy. And I haven't even mentioned all the people who must travel with
him and the Vatican's plane. It's just like if your President Reagan went
somewhere."

"Why so many policemen for the Pope in such a peaceful nation like
France?"

He looked at me, surprised. "You wouldn't believe how strongly
some hate anything that has to do with the Catholic Church. They'll go to
any lengths to strike out. In France, it wasn't until after the Pope had left
that the police revealed they'd uncovered a plot against his life." He shook
his head disapprovingly.

"Oh, if he would only stay in Rome and just take care of the affairs of
the Church there. . . ."

When he took me to see the inside of his church, I was unprepared
for its beauty. The outside was dull, like a large gray stone box, with worn,
insignificant carvings along the eaves. But now I saw a cathedral built by
the hands of angels.

"Beautiful, isn't it?" the priest's voice floated to me from somewhere.

I nodded wordlessly. The carving of the wood railings and columns,
the perfectly spaced polished wooden benches, beautiful tiles, golden organ pipes, and under the high ceiling arches, finely painted beams of red,
blue, yellow, and green.

Father Bryan was standing beside the altar. Behind him was an altar backdrop of such intricate carving that I had to touch it to see if it was made of wood or ivory. I ran my hands over what turned out to be pale marble.

He explained it was from Italy. And the wood, he said, was of the same quality and richness as that used in the house.

I wondered aloud how one woman could have afforded to have such a masterpiece constructed.

"Remember, a pound sterling went a long way in 1872, when this was built," he said.

We returned to the house. He made me take an unopened can of the Argentine corned beef to stuff in Clinger. Then he rushed about the kitchen, looking for other things to give me. For the most part, though, the shelves were a typical bachelor's—empty.

I don't think he was aware of it, but the cat was just outside the kitchen window, watching intently every move of the priest's.

"Could you carry a couple pints of milk?" his voice boomed from the depths of the old round-top refrigerator.

"No. They're just too heavy in those thick glass bottles," I answered reluctantly, for I loved milk probably as much as that cat did.

Finally, he had to call it quits. The house was just too empty of food.

On the porch I thought of one more thing I had always wanted to ask a priest.

"How much money does a priest get paid a month? Are you paid a salary?"

He laughed. "I'm allowed just about enough to keep me supplied with cigarettes, toothpaste, and an occasional sweet treat."

Then he squared his shoulders and asked, "And as for you, have you given any thought to being a priest? It's never too late, you know."

My turn to laugh. "When I was an altar boy at St. Mary's in Bethel, our big old priest used to take me aside, put his hand on my shoulder, look off grandly, and say reverently, 'Cardinal Newman. Has a good ring to it. Doesn't it?' Later, of course, I found out there had already been a Cardinal Newman. But even so, I couldn't ever be a priest. I never liked the idea of limiting my life so much."

"Oh, but the Church has places for people who want to keep using whatever it is they're skilled at," he retorted.

"Naw." I couldn't think of how better to explain.

He chuckled. "You just don't like bosses, do you?"

He had hit the nail right on the head.

"That's okay," he said. "I feel the same. Here—" He slipped me a folded piece of paper. "Write when you reach America. I'm really interested in knowing if you make it."

We parted, and just in time. The cat had finally figured out where we were, and I spied him sneaking his way back along the porch.

Out on the busy, hot street, I unfolded the paper and read: *Fr. Bryan L. Irving. God bless, Steve!*

A long smile crept across my face. Not, however, because of what the paper said. But because mingled in with all the sounds of the traffic I could hear Father Bryan's voice cursing up a storm.

The cat might have made it inside.

20

On the morning that I left Bethel, Police Chief Fambry had asked that I give the honorary police badge he had received from Manchester, England, to a lady in Bolton, England, with whom he had been corresponding. He had promised to keep her informed of my progress around the world, and he told me she would be expecting the badge as a sort of token of friendship from our side of the Atlantic. So it was that when I finally walked into that industrial satellite city of Manchester on August 19, I went to the address Chief Fambry had given to me. I wholly expected to see some quaint old Miss Marple-type spinster who spent her long lonesome night hours listening to the rest of the world's stratospheric chatters.

Imagine my surprise to find instead a young, pretty blond-haired girl of around twenty-three. Rather than being small and plump and doting, Hilary was tall, thin, quiet. She lived with her eighteen-year-old brother, Jeff, her divorced mother, Edna, and her boyfriend, Jerry. Like so many in the British Isles, they occupied a cramped, though very tidy two-bedroom apartment that seemed to center around the usual small color television and squeaky-clean coffee table. (Edna slept on a pullout couch bed in the living room and Jerry slept with Hilary, while Jeff had the other small bedroom.) If Jeff, a tall and strongly built blond who looked a lot like my brother Gary, hadn't been staying overnight with some of his college friends, I might have had to spread my blanket on the hallway floor.

I found out as they crowded around me in the flat that Hilary and Jerry had come to know Chief Fambry after they had heard his voice on a citizen-band radio Jerry once owned. Hilary ran to her room and came back with some snapshots of myself the chief had taken on that cold April day I left home. I could have cried when I looked at those snapshots and saw my family and neighbors for the first time in almost five months and fifteen hundred miles. So many memories, now so far away and slowly fading.

For three days, I rested there, and even took in the Bolton Marathon, the largest marathon race held in England each year. But the most interesting moments for me, being a journalist, were our rounds of conversation in their favorite local pub each evening. Those conversations reinforced what I'd already found by talking with dozens of others since crossing the border from Scotland.

The conversation usually ranged from rock 'n' roll to politics. One of the most persistent topics was that of "North versus South" in England. (Father Bryan had said, "This division, this attitude, of us against *them* is so typical of the English mind. The line that supposedly divides the country runs right through this area, and you have those who say they'd never live in the South, because they're snobs, and people in the South who say they'd never go to live here, because we're poor and dumb. It's really so petty, isn't it? But then that's how so many people's minds are. What it is really is boredom, a lack of goals and dreams anymore.")

Jerry did most of the talking, while Hilary sat and listened patiently. (Such a vast difference between the Irish and English girls. The Irish girls would never sit still for being out of an argument or discussion for more than five minutes.) Like so many others, Jerry saw Britain's present economic and employment woes as connected to weak leadership and an overall decline in the country's spirit since the breakup of the empire. There was a general listlessness throughout the country, he said, with too many too willing to live off the government's handouts, rather than to be ambitious. He himself was presently unemployed, and looking hard, with just a small amount of unemployment money from his last employer, RCA, coming in each week.

It was difficult, if not near impossible, to get back into his old job of record producing, because of his age. In his early thirties, he was already considered too old. But he wasn't going to give up, for he'd changed too many professions in the past as it was. He could possibly find work in a larger market like London, but that was too far from home and Hilary. He'd rather keep looking, I gathered, in an area he knew was hopeless, than upset the comfortable relationship he had with Hilary.

"No one dares to do anything that will get them fired, or make their bosses not like them. In England, if you get put out of work, there's no way you'll get back into that line of work again at the same pay and level.

Therefore, no one makes any waves, or trouble, especially if you're over thirty.

"There're men I know who are only in their forties, and who have given up hope of ever finding a job they had before. They've lost all ambition, because they *know* they're going to have to work for less pay and in a different type of work from now on."

There it was again: that attitude of apathy that never failed to rile me. I was puzzled at how people still so young and healthy could be so torpid about their lot in life. I'd always thought of the English as adventurous and ambitious, for they had explored and conquered so much of the world. But so far in my walk in England, I was finding quite the opposite. In many ways, they seemed exemplified by their most popular newspapers, the *Sun* and the *Daily Mail.* Everywhere I went, it seemed people were getting their daily news of the world from those two papers, along with other, similar sensationalist, trivia-choked tabloids. The forte of those newspapers seemed to run along the lines of the royal family's romances and squabbles (a porno star was supposedly bedding Prince Andrew), love suicides labeled as modern-day Romeos and Juliets, and the depressions of the athletes.

The English seemed obsessed with the pettiness of daily life. It was with much inner consternation that I listened to Jerry tell me how England's present woes were due to forces beyond the people's control, and thus why change anything? I found myself looking forward to getting out of the dark streets of row houses to the nearing countryside of France. The Irish had been as filled with life and joy as a canary; by comparison, the English seemed a tired old basset hound. Weren't there any more lions in England?

The grassy hill country that had carried me into the monstrous sprawl of factories and smog and traffic jams that was Manchester resumed on the city's south side, much to my delight. The scenery was ever so beautiful and lush during the next several days. And the towns were just as I would have preferred—small, ancient, and filled with moss-covered shingles and leaning grave markers, as well as sneaky cats and tall roses. The rich, stone-walled farms and the occasional massive mansion kept my imagination alive and healthy, while the dairy cows with their noses buried in clover and grass kept me from being too lonely when I napped in the shade of a pasture's resident tree.

Wishing to know the land and its trout-filled brooks more intimately, I ventured off Route A6 at a point near Bakewell in the early afternoon of August 23 and crossed the sheep and cow pastures on one of the many public footpaths I'd noticed. Through a "walkway" in the farmer's fence, I passed to "trespass" across his property to the next town. The walkway was a crude wooden plank made into a step, so that the fence could be stepped over easily. I had never seen such politeness built into a fence, to say nothing of a pathway for the public to cross someone's land on foot. In England, the law gives the pedestrian right-of-way to cross stretches of open countryside that he or she might otherwise have to detour around. I thought it a jolly great idea.

I stepped through a walkway in the next fence line, and in no time was treated to the sight of pools shimmering with lovely-sized trout. I sat there in the tickle of a weeping willow until I could no longer resist the temptation, pulled off my clothes, and plunged into the icy water. *Yeoww!* I caught my breath—or at least tried to—and wondered if that was how an ice cube felt. All around me, speckled rainbows streaked to safer stretches of water and moss, leaving me to swim and splash as I hadn't done since Massachusetts.

That evening, at dusk, as I headed south, I became all the more certain that the same spirits that had once inspired writers to set their tales of love and heroism in England were still here. Just before the sky gave up the last vestiges of sunlight, when all the hills and fields were painted the color of claret, I looked up to the summit of a tall hill guarding the town of Matlock, to see the ruin of what had once been a large castle. The castle's walls and turrets viewed against the sky looked as black as the soul of the Devil himself.

Beneath the dark and almost featureless structure were the walled hillside plots of what must have been many serfs. As I watched, the castle went from gray-black to all black, and from the valley below the castle rose a ghostly mist, which slowly crept up the hillside plot by plot. On how many nights had the mist and the castle and the night sky rendezvoused? How many more of those silent meetings on the hill were yet to come?

And what of all those clothed in mail and silk who had dwelt within that stone edifice, and of those who had toiled to keep the castle's masters satisfied? They had disappeared as completely as the mist now clawing at the castle would, when the light of the sun returned. Yet I felt I was not far from them, wherever they were now, as I bedded down on my raincoat that night in a dewy field beside the castle.

I was traveling southeasterly, toward the western edge of London. I knew from walking into the large cities in America how difficult that could be, so I decided to skirt London entirely. If necessary, I would ride a train into the city from one of the outlying towns, do whatever chores were necessary, then return to my stopping point by another train.

To keep from being steered directly into London, it was necessary to get off the main roads and follow the very narrow old lanes that zigzagged more toward the little towns outside of London. Thus, the countryside I passed through remained a lush green carpet sprinkled with hedges and trees abundant with such fruits as pears, apples, and blackberries. And also lots of fat cows and spoiled sheep grazing around the edges of towns with names like Melton Mowbray, Oakham, and Uppingham.

It was while following one of those old lanes, number A6003, that I came to a little cottage on a side street in the village of Caldecott—located about forty-five miles north of London—that looked as if it were something dolls should live in. Built out of dark brown stone and topped by a slate roof that hung low over the eaves, it was a pretty place that had probably ended up on many a tourist's snapshots. I, however, was too hungry to think about my camera that day. Instead, it was all I could do to plop down on a milk crate alongside one of the cottage's walls, slip out of an unbearably heavy and cumbersome Clinger, and begin eating some of the groceries I'd purchased minutes before in a carry-out.

Hardly had I taken my first bite into my McVittie's biscuits than a man and a woman approached me from the alleyway. He was around his middle sixties, stoop-shouldered, thin, balding, and trying to light a briarwood pipe that looked to be only slightly more used and aged than his clothes. She was perhaps five years younger, taller, straighter, but also dressed in well-worn clothes. I figured it was their cottage, and I started to rise to ask if they minded my sitting in the alley beside their home. The man waved me to sit back down. Both he and his wife came right up to me, holding hands like a pair of teenagers, and started chatting as if they'd known me for years. When they found out I was American, they both insisted I come inside their cottage for something better to eat than my sardines.

They referred to their dwelling as the Rose Cottage, and their own names were Kenny "Jimmy" James and—as Jimmy liked to say—Mrs. James. Inside the cottage were a living room, a kitchen, a bedroom, and a bathroom—made cozy by thick throw rugs, large stuffed easy chairs, prints of country scenes on the stone walls, a blackened fireplace with pieces of kindling stored nearby, an antique chest of drawers, and magazines lying about.

Tea and orange pieces were served right away, and Jimmy settled into his favorite recliner to repeat his attempts at keeping the pipe lit. In no time, it became apparent he was a man who loved to talk about anything and everything, with all his emotions and biases right out for everyone to see. While Mrs. James rounded up some dinner in the kitchen, Jimmy passionately discussed with me such things as the antinuclear demonstrators who were trying to disrupt the importation of American missiles into England ("Surely those women must stink!"), the American foreign policy ("They've got guts! They're not afraid to tell it like it is"), the Russians ("Barbarians, I tell you! Murderers and liars!"), the stagnation of the English society ("Give Maggie a chance"), the English foreign policies ("All this diplomacy makes me so infuriated! Words but never any action or results"), the nuclear-missile buildup in the United States and Russia ("It's insane, I tell you. No one can win. Why must they keep wasting our money?"), and then, for a very long time, his favorite subject of all: his memories as a fighter-bomber pilot of the Yank flyboys he fought alongside in World War II ("The best men I ever had the honor of knowing! Smart as a top. Did they have guts! We were supposed to teach them how to bomb the Germans at night, and they did it in the day! We thought for sure they were going to come over here and tell us the 'right' way how to fight our war, but gads if they didn't keep their mouths shut and listen. Smart and quick learners they were. In no time, they were flying circles around everyone. Not the least bit afraid of anything! There could be a whole room of our own airmen standing around looking at each other as bored as could be, and all it took was *one* Yank to walk into that room to completely lift everyone's spirits, and get them laughing and feeling like a million.")

All the while, he sucked on that pipe as if he might try eating it, while throwing his hands up to mimic frustration or admiration every few seconds.

Not until we were gathered at the table to begin eating her meal of roast lamb, potatoes, corn, salad, cheese, milk, tea, and cake served on a fine linen tablecloth, with her best dishes and candles, did Mrs. James finally tell a war story or two of her own. Her best by far and away was of the time she danced with the handsome, tall American actor Jimmy Stewart, who at the time was a bomber pilot like her husband-to-be. She had been a nurse, and when she described the way the young and almost shy

Stewart had swept her across the auditorium's floor, her eyes closed half-way and her fork hung limp in her forgotten hand.

The Jimmy she'd married, and whose diseased heart and sparse income she'd endured all those years, was a conservative right-winger. But still it was a treat for me to be able to sit back in the cool house and watch his performance up close.

After dinner there was more talk and, of course, more tea. But not for long. Jimmy grew very weak and tired-looking quite suddenly, and he had to be helped to bed by his wife in much the way my mother helped my father. Watching his bent and thin, wheezing figure being led away to the bedroom, I felt such a hard tugging on my own heart that I couldn't keep my lower lip from quivering as little rips of homesickness again opened up in my spirit. How crazy to know that I could go for weeks with hardly a pain for my home and family, only to have it rush back harshly at the most unexpected moments.

Jimmy and his patient wife were a simple and deeply loving couple, with a relationship as rich as anything in the heavens. Jimmy loved life so, but he knew the end would come any day now, and so did the heartbroken Mrs. James. I knew that look of sadness in their eyes, because I'd seen it in my own parents' eyes.

They were, sadly enough, the closest I had found in all of England to what I had always envisioned the English to be like. They had guts, and they had something even more important: They believed life was truly extraordinary, something wonderfully magic and challenging, unquestionably worth being excited over.

As I continued onward the next day to Kettering, Woburn Sands, Leighton Buzzard, and then Hemel Hempstead, on the edge of London, I thought of Jimmy often. He probably wouldn't be alive for much longer. But that was okay. Wasn't it? Surely, if there was a loving God, no soul so filled with adventure and enthusiasm could be denied its eternity.

I reached Hemel Hempstead on a weekend, and the Monday following was what was called in Great Britain a "bank holiday." For three days, nearly every shop I came to was closed. And all I had to my name was two pounds, since I'd missed the banks on Friday. I knew that even if the shops had been open, the two pounds wouldn't have lasted one day, let alone three. But, no worry. I simply knocked on a few more doors than usual, and survived on a lot more glasses of water and tea than normal, along with their usual attendant sandwich or cookie. Many a meal came my way, too. And in one instance—from the Hemel Hempstead Police Club, of all places—a five-pound note.

I'd made my way through the British Isles to London more by trial and error than by any precise sort of planning or decision-making. Yet in the six hundred miles I'd walked since Dublin, I had found much of that good fortune that had characterized the eastern United States phase. There were no tragic memories to spoil the first phase of my foreign trek. None, that is, until just sixty miles from the end, on September 1.

In the beautiful thoroughbred pastures to the east of Reading, near where American nuclear missiles were to be based any day, a small group of antinuclear people happened upon me. I was surrounded and called a murderer, because I had my little American flag pinned to Clinger. In the scuffle that ensued, some of the protesters tried to rip the flag from my back. I was able to preserve the Stars and Stripes in one piece, but not without first showing a jaw and a stomach how much punch one ex-roughneck can pack.

Having won the battle, I nearly lost the war, however, because of the tougher loss suffered by my heart.

And so that evening, after much contemplation, I decided to put the flag into my pack to avoid any further controversy. I felt afraid, embarrassed by my own nationality for the first time in my life. And I wasn't at all sure how to handle that strange shame I hadn't known was inside me.

But my decision was temporary.

As I neared Portsmouth, it occurred to me that as an American, I would probably be criticized often—especially as I advanced into the Third World countries. So I had to learn to live with that criticism, not hide from it. How could I really say I had tested mankind if I'd gone to face it with less than the truth on my part? To hide my Americanism, even if that was possible, was the act of someone not confident and secure in himself. And that was the last thing I needed the next time I faced hatred in person. Next time, my life might be on the line. Not just a flag.

And so, on September 6, I walked into Portsmouth—home to the royal navy that once conquered the world—with my own nation's colors showing proudly.

Steve Newman, the week he left home for his worldwalk.   O. H. Sharp

Steve's boyhood home in Bethel, Ohio, from which he started his worldwalk and to which he returned four years later.

Virginia, U.S.A. Clinger beside Steve's "hotel," a barn.

Dublin-Belfast Road, Ireland. Road signs in both English and Gaelic.

A five-hundred-year-old bridge over a country stream in Scotland.

Stone walls of northern England.

Saint Romwald Church in Wellingborough in the middle of England. It was built in the eleventh century and is still in use today.

Ancient fort, "Le Château," in Vitré,
N.W. France. Built in 1530, it was
formerly a Huguenot stronghold.

Harvesting the grapes. Southern
France.

French village woman at side
door of her church. She offered
to say a prayer for me.

A *churra,* a Spanish fried confection. Woman in Algemiri cutting a fresh ring with her scissors for a customer.

Collecting almonds in Spain by the age-old custom of knocking them from the trees onto a cloth on the ground.

Shy Moroccan girl hiding behind a goat.

Mother and daughter in East
Moroccan desert region.

Moroccan nomad.

Algeria. Pots and pans vendor
making the rounds on his bicycle.

With Clinger and umbrella in the
Atlas mountains during a sleet
storm in Algeria.

Pretty canal in northern Italy, along
the Adriatic Sea.

My only cooking gear in Italy: an old
ravioli can with a wire handle. I often
cooked spaghetti or macaroni in it,
using the seawater of the Adriatic.

A small boy
enthralled with the
pigeons in the *piazza*
of Pesaro, Italy.

Yugoslavia. Church set in canyon wall in the mountains in the province of Kosovo.

Prizren, Yugoslavia. Minaret of a mosque poking up above the other rooftops.

Greece. Roadside shrine for a farmer's fields.

From their front doors, a grandma and a little girl in a Yugoslavian village watch warily as I walk up their street very early one morning.

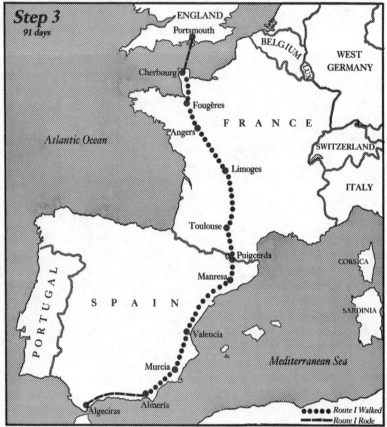

Step 3
91 days

ENGLAND
Portsmouth

BELGIUM

WEST
GERMANY

Cherbourg

Fougères

F R A N C E

Angers

Atlantic Ocean

SWITZERLAND

Limoges

ITALY

Toulouse

Puigcerda

CORSICA

Manresa

S P A I N

SARDINIA

Valencia

P O R T U G A L

Mediterranean Sea

Murcia

Almería

Algeciras

●●●● Route I Walked
▬▬▬ Route I Rode

September 10, 1983 to December 9, 1983   1,395 miles

21

The diary page on which I was writing quivered every so often, causing my pen to slip and my eyes to feel even more muddled. That, and an incessant distant throbbing of engines somewhere far, far below me, was the only way I had of telling that I was at sea. I looked at the date at the top of the page. *September 9, 1983.* Guided as much by nervousness as by excitement, my fingers wrote, *Today I left Portsmouth, England, by ferryboat, to seek what I hope is my next treasure chest of romance, beauty, and friendship—France. . . .*

As far as I knew, I was the only American on board the ship to the Normandy port of Cherbourg. There were many British subjects in their scrubbed tweed expressions and the usual odd raw Irishman or two, but none of my own.

With 1,750 miles of walking behind me and my fifth country only a few hours away, my confidence was soaring. Except for a touch of homesickness, I had never felt better, it seemed, in all my life. Physical discomforts like blisters, sore knees, and aching muscles were hardly a factor anymore, and, as crazy as it sounds, I actually *enjoyed* having Clinger on my back. I considered him as much a part of me as my khaki pants and straw hat. So well balanced and comfortably fitting was he that I thought of him more as a friend than any burden. The metal supports in the hip belt that were supposed to put the weight of the backpack onto my legs were working beautifully. My back wasn't entirely free of exhaustion, but it was nothing like it should have been. When I thought back on all the tourists I'd seen in London groaning with bent backs beneath the sagging lumps of those new internal-frame packs that were currently the fashion, I was thankful I had let function, not looks, dictate my gear selection.

While physically I was in excellent shape, mentally I was a little bothered that many people in England had warned me the French were an arrogant and rude race. Still, I couldn't help but be carrying inside me an excited heart. For I had lots of experience on my side—the experience to know that there were undoubtedly many, many good and caring people among all that supposed inhospitality. And, besides!—my precious dream was still as alive and kicking as ever. What possibly could be more fun in this life than living out one's imagination on such a grand scale?

I pushed my diary across the table and looked down again at the Rand McNally road map of France and Spain I had purchased in Portsmouth. Maybe to others it was only a big piece of laminated paper with lots of very thin and crooked red, blue, and black lines running across it, but to me it was an enchanted treasure scroll covered in innumerable *X*'s.

I suddenly had to smile extra wide: Heck, I really *was* in that map. Somewhere right . . . there! Yes!—right there south of the *C* in Channel and north of the *g* in Cherbourg.

My finger traced the route I would probably follow to the Pyrenees: Cherbourg, Fougères, Angers, Parthenay, Civray, Limoges, Brive-la-Gaillarde, Cahors, Toulouse, Bourg-Madame. Nothing but pleasure shot up through my finger. That was around one thousand miles of almost entirely rural farmland and little villages whose names were so fine I had to lower my eyes almost to the map to read them. Lots of peace and quiet, I thought.

"Just the way I like it!" I practically sang out as an elderly Frenchman passed by.

He looked at me, startled.

I grinned and pointed to the map.

He saw Clinger on the bench beside me and nodded enthusiastically. *"Wee, misyer!"* he said. Then, moving his legs up and down and wagging his hip, asked, *"Ahh peeay?"*

I hesitantly nodded, hoping he was asking me if I was walking. I sketched the earth on a blank diary page and walked my fingers around it several times, to better explain myself.

At first he thought that was very funny. But then he shook my hand firmly and proclaimed something real grand that sounded like:

"Say impussaybull!"

I nodded heartily with those around me, proud as a rooster that this wise old man had praised my journey. Yep, this walk certainly was every bit *"say impussaybull!"*

As was every Normandy village I had entered the past three days since leaving Cherbourg, tiny Gavray was musty, ancient, and shrouded in a soupy fog that made it seem all the more removed from the present. Dripping from the rain that had been sprinkling nonstop for ages, the cement and stone of its tightly packed shops and shuttered second-floor homes were as gray as I imagined the worlds of lost spirits must be. Barely two hours past sunrise, the dark stones of the streets were still as empty as if the night had not yet dissolved into the dawn. And as the waffled Vibram soles of my boots woke up each slumbering narrow sidewalk, which was usually also someone's front yard, I knew I was falling deeply in love with still another country and its people.

In this lush area of rolling hills, moody skies, and bright-eyed beautiful people, the essence of romance was everywhere. Even the language flowed from lips and radios like the notes of a sweet love song.

Perhaps it was good I was walking across such a place in the dark, rainy days of an early autumn, rather than in the sunshine of spring. I sincerely doubted I could have stood to leave behind such scenery and beguiling dark eyes, had a little more birdsong and flower been added to the poetry I was a part of.

Strolling south from Cherbourg, to Briquebec, to St. Sauveur-le-Vicomte, to Lessay, and then to Gavray, had been like floating through a timeless painting. Sometimes, such as the night I passed the crumbling towers of a Norman castle in St. Sauveur-le-Vicomte, I could hear the clanking of knights' armor and the hoofbeats of their battle-weary horses, if I concentrated just so.

In the small, gray-stoned villages of the countryside, far down the arteries and veins of roads leading into the heart called Paris, life still clung serenely to the past. Most of the families lived in the same mortar-and-stone homes their great-great-great-grandparents were raised in. And, fittingly enough, their children were being baptized and later married in tall-steepled churches with gargoyles and Gothic cloisters that had been sanctified against evil and Satan long before America was known to their kings and queens.

Every farmyard in France's northwestern corner had its small herd of black-spotted dairy cows, its cranky geese and quacky ducklings, and a loud dog. Every house had its shutters opened by ten and closed by seven. Every garden was filled with vegetables and fruit trees.

Each town, whether a one-café, four-house village, or a large one like Cherbourg, radiated outward from a soaring, sharply pointed church steeple of crockets and lightning rods. And because God's house was always on the highest point of land, I never lacked for a direction needle to the next settlement.

At times I felt as if I were merely traveling from church steeple to church steeple, like some wandering medieval pilgrim of Chaucer's.

Caught in the spell of happy faces and sad love songs, I found it difficult to believe that four decades earlier, tens of thousands of soldiers had died beside the same back roads I was following. Yet hardly an hour passed that I did not pause to gaze at another high roadside crucifix planted into a cement base covered with the casualties of *"la Guerre."* And the deeper my feet brought me into the past, the more I grew as puzzled with the French as I was titillated. I couldn't understand why they chose to keep their painful history so dominant in their lives, as if it were a scarlet letter they had grown perversely attached to. It was confusing until that misty morning in Gavray when a most unexpected child from the past reached out to return a gift I had not even been aware I'd given to her. And then, only then, did I understand fully the Frenchman's strong attachment to the sorrows of past generations.

While passing Gavray's town hall, I decided to go inside to see if the mayor, *le maire,* was at work yet, and would be willing to sign my Witness Book for the village. No one was downstairs in the old, drafty building, so I went up some steep stairs with Clinger still on my back, to see if anyone was in the offices on the second floor. But it was all so quiet that I began to think I was alone.

Timidly, I pushed on a door that was partially closed, and stepped into a long, plain room of worn carpeting and filing cabinets. A furtive creak escaped from the floor beneath my boot. At a simple wood desk at the far end of the drab room, a woman similar to my mother in age and appearance looked up from her paperwork. Beneath her wispy, gray-peppered black hair, her dark eyes broadened like those of a raccoon trapped in a headlight. She gasped and grabbed at her heart. I panicked, thought she had had a heart attack, then calmed when I saw her jumping to her feet.

"Américain?" she asked excitedly.

"Oui."

She hurried out from behind her neatly piled papers, saying in a voice filled with excitement, "Yawnkee! *Oui?*"

"Oui!" I laughed with delight. I couldn't for the life of me figure out why she was so glad to see me, but I certainly wasn't going to complain.

She couldn't have been any higher than my chest, but she practically tackled me in her eagerness to reach my side. She was the town-hall secretary, she said, and the only one in the office, because the mayor was working on his farm, helping with the fall harvesting. My knowledge of French was such that most of what she was saying made no sense to me, but eventually I guessed she was begging me to stay in the room and not leave. She wanted to go get something or someone from somewhere down the street outside. I nodded till I thought my head might fall off, but apparently that wasn't enough insurance for her. She grabbed my right hand, led me to a side wall partly covered in framed black-and-white photos, told me to look at the photos, and *please* not to go anywhere while she was gone. Then, like a jack-in-the-box, she was through the door, and slammed it shut behind her. I listened for a few seconds to her pumps tromping down the steps, like a sound effect in a puppet show.

As I studied the photos, it became obvious they were of the village during World War II. Gavray had been in the very thick of some of the heaviest fighting between the Allied forces and the German Occupation troops, and the scenes of destruction framed on the hospital-white wall were stark reminders of how powerful bombs and bullets were. Peaceful Gavray had suffered terribly.

The ticking of the wall clock grew from a background noise to a monotony. Five minutes, ten minutes, fifteen minutes . . . Where was that strange-acting secretary? Clinger was hardly getting any lighter, so I slipped him off. I'd give her five more minutes, then leave. Maybe I'd totally misunderstood what she'd said. I ran my eyes over the photos again, a bit irritated. Maybe I was supposed to have followed her. Or maybe she'd gone home.

Thump thump thump thump thump . . .

There was no mistaking those pumps racing up the stairs. Sure enough, the door swung open wildly, and there she was, out of breath, red-faced, as excited as ever. Standing as tall as she could make herself, she expanded her ample chest with a deep breath, hid her left hand behind her back, and then exploded into one of the darn-craziest things I'd ever seen a perfectly sane person do: pretending she was waving some sort of little flag in her right hand, she high-stepped her way back and forth across the squawking floorboards quickly, with her voice shouting out the American military fight tune that goes something like, "Daaa-daaaa da-da-daaaa da-da-daaaa, daaa-daaaa da-da-da da-da-daaa da-da-daaa!"

As if that weren't enough to keep my jaw hanging to my chest, she'd glance at me briefly every several seconds, grin broadly, wave the imaginary flag more briskly, and yell for all the world to hear:

"HOOOORAAAY, YAWNKEEES! HOOOORAAAY, YAWNK-EEES!"

I was convinced the local gendarme on duty at that hour would be rushing up any second to see whose death yells were making the village's shutters fly off their hinges. I wasn't just embarrassed—I was scared! Had she lost her mind? Just what the heck was going on?

Finally, she stopped right in front of me. I looked way down at her with an expression that I hoped said, "Are you *crazy*?" And she in turned raised her eyes to mine, like some naughty schoolgirl. Which was when I noticed, to my surprise, that she was . . . crying.

My heart melted as if it were a lump of butter on a flame. What had I done to make her cry so much? I felt a lump growing in my own throat.

Slowly, very slowly, she pulled the left hand from behind her back, and raised it up, up, up to me with her fingers clenched shut. When the hand could go no farther, she lifted her fingers from her palm one by one. There, nestled snug in the cradle of her palm was a chocolate *Lion* candy bar, the most popular brand in this country.

Suddenly, it was clear to me what she had been doing. She would have been a girl of about sixteen when the Allied soldiers liberated Gavray. She would have been on the street curbs, along with many others, waving her little American, Canadian, or British flag at the passing troops, as well as shouting the popular slogan of "Hooray, Yankees!"

When that morning I came into the office and surprised her, it must have been almost like *déjà vu*. There, standing tall and ruddy-cheeked before her was a young American again, red hair and all, with his backpack piled high onto his back, just like those soldiers with their gear on that unforgettable day of her past. And the candy bar? I looked at it and smiled. After almost four decades, she was undoubtedly paying back to me the Hershey's chocolate bar given to her by one of those smiling Yanks. The reason she had been gone so long was that she probably had had to run several blocks, maybe across the whole village, to get some shopkeeper to open his shop so she could have that candy bar. Then she would have run all the way back, as fast as her thick, aging legs could carry her, wondering if I was still in the town hall, or gone away as mysteriously as I had appeared. No wonder she was so out of breath when she'd opened that door. How amazing that she wanted so much after all those years to repay that gift.

And yet there was more to it than just the return of the candy bar. For she was crying now more than ever. So much so, she couldn't even speak.

I slowly turned my eyes to the framed photos on the wall behind my right shoulder. Yes. Yes, of course. In the horrible turmoil and wreckage in those frozen scenes of the war, there were probably her parents buried in some crumbled building or cratered makeshift cemetery. What she really was saying to me was how happy she was to be a free person. How, even after all those years, she was still so greatly in love with those brave young soldiers who had freed her and her home of that horrible tyranny.

I felt tears of my own wanting to escape from the corner of my eyes, and I thought it best I continue on. I placed the candy bar in a side pocket of Clinger and heaved him to my shoulders. On the way to the door, I paused and managed to thank her for the chocolate bar. She nodded with a nice, gentle motherly smile.

Continuing on down the small sycamore-lined road, I came after a while to one of the most moving sights I had ever seen. Stretching before me, for what seemed miles, was a long, velvety field sprouting thousands upon thousands of identical white marble crosses. Gleaming like long, straight strings of pearls on an emerald sea of grass, the crosses bore the names of my countrymen who had landed on those foreign shores on D-Day, but never made it back home.

As I stood among those crosses at St. James, and read the names and ages on their outstretched arms, I couldn't help noticing how many had come from small, unknown places as I did, and that most were younger than I. I noticed a man standing by himself in the middle of another field of the crosses. I worked my way toward him, and when I was near, he asked with a rich southern drawl if I also had come to pay my respects. I lied and said I had. Something, perhaps the red in his eyes, had told me the American knew someone buried there. I didn't want to risk hurting his feelings by admitting that I had not even known of the cemetery.

He explained to me that he had come to see the grave of his older brother, who had died in the Normandy campaign. It was his first visit to the cemetery. All those years he had wanted to come, but he had only lately been able to afford the trip. As we were talking, the caretaker—another American—came and joined our discussion. He told us that there were over forty-four hundred American war graves in the cemetery—but a tiny fraction of the nearly one million total casualties in the area. These had been the boys who, for some reason or other, didn't get sent back to America for burial.

As I slowly walked further into that day and the French countryside, the images of those photos in the Gavray town hall, the secretary with the candy bar, those crucifixes beside the road, the long lines of crosses at St. James, the names on their outstretched arms, and that man crying in the midst of a sea of graves kept going through my mind. Until, at last, I had to stop, sit down wearily upon a log, and cry myself for a long, long time.

That day taught me a crucial lesson. Should I ever decide to give up and go home, I knew right then and there that I would be nothing less than a coward. For no matter how tough or dangerous or lonely the worldwalk should become in the many years ahead, my pain and anguish could never begin to match that which those boys under those crosses had gone through, in the last seconds of their life. Lying there in the cold mud, their bodies shattered and bleeding, they must have known they were never going to see home again.

I rose just as the sun was setting. I rinsed my face in a cool stream. *No, I can never give up, no matter what,* I thought. Those soldiers had come and died so that someday I would have a free world in which to live my dreams. To give up would be saying to all those people who had helped me, and who were reading my stories in *Capper's* and the *Columbus Dispatch* in Ohio that the world really was a dangerous place, that our soldiers had died in vain. And I was not about to do that, because I knew it was just not true.

Now, I knew finally what a lot of French people in Normandy and Brittany knew, what people all over Europe, wherever wars had been fought, knew: To forget the past was to doom the future.

I took a deep breath and pushed on. I had had to come all the way to France, where I didn't even speak the language beyond a few tourist phrases, to realize how proud I should feel to be an American.

I didn't rush France, and France didn't rush me. It was as simple as that. France, like the wines she produced, seemed to get better and better with time. Or, in my case, with each kilometer.

Those first nine days there were the gray skies, fat dairy cows, and daily rain showers of Normandy and Brittany. Then, for about 120 miles, from near Rennes to the medieval hill city of Parthenay, the poverty of the villages and the cloudless, hot sky reminded me of Mexico. I feared that the heat of Africa was already upon me. For four long days, the fruit trees and streams were few, while the lizards, spiders, and rocks were many. Walking in the middle of the day was out of the question; I had to content myself with napping in the shade like a lazy tomcat.

My clothes needed washing badly, yet nowhere did I find a coin-operated washing machine, not even in the largest of the cities I passed through. But west of Parthenay, I discovered a beautiful little spring-fed pond, and once again I was able to enjoy France in comfort. Well . . . almost. For there was still the very discouraging problem of language.

Before I had entered France, over 490 miles before Parthenay, I had been concerned that my unfamiliarity with the language would cause me many problems. But many former travelers to Europe had told me that most Europeans knew English. To my advisers, the fact that I knew hardly any French, and yet had one thousand miles of France to cross to reach Spain, was no obstacle at all. But, oh, were they ever wrong!

For starters, upon landing in Cherbourg, I had with me 2 pairs of new Adidas running shoes, worth a total of $120, which had been given to me as presents in Bolton, England, and which I wanted to mail ahead to Limoges, in southern France. To carry them was plain foolishness, since the Rocky Scrambler boots on my feet were still serving me well.

But no one at the *poste* spoke a lick of English, and my clerk was obviously new at her job. She couldn't seem to understand that my sending a package to myself in care of the post office in Limoges was a perfectly normal thing. I tried to tell her that I wouldn't be arriving there for at least one month, and that the postal clerks would have to hold the package for me. What in my own country would have been a two-minute chore turned out to be fifteen minutes of stuttering and pleading looks. When I left the post office, I honestly doubted I'd ever see those shoes again.

I rushed to a bookstore and frantically purchased a Berlitz English-French phrase book. And for the next several weeks, I gave myself a crash course in learning and memorizing spoken French. The book and the people I met were my teachers, and the roads and an occasional shade tree or coffeehouse my classrooms. Many days I spent walking with my nose in the book, my lips repeating, repeating, repeating some new noun or verb until a honking auto would remind me that I was again weaving into the traffic. It was anything but easy. Still, I was determined to understand at least some of what I heard, because I loved the country and the people so very much. "How will I ever learn much about life in France if I can't speak to anyone?" I lamented, with no small amount of frustration.

Since I was traveling almost entirely through the rural areas, not the cities and tourist centers of most other visitors, I found English speakers to be a rarity. And, really, that made sense. After all, why would any of the farmers need to know how to speak English to grow their corn or grapes? Or a village shopkeeper to make his sales? They never saw Americans in their day-to-day living, just as we in Bethel never saw any Frenchmen in our daily lives in the village. Indeed, most of the many new friends I made surprised me by admitting they had never before met an American. It just wasn't true that Americans were everywhere.

Therefore, almost none of the French people I met in that first half of my Francewalk had ever spoken more than a handful of English words. Yet, ironically, that handicap was to make our brief meetings all the more special. Because we had to put so much effort and thought into both listening and speaking with each other, our moments together became more alive and emotional than they might otherwise have been.

Sure, it was exhausting, too. But definitely worth every furrowed eyebrow. Language, I found, was not actually a barrier, if one really wanted to learn.

There was always some way to get my thoughts across, even if it meant I had to act them out, mime fashion. Which was okay, because usually that led to much laughter by everyone concerned. Many a new friend I made that way. In St.-Hilaire-du-Harcouet, there was an eleven-year-old schoolboy named Xavier Gougeon, a big fan of the Dallas Cowboys football team, who loved my acting out how those giant linebackers pictured in his magazines grunted and growled on the line of scrimmage. In St.-Georges-des-Gardes, on a stormy gray Sunday afternoon in a cookie factory whose chocolate aromas had been pulling me along all day, all the workers who were studying English at the factory's night school sang me "Happy Birthday" because it was the only song they knew, after which I gave a rousing performance of "Old MacDonald Had a Farm" that had them practically falling into their vats. And when the bosses refused to let me leave until every spare inch of space in Clinger had been loaded down with fresh cookies, I knew already that France was destined to be one of my favorite places in all the world.

Then, too, at a public bathhouse in St.-Maixent I met twenty-seven-year-old Alain Amiot, who enjoyed my acting out how grungy and stinky I felt that day, and who took me to meet his wonderful family and fiancée, Cosette, in La Mothe-St.-Heray. Through Cosette, who was forever biting her lower lip and skimming through her French-English dictionary in the two days I stayed with her and Alain's large farm families, I met over the course of three days such local legends as a lonesome, haunted thousand-year-old church on a gravel lane far from any town, a honeycomb of tight, claustrophobic underground passages, and a small, round cave, marked with strange drawings, in which prehistoric man had worshiped.

And a mysterious old hermit who lived in a five-hundred-year-old home deep in the forest.

Limping from a wooden leg he'd worn since the last war, the hermit not only shared with us the large dolls he had carved and dressed in the images of past French queens, kings, and royal mistresses, but also a look into a shuttered and padlocked gristmill straddling a deep and fast stream on his property. Looking at the profuse spiderwebs that stretched like rotted sheets from the musty, cold gristmill's ceiling beams to the hole in the cement floor through which his only son had, at the age of five, fallen and drowned in the creek below, I felt a deep sense of sadness. No wonder the old man had never used that mill again.

Maybe it was because I had not gone to Paris, to its doubtless many hustlers and tourist traps, but had stayed entirely in the countryside with those who hardly ever met my kind, that I encountered scarcely any of the rudeness other travelers to France had complained to me about. Whatever, I was feeling even more blessed than ever by the journey's progress. It was everything I had hoped, and more . . . for example, Nicole.

I met her in Argentré-du-Plessis. A beautiful dark-haired young poet with large brown eyes as deep and mysterious as the waters of a hidden canyon, and high, full cheeks that seemed those of an empress, Nicole was serving the *café* and *vin* in a little pub crowded with black berets and dark-suited farmers who were temporarily kept from their work by the same cloudburst I was hiding from. She was a welcome guest at my table all that afternoon. Though we did not speak a common language, it hardly mattered. I could have sat for days listening to her sweet voice reading to me her poems, and she and the farmers probably would have enjoyed a few more hours of my mimicking their longtime enemies the English.

Unlike the farmers, I did not disappear when the sun returned. All the rest of that freshly showered afternoon and evening, Nicole led me by her soft hand and softer voice to those magical places of flowers and leaf-covered paths she had written about. What we could not communicate with our lips, we left to our eyes and hands to say. And before that night would end, I myself wanted to leave her a poem to remember me by. I was the last person in the world to be composing such a thing, for I had never tried before. But when I gazed at her beauty, I felt inspired. And so, late into the night, after she had returned to her parents' home and I to a kindly neighbor's hayloft, I labored by the light of a candle onto a page torn from my diary:

Nicole, I have to be faithful to the call;
But before I leave let me extol
The beauty that Lady France does enthrall
In my heart, mind, and soul. . . .

Come morning, her soft, deep voice coaxed me from my burrow in the hay. Sleepily, I pulled on my clothes, crawled to the edge of the loft, and peered down. There she stood, her soft eyes as inviting as two wild-flowers, come to take me to breakfast as she had promised.

"*Bonjour,* Steven," she said with a lovely smile.

I motioned to her to join me, and she climbed up the ladder to sit only an inch from my right shoulder. To keep off the chilly drafts, I pulled the blanket up over our shoulders, as if that ragged thing were the cape of some prince.

Shyly, I showed her the poem. Her eyes lit up, and she insisted I read it, even though she wouldn't understand what I was saying.

I had never serenaded anyone before—I was always timid and self-conscious in the presence of a beautiful lady—but after clearing my throat, I read each of the poem's stanzas.

Judging from the bright gleam in Nicole's eye when I finished reading, it seemed my clumsy little poem had been as special to her as I had hoped it would be.

Without saying anything, she took it and studied it. Watching her eyes move from side to side, occasionally pausing as they caught a word that looked vaguely familiar, I thought she was reading it as much with her mind as with her heart. Did she care about me, as I did about her? If only she could say. What a horrible curse this thing called language could be sometimes.

I would have given anything just to have leaned over those few inches separating us and kissed her. But, again, I was too shy.

I told her to keep the poem, and then I stood and quickly busied my mind with preparing for another day on the road.

Our breakfast was the normal farmer's fare of yesterday's leftover bread dunked in a large bowl of strong coffee flavored with many tablespoons of sugar and condensed milk. Though that didn't seem like much, I had learned to like it for the warmth it gave me on these cool, damp autumn mornings and for the energy the caffeine supplied.

When at last it was time to say good-bye to Nicole, I touched my heart and said simply, *"Ami."*

She nodded, then stepped forward and presented me with a book of her poetry. I smiled, remembering for some reason a time in my boyhood when I'd given the girl next door a bouquet of wildflowers.

I kissed Nicole on the forehead, and we parted.

In the south of France, near the Pyrenees, all the best aspects of the country seemed to be merged. How was it possible that a land could be so blessed!

Walking in the morning was such a joy that I came to look forward to it all night long. I was awakened by the songs of hundreds of birds. Then, precisely at seven, there would come the ringing of my "alarm clock," the long, slow, distant tolling of some village's church bell. Even the sun knew it was only natural to be lazy in southern France, and it rose from the cotton-candy fog ever so slowly, as I did from some farmer's cot or fragrant loft. After which the morning only became more mesmerizing, with dew droplets clinging to the vines of fat grapes and to the broad leaves of sycamores in such profusion that they sparkled like finely cut diamonds.

If the world had a face like that of the man in the moon, unquestionably the lower lips of its smile would be the Pyrenees' chain of peaks that make up France's southernmost border.

The tranquillity of the land shone in the customs of the people there. At long last, I found a people who enjoyed lingering over a meal longer than I—dubbed by my friends the slowest eater anywhere. Apparently, the French had decided that the things in life to be enjoyed the longest were food and friends.

A dinner I shared with the "family" of a former Third World rebel near Bourg-St.-Bernard was typical of those the households of France shared with me. The strongly muscled, gray-bearded, forty-six-year-old Guy Thibault and his thirty-six-year-old energetic wife, Isabelle, lived in a rambling old yellow farmhouse in the middle of a countryside bursting with fat pink and purple grapes. Along with their three young children, there were six other "youngsters" also keeping them constantly busy: six recovering drug addicts.

Guy and Isabelle had converted the huge old farm's buildings into a combination house-dormitory-school-workshop for young men from Europe and North Africa who were recovering from past drug addictions. When I had stopped at their front door to request a drink of water, there'd been such an excited clamor by the young men, most of whom had never met an American before, that I could hardly refuse their invitation to be one of the family for a few days. With me, there were twelve of us at dinnertime. Which quite truthfully was about the same number as in some of the regular farm families I'd stayed with, where grandparents often lived under the same roof, too.

As was the custom in many homes, we ate the evening meal in the large front room that, depending on the time of day, served as the living room, dining room, or someone's bedroom. On that first night, Guy and Isabelle served a strong before-dinner wine. It was followed by a large bowl of soup made from tapioca and tomatoes served with a lighter wine, lots of long loaves of bread bought that day from the *boulangerie,* and plenty of fresh liver pâté.

Then, into the soup bowl was put a large salad of fresh home-grown garden vegetables. After which, again using the bowls, we feasted on the main entrée of garden tomatoes stuffed with beef, pork, and onions simmered in a light oil, along with yet more of a seemingly endless supply of bread and homemade wine. Finally, there appeared the customary after-dinner treats of delicate chocolates, cheeses made from goat's and cow's milk, yogurts, grapes, apples, peaches, and walnuts (again, home grown), still more bread, and then the period on the exclamation mark—the cognac-spiked *café*.

We sat down at seven-thirty, and were not to rise again from that table until ten-thirty, and that was after having earlier enjoyed a two-hour lunch! Now *that* was true art.

One young addict, who had studied English for seven years at school, perhaps best summed up France when he observed:

"We understand that in America, you put money first and love second. Here, we put the love of life first, and then, if there is any, money second."

When Isabelle translated for the others, the happy house fairly shook with laughter.

As usual, the stars outside had a lot to smile about that night. And I did, too. Something told me my heart would be very sad, indeed, when it came time to cross those Pyrenees.

My being an American was supposed to have been a serious handicap in France, according to some American overseas travelers I'd talked with in the United States. They described the French they'd met as being often unfriendly, even purposefully rude, to Americans. And those same Americans invariably described the French as a "dirty" people who generally lived in "filthy" cities.

All of that was, I found, largely nonsense. There was no less concern for hygiene by the French than in comparable American or British settings. In fact, the French in the rural areas were often nothing less than admirable in their life-styles. Despite considering eating their greatest passion in life, they were seldom fat. The men and women seemed healthy, fit, and very well groomed even into their old age. The young women were especially pleasant to look at and to know. They liked to talk about art and politics and philosophy as much as did the Irish ladies, but in a much more sensible and unemotional manner. And unlike the English ladies, the French women and girls knew exactly how to dress and preen themselves so as not to make it seem an effort.

As for the rundown look of their villages and cities, that was mostly a by-product of age. In America, a building older than seventy-five years was usually too rundown and neglected to be used any longer. In France, many of the buildings still in use were 300, 400, or 500 years old.

My "souvenirs" were my memories and my published stories. And the French people I met along their gorgeous nation's "blue highways" highly respected that.

As I hoped, my walking all alone and in no hurry past their houses and shops put a question mark in their minds that prodded them to stop me and chat. When they learned I was an American, they clustered about me, sometimes in crowds of more than a dozen.

Most of those who came to talk to me were young, in their teens, and most of their questions concerned jobs, wages, and the life-styles of my countrymen. There was, I noticed, a sense of pessimism among the young concerning their own future. They were all too aware of how tight the job market was in a nation the size of France. Many expressed a desire to try living and working in the United States for a while.

The fascination and admiration for Americans and our products was particularly strong in the areas of France that American soldiers had passed through in the two world wars. Jerseys with pro-football insignia or American university names on them were numerous. As in Ireland, much of the programming on French television was devoted to American sitcoms such as *Dallas, CHiPs,* and the latest craze, *Flamingo Road.* Even *Lassie* was still popular.

But by far the strongest communicator of American values to the French youth was American music, particularly rock and disco. In the crowded open-air markets, in bars and at private parties, I heard my language being sung. It was so weird to walk into a medieval village of black-bereted farmers and little "flying nuns" and hear KISS or Glen Campbell or Michael Jackson belting forth from the municipal loudspeakers along each main shopping street.

I tried to live like the French people as much as possible. Much of my day was spent going to the butcher's and the baker's shops, standing in long lines, and haggling over prices. Again and again, I realized that words are not as important in communicating as desire and curiosity.

I made so many new friends in those forty days it took me to cross almost the length of France. Several of them fondly referred to me as the "macadam cowboy," or road cowboy. And I had enough new experiences to fill a ranch. Even as I was stepping across the cement bridge from Bourg-Madame, France, to Puigcerdá, Spain, near the eastern end of the Pyrenees, France was still reaching out to me. My last memory of that paradise was of a sidewalk-vendor girl planting a kiss on my cheek and placing in my hand, to help me ward off the late October cold, a bag of her freshly steamed hot dogs. What a nice world we lived in, I thought, as I disappeared into the snowy peaks of another new adventure on that cold October 17 morning.

Oh. . . . Those shoes I'd mailed in Cherbourg? Well, they had been waiting for me at the post office in Limoges. All safe and sound, and with a big, bright URGENT stamped on the package.

22

I forced myself to climb another step up the slick, icy road, further into the wall of snow swirling and howling around my frozen ears. At a curve in the road that hung suspended in the sky, like an eagle's nest on a cliff in the Rocky Mountains of Montana, I stopped and grabbed tightly onto the guardrail—and felt my life depended on how tightly I gripped that flimsy railing's rattling planks. My lungs gasped desperately for more oxygen. I wanted to cry aloud at the frostbite that made my fingers sting as if they were being pinched between red-hot pliers. But I was too weak to do more than wonder groggily when salvation would come.

How could the world have changed so quickly for the worse? Was it really possible that just two days before, in France, I had been sweating in summerlike heat and snitching grapes from sunny fields? This was insane! From summer to the dead of winter in just a matter of maybe twenty miles? And I wasn't even to the Puerto de Tosas pass yet. Whatever had happened to the warm and sunny Spain everyone had assured me was just over the Pyrenees?

Looking out over the jagged snowy peaks that seemed to stretch forever to the west and the east, I could barely believe the rugged beauty of the scene: row after row of formidable dark fangs scarred with the cavities of avalanches, and buried beneath a plaque of ugly gray rock. I felt like a Jonah fallen into the jaws of a huge land monster. By far and away, these mountains were the toughest and most challenging terrain I'd faced yet. As well as the most dangerous. They resembled in some ways the Sierra Madre in California and Nevada, but their coldness and moodi-

ness made me think of the Rockies in Wyoming. A dangerous yet spectacular combination.

My distended nostrils were thirsty for oxygen, yet it seemed that the
waves of wind trying to tear the very flesh off my face had not a drop to
spare for my insides. I shivered violently again, and wondered seriously if
on this high asphalt perch and in the throes of this unexpected snowstorm
was where death would finally catch me. All the forces in Jupiter's domain
seemed intent on ripping me from the mountainside and smashing me on
the rocks below. Again and again, the snow clawed at my uncovered head,
and from unseen canyons there rumbled the sounds of a discontented
Mother Nature.

Obviously, the road I was on had been barred to traffic because of the
high winds and freak snow; not a single vehicle had slogged past all day. I
was afraid that it was deadly hypothermia that was making my head and
body feel so weak. Since leaving Puigcerdá yesterday, I'd not seen a village
or house, and the road seemed to grow steeper and more curved with each
kilometer. What if the snow on the pass was too deep? What if the storm
lasted for even one more day? Was there any way to get help?

I told myself I should have known better than to be so ill prepared.
My training in the mountains of Wyoming, before the journey started, had
taught me the dangerous moods of those parts of the planet. But I had
remembered nothing.

The gentle climate of France had lulled me into a state of careless-
ness. All I had to wear was light summer gear and a sweatshirt a very
worried Isabelle Thibault had made me take. I just wasn't prepared for the
cold weather. I had both of my short-sleeved cotton shirts on beneath the
sweatshirt, a pair of lightweight khaki slacks on my shaking legs (I'd
discarded my heavier jeans weeks ago), two pairs of socks on my feet, and
a third pair on my hands. For all the warmth those thin clothes gave me, I
might as well have been naked.

What water was left in the goatskin bag tied to Clinger's frame was
frozen. I knew there was just one sandwich left in the pack. I was in big
trouble. Still, I told myself not to panic. I'd been through worse in the
past.

In December 1975, I'd been in the Red Desert of southwestern Wyoming wrapping up six months of uranium prospecting when a far worse
storm struck. For two days and nights, I, accompanied only by a young
collie pup, Charlie, had huddled in my stranded pickup waiting for rescue.
Finally driven by hunger and thirst to attempt an escape from that vast
high-altitude basin of the Great Divide, the dog and I struggled through
fifty-two miles of constant screaming winds and stinging snow to reach the
nearest settlement, Wamsutter. For a day and a night, we stumbled and

walked in the below-zero blizzard. When Charlie's feet became so cut from the cold and ice that he could no longer walk, I had taken to carrying him. Though my lips swelled shut with dehydration and I was crying from the endlessness of the pain, we made it. Perhaps I might have given up, but I could not stand the thought of anything happening to Charlie.

So now I toughened my spirit with the reminder that I'd lived through worse. And my lungs found the full breath they needed. I leaned into the wind and moved slowly, foot by foot, to the pass. The wind-driven snow stung like shards of glass. I prayed that I would not have to spend another night trying to sleep in a crazily angled tent. Surely, if France had been heaven, then this was a sort of purgatory. There was no way I was going to stop again, until Nature had regained some of her sanity.

It was well after dark before I gave up the search for the earth far below. I seemed stuck in the clouds with those massive, craggy giants. I still saw no lights of homes or villages. And again I worried about the shivering I could not control. If hypothermia *was* setting in, my only chance of survival was to get under cover and save what heat I had left in my body.

I found a small stand of pines around a curve. Out of the direct path of the wind, I erected my tent on a 45-degree slope, then settled down onto some of the sharpest rocks a man ever had for a mattress.

A howling and the shaking of tent cloth woke me in the middle of the night. I was trembling like a sick animal and scrunched into a ball at the downside of the tent. The angle was so steep that the only thing keeping the pegless tent on the mountain were the pine-tree trunks it had slid down against. I didn't dare to think about what would happen if the tent slipped between the tree trunks and tumbled down the steep rocks with me helplessly flailing about inside.

It was eight o'clock in the morning when I next awoke. Though the air was so brittle with cold that I felt I could reach out from under the blanket and shatter it with my fist, the shivering fits I'd had during the night were almost gone. But folding the frozen tent was not an easy chore. My fingers stung so badly, I had to stop every other minute to blow some warmth onto their tips.

The road continued to rise slightly for about a mile. Then I came to a deafening howling. I was at the top. I paused at the summit and treated my eyes to what was surely one of the most spectacular vistas on the planet. I was sure that if I concentrated, I could see the Mediterranean Sea to the east. And if I imagined hard enough, the dark hulk of North Africa, far away to the south, would somehow materialize.

I knew that by going to Africa, I was probably adding almost three thousand miles and over a year to my trek. I would be crossing the entire length of Spain, the widths of Morocco, Algeria, and Tunisia, and the length of Italy before I was again on the same latitude. I must be crazy. But I had to do it if I was really to explore the world.

The descent into northern Spain was quick and steep, almost one hundred meters every kilometer. I could have been out of the clouds by as early as noon, but along the way I came to a roadside spring that gave me a chance for a bath and to hand-wash some of my clothes. The water was like liquid ice, and the breezes still chilly, but I braved it. There were few things that gave me a shot of energy like a good, refreshing bath.

The road had been reopened, and every so often a car would drive past with its driver very surprised to see someone standing half-naked in a stream in the snow. One driver was so shaken he nearly smashed his car into a rock cliff.

At dusk a station wagon with British plates pulled over to the side of the road I was walking on. The driver was a Scottish lad of about twenty. His mother was in the front seat beside him, and his younger sister in the back with all the suitcases. The mother, a cheery person who looked rather professorial in her wire-rimmed bifocals with their neck chain hanging down onto her prominent chest, did almost all the talking.

"Would you like a lift?" she asked.

I naturally declined, then told her what I was doing.

"You've lost a lot of weight, haven't you?" she asked.

I felt even more conscious of how little I'd eaten in the past two-and-one-half days, and how battered my face must have been from the exertion of getting across the Pyrenees.

But right away she made me feel better by saying, "You must be in great shape."

"I am!" I replied in all honesty. I hadn't really given it too much thought, but she was right. I hadn't felt so tough and healthy in years. When I told her how far I'd walked since my last meal, she immediately commanded the wide-eyed son and daughter to find some food for me in the car.

The daughter pulled two apples from under a suitcase. "They're fresh off a farm in France," the mother said as she handed them to me. *Will I ever be done with French apples?* I thought. It seemed I had snitched from the trees, or been given, enough apples while in France to last me a dozen lifetimes.

I asked if they were on some sort of vacation, because they seemed so happy and excited.

"We were only going to go to the south coast of France," the mother replied. "But I've a son who lives in Tarragona, south of Barcelona, and we decided, 'What the heck, let's go visit him as long as we're down this far.'"

She didn't know the son's address, or even his telephone number. But she was going to take a chance and try to find him anyway.

"And what if you don't find him?" I asked.

"Oh, we'll at least have seen this part of Spain," she replied like a true adventurer, jangling her glasses for effect.

For the next forty minutes or so, everything and anything seemed fair game to chat about on that cold and lonely stretch of road. But at last I had to let them go and face the dark road again on my own. In the time we'd been rattling on, no one had passed, and night had again returned. I hated to let them out of my grasp; I met so few English-speaking people now. But they and I had long ways yet to go, and the road wasn't about to get any shorter on its own.

"You sure you won't take a run with us for a ways?" she asked, with worry on her face. "We won't tell anyone, I promise."

No, I would walk. Maybe some people wouldn't have thought sneaking a ride down to the valley in the night was a big deal. But for my own sense of accomplishment, I wanted to keep the journey true and pure. It would mean a lot more to me, and others, in the end.

"Ah, well," she sighed. "You sure have guts."

While I repacked my log books, she again had her children scrounge around for food. All they came up with were two oranges and a half-eaten French *Lion* candy bar.

"Maybe we'll see you on the way back!" she shouted encouragingly as the car pulled slowly away.

Boy, I sure hope so, I thought warmly, the chocolate serenading my tongue.

TUNEL DE SANT QUIRZE, read the long, narrow metal sign in the weak light of an overhead bulb. I paused at the entrance to the long tunnel and peered cautiously down its wide, dark mouth. There certainly wasn't anything saintly looking about the way it seemed to lead to absolutely nowhere. Or to the trash lying piled along the road beside the opening, or to those sounds of dripping water echoing faintly inside the passageway.

I looked back at the small lights of a gasoline station I'd left about five minutes before. The idea of walking alone through such an enclosed black space in the middle of the night did not appeal to my worry cells at all. Especially considering what I'd passed through the past three days.

My descent from the clouds might have brought warmer temperatures and, finally, some food, but that was about as far as the blessings went. In the narrow and densely populated valley I followed southeastward toward the giant city of Barcelona, the air stank and the water was polluted; many animal corpses floated down the narrow and steep-walled river; machine-gun-toting soldiers guarded the family barracks of the national police; some factory windows were pocked with bullet holes; the hammer-and-sickle emblem of the Spanish Communist party was painted on crumbling walls in every town.

I hadn't exactly cared for some of the tough faces I'd seen watching me from the shops and homes all day long. And something told me there had to be more than a few would-be-robbers aware that I was going to be passing through the tunnel about now. And wouldn't you know it: There'd been a long string of traffic all day on this road, and now—nothing.

I swallowed my last bit of common sense as I risked life and limb to chase after the faint glob of light at the far end of the long man-made intestine.

I hadn't gone fifty steps when I heard something behind me. Someone had definitely kicked a loose rock back on the road. I slunk closer to the wet slime of the curved wall on my left. Maybe being in the middle of the road wasn't such a good idea. Whoever was behind me might see my silhouette against the far opening.

My ears strained so hard to hear any kind of sound that the water dripping from the tunnel's roof sounded like cannonballs dropping. From the blackness around me all sorts of gruesome specters jumped out at my imagination, like props in a carnival's haunted house. I tiptoed as quickly, and quietly, as possible. No doubt the stranger had followed me clear from the last town. I'd passed some pretty suspicious-looking dudes holding up some walls back there.

The pesetas and traveler's checks in the money belt around my waist felt abnormally large and bulky. Any second, there would surely be a powerful tug on my pack, and I'd be spun about to scream at the flash of a gun or a knife blade tearing through my rib cage.

That did it! I was off like a track runner.

Clinger bounced crazily on my back like a drunken jockey. In my ears, the other's footsteps kept right behind mine. My heart tried its best to trade places with my stomach.

Suddenly, a tremendous explosion of light just ahead blinded me. I leaped aside. A growling truck roared past, inches away. Its horn scolded me so sharply, not a hair on my head stayed put. Somehow I remembered to turn around, to search out my pursuer in the truck's searchlights.

There he was! He . . . he was still down at the other end. I couldn't believe it; he was barely into the tunnel. And sure as I had been scared to within an inch of my wits, he wasn't any killer. He was a priest! There'd been no mistaking the white cleric's collar and the black cassock.

I walked out into the cool night. Up a little further, I passed a red Renault parked on a narrow, unlit shoulder. Something else suddenly became clearer about the fright back in the tunnel: The priest had been carrying some sort of large metal can with a bent spout in his right hand.

I played for a second with the idea of waiting for the priest at the stalled car. He might need help putting the gasoline into the car and getting it restarted. But then I took off, walking faster than ever. My poor frazzled imagination knew there were probably as many "priests on lone country lanes in the middle of the night" stories as there were black-dog tales.

My nerves were ready for a rest after that tunnel. When I came to a freshly cut field of clover and mint beside the river I was following, I decided that would be my campsite for the night. It smelled just too good to pass up. Down near the river, out of sight of anyone on the road, I pitched the tent and dropped right off to a well-earned sleep.

Sometime in the depths of the night, I was awakened by the sound of what I thought were pebbles being thrown against the tent's sides. Knowing that there might be someone just on the other side of a tent wall was scary. There was no way I could see them; yet they knew exactly where I was.

The only defense, I decided, was an offense. I sprang from the blanket, quickly unzipped the tent door, and poked my head out.

JEEEZAL PETE! AWWWWK! RATS!!!!

Six, seven, eight—they looked as big as house cats in the full harvest moon. I pulled my head back into the tent as quickly as if I'd seen some Martians. My fingers couldn't yank that door's zipper up and around to the last pair of teeth fast enough.

I didn't think for a minute there was anything less than an army of rabid rats outside, figuring out how to pull me into the river mud.

During the afternoon I'd passed a puny rabbit stumbling around in a field between the river and the road along one of those stretches where the river water was particularly green and foamy. From the way the rabbit lurched, and from the way its fur was discolored and falling out in clumps, there was no doubt it was a mighty sickly creature. Even its eyes were glazed and crusted. And whatever that rabbit had, those rats probably had, too.

Earlier, I had cut off a chunk of hard sausage to eat, and I had set the greasy plastic wrapping outside the tent door on the grass. That must have been what attracted the rats in the first place. And now they wanted the rest. I felt for the remaining sausage, and found it lying against the tent wall, right where my face had been snoring away. Ughhh! I wanted to leave then and there. To think that only a few skimpy millimeters of fabric had been between my nose and their teeth!

I eased myself back to a prone position, tucked my legs and arms safely away from the edges of the blanket, and eventually coaxed the sandman into making another visit. As I dozed off, the last thing I thought was how much like an old man "sunny, easygoing Spain" was beginning to make me feel.

23

By the fourth day, I'd had enough of the valley to Barcelona. Rather than continue toward that two-thousand-year-old city, I turned away from the dust and traffic and filth to head southwest across the high, semi-arid, sparsely populated plains that make up most of Spain's interior. Maybe there I would find those friendly people that Spain was supposedly so full of. And even better, maybe I would find myself returning to the peace and quiet of the rural areas that I enjoyed the most.

It was a rough, long climb of many days through virtually forgotten valleys and canyons before I reached the brown plains and their walled plots of olive and almond trees. But once away from the insanity of the urban jungle around Barcelona, I felt a hundred times more alive. The quiet, sunny days of bare-chested temperatures, and those high-altitude night skies with their unobstructed panoramas of the Milky Way, returned to me a lot of the magic the rats and the pollution had chewed away.

Even though I was zigzagging my way across the tabletop of the Iberian Peninsula that makes up Spain and Portugal, it seemed I was always looking *down* onto that immense harsh plain from some ridge, rather than being right on it. It was as if I were a cloud of my own, and, indeed, I hardly moved with any more speed than my white fluffy companions just overhead. I understood why it was that out of a very poor nation like Spain there had emerged such a wealth of artists and visionaries such as the world has rarely seen even in far richer nations. When one has a billion stars throwing down kisses from the farthest reaches of the universe each and every night, it isn't all that easy to keep your mind on your material poverty. As the land and winds invaded my soul, I felt that I was never more than a simple reach of the arm from the immortals.

In time, I learned to watch for certain stars and constellations to tell me if I was still heading south toward Muhammad's provinces in North Africa. I even came to know the satellites that crept across the sky each night, and the very second on my watch that they would be brushing across my nose and prodding me to call it another day, another adventure.

"Una cerveza, por favor," I said to the bartender.

"¿Grande o pequeño?"

I held my hand a foot above the gouged counter. He understood right away, and eventually returned with a tall beer.

"¿Cuantos dineros?" I asked, feeling into my pant's pockets for some more rumpled bills.

He sneered in a way that I immediately recognized as being a Spanish smile. The friendly wave of his hand said it all: "This one's on the *casa,* my friend."

"Muchas gracias, señor."

I returned to my little table by the wall and continued to fill my diary with tardy words. It was nighttime, and though I'd been at the book all day, I wasn't about to lay the pen down quite yet. For one thing, it was a good five miles to my camp in the woods, and since the temperature was around freezing, I wasn't all that eager to go back to the shivering I'd done my share of the past two nights out there in those hills. But then came nine o'clock and closing, and I had no choice but to amble on down the lane to my hideaway. I still had only that bum's blanket from Staten Island as my bed and my walking clothes as my pajamas, but I wasn't quite ready to change to anything fancier: After all, the temperatures at night had to rise eventually. I mean, here it was nearly the end of October, and I was getting so close to Africa I could *feel* it. It just didn't make sense to be carrying the weight of extra blankets when surely any day now I'd be waking up in the glow of the Sahara. Still, I sure as heck wished someone would tell these nights on the plains that.

A little yellow Renault gasped beside me and stopped. Its driver poked his black beard out the window and offered me, in Spanish-accented English, a lift. I recognized him as Jordi Canas, and the pregnant young woman beside him as his wife, Muntsa. Jordi had given me a lift into the village, Moia, the last two mornings from near where I had my tent and Clinger hidden away. He worked in the small city of Manresa, about fifteen kilometers ahead of my campsite, but this morning he had come back to the village because the water pipes where he worked had frozen.

"Someone came to my house and told me you were walking out of the village. We worry, my friend, that you will not be safe walking in the night. It is too cold, and you have no jacket. Please, Muntsa and I wish to have you come to stay in our house tonight."

He needn't have said another word. I hated being cold as much as the next man.

"We have an average of one hundred nights each year where the temperature goes below freezing," he told me as the little bug of a car whined and jolted its way down the dirt lane to where my tent was. "This is about the time the cold nights start."

The news that there were about ninety-six more cold nights to go on these plains hit me like a hammer. More and more, the Mediterranean coast was looking appealing again.

Jordi pulled the car off the road at the woods I was camped deep inside of, and pointed the lights into the trees. He was very curious (as was probably the whole village) to know how I could be so well hidden in the midst of such open territory. He followed me into the woods, and then from side to side for many minutes. In the headlights the forest looked very different, and even I couldn't find my campsite. Then I stumbled onto it. Jordi was amazed at how difficult it was to spot something the size of a tent in just a little patch of scraggly trees.

I placed the journals, my groceries, and the liter bottle of water in the tent, and we dashed back to the car's cold seats. I was confident that no one would steal my gear while I was in Moia. I knew from plenty of experience in sleeping out on the walk that robbers do not go tromping about in the middle of the countryside on cold or rainy nights. They are as lazy as the rest of us when it comes to choosing between a warm bed and work.

My guardian angels lived in the center of Moia, on a claustrophobic side street beside the town hall, the Casa de la Villa. Their three-story, narrow house was, like most homes in a town setting, without any front or side yards and packed against the other buildings like the blocks in a wall. Over three hundred years old and formerly a warehouse, it was in various stages of "weekend remodeling" by Jordi and any friends who could be persuaded to work for *cerveza,* good feelings, and big helpings of Muntsa's delicious cooking.

My bed was a mattress and box springs on the floor of the living room. My heater was the fireplace, and my crickets the ticking of a grandmother clock. It had been two weeks since I'd last slept under a roof. And man, oh, man, did it feel *good.* If I ever made it back to Bethel, there was no way I'd ever again take having a roof over my head as anything less than fantastically wonderful. Ditto for showers, hot water, meals, and washing machines. Daniel Boone was looking more legendary by the day, in my eyes.

When I'd left Bethel on the worldwalk, I'd estimated that I would be spending around 70 percent of my journey in others' homes. Boy, was I off. To date, I had walked over 2,700 miles, and been on the journey 204 days. In that time, I'd slept in a home eighty-six nights, or around 40 percent of the time. The rest of the nights had found me sleeping everywhere from cemeteries to abandoned houses, park benches, convents, under many a bridge, even on the side porches of occupied houses. Never did I ask for permission, and yet amazingly enough, only once was I caught trespassing. That had been in France, in Normandy, when the rain caused me to stay late in my tent in a farmer's field one morning. The gendarme sent to see who was inside my tent, checked my passport, and kindly let it rest at that.

In the morning, Jordi dished up a breakfast of eggs, bacon, toast, and coffee—and some of the still-sleeping Muntsa's almond cookies from a covered dish on the counter. I thought wistfully of how, before the walk, I had enjoyed eating every morning a breakfast of four eggs, four pieces of bacon, a large bowl of cereal, a couple of glasses of orange juice, and sometimes my favorite—a chocolate malt. And now, except for the kindness of people like Jordi, I usually had nothing more than whatever was inside Clinger when I awoke: a candy bar, or a piece of leftover bread and some sausage. Sometimes, when I passed no towns or houses, that bite of sausage and piece of bread might be all I had to eat for days. And yet I could still find the energy to walk twenty-five miles each of those days. My respect for the human body was growing every mile. When we had to be, we could be as tough as anything alive.

Jordi served up another cup of coffee and seemed eager to talk with me as much as he could before giving me back to the roads. The house, he went on to tell me, was a gift of sorts from his father-in-law. It was the custom in Spain to pass such things on to a son-in-law, eventually.

"Very few young couples in Spain own their own home," he said. "It's just too expensive, and wages are too low."

He made around sixty-five thousand pesetas a month working for the government, which was about five hundred dollars. But Muntsa did even better as a kindergarten teacher: eighty-five thousand pesetas a month, or about seven hundred dollars. With their combined wages, they could buy

the necessities they needed and pay back the bank loan at twice the rate
their contract stipulated.

Life was good for them—much better than normal for a young married couple.

"Many of my friends have higher degrees, but there is no work for
them to use their educations in. It is very frustrating, because they had
expected to make a lot of money. But, instead, they are baking bread or
driving taxis, for maybe twenty-five thousand pesetas a month.

"Others stay in school. For them there is *nada.*"

He had gone to school at the University of Barcelona for seven years,
and had graduated with a master's degree in biology. Unable, however, to
find any related work for the first year out of school, he and Muntsa had
survived solely on her teaching salary.

His occupation for the moment was explaining Spain's fauna to
school children from a government-sponsored traveling exhibit. Each day
he drove to Manresa, fifty kilometers to the south of Moia, to explain in
classrooms the plants they had arranged in the town's exhibition hall. He
usually put in many extra hours every week, at no overtime pay. But he
hardly minded. He was all too thankful to have work for his degree.

Things could be worse, he assured me. Under the last ruler, the
dictator General Franco, conditions had been very bad. And though life in
Spain was not the best, Jordi was positive it would steadily improve.

"Under Franco, it was like there was a big dead weight on our shoulders. Everyone was so afraid. After dark, there wasn't as much laughter
and song as you see everywhere now.

"We students at the university hated him so much. I protested with
my friends several times for a democracy." He rapped the table for em-
phasis, then looked at me with a big grin and exclaimed, "Oh, how we
danced and sang with joy, when we heard the news that Franco had finally
died!"

Now, though, some of those very same protester friends of his were
wondering just how acceptable the idea of a democracy was. For one
thing, there was still a lack of work.

"And the United States—our role model, you could say—is fighting
in so many places in the world," he said irritably. "We are so baffled why
your President Reagan wants to direct everything that happens in all the
countries. It's as if America is trying to be like Rome was."

"What country are you from?"

"Why, America," I answered, surprised.

I looked more closely at the short, dark-haired villager I'd accidentally bumped into. He looked to be the last person in Spain to be speaking such refined English. With his broad shoulders, thick, crooked boxer's nose, faded denim pants, old corduroy jacket, a straw carrying bag hanging from his left shoulder, and a large, dark sickle in his right hand, he didn't look the type to be so well schooled in my language.

"Follow me," he commanded, offering no explanation.

He rushed down a shadowed street of stone and cement homefronts pressed as tightly against each other as pieces of a puzzle. Further and further, into a narrowing vista of cobblestones and dust and cracked flowerpots on crooked ledges, I allowed myself to be led without a clue as to why.

Clear to the other side of the little village of Calders we went. Then, turning to the right, my mystery guide pushed open a steel door in the base of a three-story stone building. I followed his strong back through the door and across the dirt floor of a root cellar cluttered with burlap sacks, sleepy-eyed cats, large wooden casks, and rusted bicycles limp with flat tires.

He turned and nodded at the bicycles. "Usually, I ride a bicycle to work. But as you can see, *mine* has a flat. And right now I don't have enough money to have it fixed. Sooo . . ." He scrambled up some wooden steps sagging and smooth with probably decades of use. They were so steep and narrow that going up them was like climbing a ladder. I had to slip out of Clinger, so I could fit my way through the hanging tools and junk on the sides of the stairwell.

"Do not hit your head," he warned.

On the other side of the rough plank door at the top, we emerged into a kitchen barely large enough to hold four people. It reminded me of *Hansel and Gretel.* Bent pans, iron pots, and oil-burning lamps clung willy-nilly to gnarled roof beams. In a cavernous arched stone fireplace of sooty sides, there hung above a crackling wood fire a witch's pot in the crook of a meat hook, its frothy stew all black and bubbling and spitting.

Even before I'd stooped to enter the room, my nostrils were aware of what smelled to be the best food aromas since France. And when I saw a pretty auburn-haired woman bent over a sizzling wok of chicken necks and wings, the "hungries" attacked me like a gang of football tacklers.

Said the man: "Please forgive me, er—"

"Steve," I answered.

"Please forgive me, Steve, for rushing you here. But I didn't want you to go away before I had a chance to bring you to my house to meet my wife." He pulled me to the lady's side, and in Spanish said to her, "Imma, do you know who this is? He is from America! I met him now on the street."

She seemed thrilled for her husband, whose name was Pep Cruell. She nodded at me with a big smile, while chicken entrails hung from both her hands. I was content just to nod back.

Imma, Pep said proudly, was a very talented batik artist, and apologized that she knew little English. That was no problem, I assured him, because I could speak fairly fluent Spanish. And to prove it, I asked her what she was cooking.

Shyly, she answered, "I'm trying to learn to do 'macrobiotic cooking.' I hope you will let us test it on you."

She could test it on me as long as she liked. It was torture being there without any of it already on its way to my stomach.

"Imma will bring the food around two P.M.," Pep said, planting a kiss on her forehead.

It was as if he had said I was being condemned to starvation. "Bring it to where?" I asked, confused.

He laughed at our mix-up in communication. "I am sorry. She spends every morning fixing a big lunch to bring to me in the almond trees, where I work. I was going there when I saw you in the village. I wish that you will please be our guest today and tonight, and that you will come to see where I work. I have many questions to ask about America, especially that place with all the Spanish names—California. You are my first American. I did not want to miss this chance to learn about your country. If you are tired, you can stay here. I will hurry to do my work, and come back soon."

I chose to go to the fields with him. I thought the experience of harvesting almonds would be interesting. Also, I could practice my own schoolbook Spanish. So Pep said good-bye to Imma, and like Tweedledum and Tweedledee we hurried off to the sun and dew of the gnarled groves on the edge of the village.

All morning we shook the dark, small, hard nuts from trees that were almost twice my height. It was slow and physical, but actually very easy once a rhythm was found. As if the trees had done something terrible and had to be punished, we went to each and every one and smacked its many outstretched crooked fingers with long switches. Then, quickly, we'd step back to watch the small, oval-shaped nuts shower onto burlap cloths on the ground. The day was deliciously warm and cheery, with enough sun and fragrance to be straight out of a postcard. All morning the dry, thin air sang with the whacking of our poles against the trees, and the almonds leaping from the limbs like so many surprised locusts. The noise the nuts made tumbling into each other was like that of a million dry leaves whipping across a dusty road in the wind. Empty burlap sacks that earlier had looked mighty spacious to me were quickly filled and placed into fat brown rows as high as my chest.

It felt good to be doing some sort of labor other than walking with a backpack. The sun was hot enough that I stripped to my pants, and then to some jogging shorts someone had recently given to me. No sooner would I perspire than the thirsty breezes would snatch at the moisture and leave me tingling all over, as though I could somehow feel each and every atom in my clothes-weary flesh.

It wasn't until around two-thirty that Imma, their seven-year-old son, Pepit, and that fantastic-smelling lunch arrived. In Spain, declared Pep with appropriate joy, lunch was the most important part of each day. I was fully expected to be every bit as lazy and voracious as I wished for the next two to three hours. All the rest of Spain was likewise shutting down even as we talked and laughed, and Pep joked that now was the time to be making love to my taste buds and snore bugs.

Under the picnic-perfect Mediterranean sun, we filled ourselves with the main dish of eggplant, rice, chicken, peppers, carrots, onions, celery, and garlic, and the generous side dishes of a flat gray tortilla called Indian bread, steamed and buttered garden-fresh cauliflower, three tart bottles of wine, and airy chunks of homemade bread iced with a homemade marmalade made from the nectar of a fruit that Pep said resembled an apple but was bitter uncooked.

Physical work, a warm and pleasant late-autumn sun, delicious food and wine, Spanish words spilling off happy lips . . . This was a scene from a Hemingway novel, and yet *I* was in it, not merely reading about it.

Around four, our snoozing heads woke one by one, as if an alarm had gone off. There was no way we could have known the time for the siesta was over, but the slight coolness beginning to flavor the air ever so lightly was probably a good enough hint. Imma gathered into her picnic basket the empty wok pan and wine bottles, and Pep and I reached for our "tree whips." Pepit ran on ahead of Imma, for he still had a couple of hours of school.

The work went faster and easier now that our bodies were rejuvenated by rest, good cooking, cool, pure, unpolluted air, and, most invigorating, the Spanish sunset. After spending almost a fourth of my life watching sunsets from a prospecting camp in the unearthly folds of the Red Desert, the roaring floors of oil rigs in Montana and Wyoming, and now all those months on the road in lands of leprechauns and kings and cathedrals, I considered myself something of an expert appraiser of such sky paintings. And even Salvador Dali would have rated the sunset that evening to be worth all the diamonds and rubies known and unknown. Every shade of red and orange known to painters soaked into the earth and plants, and from even the creeping shadows there shone a nearly invisible blush that suggested they were not forgotten either. As always, I was reminded by the halo of the sun that I had much to rejoice in every single day I was alive.

By anyone's reckoning, the day had been the stuff of many an office worker's daydream. And in the home of the siesta, it was only beginning.

Pep and I worked past that sunset and collected nearly one thousand pounds of the fingernail-size nuts. We waited for the grove owner's son to come in his pickup and collect both the harvest and us. There were eight bags of the nuts, weighing 100–120 pounds each. It seemed a lot to me. I figured Pep had some nice money coming. But that wasn't so. In fact, he was in a bit of a huff, because two of the sacks were larger than the rest. With everything to be divided three ways—among him, the owner of the trees, and the owner of the land—he didn't know who would get the larger sacks, and thus more money. The poorest of the three, Pep was sure he would be the one who'd have to settle for the smallest share of the nuts.

Still, if he could keep up such a brisk pace for the whole two weeks it would likely take to harvest the grove, he'd have about five hundred dollars' worth of nuts as his share.

"That's not bad money for two weeks' work, even in the States," I assured him.

"Not that bad, is it?" he said, feeling better. He frowned. "Of course, don't forget, Imma and I still have to take off the shells. And that will take a long time."

If it had been me, I would have been too depressed even to attempt such a living, I thought. I could never kiss my American flag enough.

Pep and Imma normally did the shelling each night in front of the fireplace, with their sons Pepit and twelve-year-old Pol helping, when they weren't doing their homework. Tonight, though, it wouldn't be possible, Pep explained, because the wood for the fireplace was still too green to burn, and the house would be too cold.

The grove owner's son dropped us off at Pep's house. We went inside only long enough to get Imma and the boys and head to the third phase of a Spaniard's day (after work and lunch), the local pub. The bar was only one minute away and didn't have any sign out front. I ducked through a low door to come into a quiet room of beamed ceilings, rough white plaster walls, and a roaring fireplace that made the room as warm as hospitality can get. It was surprisingly empty, which allowed us prime seating at the fireplace's hearth. I leaned back in a stuffed chair in a semicircle with the others, and Pep ordered a round of Damm beer. I knew I probably had more money in my pocket than he saw in a whole year, and I offered to pay. But he wouldn't listen. He had the bar owner add the beers to his tab, which was already over the five-thousand-peseta mark.

While we relaxed and talked in both English and Spanish, Pep would take chunks of bread from the boys and Imma and skewer them onto a wire, dip them into olive oil, and then roast them over the open flames. They were delicious, especially when Pep sliced chunks of raw garlic onto them. It was again a scene taken straight from the Hemingway novels of my youth.

We returned to the three-hundred-year-old home's cozy rooms of low ceilings and cramped walls covered with the crayon drawings of Pepit and of Pol, who went to the middle school in Manresa. They had no television, so while Imma worked on some dinner in the kitchen, the boys went to the stone floor beside the fireplace to draw, and Pep and I sat expanding our chests and furrowing our brows with still more talk of adventures and dreams.

Since I could speak Spanish, the entire family was able to join in, whenever something caught their ear. The charm of the evening climbed up a notch more when Imma came in with a rice and fish casserole, French-style bread lathered with soft cheese, and a crisp salad shiny with freshness. And the evening really took off when the boys each presented me with drawings they'd done beside the fireplace. One was of me with pistols shooting down tarantulas and scorpions on my path. Another was a simple line drawing of me in the scraggly beard I was still wearing from the dry miles since the last town. And still a third one was of me in my pack and colorful clothes walking around the edge of a bright green earth surrounded by yellow stars. Future Picassos, truly!

At last the house was quiet. The children had gone to bed in their room crowded with posters of Superman, Spiderman, the Incredible Hulk, Daniel Boone, Davy Crockett, and Captain America. Imma had gone to sleep beneath her batiks of dragons and stars and butterflies. Only Pep and I and a bushy white kitten were left to keep the flames in the fireplace company.

During the day, while we were gathering the almonds, Pep had questioned me incessantly about the States, particularly California. I now asked him why he had such a burning desire to visit that faraway land.

"I want more than anything to sail around the world and eventually land somewhere like California," he said softly. "That is why I couldn't let you go this morning. Not when I had the chance to find out what it is really like, from someone who has been there."

Pep had also struck me as being very admiring of Americans. It seemed to me we could do little wrong in his eyes. How had he formed that opinion of us, since he had no television, and was too poor to have a newspaper subscription? Why was it that we were such independent and brave people in his family's eyes, but not in others'?

He excused himself, went into the bedroom where Imma was asleep, and returned with a huge paperback book he handled as carefully as one might the family Bible. He placed the five-inch-thick book on the dining table and motioned me to join him there. I went over and looked down at the front cover of the book and nearly raised my brows off my face. It was something I recognized from the "flower children" days of the seventies.

"*The Last Whole Earth Catalog!* Where in the heck did you ever find that here?" I asked. The book, published in California by an "alternative life-styles" clique, was filled with listings of books dealing with the "natural" and usually cheapest ways of doing everything from natural childbirth to bartering to Pep's favorite, building boats. It even had a section listing books about walking.

The book, Pep said, had been given to him by a friend in Barcelona. He had ordered it through the mail direct from the publisher in California. The five-pound book had cost around twelve dollars, with another five dollars for shipping.

"That's not too much, do you think?" he asked, probably for his friend as much as for himself.

"Oh, no." After all, there were a lot of good stories in it, too. Like one that described how astronauts use the toilet while in space.

"I built a small rowboat from directions last year," he said thoughtfully. Then, looking me in the eyes: "It wasn't difficult at all. I know I could build a boat that would make it around the world. I know it!"

The boat he'd constructed was still in the back of the root cellar. He lit two candles and led me back down into that hole to show me the crude plywood boat. Had I come across it on the street, I would have guessed it to be a box. But I didn't say that. I admired it, and agreed he had much potential as a sailor.

"I have no car to take it to any lake. So I had to fill the boat with water to test it for leaks," he said, rubbing its side proudly. "She didn't leak at all, not one drop."

Then, to himself more than to me, he added, "Ten years . . . That is when I will try to sail around the world to America!"

That night I slept on a thin mattress on the floor beside the fireplace. The next morning, as I was leaving Calders, I heard my name being repeatedly called from somewhere far away. I turned and looked back up to the village the road was dropping away from. There was Imma, high atop one of the terraced neighborhoods, a straw carrying bag in one hand.

I cupped my hands to my moustache. For all I was worth, I shouted joyfully, *"Muchas gracias!"*

I doubted she could hear me.

But she did. For, ever so faintly, came the reply: *"De nada! . . . Mí amigo!"*

24

I ventured deeper into a Spain that, with each kilometer, became more rugged, browner, and ever poorer. It was to be a period of bathing in muddy, leach-filled trickles, of tight little valleys that screeched with the death cries of pigs being slaughtered and reeked with the stink of those still waiting. Of dark and narrow village streets where eyes peered at me from behind grimy window panes and beaded doorways, and of hotter days with even colder nights.

Unlike the other countries I'd visited, Spain's interior was not a buffer zone of gentleness from a harsher seacoast. Instead, it seemed a desert of unrelenting hardships and raw perplexities. The howling of the winds and the screams of the slaughtered animals accentuated the pain and loneliness coming back into my own soul. From a distance, this was a people who seemed to live in treeless jumbled brown colonies atop the earth's dried nipples.

Although there were many terraced hillsides of olive and almond trees, and a few dried river bottoms sprouting small vegetable gardens, there were also oceans of sagebrush, rocks, and . . . nothingness. Space so huge, so immense, that at times I felt as if I'd been set adrift on another planet.

Somewhere between poor and almost poor, the people were suspicious and frightened of my strange figure crossing their twilight zones. It was as if somewhere I had made a mistake, had turned the wrong way in the universe and come to a world of fearful, cold stares; of black-garbed figures slinking back into musty doorways like snakes into a stone wall; of dirt-encrusted dwellings clustered about the tops of ugly hills. As much a part of the dust as the boulders and scrub pine, those stranded souls sometimes actually ran from me when I turned the corners of their streets. It hurt me to see the old people flee as my tall figure approached them on the narrow, enclosed vistas of the side streets. And I found myself snapping angrily at the young boys who crowded around to stare wordlessly whenever I tried to rest from the fireball above my burned skin.

It was time, I decided, to exit to the sea. The land that had forced my imagination and soul to be even more restless than ever had brought me to the brink of striking out. The laughter was gone. I was losing my sanity.

I turned my back on Madrid and fled to Valencia, to the promise of orange groves and white-washed fishing villages, to the glimmer of azure both above and below. But the land struck back, throwing at me two days filled with rain and bitterly cold winds from the west, the direction I was trying to forget and ignore. On the second night, still dozens of kilometers from the sea, I was so weary from all the walking and all the shivering that I needed shelter and warmth very badly. But the mountain range I was straddling offered none. Only more rock, more blackness, more rain.

On the crest of a windy mountain, I paused long enough to gaze out into the darkness stretching far ahead and below my soaked feet. Scattered few and far between were the yellowish glimmers of villages clinging precariously to the surface of a tar pit.

There was so much emptiness between those lights. And between them and me, too. I felt more fragile and helpless than I cared to admit.

I pushed on. But the sense of isolation grew keener with each drop in the temperature. With my tent and blanket as soaked as the clothes on my back, the night held little promise of comfort. This was turning into a nightmare comparable to that on the Pyrenees over a month before. I repeated some silent prayers for a shelter of any kind from the rain. But there didn't look to be any hope. No one was foolish enough to have a home or farm up so high, where it was cold most of the year.

Suddenly, ahead there appeared a wobbly globe of light. Accompanying it was the whine of what sounded like a moped cycle. It danced slowly toward me. In the refractions of the raindrops, its weak light was like a small witch ball in the hands of a bodiless spirit.

Its beam blinding me, shining in my face as though I were an escapee from all that was normal and sensible, the still-invisible scooter stopped ten feet in front of me, its engine slowed to idling speed. I stopped, too, and waited, my heart pounding. I discerned a shadowy rider in dark clothing dismounting from behind the pulsating light. The stranger said nothing, only moved unsteadily toward me. I tensed, pulled my shoulders in against the pack's straps, raised my forearms just enough to cock my elbows, and flexed my fingers. The rain dripping off my cap's bill and the light's rays pricking my irises made a mockery of my night vision. The wordless driver stopped just two feet from my side. I still didn't know whether to scream or smile.

A pair of leather-gloved hands reached up to a black skullcap that hung down over the ears, like an aviator's cap from World War I. The cap flopped off to reveal a very old and wrinkled . . . peasant woman? I backed off, hoping the person would be drawn into the light.

So bent, so fragile was the lady who stepped forward, that I wondered if I might not be seeing things. Her black clothes clung soggily to her. The gray hair above her sunken, furrowed eyes glistened eerily in the light. She spoke in a hoarse whisper. Inside me something lurched, as if the sound of words from someone at such a late hour, in such an out-of-the-way place, was too much to accept. Someone so old and helpless should not have been so far removed from the warmth of a fireplace and shawl on such a forsaken night, I thought.

"Do you need a place to sleep?" she asked unemotionally, in Spanish.

"Yes. I'm very cold," I stammered.

She walked off the road almost right where we were standing. I followed her into a grove of bare, spindly limbed trees that reached out every so often and tapped me on the face. Wordless as ever, she hobbled on, never once even looking to see if I was still following. I sloshed along, too weak and racked with shivers to worry where this being no higher than my elbows was taking me.

After about five hundred meters of rough climbing, she stopped. Her crooked fingers pointed to the side of a rock cliff. There, its entrance even blacker than the night, was a cave that had been dug out of the rock. I entered and struck a match. It seemed to have been used for storing tools for harvesting almonds.

I thanked her and asked if I could pay her for her help. She looked at me dully through the dying flame, as though she did not understand the meaning of my words. Darkness suddenly doused the light. I struck another match. She was gone. I hadn't heard a thing. Down the mountain her puttering chariot charged. I watched it wobble across the sable void and wondered how she'd returned to her mount so quickly.

I scraped together a little fire from scraps of reed and lumber. Uneasily, I huddled on the dirt floor beside the scant heat, my blanket wrapped about me like an animal skin. I kept expecting her to return. But she didn't.

The next morning I left the cave and headed directly into a dazzling sun. On my face was the start of a beard, for I was tired of torturing my

burned skin with cold water shaves and had decided to let my whiskers
grow at will. I felt dirty, raw, tough.

In other words, a bit like Spain herself.

The coastline was a whole different face of Spain. Tall white condos,
resort hotels, sleek modern highways, truck stops festooned with French,
Spanish, German, Italian, and British flags and signs . . . I was thankful
it was the off-season for tourism. The traffic and the noise might have been
as much a curse as the silence had been in the highlands to the west.

On the sixth of November, after almost three thousand miles of the
journey, I saw the Mediterranean Sea for the first time. It was just before
ten o'clock in the morning, and the sea's waters reflected the gray sky as
effectively as a mirror. Looking out from beneath a fig tree across to where
the sky and sea were grafted together, I almost expected to see the flapping painted sail of Odysseus' ill-fated ship searching out his homeland of
Ithaca.

The rain came down hard that same day around eleven, while I was
between towns, in a barren stretch that didn't even boast many cacti. I slid
on the seat of my pants down a steep hill to get to shelter under a bridge.
Just as my boots spilled over the edge of the rocky arroyo at the bottom,
Clinger shifted on my back and caused me to go tumbling. I picked myself
up out of the sand and the aches three feet from the low opening to the
space under the bridge. I minced no words at what I thought of my bad
luck, only to shut up right away when I discovered I wasn't the only one
there at that bridge.

Just fifteen feet away, a ragged human form was lying under the
bridge, beside a campfire. On a filthy blanket, screened by the smoke of
the fire, his bearded and darkly dirty skeleton made him seem like a
solitary holdout from some unspeakable holocaust. I glanced into his
deeply sunken eyes, then just as quickly looked away. He was as calm and
unperturbed by my wild entrance as if he had been expecting me all along.

I didn't know what to say. It was as if I had trespassed into another
man's house. The rain was trickling down my neck, but I stayed standing
outside in the gulch, not sure whether I should go on or even speak. The
hermit shifted on his elbow and waved me in with a set of long fingers
topped by jagged black nails. I slipped out of Clinger, bent way over, and
cautiously stepped into a smoldering, crackling haze that filled my nostrils

with the pungency of rot and musk. I felt as if I were entering the crypt of an Edgar Allen Poe dream.

He took a small twig from a pile beside his head and poked it into the flames. His calmness was unnerving. I wished he'd say something. I settled into the rocky sand and eyed the crooked staff beside the man's thin legs. My eyes crept from side to side, looking for hints that others might be there with us, too. Already my imagination was turning its pages, reading into the murky hideout's beast the makings of everything from an escaped killer to a dying leper. The only possessions to betray the man's destiny were all scavengings. They were as few and humble as those of a hobo: his cheap, dirt-crusted clothes, a blackened pot boiling away on the fire, a battered tin cup with a bent fork and a rusted butter knife resting in it, a clay ewer with a busted handle, some thin strips of torn packing material for a mattress, a scrawny wool poncho that was also his blanket, an old leather woman's purse with a broken strap, and, in his hands, a dog-eared yellowed book that fluttered apart with each gust of wind.

I was sure we were alone, but I wasn't certain if that was good or bad. The storm sent a chilly mist gusting over our bones. The fire hissed, the pot spat, and the smoke hugged the other man's eyes, as if he were a long and patient companion. His black whiskers seemed frizzled from years of staring into a campfire. I brushed my hands through the heat and the silence:

"¿Cómo se llama?"

His eyes raised from the book with surprise glistening in their yellow pits. He apparently hadn't expected me to know any Spanish. He didn't seem willing to tell me his name, but then he answered very softly:

"Ricky."

Aha! The man did speak. One of my imagination's creations had been that of a deaf mute. I decided to go for broke. I told him my name and that I was walking to the south coast, to the ancient port of Almería.

"Me llamo Estebán. Soy Americano. Yo voy a pie a Almería."

That I was walking immediately endeared me to him, just as it had the bum on Staten Island I'd bought my blanket from. When I went on to state that I was trying to make it in such a manner around the whole world, he burst out with amazement:

"¿Todo el mundo?"
"¡Sí!"

Whatever it was he was cooking in the pot started to raise quite a fuss just then, so he had to poke a stick under the pot's wire-hanger handle and lift it off the flames. He set the pot on the ground, and the bubbles of the contents dissipated enough to let me see it was rice. Ricky saw how interested I was in his meal and held some fingers to his bushy lips.

"¿Tiene hambre?" he asked kindly.

As a matter of fact, I was *very* hungry. I nodded eagerly. Rice was rice, and I wasn't going anywhere. Even if he did have some horrible disease, or the water he used to cook the rice was from some ditch, the boiling should have killed any and all germs—I hoped.

Ricky sat up and grimaced something terrible with pain as he scooted himself onto his one good leg. The other leg he kept stiff and straight, as though it was lame with arthritis, or worse. Using his staff, he hobbled to the purse. He snatched it, then came back to sit again beside his side of the fire. He pulled out an extra fork, a plastic cup that had seen better days years ago, a leftover hunk of bread, and a small jar of Kraft mayonnaise. Onto two pieces of the bread and into the swollen rice gumbo went the mayonnaise. With each plunge of the mayonnaise into the turpid rice scum, I swallowed hard. Whatever was he thinking?

"Mi comida favorita," he said. *"¡Mmmmmm—deliciosa!"*

The mayonnaise-and-rice stew wouldn't have won its way into any Betty Crocker cookbook, but it was a hot meal. And besides, it was raining outside our little "kitchen," and I had a lot of space to fill behind my belly button. We each ravaged our half of the stew as if it were the best in Paris. There wasn't even a stray grain of rice clinging to the side of my cup when I leaned back at last.

No longer did our cubbyhole beneath Route N340 seem like a grave to me. Any man who shared a meal with me was a friend for life, as far as I was concerned. I reached over a side of Clinger and fished out a blue pack of French cigarettes to give to Ricky. I didn't smoke, but I figured if anyone would appreciate the taste of smoke, it would be Ricky.

Sure enough, he lit into the short, harsh-smelling cigarettes as a child would a cinnamon stick. I had plenty more where that came from, I thought happily. Back in France, about five miles before I reached the famous porcelain-manufacturing city of Limoges, a long, long convoy of French troops, under the command of "le Capitaine Roisin Philippe, Commandant de la 4e C.C., 22nd Marine Infantry" had pulled to the side of the road and loaded me down with enough canned rations and packs of cigarettes to break a donkey's back. The food, even though it was meant for soldiers trying to survive in the field, was typically French—delicious beyond comparison—and I had feasted on it for days.

But the cigarettes were another matter. I had decided from the time I spent as a youngster gagging behind the shed with my older friends that getting sick on such things was better left to the more sophisticated and cooler cats. Yet I carried the cigarettes, because I knew they were some of the best "friend makers" under the sun, especially in Europe. It seemed most Europeans lived on the things. Nothing could break the ice and get a conversation going with a stranger like offering a smoke.

I asked to see the book Ricky was so engrossed with, and he gladly handed it over, as if to see if I approved. It turned out to be a librarian's orphan. *Parte Segundo, El Paleolítico Superior y El Mesolítico* (40,000–8,000 B.C.). The chapter he was reading wasn't any more decipherable. It was titled *"La Primera Civilización de la Historia y Su Expansión Ecuménica: La Gran Época de la Caza."*

"¿Comprende este?" I asked. The idea of a college professor, let alone Ricky, being able to read through even ten pages was absurd.

But he said he not only understood the book, he had read it many times over!

"¿Qué?" I retorted.

Suddenly, this strange man before me ceased to be something of the gutters and trash bins. I sat up straighter, filled with a great surge of curiosity about him. Though many times I stumbled on my words or had to kill a thought in its bud for lack of sufficient vocabulary, I talked with Ricky about his history for at least an hour.

He was pretty sure that I was his first visitor in the three years he'd lived alone under that bridge. He had been a truck driver before a crushing injury to his leg ended that. Before he lost all his savings to the doctors —and his membership in the human race to his despondency—he had actually been well off financially and married with two children. But they, too, were now memories that hurt his head and heart to remember.

His grown children no longer knew about his present condition or his whereabouts, he said with obvious hurt. He wrote to them twice a year— on their birthdays and at Christmas—but no longer received any mail at the General Delivery in the town where he scavenged his food and water each day. Not once in the past ten years had they written, even after he had walked three hundred kilometers to visit them and the grandchildren he so proudly described.

What about his own mother and father? Were they still alive? Couldn't they have helped him?

On the contrary. He had been an orphan from as far back as he could remember. He had never known parents, or what had happened to his. It was as if he had been born to be alone and forgotten from the very start, I thought. No one had ever adopted him. He was one of the forgotten and unwanted that come and disappear in this world by the millions, and are hardly ever known, or missed, by the rest of the laughing and loving masses.

He had learned, he said, not to miss humanity. The tattered book, which had come from a trash can, was his only friend. That, and the animals of his gulch.

Limping heavily and having to stop every few meters for rest, he took me down the trickling arroyo, in the direction of the sea's murmurs. His black whiskers, frizzed by the rain, led the way to all the little friends he wanted me to meet in that scratch in the earth. From one bird nest to another we trod. All the while Ricky was telling me in a low, happy voice how many *"bebés"* had hatched right before his eyes here, and there, and there. He was a father again. He even showed me an entrance to a mouse's home, and paused over it as if he expected the lady of the house to come out and serve us a plate of seeds and cups of mint tea.

I told myself it had to be because of the rain and the lusher undergrowth nearer to the sea, but whatever the reason, there was more birdsong and movement of animals here than I'd noticed anywhere else in Spain. Ricky seemed to think it was all as usual as he moved along like a gardener—shuffling, pausing, squinting his weedy face, pointing a finger at a flower or insect.

Such a startling contrast there was between us: He confined by injury and poverty to his hole; I free as a bird. He with scant possessions; I with a huge pack loaded with expensive camera gear and gifts of clothing and food from a world that couldn't seem to do anything less than love me. I, young, healthy, and still able to turn the occasional lady's eye; he, old, sick, and as ugly as he was forgotten.

When we returned to the bridge, the dusk was even grayer from the smoke of the smoldering campfire. I hated to leave him in such a cold and forlorn spot. A part of me felt a strong desire to help him. I offered him some pesetas, but he politely refused. Instead, he gave *me* something—a pomegranate.

Back on top of the highway, I searched for something to remember this very special human being by. On the end of one of the bridge's abutments, I saw in the sweep of a passing headlight a marker reading 8/125. I wondered if I ever addressed a letter to Ricky the Hermit, Highway N340, Bridge #8/125, just south of Benicarló, Spain, would it reach him?

I walked away into darkness, the faint smell of a campfire briefly scenting the sagebrush and sea.

Several miles farther along into the night, the rains returned, more heavy than I'd seen since northern France. I retreated into a tavern in the town of Alcalá de Chisvert for a while and watched on the television a special by the famous French sea explorer Jacques Cousteau. He was exploring the Nile River. Along with a giant seaplane equipped with a kitchen, living quarters, and a laboratory, his equipment included Land

Rover trucks, a hydroplane boat, tons of cameras, and some large speed-boats.

I left about forty minutes later, the television blank from a power outage and the rain still falling. That night I slept in my tent in the mud three kilometers north of Torreblanca, curled up between my blanket and rain jacket, dreaming of Ricky under his bridge.

I rose the next morning, having decided to shave my beard. I hadn't been able to get Ricky out of my mind. Suddenly, the idea of me in a scraggly beard, especially with my thin face and hungry-looking eyes, didn't strike me as being so *bravo*.

First I attacked the beard with a pair of round-tipped children's scissors, then used water from a puddle, soapsuds, and a dull disposable Bic razor. Every scrape of the blade across my thick stubble was as if someone were tearing snagged fishhooks from my face. It was all I could do to not cry. I had gone through the ordeal of shaving with cold water a hundred times since leaving Bethel, but that didn't mean it hurt any less.

It was twelve-thirty before I got going. After shaving, I had snuck to an irrigation trough beside a nearby farmhouse to quickly bathe, as well as wash my clothes with my bar of soap.

All day long, those wet clothes inside Clinger felt as heavy as bricks. Up many long hills and through the towns of La Ribesa-Cabanes, Oropesa, and Benicasim I continued with few rest stops, however. I wouldn't let myself call it quits until just before nine—when I was satisfied the worldwalk's three-thousandth mile was behind me.

25

Being a journalist and trying to carry my "office" along on my back around the world necessitated that I pause long enough every few weeks to trim down the weight of the accumulated paperwork. I would have loved to have had the notes and interviews and spent film and recording cassettes piled away in a desktop filing system. But since I had to carry those things daily, I was forced to try to be tidier and more practical.

So most of November 12, while the previous day's soggy laundry was hanging on the pine trees I was camped among, I busied myself in my tent with a round of "office cleaning." And by the time I was on my way back down Route C3320, it was five o'clock and nearing sunset. I knew I would have to rush to get in any kind of decent mileage for the day, so I put my chin down and swung my arms widely and forcefully—for about one mile. Then I decided, as always, that rushing on a walk around the world made about as much sense as trying to add another five minutes to one's life.

A few miles along, I entered the town of Almusafes and stopped in the park to eat dinner. The usual dozen or so kids clustered around me, excited by my height and red hair. There were also the guessing games as to whether I was Irish, German, or French. No one, it seemed, ever thought I might be American, because the American was such a rare sight outside the large cities and well-known resort strips. When I left, it was with yet another bunch of inquisitive and excited kids tailing me, wanting to know *más, más, más,* about America.

The night was warm, though rainy from time to time, and scented with the flowers and fruits of a climate that was a stranger to ice and snow. At long last, after putting over 370 miles between myself and the Pyrenees, I had gone through the door to the sunny south of Spain. Just knowing that I could forget about shivering for a long time now did more for my progress than anything else could have. I celebrated by raiding an orange grove. When I entered the medium-sized city of Algemesí, my fingers were so stuck together with the sweetness of some twenty oranges that I looked as guilty as Winnie the Pooh with a honey jar.

And wouldn't you know it, no sooner did I enter the city than a policeman waved at me from a doorway on the other side of the main plaza. Realizing my face probably didn't look any less like a sunburst than my hands, I approached the blue-uniformed silhouette with a hundred sympathy-inducing stories rushing madly through my head. It didn't occur to me to say simply that I had *bought* the fruit that had transformed me into a giant flypaper.

Above the officer, in the glare of a single uncovered bulb, the words *Casa Consistorial* jumped out from the crumbling stone façade of the two-story city building as vividly as if they said *House of Conviction.* If only there had been the usual fountain in the center of the broad square, I could have washed away the evidence of my sin. But there was only a meager patch of grass and a date palm.

"Buenas noches, señor," the prematurely balding young policeman said, stepping down to the sidewalk to shake my hand.

There was no way to avoid his extended hand. I forced a smile and stuck my hand into his. He grimaced. Quickly, I started talking about my journey, to get his mind off the possibility I'd been snitching his neighbors' fruit. He listened with amazement and then invited me into the station. We stepped through the tall doorway to a cramped, cold room with stout iron bars on the windows, and just enough paper scattered on the desk to make it look as if someone had been working.

His name was Alfredo Canet Selva, the "man behind the desk," or the night commanding officer, he joked. He was twenty-four, clean-shaven, soft-spoken. And he turned out to be a good friend right from the very start. He even offered me the use of the prisoners' shower, which I gladly accepted.

Leading me to the back of the building, he showed me the lockups for the town's rowdies. They were in a sort of dungeon that he said had been built hundreds of years before. I believed him. Peering into the dark, lightless holes of the two cells, I saw something that looked not too different from the cave I'd slept in on my last rainy night in the interior.

Alfredo treated me to dinner and coffee at an adjoining *taberna.* Like the city itself, the tavern was a merry and bustling place. Though I was

virtually on the edge of Africa, the hospitality here was every bit as May-
berry R.F.D. as Aunt Bea's apple pies.

Someone suggested that Alfredo introduce me better to Algemesí by
taking me on night patrol in the car. That proposal met a chorus of
hurrahs, and so it was settled that for that night I would be a policeman.
But first there was the problem of a badge, and off to the station we rushed
to fit me for my duty. From a drawer Alfredo took a heavy thick metal
badge about three inches high and two and a half inches wide, and pinned
it on my shirt. It sure was a pretty thing. Set against a background of
silver rays spreading outward from the center was the town's crest of a
conquistador on a white horse rearing below a golden crown in a blue sky.

Just then the night patrolman, a taller, older, and stronger man
named Rafael Esteve, came hustling in from the cooling night with the
keys to their white patrol car. Like Alfredo, he was dressed in a dark blue
shirt, dark blue nylon windbreaker, brown dress slacks, and black patent-
leather shoes. He was just as mild-mannered as Alfredo, but more quick to
break into laughter or leap from the chair in excitement.

Into the car went Rafael and I, while Alfredo stayed behind to watch
the fort. The car was a tiny white station wagon that could barely hold the
driver. There were no weapons in it, no cage wire, no lights on top, not
even any radio communication equipment. It seemed more appropriate for
going on picnics than for hauling criminals.

Lots of young people were out walking along the streets, or buzzing
about on mopeds. There was a festive air. And even many old people were
strolling until after one in the morning. In France, the streets of a city of
around twenty-two thousand would have been as quiet as a graveyard by
ten, but in Algemesí there were laughter and loud voices right up till the
dawn.

"Does Spain have any *real* motorcycle gangs, like the Hell's Angels?"
I asked Rafael. Even the smallest village in Ohio had its share of big,
hairy, bad-looking Harley-riders. Maybe they were just riding monster
bikes for the fun of it, but they got the imagination flaring and the knees
knocking from time to time. Whereas in Algemesí, the young boys on
their mopeds, buzzing past the police station and around the old square
every half hour, looked too much like a circus act to be taken seriously.

Quite simply, he said, the average Spaniard was too busy trying to
scrape together an income to be spending the large dollars and time
needed to raise hell on expensive machines like Harleys and BMWs.

As he puttered down the main streets and beeped at the police station
each time he passed it, Rafael kept me busy answering questions about the
United States. He had an astounding number of misconceptions about the
level of crime and violence in America. But even as I tried to laugh off his

negative images and correct them, I knew I was beating my head against a wall. His country's media would continue to tell him otherwise about my homeland.

Rafael took me on a brief flashlight tour of the town-hall building, where he showed me a large statue of a Christian conquistador on a white horse trampling a small, dark-skinned, turbaned Moor to death. That statue had been used as the emblem on our badges and on the ceiling of the crumbling council meeting chambers. To me, it was a case of the future and not the past. In a matter of weeks, I would be with those Moors myself. And so I stared now not at the perfect white-knight hero of Algemesí but at the screaming and dying Moor. Was this an accurate picture of what was just ahead in Morocco? The Moor looked tiny and wiry, and yet anything but harmless with his fierce eyes and rough face.

I slept in my tent, in a parking space between the police station and the church. Alfredo and Rafael had offered me one of the jail cells, but I'd declined. There was no telling what creatures occupied *those* cells between prisoners.

During the night, many turbaned dark heads with wild black eyes kept coming at me. Some had knives. Others, dressed in military uniforms, dragged me into dark rooms, where I cried with loneliness. Once, I dissolved to a crowded street in what I thought was Africa, begging each dark stranger to tell my parents that I was still alive, still searching for home.

I woke with my heart pounding, lit a candle, and ran my hands through my hair. The bell in the church's clock tower tolled four times.

My homesickness was getting worse. And it had to be because Africa was so close—three hundred miles by land and one hundred by sea, by my last calculations.

In Spain, I still felt a slight umbilical cord connecting me to my country. Maybe it was the huge part the conquistadors and missionaries had played in our history. Or my memories of the Basque sheepherders I had befriended in Wyoming's Red Desert during my prospecting days. Or simply that I spoke Spanish, too.

But North Africa? It loomed in my mind not as simply another culture or series of countries, but as a hole—a black, empty hole that was going to pull me in and smother me with tragedy, if not death. All I could

remember of it were the many recent headlines about Americans being
shot and kidnapped there.

Breakfast was an immensely popular treat called a *churra*. It was
made for me by a jolly sidewalk vendor whose pushcart was at the foot of
the Catholic church's steps.

Like many of the other churchgoers on this fine second Sunday in
November, I watched with delight as the aproned man squeezed a long,
thin string of dough from the end of a metal tube into a deep vat of boiling
oil. Around and around he laid the unbroken string onto the sizzling oil.
In seconds, the dough expanded from a quarter-inch thickness to probably
an inch, with the entire *churra* being at least two to three feet across.
When it was brown, after about a minute of cooking, the man's wife lifted
the whole thing out of the oil with long wooden sticks, set it onto a
wooden block, cut it into six-inch pieces with scissors, sprinkled sugar on
the pieces, then apportioned them into small paper sacks that quickly
became soggy from the oil in the *churra*.

It was mostly doughy tasting, even with the sugar. But it was still a
bargain at forty pesetas (twenty-five cents) a sack. Some even purchased
entire *churra* rings uncut and packed to go in cardboard boxes similar to
those used for pizzas.

Rafael and Alfredo's shift had already ended by the time I woke,
around nine. So I had to go without saying good-bye to them. They had
been the nicest policemen I'd met so far. Indeed, the policemen in Spain as
a whole had to be the friendliest in the world, I decided. Not once had a
policeman in Spain asked me for identification. In France the gendarmerie
had checked my passport almost a dozen times.

Just before noon, I entered the large and even poorer city of Alcira.
Much of Alcira was a stifling conglomeration of tall, tightly packed apartment complexes of drab cement bristling with television antennas and
laundry-colored balconies. But there were thousands of caged canaries on
those balconies, their vocal cords filling the dusty, dry air with sweet
notes.

The next town, Carcagente, was smaller, with trash and loose dirt
piled on the streets and every vacant lot. I wanted to pass directly through
it, but first I needed to eat dinner. Finding an open store or café on a late
Sunday afternoon in Spain was not easy. With around twenty children
leading me on, I was directed to one closed shop after another until, at

last, I realized there would be no dinner this evening. Darkness was closing in, and the only places open would be the occasional bar, with expensive and hardly filling snacks.

I continued on, my stomach growling.

When I was nearly to the town's edge, a shout from behind made me stop. Several of the boys who had been helping me look for an open grocery store ran up to me. They were out of breath. The oldest, around thirteen, handed me a plastic sack. In it were four sandwiches wrapped in aluminum foil, two cans of sardines, two oranges, and a little can of pâté.

"My mother fixed this for you," he said.

He and his mom must have moved at the speed of lightning to have gotten the food together and to me so quickly.

"What is your name?" I asked the boy.

He looked so proudly at the other boys. "José Antonio Armiñana Sanchez."

I promised to send him a card someday from America, and he went away as happy as if I had said I was going to send him gold. I took Clinger off, sat against a fig tree, and wolfed down the delicious food.

Later, around five-thirty, I passed through the village of Puebla Larga and followed what I thought was the same road into steep, rocky hills covered with cacti resembling giant Mickey Mouse ears. By the time I realized I was lost, it was too far back to the village to think of turning around. A faint tinge of dusk on the horizon to my right assured me, however, that I was still heading south. So I pushed on, hoping that the road would eventually find its way back to the main road.

Around the very next curve in the road was a tiny village named Rafelguarde. In the light of a street lamp I squinted my eyes and studied very closely my road map. It had innumerable folds and rips in it from my taking it out of Clinger many times each day to study it. From what I could see, there was no Rafelgarde along the inland roads connecting the cities of Valencia and Alicante. Or, for that matter, any similarly spelled.

I shrugged and packed the map away.

I looked again at the crowd in the street. They were waiting to get into a nearby plain-looking building that apparently was a cinema house. I thought as long as I was lost, why not? According to a movie poster on a portable stand by the door, tonight's film was a Monty Python British comedy called *Time Bandits*. (*Héroes del Mundo* on the poster.) The admission? A mere sixty pesetas (thirty-five cents).

A fat old lady seated with a shoe box in her lap took my ticket at the door and gave me a big happy smile in return. Inside, behind a long table, were two harried women trying to keep up with all the kids waving coins and yelling for sodas, sweets, and homemade Popsicles. I pointed to some

bottles of beer in a carton behind them. They served one right up, popped
its cap for me, and took only forty pesetas. It was perfectly okay for me to
take it into the auditorium, they said, and they even offered to watch
Clinger for me.

The film was one of those that should never have been allowed to
leave the editing room, it was so choppy, so scratched, and of such poor
sound quality. And the actors' lips were always about five seconds behind
the dubbed Spanish voices.

When the movie screen went completely black about an hour into the
ninety-minute-long film, it was actually a relief. But then, to my surprise,
the lights all came on, along with what seemed the screams of a thousand
rioters. What was happening? Fire? Terrorists? Where was everyone running to so frantically?

"It is the intermission!" a young boy said as he pushed past to get his
share of candy and soda pop.

For the next twenty minutes, it was total mayhem, as no one attempted to keep the kids in order. It was as if the cinema had become a
giant playground, with kids of every shape, age, size, and scream imaginable in the middle of a giant tag game.

After the film, a dozen of the still-hyper children tagged along with
me in the darkness. The oldest was around ten, the others from probably
eight down to five. At the town's southern edge, I stopped while there was
still some light and asked if they intended to follow me all night. No, said
a little girl with a big blue bow in her hair, just to their houses.

All I saw ahead were dark, empty farm fields. The oldest boy explained that their village was about three kilometers farther on. All of
them had walked to the movie in the dusk and were now returning the
same way.

"Aren't you afraid to walk so far in the dark where there are no
houses?" I asked at one point.

"Oh, no," they took turns repeating. They just didn't seem to know
about such things.

When they were safely back in their homes, I continued to climb a
road that grew narrower and steeper. Then, over a hump I went and down
to the main road, C3320, that I should have been on all along.

Shortly afterward I settled down onto my blanket on the second floor
of an abandoned house beside a quiet spot in the road, two kilometers
north of Játiva. I looked over my map again and figured I'd gone five to
six kilometers out of my way, when I was lost. But it hardly bothered me.
I'd met Spain up close.

My walk through the southeastern corner of Spain blossomed into
yet another of those footloose love affairs with the people and their cus-

toms, even though the land was the ugliest yet. Mostly low, barren mountains covered in rocks, sage, and cacti with three-inch-long needles, the scenery when seen in the middle of the day could be mistaken for hell. But come the evening, it softened into the prettiest browns imaginable.

Some evenings, like the one when I looked down into Xativa and saw its white adobe houses, tall church tower, and crumbling fortress walls still faithfully guarding that city's tan clay roof tiles, I simply jelled into one big goose bump. The white buildings literally glowed in the pale refraction of the cloudless sky, and the bell tower rose into the rapidly cooling still air with breathtaking clarity. How ugly the world could be one minute, and how spectacular the next!

My next letter to my mom and dad ended with: "Let no one convince you there is no heaven, for it is all about us."

Almost as if the real heaven had been looking over my shoulder when I wrote that letter, six days later I met someone named Angel, as I was entering the large city of Murcia. And like angels, he and his best friend, Vincente, had me join them for lunch at their favorite tavern, El Candil (the Oil Lamp). Over plates covered with three kinds of sausages, roasted almonds, escargots, small bread slices, and some teeny cups of *very* bitter and thick coffee, Angel, twenty-seven, and Vincente, twenty-one, explained that though they shared the same last name, Martinez, they were not related by blood—only by their common love of adventure, travel, and mountaineering. Angel was short, muscular, and bearded, with thick, curly brown hair. Vincente was taller, clean-shaven, and extremely handsome—the streetwise, semi-tough James Dean type. In his jeans, dark T-shirt, sunglasses, and black leather metal-studded motorcycle jacket, he was quite a contrast to Angel's khaki slacks and dress shirt.

Angel wrote the occasional magazine and newspaper article about mountaineering and travel, and Vincente did construction work.

Both were excited at what I was doing. They brought me to Angel's apartment to talk more of our adventures, and to see his souvenirs of his own travels. On the way there, Angel said I could stay at his apartment for as long as I wanted.

In the apartment's front room were two crude workbenches covered in mountaineering gear and sleeping bags. Leading off it were rooms filled with mementos: shelves lined with seashells, fossils, meticulously mounted bugs and butterflies, African carvings, and snapshots, maps, and posters from climbing expeditions Angel had been a part of. One poster for a Murcia bank really caught my imagination: It was of a lone man standing atop a huge rock monolith, his arms outstretched to a golden-red sky melting into a horizon of silhouetted mountain peaks. It was too beautiful to be real.

"It is real," Vincente assured me. "And that man—that is Angel."

I looked at it more closely and saw that it was indeed Angel.

"Where is this place? Please show me on your maps," I practically begged him. Even if it meant going to some far corner of the world, I wanted very much to see that setting some day.

"It is *here!*" Angel said.

Murcia? That was too good to be true! I decided that my remaining 140 miles to Almería would have to wait until I had visited that place.

"How would you like a worldwalker for a guest for a few days?" I asked Angel.

He and Vincente had a cot cleared off in less than a minute.

The next afternoon we were in Vincente's old white Renault heading upward into the sky on a road as curvy as a snake gets when you grab it by the head. The mountainsides towering above us on the one side and plummeting down to infinity on the other were semi-arid and bushy, with an occasional patch of short pines.

The weather was beautiful and we were going rock climbing. Well, Vincente and Angel were. I planned only to take photographs and admire from below the monolith that was in the bank poster.

It was almost ten years to the day that I had nearly lost my life in a mountain-climbing accident in Wyoming. Until then I had been carefree and loose with heights. I'd parachuted out of airplanes, jumped off cliffs into canyon rivers, and, of course, suspended myself from rock outcrops on nylon ropes that made me look like a human spider to anyone far below. But then came that time while rappeling down a two-hundred-foot cliff that I pushed myself backward into space—only to plunge out of control when the thin rope slipped out of the guide on my harness belt.

I glanced nervously at the edge of the road that dropped off to our left. Now, it was all I could do to stand on a high bridge or look out a jet window and not feel my chest tighten. I would never forget the tumbling backward, the slamming against the cliff's side, the screaming, the falling,

falling . . . then the jolting stop, my body upside down and my head one foot from the ground.

I grimaced at the throbbing in my hands. It was as though they remembered the rope whipping wildly through them—burning through the leather gloves, then into my palms as I squeezed that rope to stop my fall. I still felt the blisters bubbling up instantly and the seared gouges from where the rope had ripped through the flesh.

Those few seconds had seemed an eternity in hell. A hell I never cared to know again.

The panorama from the top of the mountain range where the monolith sat, like a horn at the end of a sleeping rhino's long head, was nothing less than fantastic. In the immense irrigated river valley below sat Murcia, ringed by jagged mountains on three sides and topped by a deep blue sky occupied by only a few lazy white puffballs. Further to the south of us, toward Cartagena, there were scattered rugged foothills that reminded me of Devil's Half Acre in Wyoming, with the Mediterranean Sea further away yet.

The monolith was nobly named Cuesta del Gallo (Rooster Hill), and was actually two huge rocks in one—each the same height, the one sprouting from lower on the mountainside the longer and steeper.

Like two happy children, Vincente and Angel scrambled up to the monolith from where we parked the car, their climbing gear jangling from every shoulder and elbow. I was right behind with the cameras and sandwiches and water. In hardly any time at all, they were creeping from foothold to handhold toward the heavens. I sat on the round boulders below shouting occasional encouragement, but struggling inside with a voice that taunted me mercilessly for not being up there with them. It told me I had no business staying behind, hiding behind a camera, with only the flies and my fear. That wasn't like me at all. But who could explain the tremendous grip that bad memory had on my emotions?

Still, when I looked up at the others, who were obviously loving every second of the challenge of reaching the rocks' summits, a teeny light still flickering bravely in the deepest recesses of my soul reminded me of the joy such climbing had once given me. And telling me that it wasn't natural to be living with the claws of a past monster still embedded in my soul.

"Estebán!" It was Vincente who had called my name. "Estebán, come up here. The view is wonderful!"

I didn't know what to say. He and Angel, who had paused in his ascent to wave at me, knew about my climbing background, but not that I was scared of it now.

Vincente had tied one end of his rope to the top. Now, he dangled it just inches from my feet and shouted down at me to let me know I should use it to pull myself up. It was as if he were a fisherman on the surface of a lake trying to entice a fish.

It *was* tempting. I was sure the view from up there was one of the most beautiful I could hope to see on the walk.

The frustration went off inside me like a flashbulb. I sent a loose rock careening down the mountain with a swift kick. Then my hands grabbed the rope tightly.

I pulled my way up that rock's slope, my movements firm, strong, determined. Not once did I let my eyes, or my mind, slip from the smooth nylon strands guiding my hands. I only pulled, stepped, pulled, stepped— until there was no more stone before my eyes but only a huge blue sky whose winds breathed pure fresh energy into the deepest corners of my being. I'd done it!

I turned to the standing Vincente. His smile was as wide as some of the clouds. We clasped hands and he helped me to my feet. I stood unsteadily in the wind, still scared of the way the world ended only a few feet from my boots yet determined now not to let that defeat my love of adventure. I spread my legs, and then my arms, as if I were an eagle about to launch into flight.

A current of strength I'd been missing for years shot back into my nerves. I let out a big happy shout as I pointed the compass of my soul to the Mediterranean. Now, I knew what life was all about: growing through overcoming our fears.

Suddenly, I was eager to face Africa.

All the way down, I gripped that flimsy rope as if any second it would dissolve. Again I couldn't bring myself to look at the ground below. And surely I shook enough in those few minutes to last me the whole worldwalk. But at least I felt stronger and more complete in the end for having done the climb.

Angel, Vincente, and I celebrated that most special of afternoons together by stopping at the Las Tapas (the Caps) tavern in the village of Santo Angel to fill ourselves with hard-boiled eggs in lemon juice, blood sausage, tortillas with potato stuffing, and more of those teeny cups of bitter coffee. The beers came later, when all of us and Felipe, Angel's younger brother, held a boisterous all-nighter doing what Spanish men love best—boasting and arguing.

On Wednesday, November 23, I prepared to leave beautiful Murcia and my newest friends with my heart as heavy as lead. When I said good-bye, out on the city's main street with most of Angel's family and friends around me, it was five o'clock. There were so many gifts on my back that I was worried about how I was going to get out of the city with my spine intact. Along with three fossil shells of Angel's, I had a large sack of sausage sandwiches from his mom; several meat pies, or *pastels de carnes,* (the food specialty of Murcia) from Vincente; several bags of hard candy and a can of Argentine beef from Angel's sister; a liter of white wine from Felipe; and, thankfully, simply a note from his father reminding me to send him butterflies from *"todo el mundo"* for his prized entomology collection.

"Con pan y vino, se hace el camino [with bread and wine, you have the road]," Angel said as we squeezed each other's hands the final time.

"No, Angel . . ." My smile quivered. *"Con* amigos, *se hace el camino."*

So high was I feeling from the glow that was southern Spain, that when I reached the Mediterranean again on November 29 at Almería, I felt I could walk across the water to Africa. Not even the freak late-season sirocco that had belted me with a sandstorm for ten hours on November 27, in the desertlike land between Los Castaños and Sorbas, stood a chance of putting me in a bad mood.

Catching up on my notes, mailing all the accumulated gifts home, and writing my stories for the *Columbus Dispatch* and *Capper's Weekly,* as well as for the *Cincinnati Post* and the *Weekly Reader* children's magazine, which had contacted my parents to ask me for stories, necessitated that I stay in one spot for at least several days. That place, I decided, would be atop a sea cliff just west of Almería, where I could camp in privacy and have as my only companions an occasional seagull, the salty breath of the Mediterranean, and poor weary-looking Clinger.

But I came to know many Spaniards as I ventured into Almería each afternoon to buy groceries and stop at Steffany's Pub for some Cokes and air-conditioning. Sitting on the edge of the cliff in the mornings with

colorful fishing boats bobbing below on a sheet of blue, and memories of
Pep and Angel and Vincente flowing from my pen, I had to wonder how
Hemingway ever found it in himself to leave Spain behind.

So reluctant was I to leave Spain that I decided to hitchhike along the
southern coastline to take a ferry from Algeciras, rather than one from
Almería. Not only would it give me time for a few more adventures in
Spain, but it would save me a lot of money. The boat trip across the
Mediterranean from Almería was over a hundred miles long, but from
Algeciras to Tangier, across the Strait of Gibraltar, it was only forty.

And any mile on a boat that I could avoid was always a blessing to
my poor motion-leery stomach.

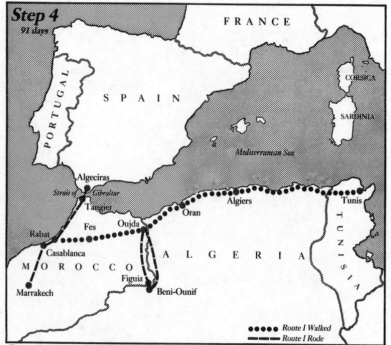

Step 4
91 days

FRANCE

CORSICA

PORTUGAL

SPAIN

SARDINIA

Mediterranean Sea

Algeciras

Strait of *Gibraltar*

Tangier

Algiers

Tunis

Oran

Rabat

Fes

Oujda

T U N I S I A

Casablanca

A L G E R I A

M O R O C C O

Figuia

Marrakech

Beni-Ounif

●●●●● *Route I Walked*
▬ ▬ ▬ *Route I Rode*

December 10, 1983 to March 9, 1984   1,202 miles

26

"It's totally insane" . . . "another world" . . . "too dangerous for a lone traveler" . . . "they kept coming at us . . . pawing, reaching . . ."

The frightened faces, the trembling words, the disgust, the fear, the hatred. All day at the port in Algeciras, Spain, the travelers who had just disembarked from the Morocco ferry stammered and cried through one horror tale after another.

Alain, a Swiss student, told of two Moroccan men bursting into his motel room and choking him. "I-I cried like a baby. I didn't want to die," he said frantically, crying again as he reenacted how one of the men had grabbed him so hard around the neck that he had been unable to breathe.

Juan, a Spanish soldier, described a society growing poorer and more desperate each day, especially now that Saudi Arabia had stopped giving the monarch-ruled Northwest African nation any more money. "In a car, you are half-safe. But on foot, you'll be robbed in no time," he warned me sternly, insisting that I must always go somewhere by taxi or bus.

Even the ticket-counter clerk tossed out words of caution: "Never, I repeat, NEVER let them know you are American or have any money with you. In Morocco, a lone American traveler has no friends. Only those who want your money."

Only one person, an American adventurer named Philip, offered hope. A Steve Canyon look-alike, he had lived, loved, and fought all over the world since leaving an America thirteen years ago that, to him, had become little more than "one giant department store."

"The Moroccans know how the tourist mind works, and they prey on it, play on your fears. It's all a mind game to them. Stand up to the jerks. Tell them to go to hell. Inside, they're nothing but cowards," he said in a low, rock-steady voice.

Less than six hours later, in the dead of a December 9 night, on an unlit and narrow street in Tangier, Morocco, a port that Mark Twain had once described as a snake pit of thieves and killers, I was to put Philip's advice to the test.

It was nine-thirty, cold, misty, with policemen all about, when my Moroccan ship finally docked in Tangier. For three hours, the ship had plowed uneasily through the storm-tossed seas of the Strait of Gibraltar. I should have been only too glad to step onto Africa. But I wasn't. I was scared.

With each roll and dip of the huge boat on the crossing, I had wished that Neptune might see fit to let me die a graceful death. Stormy seas and I went together like vinegar and baking soda. Besides, I had ended up in the deepest of the holds with a roomful of Moroccan men returning home to their tents. And with sunken spirit, I'd had to watch as they picked at their long crooked teeth with a gleaming knife blade, or spat a half-chewed bone onto the floor, or burst into a fit of screaming and crazed laughter.

Now, there was the scene awaiting me below on the shore. Lining the rotted buildings and walls about the dockyard were dozens of the men-of-prey others had told me about. Almost all of them were wearing long, dark, hooded robes that covered their bodies from their ankles to their heads, so that they looked like the faceless priests of a satanic rite. I had no doubt that beneath their loose robes were scarred fingers clutching curved daggers.

Though the other passengers disembarked with little trouble, I stayed behind, partly out of fear and partly to survey the arena below. No sooner did the passengers clear the customs tables beneath the murky bulbs of the old warehouse than they literally ran into waiting taxis. But I was determined to walk from the ship to the city lights a kilometer away—as insane as that might be.

Reluctantly, I shouldered Clinger and joined the receding line of passengers trying to leave the ship. In my pocket I had the name and address of an American doctor and his wife who lived in the south of Morocco, near the Sahara Desert, in the nine-hundred-year-old city of

Marrakech. Though I had never met them, they had written several months ago to my home in Bethel to invite me to stay with them if I came through Morocco. They were subscribers to *Capper's* and had been reading my stories of the walk. I felt it would be nice to have an American family to spend the approaching Christmas season with. Besides, in the safety and comfort of their home, I could take the time I needed to prepare for the African phase of my walk. And to take a good long rest: Spain hadn't exactly been a nursery school.

A heavy tap on my shoulder caused me to jump. It was a policeman who motioned for me and a young Jewish couple with a month-old baby to step out of the line. I did so, confused and somewhat angered. The Jewish couple, from Israel, looked as if they knew all too well what came next.

I was led by two other policemen along the ship's corridors to a small room that I recognized as the ship's security office. I had gone there earlier in the journey to have my passport stamped for entry into Morocco. The same burly officer was there in his wooden stiff-backed chair, along with someone in a brown trench coat and with a dangling cigarette.

The *inspecteur* glanced at a card on the table. I recognized it as the entry card I'd had to fill out. He asked if I was a journalist.

He already knew the answer; it was on the card.

Whom, the policeman asked, did I work for?

"I'm independent," I replied.

"*Whom* do you work for?" he demanded impatiently.

I glared at him and repeated the truth: I was independent.

He became angry and threatened to send me back. Either I tell the name of every publication I wrote for, or else I could forget Morocco.

I thought a minute, smiled, and smugly lied:

"The *Picadilly Times-Review.*"

"Tell us the address."

I was in no mood to argue. "Picadilly, Alaska, U.S.A."

He looked at the policeman in the brown uniform, who lifted the card and read my name off:

"Steven Mark Newman."

I shrugged. So?

"Newman. Isn't that a Jew name?" he asked.

"No, it is not," I replied, with a hard expression.

He seemed to like that very much.

He waved me on my way. At the gangplank, I found Clinger leaning undisturbed against the railing. I had been sure they would have torn it apart to look for *something*. The Israeli couple was also there, huddled against a wall with a policeman nearby. The policeman was looking at some long forms he'd pulled from the man's black briefcase. The fallen face of the wife told me all I needed: They were going back to Spain.

At the customs counter the officer in charge asked if I was the American. I said I was. To my surprise, he told me to go straight through to the exit. They didn't need to check my pack. I snapped Clinger's wide, thick waist belt tightly together, snuggled the blades of my shoulders deeper into the wall of cushions I had stretched across the part of the pack resting against my back, and slipped a hand into my jacket to feel for the hard, cold, rounded metal tip of my hunting knife's handle. It was right where Philip said it should be.

"Hey! My friend! My friend! Quick! You go in my taxi to hotel. Here." The driver grabbed at my pack, naturally assuming I had no choice but to ride in his taxi, since he was the only one left. I pulled away politely and explained I wanted to walk. He looked at me as if I had said I wanted to kill myself.

"No! You must take taxi. No, no! It's not safe. No walking, my friend. You will be killed. Come now, I take you right to hotel." He ran after me, took hold of the pack again. This time, I practically had to wrestle it away. He put his fingers to his head and shouted with huge eyes, "You crazy? No walking! Many bad men here. My taxi safe, good car. I your friend!"

I had no doubt he was, but once I had something in mind, I could be as stubborn as a team of jackasses. He continued screaming, flung some obscenities my way, and spun away in his taxi, his wheels ripping apart the black scummy puddles of the dockyard like so many bags of blood.

For a few moments, I was alone with only the sounds of a yelping dog in the distance, and the splash of my footsteps hurrying along a dilapidated street that grew dimmer with each stride. Then . . . they advanced from the sides, from rotten wrecks of buildings that even rats would have avoided. They came like jackals—hungry, desperate, and mean.

I walked straight, looking neither right nor left, and tried to ignore them. But my heart was tearing at my chest, my mind refusing to believe what I was seeing. My God, they looked every bit as wretched as the walking dead. Before I knew it, I was trapped in a shoving, pulling, yelling, fighting, tearing mob of robes and hoods and clawing hands.

"Cheap hotel! . . . Cheap drugs! . . . My friend! . . . I'm your friend—not him! . . . No, listen to me! . . . English? . . . Speak English, my friend? . . . *Parlez-vous français?* . . . Come here, my friend. . . ."

They fought for my attention, they fought among themselves, they screamed and choked and punched every bit as wildly as a frenzied tribe of baboons. I looked down, kept moving, so scared I couldn't utter a single word. Their hands slapped my face and tore madly at the zippers on poor Clinger. I thought any second I would lose my mind. Instead, I nearly lost something more.

He was as ugly as a corpse that had been resurrected from the torture dungeons of the Inquisition. From the oval of his pointed black hood's opening, there stared out at me a skeletal face that left no doubt I was about to die. In the faint light, its lone eye burned into mine. I made myself look at the wide, horrible scar running down the face from the hole that should have been his right eye, at the four or five yellow stalactites that were his teeth. The others stood back, as if it had silently been communicated to them that I was no longer theirs . . . but his alone.

He pulled a switchblade from beneath his robe and snarled, "Say something! Why won't you talk to us?"

I glowered at him and at the knife.

"Talk! Give me money! You want to die?" he said, moving nearer and nearer.

It was as if an atomic explosion had been triggered inside me. All the disgusts, worries, and frustrations, and now the horror of the scene, fused into one and turned my fear into violent anger. How dare *he* threaten to kill someone whose only wish was to be friendly? I whipped out my hunting knife and pointed its long blade at his one eye.

"ME die?" I screamed furiously. *"YOU* die!"

He looked as if he'd seen a ghost. His mouth dropped open, and he turned tail and ran away down a side street, behind a donkey-pulled cart.

I turned on the others, sneered death and dismemberment. They, too, fled down the gutters.

But three remained with me as I walked into the city to find the bus station and the bus to Marrakech. My "guides" kept insisting that all buses to Marrakech had left, that it was better for me to stay in real cheap hotels they knew, or in their houses, that the next bus leaving for Marrakech would not be until ten in the morning.

I tried to stop a policeman to report the knife attack and get directions to that invisible bus station. But the policeman continued walking, ignoring my shouts. And at that moment I knew for sure what I had feared all along: In Morocco, if not in all of North Africa, I was totally on my own.

I shoved my way past the hustlers and hucksters into a small tobacco shop. In Spanish, I pleaded with the owner to tell me the way to the station. He led me to the door and pointed to the street I should take. It was the same one I had just come up on from the docks. According to the shopkeeper, the station was only a couple of hundred steps from the ferry wharf, and if I hurried, I could still catch the bus to Marrakech, because it always left late.

I marched back into the same nightmare I had just come through. Increasingly, the hustlers returned, ever more vehement in their demands for my money and attention. Fortunately, they kept a respectable distance as they tried to get me to part with some of the Moroccan dirhams I'd changed a traveler's check for at the Spanish port.

Not until I was on the bus to Marrakech did I feel I was out of immediate danger, and did I acknowledge just how awfully scared I really was.

When I thought of the scene around me: filth on seemingly everything, families in rags hovering around open fires, beggars rushing from gutters and back alleys, women with every inch of their bodies covered except for their eyes, wild-looking dogs running loose and fighting over bloody goat heads tossed into the streets by the merchants, garbage of all sorts strewn about, I cried inside that this time I'd gone too far. *Dear God, I cannot possibly live walking alone across this country.*

As if to confirm my fears, as the bus pulled away from the station, two hours late, there was a loud THUMP! at my window. Outside, my hooded "friends" were letting me know they were angry I hadn't handed over my dirhams.

I shuddered. Next time, I knew, there wouldn't be any window between my body and their fists.

What a relief it was to see Tangier swallowed up by the night. But the bus ride turned out to be another nightmare.

At the turn to the airport, we ran into our first police checkpoint. An hour later, the bus stopped at a second roadblock, this one on an isolated, completely dark stretch of road. Again plainclothes policemen in leather jackets came on board and demanded to see every Moroccan passenger's "national ID" card. Sitting there in the unlit, cold interior of the bus, with the passengers afraid to look up at the machine-gun-toting officers, I couldn't help feeling I had been transported back to the time of Stalin and Hitler.

From what I could see through the rain sliding across my window, as the bus droned on through the night, the terrain outside was flat and sparsely covered with some sort of desert scrub. We frequently passed robed men and veiled women standing along the road's shoulders, even though there seemed to be no village or town nearby. What could those stragglers be doing out there way after midnight, and in such weather?

The third police roadblock was around 1:00 A.M. Again, in the black nothingness of an unpopulated stretch of desert, leather-jacketed thugs demanded everyone's national-identification cards. This time, there was a scream. Everyone quickly looked down and tried to sink lower into the hard seats. A Moroccan woman in a white dress and veiled face was dragged off as she pleaded something in Arabic. I waited with pounding heart for someone to object to the police brutality. But there was silence as the bus driver hurriedly rammed us deeper into the darkness of a continent I was fearing more each minute.

The bus slipped into Rabat, the capital of the kingdom—and my pessimism increased. As the residence of the monarchy, as well of other nations' embassies, it should have been a beautiful and impressive place. Instead, one filthy, unpainted, and unfinished cement-walled building after another passed my window. And idle men were milling everywhere.

I realized that in such a place I'd stand out like a blazing sun. Even in my worst clothes, I'd look rich by comparison to those outside my window. Anyone could—and would—deduce that my backpack must be filled with objects worth many, many dirhams.

This is absolute craziness, I had to admit to myself. *There's no way you can walk across this country. You'll never live, Steve.*

In Casablanca, I was transferred to an old school bus for the remaining four-hour ride to Marrakech. The luggage loader saw fit to charge me three dirhams (about seventy cents) for handing my backpack up to another man on top of the bus, who was strapping together a small mountain of everything from chickens to rugs to mail bags. All I had was a fifty-dirham note. I went to the ticket counter, but they didn't have change for a note that wouldn't pay for the ink on a ten-dollar bill.

All too happily, the loader took the fifty-dirham note and rushed out onto the streets to get change. I kissed that money good-bye. But then I was surprised (shocked!) to have him return with the proper change. I gave him the three dirhams, but he wanted one more for getting the change!

On board the bus, I looked once more through the plastic bag I'd stuffed with the camera, log books, tape recorder, tent, and blanket. I didn't trust those Moroccans an inch.

Against a chorus of bumps, creaks, and squawks, I tried to carry on a conversation with an attractive blond-haired French woman seated beside me. It was difficult enough to try to make myself understood speaking French with my mouth operating normally, but trying to do so with my mouth closed against the dust and flies was like talking while gagged. Still, she was a salesperson, and had learned to put up with a lot stranger conversations in her time. Her name was Marie-Jo Boucher and she was from La Chapelle-Pontaneyaux.

She explained to me that she was in real estate, and was in Morocco for two weeks to sell Swiss ski-resort condos to French nationals living there. I looked at the moonscape in the background behind her head and thought that maybe her idea wasn't all that crazy. One year of that desert, and I'd probably pay her asking price of 200,000 francs just for an igloo in the Yukon.

She was nice enough to spend a lot of the time to Marrakech teaching me Arabic phrases she thought I would find useful in North Africa. I wrote them down as she said them in her French accent, knowing that Muhammad would have turned in his grave at the way I spelled the Arabic sounds. But at least they gave me a faint feeling that maybe I would be willing to walk across Morocco after all. Just in case, I thought of key words I would need, and she gave the appropriate phrase or word in Arabic:

Bread: *Rooobs*
Water: *Eyema*
Milk: *Leeeb*
Beef: *Veeown*
How are you?: *Labess?*
Good morning: *Sba el rere*
Good-bye: *Slama*
Thank you: *Shokhan*

I thought of the beggars who boarded the bus at every stop and went through asking for money. There had to be some way to let them know I was not an endless source of handouts. Marie-Jo thought a minute, then told me to say, while pointing piously upward, *"Allah ajeeb."* (God likes to give.) And if they were still persistent? She laughed and stamped her foot and mimicked herself getting very angry and shouting *"Makench flooss!"* (I have no money!)

I laughed, too. It felt good to have something about Morocco that I *could* laugh about. My spirit sparked for the first time since I had left Spain. Outside in the east the sun poked above the gray, barren wastelands at long last. I sat up and noted with excitement, rather than fear, my first sunrise in Africa.

There were few other vehicles on the road. Most people were on foot, or donkeys, or camels, and all were dressed in the traditional caftans or veils. The laborers on the roads and in the fields were already at work, even though it was barely past seven. Their tools seemed those of a century before: horse-drawn plows, picks and shovels, and hoes. Donkey-pulled carts and camels far outnumbered any motorized traffic.

The bus stopped at seemingly every little roadside market that popped up out of the flat, treeless plain. And right on cue, at each stop, hobbling skinny men on crutches would pass along the bus aisle begging in a singsong voice for a bit of a handout. Then would come the blind people, led by others to the front of the door to reach out to those going for refreshments. Then the aspiring evangelists, serious-looking young men in striped robes and red fezzes, would beg aloud in arrogant tones for money for Allah.

My French lady friend would not budge from her seat to experience the outside world, but I couldn't sit still with all those delicious smells coming from the cooking grills at each stop. Close to Marrakech, I finally got out of my seat, ventured down the aisle to the door, and stepped off into a maddening rush of everything from shoeshine boys to yet more beggars missing all sorts of appendages. I followed some passengers to what seemed to be the Moroccan version of a quarter-pounder. A purchaser went to a stall where goat carcasses hung from hooks, pointed to the part of the goat he wanted to eat, and then waited patiently as that part was attacked with a giant butcher knife. After having his purchase weighed on a scale, he would hand the bloody meat to a young boy, who fried it over hot coals and then slapped it between hunks of bread that looked like the cow patties back home.

I had just about decided to try one when a fly-covered goat head on a nearby table caused me to hesitate just enough to miss out on the treat. Rushing back to catch the bus, I had barely enough time to grab a large bottle of Coca-Cola and two hard-boiled eggs. The price for everything was only two and one-half dirhams, or forty cents.

Things were definitely looking up.

Mercifully, my motorized stagecoach ride ended about half an hour later in the Marrakech bus station. Naturally, the man who unloaded Clinger from the top threatened to hold my dear friend ransom for two dirhams. This time, I paid without even a peep of complaint. I was beginning to soften considerably, a definite sign that I was actually starting to like where I was.

There were the usual hustlers who rallied at the sight of my backpack, but they didn't seem quite so dangerous in the sunlight. I told them I was visiting my parents. I don't think they believed me, for they kept asking where my parents lived. Then I hit upon the—I thought— brilliant idea of speaking in Russian, which I had studied for two years at the university. That did the trick. Everyone knew all Americans were millionaires, but Russians?

I looked at my slip of paper with the doctor's name and address. *Dr. & Mrs. Clifford W. Jaquith, Post Restante Guelez, Marrakech.* I hadn't the foggiest idea where Post Restante Guelez might be. The only clues I had were some scribbled instructions Mom had given me on the telephone, when I'd last called in France. According to what I could decipher of my notes, I was to go down the Rue Sourya, then take the branch-off to Mohammad V, where the movie boards were posted, then go to the end of the street (what street?) to a dead end at a wall. There I was to look for a gate on the left with their name and four white birds on it. That was it. Nothing more.

And I didn't have a map of the city, or a telephone number for the Jaquiths (if they had one).

I flipped a coin and set out in the winning direction, and along the way I asked every policeman, beggar, and even two Swiss tourists for directions and help. Within an hour, I was at the gate with the four white birds painted on it. It was kind of a miracle, though, because my instructions were all backward!

The gate resembled something from a prison camp. It was wide, at least seven feet high, and made of solid, gray-painted steel. Along the length of its top and of the fence around the little front yard was coiled barbed wire, like that I'd seen in Belfast.

I pushed the doorbell once, twice, several more times. No answer. I sat down on the walk to fix a sandwich. Across the street, several crouching beggars and a urinating child fixed their eyes upon my mouth. It was the first time I'd felt guilty for eating a peanut-butter sandwich.

Just as I was trying my best to swallow the last of the sandwich, a frail, white-haired old gent shuffled up to the gate with a small bag of groceries. As he struggled to unlock the thick padlock on the gate's two-inch-thick bolt, I introduced myself. Without hesitation, he had me enter and locked the gate securely behind us. But it was clear he had not expected me. I asked if he had received the letter I'd sent ten days before from Almería, Spain.

He paused at the door of his apartment, turned his gentle face to me, and with a childlike twinkle in his blue eyes said, "Oh, sometimes it takes four or five weeks for a letter mailed in *Morocco* to get to Rina and me."

He chuckled, then added merrily, "You wouldn't believe how crazy things are over here."

. . . Oh?

It was Monday, December 19, the Moroccan king's birthday. Or so I had heard. Most of the shops that I could see from the balcony of my second-story bedroom in the Jaquith apartment were closed. The streets, too, were mostly empty. The quiet was almost unbelievable. All the other mornings I'd spent in Marrakech with the Jaquiths had been filled with the clatter of horses' hooves against asphalt, of mopeds buzzing like gigantic insects, auto horns honking wildly, donkeys braying at robed owners, and veiled women chattering excitedly like black-and-white sparrows. For a city that was surrounded by desert, the voices and sounds of life were as thick as those of any jungle.

So where was everyone on such a nice day of hot sun and blue sky? Wasn't a royal birthday all the more reason for making a commotion?

"Try the souk, the open-air marketplace in the ancient walled area of the city," advised Rina.

I looked up from the huge bowl of hot oatmeal and yogurt that she had promised would put a pound or two back on me. It wasn't like my latest Mom-away-from-Mom to encourage me to go on my own into the depths of the city. Both she and seventy-four-year-old Clifford, whom she had married "in a cave in New Mexico twenty-one years ago," thought Morocco was as close to hell as one could get, without actually being in the real lake of fire itself.

"Don't you think that's dangerous, Rina?" I answered her now. "You said you and Clifford have seen a lot of bad things happen to foreigners in that market."

Just a few days before, she and I had gone through there to visit one of her Bible students, and I'd watched from our passing taxi as two arguing Moroccan men stabbed each other on a crowded street. Even the neighborhood around the Jaquiths' place was nothing to be complacent about, and that was in a supposedly safe newer section of the city. Each day as I roamed its streets to get more acclimated to the customs of the Moroccans, I saw enough beggars, cripples, and homeless on each block to shock all but the coldest of American senses. Poverty and cruelty still reigned here.

Yesterday, for example, I had gone to a nearby vacant lot to burn the trash, a chore done once a week by Clifford. Even as the mostly paper garbage was in flames, the ragged poor hurried to reach in to retrieve any magazines or pieces of cloth. According to Rina, they were probably hoping to find anything with color to put on the bare walls of their wretched dwellings.

She looked up from her dishes and stared out the window at the summerlike weather and all the birds that seemed to love her homemade feeders. When she pursed her lips like that, I knew it could mean only one thing—a sermon. She'd given them all over the world, from Miami to Israel. Rina hardly ever let a breath pass from her tall, strong farm body without a praiseful word to the Lord or a quote from the Good Book.

"Isn't it so nice, knowing the Lord directs our lives and is always with us!" she sang out.

I nodded numbly, my mouth full of oatmeal and my mind full of the stares of the hungry I knew were waiting just outside the fortified gate.

Off I went to the Djemaa El Fna at the end of Mohammed V, the city's main drag. Sure enough, there everyone was, along with sword dancers, snake charmers, mule-pulled carts of produce, and an interminable horde of hawkers, beseeching in Arabic or French to "Make price, my friends! Make price!"

And, alas, there were also those "leeches": the men and boys who attached themselves to every tourist with a ferociousness that was downright criminal.

No sooner was my "rich American tourist" red hair seen approaching the fringe of the souk than I was rushed. In less than a minute, I had human teeth, curved daggers, and jars filled with dead flies (to be drunk in tea as an aphrodisiac) pushed into my chest and face.

"No! No! No!" I shouted.

"I don't want this!" I kept pleading to screaming, shoving, pressing brown faces whose desperation scared me.

I felt as if I were caught in a thorn bush, with a few hundred snakes thrown in for good measure. In desperation, I thrust a silvery dirham into a young, innocent-eyed boy's hand. Please, I begged in caveman French, lead me someplace where life is more than just writhing arms and spitting, hissing heads.

With the audacity of a dauntless prince, the wiry little lad grabbed my hand, pushed aside beggars and foul-breathed camels, and yanked me deeper and deeper into a sunless maze of bamboo-roofed alleyways that would have confounded Rubik himself. Slowly, the leeches lost their grips and dropped away. Until, at last, there was only the boy, myself, and . . . the Devil.

"Ohhhhhhhh! Myyyy, MY! English, or Amerrrican?" the tall black carpet salesman crooned. He flashed a mouth of gold and rubbed together, like a contemplative praying mantis, a pair of fingers as long as dollar bills.

Incredible. Somehow I'd picked the sharpest little hustler of the whole souk. And, worse, I'd allowed him to lead me into the belly of a ritzy souvenir shop, on a dead-end street in the furthest corner of the market, that had more expensive junk in one room than Macy's or Sak's Fifth Avenue has in a dozen.

"You can pay in pounds, or dollars also, my friend, if you wish," the suavely attired salesman kept reminding me, with what I hoped was just a friendly wink, as he gathered everything I dared to glance at into a large pile. How was I to explain to this candidate for the salesman-of-the-month award that there was no way I was going to carry four-hundred pounds of rugs, ten camel-leather purses, and a wagonload of hammered brass tea-pots and candlesticks on my back for another twelve thousand miles?

When he sought to drag me upstairs for even more delightful gifts and souvenirs, I decided it was time to flee. I dived out into the market-place, to flee back up Mohammed V with the leeches right alongside.

When I reached the gate of the Jaquith residence, I collapsed into a kitchen chair, exhausted and suffering combat shock.

"Did you enjoy yourself?" Mrs. Jaquith asked with a knowing smile.

"It was hell," I sighed. "But it sure was interesting, all the same. Just wait till you see all the neat things I was able to bargain for. Boy, did I get some great buys."

And then, ever so much like a little boy, I heaved a plastic sack onto the table and dumped out so proudly all the knives, the teeth, the flies, and so forth. . . .

On the morning of my last day with the Jaquiths, January 2, Clifford was in his usual cheerful mood.

He sat down at the kitchen table and began to peel an orange. All the while, he talked of love, and God, and his favorite subject—Rina. His wispy fine gray hair stood out from his small head like ruffled down, and his thickly veined hands pulled the steak knife through the orange's skin with all the care of a surgeon. From his left wrist hung the silver-banded watch Rina had given to him on his last birthday.

Never letting his eyes be distracted from the orange, he said in his slow-motion voice, "Have you heard the story that says that 'love divine' is the secret of everything, that it is 'love divine' the world is seeking?"

Still peeling, ever so slowly and precisely, he recited the poem. Then he sang it. I hadn't expected to live long enough to hear someone with a worse singing voice than mine. So off-key and high-pitched was his attempt that it resembled that of an untrained child.

"Love divine is perfect love, and comes directly from God to those who are His. It is the best kind of love. It is a very unselfish love."

He put the naked orange and its coiled band of peeling aside and began anew with a second orange.

"I'll always be thankful for the patient who brought Rina to me. For Rina has been the best thing to happen to me in my life," he recounted with love in his voice.

"Her body was such a wreck, and it gave me a perfect chance to help someone very much. Actually, we've been good together, because we help each other all the time—me with her body, and she with my spirit."

I knew that at that very minute Rina was in her room sitting in her stuffed chair with wool blankets and quilts over her body—a body that was already clothed in thickly insulated long johns, wool flannel shirt, wool slacks, and a heavy overcoat. The hands holding her Bible were wearing gloves. And with all that, a large electric heater of hers was roasting away at her side, even though it was probably in the eighties already outside.

She had an ailment that was so rare only two people in the whole United States were known to have it. According to her, it was an inherited malady whereby her body generated hardly any heat at all. She was, in that sense, very much like a reptile. And so she was able to live only in hot and dry places, like Marrakech, and even then had to wear clothing that was more appropriate for a Russian trapper in the middle of Siberia.

"Steven, the doctors gave her two years to live. So I guess you could say that the fact we've now been together for twenty-one years is proof enough of the wonderfulness of love divine."

The second orange peeled, Clifford fed the oranges into a blender, as he asked if I was still afraid of losing my life in the walk across Northwest Africa. I confessed that I was. I still believed deep inside that I was going to die somewhere in the next twelve hundred miles.

"God is not going to leave you for one second," Clifford assured me. "He has you on this walk for a very important reason. He will not let you die before its purpose has been fulfilled."

Then, as if to settle my worries all the more, he added, "I would like to give you some of my poems to carry along." He placed some yellowed and crumpled pieces of paper into my hand, saying, "I hope you will use these and God as your staff across this dangerous land."

Clifford went back to his reading with Rina in her hot and stuffy little room, and I worked at packing Clinger, mailing my exposed film back to the newspapers in Kansas and Ohio, and sending home any and all superfluous items I had accumulated since Spain—including all those strange items I'd purchased at the souk.

That evening was spent sewing together an old worn-down sleeping bag that Rina had taken off her easy chair. I knew the nights in the high-altitude desert of eastern Morocco were bitter cold, and so I was happy to have such a gift. I wasn't all that happy to leave behind the blanket from Staten Island, for it and I had been through so much together. But at least I knew it would be helping Rina for a long time yet.

All that night, I rode the ancient wooden train to Rabat, squeezed into a cabin crammed with snoring soldiers. The freezing night air blew through the missing window over our blanket-covered bodies. I was shaking, sitting there in the blackness with a strange world lurching and howling all around me. I took out one of Clifford's "homemade" poems from my pants pocket and read it, to remind myself that everything was going to be okay. It helped me to relax considerably. It wasn't until I got off the train in Rabat that my fears returned—along with a lot of anger. For when I unzipped Clinger, I discovered that all my food and the two pairs of Adidas shoes I'd been hauling around since Limoges were missing.

I sat in the cold darkness of my tent, my head resting heavily upon my arm. I had never felt so fatigued and alone as after that first week of walking in Morocco.

Yet the land between Rabat and the Moroccan holy city of Fez had been the easiest terrain I'd crossed yet: wide and gently rolling grassy plains. My days since Rabat had been filled with warm sunshine, green earth, and cloudless blue sky, a perfect place to be in the middle of January.

The trouble was that I could not go a kilometer without meeting two or three dozen Moroccans on the same farm-animal trails I was taking. Straddling swaybacked donkeys, with their pointed cloth slippers sticking out to the sides like skinny little wings, or swaying precariously inside horse-pulled carts, or just squatting on the ground, beside small piles of carrots or mushrooms or tethered chickens for sale, the Moroccans seemed to be *everywhere*.

And all day long, from young children to adults, I had heard a constant "Give me, give me, give me!" So much so that on several occasions it had taken every ounce of my willpower to keep from striking out at them.

They came at me in dirty town after dirty town, and from one mud farmhouse after another. Because I was on foot, there was no way for me to escape. There was no denying that the vast majority of the Moroccans I passed were dirt poor. And that their cities and villages were little more than slums. And that jobs were few, and their work usually of the type that broke a man, or woman, before the age of forty.

But did that give them the right to demand money from me incessantly?

"Everyone knows you have money in America. You cannot fool us," one shifty-eyed man argued. He demanded six dirhams from me, simply because I had talked with him! When I refused to pay, he threatened not to let me pass alive.

"You are free to travel, to come to Morocco, to go anywhere you like, to take all this time so far from America," he continued to growl. "You must have much money to have such freedom."

I would not pay, and once again was forced to pull my hunting knife. We were entirely alone, in a stretch between villages. Thank goodness he had no weapon. I didn't know how to fight with a knife any better than I had in Tangier.

The very territory I was walking, from Rabat to Tunis, had until the last century been one of the world's pirate strongholds. The Barbary pirates had been famous for killing their victims or for selling them into slavery. And if the past week had shown me anything, it was that some of those pirates were still very much around. I, with my tall stature, reddish hair, blue eyes, white skin, and towering gray pack with its American flag was as marked a prey as any of those long-ago merchant galleons.

I stayed as still as a statue in my tent and listened to every sound in the field I was hidden in. Had anyone seen me set up camp? It was a question I asked myself every night, as I dropped off to a fitful sleep beside the thick walking stick, rock, and knife that were now my guardians.

On the afternoon of January 14, the brown stone and mud buildings of the desert city called Taza wavered only a few hundred meters ahead.

The thermals the city danced behind made it seem untouchable, unreachable, even though I had been walking, walking, walking toward it all day. A city of around fifty thousand inhabitants, it still had the air of a nomadic camp. The wasteland of rocks from which it rose starkly, the herders' tents of animal hides and reeds that formed its suburbs, and the strings of camels and goats that wandered through and around its gravelled interior made its whole scene look temporary at best. It hardly seemed possible that that town had existed for a thousand years.

Strings of peppers hung along the main street I turned onto, their withered red and yellow bulbs looking like Christmas decorations that had been up for too many years. The mournful cry of a mullah spilled from a tall, white, missile-shaped minaret and reminded me that I was as far from my own society as I had ever been. Trudging up the steep street in search of water and food, I wondered how the dark eyes watching me from the shaded benches and chairs outside the buildings would react to this lone foreigner.

A commotion up the street caught my eye. It was a large buckboard wagon, like those in cowboy movies, being pulled at a fast speed by two large black horses. I watched uneasily as people scattered from the wagon and the horses sped toward where I was standing on the long downhill. I felt I, too, should be running away. But why?

Too late, I realized why: There was no driver in the wagon! It was a runaway team, a senseless mass of wide eyes, flailing manes, and deadly sharp hooves cutting desperately everywhere but straight ahead. I was frozen with terror. I was directly in those huge horses' erratic path. I started to close my eyes: I didn't want to see the hooves and wheels that were going to crush me.

But then, unexpectedly, an elderly man with a donkey cut in front of me from the blind corner of an alleyway. The unlucky man never saw the charging team of death, for he was walking on my side of his donkey. But the horses saw the stray donkey, and the one closest to me reared its head back crazily and turned into the other horse hitched beside it.

The legs of the two horses became hopelessly intertwined. With a crash and a gut-wrenching scream, both plunged to earth. Straps and horse torsos gouged with a sickening tear of flesh and bones into the sharp-edged gravel and caused the wagon to jerk toward the opposite side of the street.

I was spared by less than an arm's length. But the old man and donkey were knocked asunder, the donkey flying off to one side of me and the man being dragged farther along in the tangled harness.

People came rushing from every side. I was still alive, not even scratched, but I couldn't get my heart beating again. All I could think of was that the old man was dead and probably torn to pieces. I glanced quickly at the donkey. Its little stubby legs were bent back and sideways like pretzels. In its large, dark, unblinking eyes was the stare of death. I wanted to cry; the man had to be dead, because he had been but a matchstick compared to the thickly muscled animal.

I ran to where the wagon had halted. The smell of the crowd's frenzy and of the horses' blood and ruined flesh hit my stomach like a fist. I didn't want to see what was left of the old man, but I *had* to know if he was still alive, for he had unwittingly saved my own life.

As incredible as it seemed, there he was in one piece and conscious. I was soaked and teetering on the edge of fainting, but I threw Clinger into the choking dust and dug furiously into the side pockets for my small bottle of antiseptic and some rags.

I was so angry I wanted to kill. All those idiots suffocating the old man with their shoving and kicking and arguing weren't doing a single thing for his wounds. Blood everywhere, and yet not a single person bending over to help stop it.

I splashed the red medication on the wide tear in his forehead and the ugly scrapes all up and down his arms. I was losing the battle. His life was spurting out, and I was helpless to stop it on my own. I couldn't understand a word of the Arabic cacophony grating every nerve in my head, but I had somehow to make them realize the man was dying.

I grabbed a man my age by his shirt collar and shook him violently.

"Get a doctor! Get a doctor *now,* or so help me God, I'm going to kill you!" I screamed just inches from his frightened eyes.

Another young man eased me away from the other, and said in English, "Please, he does not understand. He cannot speak English. Don't yell at him. We have sent for a doctor. He is coming."

That I would believe when I saw it. I went back to the old man and pressed my hands into his wounds to stem the blood flow.

Finally, a doctor from the hospital arrived, on foot and empty-handed. It was the last straw; I leaped up, unable to stand another minute of the backwardness my sanity was drowning in. I grabbed Clinger and bulled my way through the crowd, blood dripping from my hands onto the backpack I was now using as a battering ram. All I wanted was to get as far away as possible from that mad scene.

A cry went up from the crowd. I turned around once more. No! Not a person had thought to unhitch the horses from the wagon. Consequently, they had sprung back to their feet and were off and away down the hill again—right toward some crowded stalls. I didn't want to know the rest. I fled to a small, scraggly park and collapsed into the meager shade of a palm tree.

Later, as I sat sweltering on a shaded café walk, trying to cool some of my anger with an icy Coke, I sent two young boys to the hospital to find out about the old man's condition. They returned hardly ten minutes later with the good news that both the man and his donkey were going to be okay. It did more for my condition than any number of cold Cokes could have.

27

"This letter says you are a journalist. You told us you weren't," the commander of the Algerian Sahara border post said to me, waving the letter in his hand.

I had to think quickly, and answer even faster. He and the other officers were watching me like uniformed blue hawks. One slip, one hint in my eyes or voice that the cursed letter was true, and I could kiss the walk across Africa good-bye.

"No! My friend was wrong. I am a photographic artist, as I told you before," I replied. "Perhaps he has seen some of my photography reproduced in a magazine, and he *thought* I was a journalist."

The tall officer pursed his lips. His black eyes flickered between thinking and interrogating. He eased the hand clutching the letter slowly back to the hip pocket of his leather jacket. I forced my mostly naked body not to move a muscle. The beads of sweat trickling down from my armpits to my ribs were—I hoped—the only visible clue that I was scared half to death.

He motioned for me to sit down again in the chair in front of his desk. I did so, quietly. I did not want to give the heavily armed soldiers and police in the room any more reasons than they already had to mistrust me.

I watched as the officer in the leather jacket went to talk with men at the far side of the room and tried my best not to appear concerned.

I was in the Sahara Desert, had just walked alone across six kilometers of a no-man's-land bristling with barbed-wire barriers higher than myself, and had been forced to strip to my underwear by armed men I had been told were crazier than the Libyans.

Of all the countries on my walk, Algeria was the one I knew least about ahead of time. To me, it was a big question mark. All the travel books I had read before my journey had simply ignored this huge North African nation. Basically, all I knew of it when I reached its border at Oujda, Morocco, was what I had heard from secondhand sources—and that was anything but encouraging.

The Algerian embassy in Washington had told me I *might* be allowed to cross over on foot from Morocco (with whom they were at odds), but that I certainly was not to let anyone know I was a journalist.

The American embassy in Rabat seemed to know less than anyone else about getting into Algeria, except that I would have to purchase one thousand units of their currency, the dinar, as soon as I crossed into its territory. They, too, warned me not to let anyone know I was a journalist. Other than that . . . maybe I would be allowed in and maybe not.

As for the Moroccans, they described their neighbors as racist, stupid, crazy, and just plain belligerent. Coming from a people who had themselves made me so angry and disgusted at times, their criticisms rated more than just a raised eyebrow.

Two days earlier, January 20, at the grimy Algerian consular offices in Oujda in northeastern Morocco, I was told I could not cross into the country from there, even though the border was but fourteen kilometers to the east. The only persons allowed across at Oujda were those who owned a vehicle, and who worked or lived in Algeria. I could not go through the checkpoint in a bus or a taxi. My only chance, I was told, was to go four hundred kilometers south, into the Sahara Desert, to the small Moroccan oasis town of Figuig, and then attempt to walk across the "frontier" (as the borders were called) to the tiny Algerian village of Beni Ounif. But, I was warned, between the two villages were several kilometers of desert that were still disputed by the two countries.

Nevertheless, I went ahead and got my visa there at the Algerian consulate in Oujda. And resigned myself to taking the eight-hundred-kilometer-long detour—four hundred kilometers to Figuig and four hundred back to the north of Algeria. If going eight hundred kilometers out of my way to reach a point fourteen kilometers away wasn't insane, then I didn't know what was.

But at least I wasn't going to walk that detour. I couldn't: My time on my Morocco visa was within a couple of days of running out—and I had had enough of Morocco. I decided to take a bus to Figuig, walk across the desert zone into Algeria, then catch another bus (if possible) or hitchhike back to the northwestern corner of Algeria. There would be a tiny gap in my worldwalk, but I would consider it a reminder of how silly bureaucrats could be.

On the long, bumpy, dusty bus ride to Figuig, I consoled myself that at least I had survived Morocco. But when I stepped off the bus in the middle of the night in bitter-cold Figuig to find myself in a fierce sandstorm with nowhere to sleep but in a dilapidated, unpainted cinder-block, spider-infested place on a dark alleyway called the Motel Sahara, I wished I could *run* to Tunis and catch the first boat back to Europe and civilization.

Getting past the border officials of Morocco and Algeria had been nothing less than nerve-racking. First the Morocco police, then the military, had checked every bit of my gear and filled out paperwork on me. To my surprise, they passed me through, and my last sight of Morocco was of four large canvas army tents billowing beside a palm-tree-ringed oasis.

At the Algerian post, my gear and I had been searched, inch by inch, for drugs, weapons, alcohol (forbidden in an Islamic society). Since I had listed my profession on their forms as "photographic artist," to try to reduce any suspicion about all my journalistic gear, I had made sure to hide all papers that identified me as a journalist. To my relief, I had picked the one place to tuck those papers that they didn't search—my Webster's dictionary. As I had hoped, the inspecting officer had looked at the dictionary cover, seen that it was in English, which he couldn't speak, and then thrown it aside with disinterest.

But they had found a personal sealed letter in the inside pocket of my jacket, addressed to someone in Algeria. Without hesitation, the Algerians had torn the envelope open and read the letter. Written in French by a student I'd stayed with in Oujda to a friend in Oran, Algeria, the letter had mentioned that I was a journalist.

The officer in the leather jacket finally returned. He told me to put my clothes back on. I dressed, aware that he was staring at me the whole time. Were they going to take me away to a jail? Or was I going to have to go back to the Moroccan Army tents by the oasis, and try to explain that I needed back into their vacationland?

I sat back in the chair. The officer's eyes skewered mine.

"You aren't a journalist?" he asked calmly.

"No," I replied just as calmly. I was gambling that he was calling my bluff. He was.

"Sofee," he simply said, leaning back.

I could have shouted and danced. I recognized that sound as meaning "okay" in Arabic. Who would have believed I had made it in, after all those obstacles and skeptical eyes?

But I could go. And I did.
But the letter? They had put it very carefully into a desk drawer.

Once I was past the border-post officers in the Algerian Sahara, I thought I could relax for a minute. But the confoundedness that is Africa came roaring at me in enough shapes and sizes to drive me back into a fidgety wreck.

For starters, another sandstorm blew along. Then I couldn't connect with any buses heading north to near the border at Oujda. And after two days of digging out from under sand drifts to chase after tootling buses that had no intention of stopping, I had decided to brave the heat and hitchhike north. Fortunately for me, a merciful bus driver pulled over.

By the time I was back to the coastline and finished with my eight-hundred-kilometer detour on January 23, I was ready to be over and done with North Africa.

On the third of February, fifty miles short of my four-thousandth mile of walking, I set up camp in the forest near the former French seaside resort of Cherchell. Facing the threat of a rainstorm, I walked into the rotting city of around forty thousand people hoping to buy a broiled chicken and some fresh vegetables for dinner. The crumbling cinder-block row houses and old colonial-style lampposts I passed were plastered all over with the stern, white-haired face of the socialist nation's "president for life," Chadli, his dark eyes following me everywhere. As one shop-keeper had explained it to me, with a roll of his own eyes, there had been a national election a few weeks before. And Chadli had been a candidate. The *only* candidate.

On that particular day, there was a very different sort of face watch-ing me approach the open-air marketplace. That face had a horrible slash scar across its left cheek, and the conniving look of a hungry fox in its deep eyes. To my dismay, its owner came toward me in a cloud of ciga-rette smoke and asked in French if I was from France.

I preferred to answer with a quick no and move on. But I felt such curtness would not have been in my best interest. Since I was so obviously a foreigner, I knew I was under constant scrutiny from the many, many idle men and boys who hung about the fronts of the teahouses and cafés. Though the Algerians had—thank God—turned out to be unlike the Moroccans, never begging anything from me or attempting to harm me, I still was unnerved by the fact that there were so many hundreds of eyes staring at me on each street I passed. It seemed that where my eyes moved, their eyes moved—as if even my thoughts were exposed.

So I knew that when the scar-faced man approached me in Cherchell, I could not let my fear show or I would lose respect in the eyes of all those others who were watching. Therefore, I not only took time to talk to the stranger, but I even accepted his invitation to a steak dinner inside the hotel.

I relaxed considerably as the first steak turned into a second one accompanied by a couple of bottles of locally grown wines that should have been well on their way to France, since drinking wine was normally taboo for Moslems. My wariness increased ever so slightly when I saw the fist-sized lump of dinar bills he pulled from his pockets to pay for the dinners. Still, I was willing to follow him out into the dusk and the en-twining alleys of the old city to see what he had promised would be a very interesting "private club." Oh, if I had only known . . .

The private club turned out to be a speakeasy that could be entered only after a code was rapped on the planks of its low, thick door. Inside a sunken hole of a room was the stench of enough whiskey, tobacco, sweat, and intrigue to choke even the steeliest of adventurers. Lit only by smoking oil lamps set on the wall end of some of the long wooden tables, the pit held a small army of shouting ruffians. Glistening on their happy, shouting dark faces were spittle and the grease of the broiled chicken I'd never gotten around to buying. Though it was a merry crowd, there still pressed behind my rib cage the strong feeling that I had about as much business in such a place as a mouse did in a den of cobras.

All too quickly, I was rousted out of the doorway by a mob of half-drunken Algerian marines and made the guest of honor at their table. Scarface, much to his obvious displeasure, had to work his way to the other side of the room. Even through the shadows and haze, I could see his glare as the marines clustered more tightly about me every second.

"Are you with that man?" asked a stern voice to my left. It belonged to a sergeant built like a bulldog. The worried look in his bulging round eyes left no doubt that I was in more trouble than I had the courage to admit. "He is no good—a very bad person!" he cautioned me in a low slur. Then, in a lower tone yet: "We have heard that maybe in the years before, he has killed two or three people from other countries with light hair like you. You know—tourists."

The sergeant decided he and his men would protect me by working their way, in a friendly manner, to the other side of the room and block the killer's view of me. Then, while they were crowded about him, I was to bolt for the door and run as far and as fast as I could.

They moved on to Scarface like a herd of merry musketeers, slapping others on the back, singing out French like sea lions would mating calls, and just generally having a good-old-boy time. At the agreed-upon signal from the sergeant, a lifting of his Johnny Walker whiskey bottle in his left hand, I moved swiftly to the door. I paused there just long enough to glance at the group of bellowing marines to see if the killer had discerned my flight. As far as I could tell, he hadn't. The same couldn't be said for the rest of the place, however. At least a dozen of the rabble-rousers had the thumb on their right hand poking straight up—the Algerian sign for "Good luck!" I managed a smile and even a quick flash of my thumb before dashing off into a driving rainstorm.

Running, darting and pausing, running, pausing, running . . . My boots clattered through puddles and trash like a pair of mindless strays. I was completely lost. Lumps and bumps and clumps of every shape and size blocked me, and tackled me, and confused me in the unlit back streets. I was as turned around in the ancient puzzle as a rat in an electro-cution maze, while strange forms leaped at me with each explosion of lightning.

I knew the killer must have discovered my escape by now. Any sec-ond, a knife blade would flash out from behind a doorway to slice my neck apart. For all I knew, I was running in circles and was right back at the speakeasy. I had to do something before I ran myself right into the killer's hands.

I ducked into the cold dampness of a small teahouse dimly lit by some candles. As always, the men in it quickly crowded about my seat in a far corner.

Just then, in the brilliance of another streak of lightning, the scarred face thrust its burning eyes through the open doorway. In the blindman's black that followed, a sharp *crack!* resounded through the heavens. My nails dug into the table. Surely, he had spied my pale face among those of the other men. I waited for what seemed an eternity.

He never saw me. And eventually I found inside myself enough cour-age, or perhaps foolishness, to push on through the rainy night to my tent. I fully expected to meet my foe once more. But, of course, I never did.

Thank God . . . again.

28

The snarling, long-tusked boar charged at me again, as a spray of deep snow plumed from its black hunchbacked body, sparking the moonlit air.

I shifted Clinger higher onto my pelvic bones, dug the cleats of my Vibram soles deeper into the white ground, and gripped the narrow end of my walking stick, like a baseball player about to try for a home run. If necessary, I was ready to wait until I smelled the beast's breath before crashing my club against its skull.

Closer and closer, it hurtled. Higher rose the stick, faster went my heart. One of us was going to be turning the snowfield red, and I had no intention of it being me.

Just as the stick quivered for what I thought would be the last time, the wild boar baffled me again by plowing its hooves into the crust of the mountain and stopping ten or fifteen feet away. Four times now, it had dared me, only to stop at the last second. I looked at the animal's thick, bent fangs, at the long slope of its ugly head, its strongly muscled body, and I realized I was being played with.

"Will you make up your mind, you nincompoop?" I sneered at the face of snow and bristles. "Either eat me or go home."

But the boar was already home. And that was probably the reason he was charging every so often. I was the trespasser. The windswept summit of the Atlases I was trudging across was as much *his* territory as it was any goatherder's or hiker's. I doubted he saw much of my species in this part of northeastern Algeria at this time of year. And certainly not so long after the sun had kissed the neighboring peaks good night.

I remembered reading once in an Ernest Hemingway story—*The Short Happy Life of Francis Macomber?*—that a lion saw everything in silhouette. And I wondered if the same went for wild boars. If that was true, then my tall, massively humped back must have looked mighty strange, if not downright threatening, to the boar against the brightly reflective snow and the huge moon's disk.

My favorite tactic for frightening away dogs in the dark was to stick my arms straight out to the sides and then walk backward toward them, growling loudly and deeply like an upset bear. It worked like a charm every time. The poor dog's hair would rise a mile when it saw that what it had thought was a passing man was actually a headless bear, as tall as a tree and as fearless as the family cat. However, I wasn't quite willing to try such a shenanigan with the wild boar, because I had never quite been able to agree with those folks who said a pig had as much smarts as a dog. But certainly if he was going to persist in following me all the way to Tunisia, I might be tempted to try the bear act.

I walked away slowly, whistling the same sort of nonsensical notes that I had many, many a night in my youth, when I was returning home through the woods and cornfields with a heavy stringer of bass. On those midsummer nights, when the bats were swooping just inches overhead and the fog made even the most well-worn trail look like a pathway to the Devil's hideaway, I'd found a happy whistle was the best way to ward away those in the spirit world that weren't feeling as nice as I was.

Eventually, the boar had to get tired and go away, I figured. But he didn't. Spitefully, he waddled on along twenty to thirty feet behind and to my right. I didn't even need to turn to know he was there, because he made so many snorting noises through his snout. And so I crunched on in the snow and wind and stars, whistling Dixie to him and getting more and more insults in return, until I had to begin to wonder how anything could be so foul-mouthed. I turned to yell something back, and nearly crossed my eyes. No longer was there only the one boar, but thirteen!

As long as my legs are, it was all I could do to stay out of reach of their tusks before I could swing myself and Clinger up onto a nearby tree limb.

Into that patch of woods the boars came, rooting for something better to eat than frozen pine needles. Like a monkey in jeans, I watched their prickly backs and jagged rows of teeth pass back and forth all night just a few feet below. It was cold enough to make my fingers feel like popsicles, but I could not let go of that tree's skinny trunk. One slip, and the boars could tear into my fallen body. My only worse night on the worldwalk, in terms of physical discomfort, was the one I spent on Staten Island in a conduit pipe, oscillating between battling bloodthirsty mos-

quitoes and stifling in a sleeping bag meant for twenty-below-zero temperatures, not the ninety above it was.

Yet unlike that June night in New York, I actually enjoyed myself in
that tree. As miserable with cold and as cranky as my muscles were, I
delighted in the precariousness of the situation: It was as if I were living
out in real life a scene from those adventure stories of my childhood. My
favorite hero in those days was Tarzan, and if being trapped on a tree limb
in a forest swarming with bristles wasn't like being with the ruler of the
apes, then I was dreaming everything.

What an adventure the scenery alone in Algeria had turned out to be:
One day I might be dipping into fairy-tale forests, listening to the roar of
tall waterfalls and the whispers of cone-covered pines; the very next day I
might be shivering in the gloom of Himalayanlike peaks; or cautiously
stepping along a cliff-hugging road that dropped away to a thundering
surf of boulders and foam, hundreds of feet below; or walking fertile
valleys of grapes and oranges tucked among sandy beaches.

I passed dilapidated seaside-resort hotels, lonely old French cemeteries with large clumps of unmarked graves, padlocked cathedrals and
desecrated testimonials to a bitter colonial past, tiny villages of barefooted
children crowded around muddy water wells, stooping women burdened
with babies or firewood on their backs, dark-faced men with twitching
eyes. . . . I couldn't have picked a longer or more rugged way to cross
northern Algeria than its coastline.

My body had suffered greatly. So many times I had been burned,
frozen, and soaked in the 26 days and 550 miles since I had started the
Algerian phase of the walk. But was this not the stuff of which *real* adventure was made? For me now, the land of Homer's warriors, Robert Louis
Stevenson's pirates, and Frederick Forsyth's mercenaries was a part of my
everyday life—the dirt under my nails, the rain soaked into my sleeping
bag, the blisters on my toes, and the cold in my sinuses.

After two-and-a-half months, I was starting to appreciate the Arab
culture and Africa, to realize I had let my prejudices frighten me far more
than necessary. Africa was reminding me in its own raw manner that both
the good and the bad, the ugly and the beautiful, were important in making life exciting, challenging, and, in the end, fulfilling.

Around sunrise it must have occurred to the boars that the service
might be better elsewhere. Off they went, one by one, and I dropped to the
snow with enough stiffness in my joints to qualify for old-age benefits. But
at least I was still all together.

Which was enough incentive, I supposed, to shuffle on to the next
adventure.

Abdel Hakim Brahmi from the village of Ziama Mansouriah loved talking about going to America someday. And he wanted to know whether it was true that American women were "free" and thought only about sex every minute of their lives, like the ones he'd seen on *Dallas* and *Dynasty*. He was typical of the dozens of Algerian men who had befriended me during my first six hundred miles in Algeria, with the major difference that he could speak some English, in addition to the usual Arabic and French.

About the same age as I, also single, and a hard worker and a restless dreamer, he was one of the nicest persons I ever had invite me to his family's home. We met the afternoon of February 15, when I had had about all I could stand of a bone-chilling squall that had been dumping sleet on my shoulders since just after dawn. In the hospital where he labored as an X-ray technician, he found me huddled with the rest of his co-workers around a single little portable kerosene heater, in what was apparently the operating room.

The Algerians, unlike the Moroccans, could not stop showering hospitality on me. Ironically, their insistence that I continually join them for tea or food was wearing me down more than anything on the walk had done yet. The lack of privacy was beginning to overwhelm me. Besides, I had a steady cluster of school-age children tagging along with me each morning and afternoon, throwing their questions at me in unbroken streams.

And while I truly appreciated a bed and a home-cooked meal, having those in Arab Africa was not altogether easy.

I had still not forgotten my first introduction to dinner in a rural Moroccan homestead. One bowl of food had been placed in the center of the floor mat I sat upon with five other men. There was no silverware, and just a single drinking glass beside a pitcher of well water. The six of us slurped our way to full stomachs in grand bare-knuckled fashion.

Meanwhile, every bite of that insanely spiced Moroccan mutton casserole left me crying involuntarily. All that had stood between my burning up or surviving was the single little drinking glass, with its floating whiskers, food scraps, and—well, I simply had to make my eyes haze over.

Thankfully, the Algerians were aware of the fork and spoon. But they, too, had a form of torture to offer a guest they took a liking to—a drink meant to be an honor that was served many times over during the meal. The first time I drank it, I thought I was being encouraged to return to the dinner table the *couscous* I had just enjoyed. The only way I can describe it is that it was like throwing up in reverse. My guess is that the milky glop had in it something akin to convulsed yogurt, convoluted goat curds, and coagulated cottage cheese mixed in either agglomerated cream cheese or agglutinated mayonnaise. Had I not learned early on a valuable piece of Algerian etiquette—namely, to discourage refills, turn your glass upside down—I might never have reached Abdel's sea-cliff village with my insides still in relative harmony.

And what a shame that would have been, for his dear mother treated me to a truly great home-cooked meal, while afterward his father enthralled me with fascinating accounts of the extremely vicious war for independence the Algerians had fought against the French from 1954 to 1962. As Abdel translated for me, his father showed the scars that still remained on his body from being tortured by the French with live electrical wires, and shared with me the certificate from the government that said he was permanently disabled and eligible for a lifelong pension. With the mother of his ten or so children looking on very pleased, he took from an old photo album a yellowed snapshot of him as a freedom fighter in his hideout just across the border in Tunisia.

Abdel's father was not only one of Algeria's aging revolutionary heroes, but a lucky one. He had lived. Half a million to a million others hadn't. In a Moslem cemetery on the mountainside overlooking the village, Abdel showed me several long rows of identical tombstones. They marked the result of the day the French came into the village, lined up all the young men of fighting age, and executed them in retaliation for a guerrilla attack.

Had Abdel's father simply been at home that day, there would have been no Abdel.

And, for me, probably no memories of Ziama Mansouriah.

In eastern Algeria, closer to the Tunisian border, I discovered that police surveillance is very much a part of life in that society. Twice my camera landed me in a police station, to be questioned at length by a thin, trench-coated, moustachioed, and cigarette-smoking police inspector anxious to get at the "real" reason I was walking alone across their country.

The first incident was in Azzaba. While eating lunch, I had snapped a photograph of a mosque that had originally been a Catholic church.

Within minutes, two plainclothesmen and a uniformed officer were standing over me, demanding that I follow them to the police station. I did so, not at all sure what it was I had done wrong. At the station I was seated in a chair. Then, for at least an hour, I was questioned almost incessantly in French by the inspector and by another man who was much younger, extremely abrasive, angry, and not a local policeman, as far as I could tell. The younger man seemed to be a government person, who already knew much about me and was angry that I was walking across Algeria and not behaving as a tourist was supposed to do. He threw out the word *spying* more than once, and was perplexed that I had none of the standard tourist gear like suntan oil, bathing suit, or even any map or information books.

I tried as best as I could in my limited French to explain to him that at the border with Morocco, the police had taken away my map of North Africa, and since I had been unable to find any others inside Algeria to purchase, I was forced to stay close to the coastline for a directional landmark each day. Or else, if I veered away from the coast for a change in scenery, to be constantly asking strangers if I was still heading toward Tunisia. But he would not believe me. Someone without any map or prior knowledge of a nation as large as his could not have made it from one side to the other without getting hopelessly lost.

The younger man more than once came at me as if he was going to rough me up, but each time the inspector held him back. When he ordered me to turn over the camera, I put up such a fuss that the matter was dropped. I had not been photographing the mosque, I lied, but had been focusing in on a group of the children who rushed toward me as I sat down to eat.

It worked. After a while, I was released. Though I was told to go track down a bus to take me out of their area, I quickly walked instead to the eastern edge of the large town. If anyone stopped me, I figured I could again act the tourist and claim that I was lost and didn't know where the bus came to pick up riders (which was true). And sure enough, as if I had a big capital *C* for *Criminal* branded onto my forehead, a French-speaking policeman stopped me just before the town's limits to ask to see my passport and national identification card. When I told him we had no national ID cards in America, he didn't believe me. And the more I claimed ignorance of the matter, the more agitated he became, till I knew I was in danger of being led back to the police inspectors yet again.

I knew I was taking a big risk, but I pulled out my wallet and showed him my Ohio driver's license. In many ways it resembled a national ID card, since it had my photo and typed-in descriptions of my age, address, and physical makeup. I was gambling that he couldn't read English at all, and that Algerian driver's licenses weren't similar to this.

The second he saw the license, he grabbed it and scoffed at me for trying to hide from him that Americans had to carry identification cards like the rest of the world. Yes, I quickly and humbly confessed, it had been pretty stupid of me, hadn't it, to think I could convince him America was any different. He had been right: There was no way any government could run a country without being able to check the name and whereabouts of everyone. Like a rooster, he puffed up his chest and smiled smugly as he examined the little plastic-coated card, then handed it back and let me go without any further hassle.

The second incident was in El Kala. Very naively, I photographed a harbor that contained what looked like several small fishing boats. A man standing beside me, who had identified himself cordially as a hotel manager, informed me after the photo was snapped that I was under arrest. When I asked why, he said I had just photographed some naval vessels, which was forbidden in Algeria. I looked more closely at the cabin-cruiser-sized boats below in the harbor and saw that one or two did indeed look vaguely military. As for the man, I knew I didn't need to look more closely at him; he was obviously a policeman.

At the police station I explained to the officers that I had not realized there was a naval vessel in the harbor. If I had, I would not have taken the photograph, I assured them. I apologized profusely. They told me that even if there had been no boat in the harbor, I still would have been breaking the law.

"If Algeria has a war, where do you think the other army will land?" one officer asked.

"The harbor?" I guessed.

He nodded. In Algeria, the photographing of anything that might be of any strategic value in a war was forbidden. That included such things as roads, power lines, bridges, railroad stations, and tracks, and even municipal buildings. The entire coastline was likely to be a strategic military area in any war, he said. I felt as if I had been thrown into quicksand: I had enough photos of the coast on the film inside Clinger to send me to the gallows.

I tried to act like a panicked but otherwise innocent tourist. Something told me this was not the first time they had hauled in foreign visitors on such a charge. I suspected that perhaps it was all a ruse to extract some money, a ploy to make me feel scared enough to pay a "fine." So as they continued to warn me of what happened to those who broke such laws in their country, I chattered on in English like one old lady to another at a quilting bee. If there was one thing that drove an interrogator crazier than not getting any answers, it was getting answers he did not understand.

"You want to go to jail?" he asked.

"Jail? Yes, of course! I would like that very much."

"You would? Why?"

"I have not been to a jail. I think it would be very interesting to see one. Can I?"

"What?"

"Can I go to the jail?"

"No, you cannot go to jail."

"But you asked if I wanted to go to the jail. No?"

"Yes, you will go to jail."

"Will you go with me?"

"*What? I* don't go to jail. Only you!"

Not for another couple of minutes did I let on that I knew he meant to be putting me *in* the jail, rather than taking me on a tour of it. Then he stumbled into another language twister, one that nearly drove him to kick me out onto the street right then and there.

"You have a lot of money, to fly to Algeria from America," he mentioned with the look of an impatient toll-booth clerk.

"No, I am poor. I walked to here."

His head snapped back. "Walk? That would take many years. How can you walk on the ocean?"

I laughed. "I cannot walk on water. I fly in an airplane."

He frowned. "That's what I say."

"You did?"

"Yes, I did."

"You said I flew to here on an airplane from America?"

"Yes!"

"But I didn't. I walked."

"Then why you say you flew in an airplane?"

"Because I did, over the ocean."

"Then why you say you *walked* to here?"

"Because I did. I am walking all around the world."

Soon enough, I was a free man. The poor inspector must have thought I was loonier than a cartoon.

When I continued on my way to the Tunisian border, some twenty-three miles away, I soon realized that a small white car with two large men crammed inside was following me. I assumed they were police, checking out my activities more closely. But there was a chance they had been sent to beat a lesson into me for wandering so brazenly about their territory. I could see myself suddenly snatched and beaten severely, if not murdered, just for being in the wrong place at the wrong time.

My only escape, I decided, was to force the men in the car to return to town before darkness or the lonelier country lanes came along. If I could somehow shake the policemen, maybe I could get to the border.

With that in mind, I walked as slowly as possible that long, sizzling afternoon. Common sense said that such a tiny car had to be as hot as a furnace in the thermals coming off the sticky pavement. Since they were unable to go any faster than I was walking, about two miles an hour, they would get no breeze through the car's windows. So theirs would be the full brunt of the heat coming off the engine, the pavement, the sun above, and their sweaty bodies.

Deliberately, I stopped to rest at one farmhouse after another, being sure to have long drinks of water at the side of the road, where the men could watch me from their wheeled oven. Twice I settled into the shade of a tree and poured water from a canteen onto my bare chest and head, and made no secret of how great its coolness felt against my hot flesh. Stretching out in the shadow of the tree, I feigned the most relaxed and comfortable of naps. But whenever they looked as though they were about to get out of their car and seek some sort of relief for their throats or bodies, I would jump up and begin to move on.

After perhaps three hours and only six kilometers, it became quite obvious to the policemen I was not worth suffering so wretchedly for. They argued among themselves so loudly that I could hear their voices. And it was with a big, happy, tired sigh that I finally heard their auto grind itself into second gear and beat a hasty retreat to town.

Near the Tunisian border later that evening, the Algerian customs officials found sixty rolls of film in my backpack. As soon as the main officer asked specifically for the roll of film I had shot in El Kala, I knew he had been telephoned and told to watch for me. I handed over that roll of film but argued that the other film consisted simply of harmless scenery and people shots. Still, one of the younger policemen kept trying to convince me to hand over the remaining rolls, while his commander and another man mysteriously disappeared into a back room.

Just then a French television film crew pulled up from the direction of Tunisia. The crew was coming into Algeria to film some sort of documentary, their boss told me. Being a reporter had taught me that policemen hated receiving any sort of negative publicity. So again I gambled. I shouted and threatened everything just short of another world war if my film was not released. The film crew's ears perked up, and from the back room the senior officer came rushing out to see what was going on. When he saw the film crew, he suddenly warmed toward me and even presented me with the film he had taken into the back room. I was sent off with a much greater degree of hospitality than I had been welcomed with.

Just to be safe, I did not stay along the road that evening. I camped in the pine forest of the low mountain range still between me and the Tunisian post. Through the trees I could see jeeps with policemen passing from time to time. I could have been wrong, but they sure didn't seem to be rushing off to any picnic.

After the dangers of Morocco and the perplexities of Algeria, Tunisia was to seem like a playground. The tiny nation of windswept meadows and pine-covered hills allowed me some peace in the eight days I took to cross it. While it, too, was poor, it nevertheless was cleaner, quieter, and more modern than the other two countries. Only when I reached Tunis, the capital, on March 8, did I again find stark poverty.

Even though the Tunisians were perhaps the most westernized of the Northwest African Arabs I met, they were also the harshest critics of America I had yet met on the walk. Their pro-Islam, anti-American government theme was voiced by all of the Tunisians I had long talks with—from the old caretaker of a British war cemetery, who shared a pot of tea with me, to the schoolchildren who followed me about. Even the four families I stayed with in that country constantly told me how holy Islam is, and how evil a society America is. The many negative reports they had read about life in America had them deeply worried about how much, if any, value Americans placed on life. While they were well aware of our material riches, they were almost certain they did not want to live as we did, if it meant so much lawlessness and immorality. Even the young children seemed to know how many murders and rapes and abortions occurred in the United States each year. It shocked them that a people would allow millions of fetuses to be killed each year, and also "hide" their parents away when they got to be old.

I assured them it was not as gloomy and nightmarish in America as they thought. But it hurt me a lot to see, through their eyes, the mess they thought my homeland was. And, worse, to know that some of what they were saying was true.

Yet though they showed a dislike and distrust of the American government, they were still unmistakably fascinated with the American individual. As in Morocco and Algeria, I sensed a desire among the Tunisians to be close to the American people. But they just couldn't quite bring themselves to trust such a "liberal" society.

Frequently, I heard such questions as: Was Chicago still ruled by Al Capone-style gangsters? How many bottles of whiskey did I drink every day? Did I believe in a God? Why was the American government trying to kill all the Indians? Were we trying to make Lebanon into a colony? Was it true poor people in a country as fabulously rich as America were starving to death? Why were we so racist?

An experience I had near the village of Tebaba perhaps summed up best my whole Northwest African experience. There Kaled, a bright and curious eleven-year-old boy, took me by the hand and led me from the Garde Nationale post to the enormous farm of his grandfather, in whose house his family lived.

The squat concrete house sat atop a hill, on the side of which were crowded the smoky, cavelike stick and rock shacks of the farms' workers. As it turned out, Grandfather was not only a large landholder but also a member of the National Assembly and quite powerful politically. His name was Abdelaziz El Bahri.

Though I was led to the household completely unannounced, the large family immediately welcomed me inside. All that rainy day and into the evening I was fed and entertained. I was even allowed to sit in on a fascinating Koran prayer-chant session done in loud and rapid voices by four Muslim holy men.

But the next morning, as I heaved my gift-heavy pack to my back, one of the men relatives came to me and handed me my hunting knife. The others watched smilingly. I hadn't even realized it had been taken out of my backpack. As each one of the family stepped up to plant the customary kiss on my cheeks, the message of the knife flashed through my mind: As close as I and North Africa may have tried to become in the past three months, there was still the painful fact that we had not learned to completely trust each other.

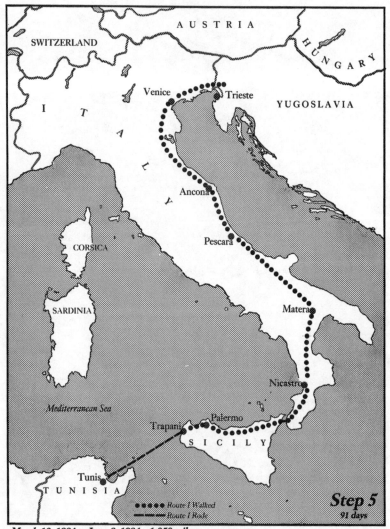

SWITZERLAND

AUSTRIA

HUNGARY

ITALY

Venice

Trieste

YUGOSLAVIA

Ancona

Pescara

CORSICA

Matera

SARDINIA

Nicastro

Mediterranean Sea

Trapani

Palermo

SICILY

Tunis

TUNISIA

●●●●● *Route I Walked*
——— *Route I Rode*

Step 5

91 days

March 10, 1984 to June 8, 1984   1,050 miles

29

The voyage to Sicily was aboard an Arab ship that rocked mercilessly in my worst sea storm yet. As I leaned my elbows on the railing of the ship's stern and stared at the Dark Continent sinking into the froth of the Mediterranean, I felt as if all those dark eyes of Africa were still burning into my mind.

Such a heavenly paradise North Africa could have been, blessed by Nature with its sun and beautiful scenery, if only another race of beings— ones who didn't know war or jealousy or religion—had settled it.

The grim face of a soldier I'd passed on my way to the dock was a perfect example. Young and lean, he had been standing guard before a large shed marked GRAIN STORAGE. The intensity in his eyes, the firm grip on his automatic rifle, and even the defiant way in which his legs were spread and planted into the mud left no doubt danger was very much a part of his life. What a contrast he was to the American marine guards at the American embassy in Algiers. A super bunch, those six soldiers had shared their rambling old house with me for two days and nights, while I haggled with the Algerian officials over a one-month extension on my visa.

The world I had just survived was far poorer and more overcrowded than I'd ever imagined possible. Most North Africans were too poor to afford even a nickel's worth of electricity a day; the purchase price of a car would likely cost a hundred times their annual wages.

In Morocco, I had met a young soldier who said he had saved for two years to buy the bicycle he rode up to me on. It was a basic plain single-speed model that many a bicycle shop in America no longer even carried —a model that would have cost me at most one day's wages. Then, again in Morocco, in the eastern desert, I had stayed with a sheepherder's family in an animal-hide tent with a television antenna poking from the top. The television was a small Japanese black-and-white model that ran off a car battery. When after four hours the battery ran down, the family would load it onto the back of a donkey or camel, and bring it thirty or more miles to a town to be recharged.

Had I been limited to one memory of the poverty I had encountered, it would have been of the time in Morocco when I had found myself one moonless night struggling to walk across a desert while being plummeted by a freezing westerly. With nothing larger than boulders to hide behind, I had had to keep walking long after my body should have been sheltered.

So stiff had my fingers become that I could not even unpack my sleeping bag. On and on, I had trudged that unfriendly night, not a sign of life anywhere, not even a blade of grass, when all of a sudden a darkly robed and hooded figure had come running at me from seemingly nowhere. Too stiff and sore to resist, I had expected a knife to come out from under his robe, only to be surprised by a handshake. He was a teenage road-construction laborer, who had seen me out on the desert earlier in the day and had come out looking for me, to see if I needed help. He immediately led me to the camp, where the workers' dwellings were nothing more than unheated tin shacks with cots and kerosene lanterns for furnishings.

Through one of the foremen, who spoke Spanish, I learned that they worked nearly the same amount of hours each week as I had on the drilling rigs in Wyoming, between ninety and one hundred, but at less than ten cents an hour. An average worker in America made more in one normal month of work than they made in *two years* of hard manual labor! Toward midnight, when I had fallen asleep under a ton of blankets, and with a stomach full of sardines and bread soaked in olive oil, I could only wonder why I was so blessed as to have been born in America.

By the time the ship docked at Trapani, the westernmost point on the Italian island of Sicily, eight hours of rocking on the stormy sea had left me clinging to the ship's railing like the barnacles on the hull. Still, just the realization that I was back in Europe, at long last, filled me with a burst of energy. I was actually shaking when I stepped off the gangplank and touched down onto land. At times I had thought I would never live to see the world outside of Africa again.

In the chilly darkness before dawn, the custodian at the railroad station into which I had snuck to sleep on the floor that first night in Italy roused me from my calmest sleep in months. When I admitted to him I had no train ticket, and was not even going to be riding on any train, he merely winked and indicated I could go back to chasing some rest. He was a kindly old Moroccan who seemed to understand that I was a man who had earned the right to rest in peace.

At the door of the Palermo post office, a short, balding middle-aged man, screaming rapidly in Italian and laughing hysterically, his mouth bloody, his eyes glossy, lunged at me and started to choke me. Try as I might to squeeze myself, Clinger, and the raving lunatic clinging to my neck through the narrow *Posta* doorway, I couldn't. I cast a look of helplessness at the staring passersby, saw no help coming, took a deep breath, grabbed the fool by *his* neck, and heaved him a good ten feet down the walk.

Even then, I was still barely able to tumble into the lobby before he was back at the door with all his delirium and drool. Looking about, I noted persons in the lobby expressing a sign unmistakable in any culture —the finger pointed to the head. I nodded. That idiot had been as crazy as they come. Wearily, I sighed and set Clinger against the wall, thinking naively that life was back to normal.

Just then, however, two young national policemen, *carabinieri*, burst through the doorway. Their long hair was ruffled and hatless, and their smooth, boyish faces were red with excitement. Swinging from their hands, their fingers up against the triggers, were short, military-style machine guns.

I crouched as I handed the clerk my letters. If either soldier's gun had had a hair trigger, that would certainly have been my last trip to a post office. But the others in the post office barely took notice of the two shouting men. While my heart was beating wildly, everyone else was calmly haggling over postage.

Finally, one of the older clerks, a tiny lady with gray-streaked red hair, evidently decided she'd had all she could take of the abusive officials. Rising from her stool behind the counter, she marched out into the lobby and stared tight-lipped at the still-shouting men.

As they continued to yell orders at the other clerks while waving their weapons about, the woman put out her right hand and pushed the first husky man back into the second one. The lobby grew quiet, but only for a second. For then she began to scold the two men as a mother might a pair of unruly children. As her sharp, stern voice rose higher and higher, she continued to push against the dark blue uniform of the wide-eyed policeman. Slowly, and now red-faced, the two *carabinieri* backed clumsily toward the entrance. She was not satisfied until they had retreated back out onto the congested, noisy street.

From the others in the lobby came spontaneous, robust applause. I joined in. One elderly man near the stamp window shouted a hearty *"Magnifico, signora!"*

For the umpteenth time in the two weeks that I had been in Sicily, I shook my head and wondered whether I was actually in a delightful opera that knew no such thing as a curtain.

Once on the mainland of Italy and into the toe of the boot, I found myself among a conglomeration of apartments and tightly packed shops that reminded me of walking through the Bronx. So much life and laundry everywhere. Bodies leaning out of doors, children rushing along streets, long johns flapping from balconies, and not a second's rest for either ear or nose.

With my mind brought back to my own country by the richness of life and the smells of baking bread in the wee hours of the dawn and of pasta in the evenings, the homesickness that had never quite stopped gnawing at my insides welled up stronger than ever. My father's face haunted my dreams so much that I feared the worst, and I called home several times, sick with worry that he would not be there to talk to. To my relief, he always was, though only barely. It was obvious, even over that distance, that his health was getting much worse. He was unable to talk with me for more than a minute before he needed to go back to his respirator. Mom confided in me that she did not expect him to last another year, but my youngest brother and sister, Elliot and Sandra, who were still living at home, said Dad perked up noticeably whenever he saw anything in the newspaper about me.

I knew the load on Mom was tremendous. Taking care of Dad was a full-time chore all by itself, and there was the large old house needing constant repair, and three acres of yard. And how, I worried, was she getting enough money to meet all the food and repair bills, as well as the money for Dad's oxygen tanks and medication? Dad's social-security payments couldn't be nearly enough. And his bad heart had kept him from ever qualifying for any affordable health-insurance programs.

Dad had sold the family nursing home on South Charity Street just before I left, but what little money he had had left from that after all the outstanding bills were settled wasn't enough to offer much peace of mind for longer than a couple of years. So Mom had tried to continue working as a registered nurse at the Morris Nursing Home. But so many times a day had Dad telephoned her with sudden breathing or chest pains that she had had to give up that job, to stay at home full time. With Gary away studying at Ohio State, Edwin serving in the South Pacific on a navy aircraft carrier, and Mary Ann now living in Germany with her army husband, Mom was largely on her own. Elliot and Sandra helped with the daily chores of going to the store for groceries or to the post office to check the mailbox, but it was Mom whom Dad wanted always close by in case of an emergency.

To listen to Mom's voice cracking with fatigue and exasperation crushed me inside. I wanted to come home and help. I told her to take any money from my bank account she might need. But she would never do any such thing; she was too stubbornly independent.

Tightly wrapped in the sights and sounds of all those closely knit Italian families, I wondered whether I was being selfish in pursuing my dream at a time when Mom and Dad needed me the most. I knew Mom especially was going through a private hell. If watching the moms of the world so far had taught me anything, it was that they were continually overworked and seldom properly rewarded. I wanted to do something to let my mom know that I always thought of her in my walking, and that I was deeply grateful for all she was going through on Dad's behalf, and mine. And so, on April 7, 1984, just over a year since I had left home, I sat down on the damp countryside of the little town of Cantinella to write to her a Mother's Day letter. Mother's Day was still a month away, but for once I wanted to make sure she got a present from me that wasn't late.

Almost as if the words had been waiting there in my heart, they came forth effortlessly from my pen:

Dear Mom,
        Some wore rags, some dressed in silk. Some talked my sunburnt ears silly, others could only gesture timidly with their eyes and dark hands. Yet there was something all of them —American, Anglo-Saxon, French, Spanish, Arab, and Italian —shared in common, no matter how awkward our speech.
        That "something" was *motherly care and compassion,*

perhaps one of the greatest morale boosters any one kid far from home could wish for.

Mom, you and I have been unable for over one year to share any time together. Believe me, it hasn't been the same without your sparkling eyes, encouraging words, and endless smile. Being so far from home, and all alone at that, has been one of the most painful sacrifices I've had to make for the sake of this trek.

Luckily, though, my days have been blessed with the compassion of so many other mothers, who somehow found yet more love in their overworked hearts for one more gangly kid with a big stomach and a sore body and spirit. Of course, it's not quite the same as you, Mom, but still I don't think I'd have made it these first five thousand miles without all the fussing and care of my "Moms away from Mom."

I don't know why I've been blessed with so much love and warmth every time the walk reached its roughest stages. Maybe I'm just luckier than I give myself credit for, or maybe they've seen something in me of their own children who've long since grown into adults and departed to other regions to live their lives.

I've become certain of one thing, though, as a result of all the kindness shown me by my moms—without mothers and their seemingly depthless reservoirs of love, this world would be much less beautiful.

So many loving moms on this big planet, so many along my solitary path.

Perhaps the best way I can think of to tell them—and you, too, Mom—how much they have meant to the success of the first one-third of my worldwalk, is to say those three simple words I suspect many never heard enough of in their laboring motherhood years—I love you.

Thanks, Mom. May you have a very special Mother's Day.

Steven

After fifty-two hundred miles and thirteen months, I was beginning to suspect that I wasn't directing the walk's course so much as it was directing me. It was as if the trip had taken on a mind of its own.

In Italy, I relaxed completely and let my feet go where they might. I found myself ambling about in the heel and ankle of south Italy's rolling grassy countryside and aged village streets with the devil-may-care freedom of King Hobo himself. One hour I would be firmly in control and well on my way toward Yugoslavia, still many hundreds of kilometers away, and the next hour wandering aimlessly, as if hopelessly absent-minded. That, of course, was when I knew the walk was "doing it again to me." But, no matter. I simply kept my knobby olive-branch walking stick tapping onward. For surely there had to be some enchanting surprise awaiting me just ahead.

And what delightful treats I did sample in those weeks I spent in Italy's most sparsely populated region, a region I had had absolutely no intention of walking through. When I had left the ship in Sicily, it had been my plan to head up the quick and warm Mediterranean side of Italy to Rome, then cut across to the Northeast to Venice. But my feet couldn't resist probing the wispy mountain range cutting down the middle of Italy.

So up, up, up I went, for over twenty-five kilometers. Then, much to my surprise but perhaps not to the spirit of the walk, my size-12 feet went down, down, down the other side of the mountains to the Adriatic side.

What I descended into was the Italy I had been searching for all along: a kindly, peaceful land of gray stone-walled olive groves, meadows of margarine-colored daisies and blood-red poppies, oceans of deep, wavy grass, and misty-cool rock beaches. It was magical. What other word could there be to describe the excitement that rushed through me one gray afternoon when I came upon the cliff-top shell of a lonesome castle ruin guarding the Adriatic Sea? Or later that very same evening when I huddled close to a driftwood campfire on a tiny beach hugging the enchanted castle's tall rock foundation?

Then, several nights later, there was the *sassi* (rock), the decrepit old city area of Matera. When I first gazed down into the enormous spotlighted bowl of low hills containing the crumbling *sassi*, I thought I was gazing into the window of time itself. Glaring back at me were the ashen-faced walls and hollow-eyed windows not of one ruin but of an entire city! I stared down at the abandoned skulls in what had once been the playground of the rich and, like a mesmerized Huck Finn, impatiently awaited dawn's light with which to explore the five-hundred-year-old relics.

And if it wasn't the land bewitching my senses, then it was the Adriatic Sea. Across one vineyard, then another, I walked one hot spring morning to reach a distant band of white beach, where I had seen groups of fishermen spreading long nets into the surf. What mysterious creatures from the liquid universe could they be trapping, I wondered? When at long last I watched the nets pulled back onto the pebbles and their cords peeled apart, I saw a pile of fragile, transparent figurines.

"What are those?" I asked the smiling red faces.

"Sardines!" one fisherman exclaimed, scooping several into his mouth.

He offered me a handful, too. Like everything else in Italy meant for the stomach, they tasted heavenly.

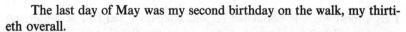

The last day of May was my second birthday on the walk, my thirtieth overall.

I had hoped to treat myself to Venice's gondolas, arched marble bridges, and deep avenues of water on the first day of my fourth decade. But by noon I had had to admit, sadly, that the fabled crown jewel of Italy was still another day's distance.

I surrendered to the shade of a sycamore, feeling more than just a little desolate. No friends, just a lot of weeds and crickets . . . Not much of a birthday at all, I told myself, settling down to a long afternoon of writing and waiting—for what, I wasn't sure.

Many hours later, at dusk, a mass of panting fur and saliva startled me from my thoughts. I looked up from my diary to find a collie. Only a few tail lengths away stood his young master.

"Buon giorno," the conservatively dressed lad said softly.

"Thank you. Good day to you, too," I replied, a little embarrassed. I figured it was probably his parents' property that I was trespassing on.

"Are you in need of anything?" he asked in fluent English.

My eyebrows raised involuntarily. He looked to be no more than fourteen, and yet he seemed so sure of himself. Ten years older, and he would have born a striking resemblance to actor Christopher Reeves.

I lifted up a collapsed-goatskin wine bag. "As a matter of fact, I am thirsty," I replied, still confused as to where he'd come from. "I could use some water."

He held out his hand to shake mine, his manner as straight and proper as that of an ambassador to a visiting dignitary. "My name is Giuseppe. This is my dog," and then he pronounced a name that sounded like "Yudda."

I jumped up to shake his hand and apologize for trespassing, but he stopped my apology with a big smile.

"Come with me, and bring your canteen," Giuseppe said. He started walking in the direction of a forest at the other end of the field.

I left Clinger, the diary books, and all my other gear on the grass beneath the tree. There was no need to worry about them being stolen, since the road to Venice was at least one hundred meters away and there were no other houses in sight. With the goatskin bag swinging from my hand by its thin leather strap, and Giuseppe and I being led down an overgrown dirt lane by a loudly sniffing Yudda, I felt strangely buoyant and yet extremely homesick at the same time. I wondered why.

Then, in the swishing of Yudda's broad tail and the bobbing brown hair of the young boy, I saw the answer clearly: When I had been Giuseppe's age, I had had a large collie sweeping my path, too. His name had been Laddie, and for many summers and autumns that big old shaggy dog and I were virtually inseparable. He had loved any excuse to get out in the woods and fields around Bethel.

"Giuseppe?"

He turned his bright eyes and lightly freckled high cheeks toward me. I almost wanted to turn away from the reflection of myself I saw in his innocent expression. *God, can I really be thirty? That's* so *old!*

"Giuseppe, what is your age?"

He tried to sound as manly as possible. "My father says I'm almost ready to be on my own. In three more years, I can go to the university in Venice."

Only a sophomore in high school. How lucky. I felt as if the bags under my eyes and the sunspots on my face had just doubled. Walking next to him, I had to admit I was not the young, footloose boy I'd thought. I was a man now. I was over the age when boyhood finally, undeniably, truthfully ended—forever. Oh, did it ever hurt!

"How many years are you?" Giuseppe asked me, as we entered the shade of the trees.

"Thirty. Old, isn't it?" I asked with a flippant sort of laugh.

He was kind. "I don't think so. My father is more than forty years." He laughed. "I thought you were in university."

Thank you.

Hidden deep in the trees was an ancient stone-and-mortar wall at least twenty feet high and two feet thick. Set into it was an enormous stone barn that had surely once held the cows and horses of a race of Goliath-size farmers. The gate through the wall was also the door for the barn. It took all the strength Giuseppe's lanky arms could muster to slide open the tall, wide doors.

I gave him a hand with the closing of the door, and from the webs and dark shadows of the loft above heard the echoes of the gate closing. We passed musty, empty stalls that resembled dank crypts robbed of their treasures, and then beneath a yawning archway we stepped, and emerged in a courtyard so beautiful it stopped me in my tracks.

Stretching far to our right was what looked to be a mansion. With lacy ironwork over many of its windows, and with its white-columned cloisters set into yellow walls with beveled window panes, the building looked like a creation from a romance writer's novel. The long yard we had emerged onto was bordered by sculptured shrubbery. The carpet of manicured grass was so emerald in color, it hurt my eyes.

"Is this a museum?" I asked Giuseppe.

"No. This is my house."

At the front door, a balding man dressed in faded jeans appeared. His smiling eyes were on the same plane as mine, a rarity in this nation of short people.

"Hello, hello. And where did Yudda find you?" he asked with a chuckle.

"I am sorry, signore, to bother you. I am walking the entire length of Italy, and I stopped to rest beneath one of your trees." I nodded at the boy. "Giuseppe said I could get some water here."

"I think we have some to spare," he kidded.

Before I could stop myself, I blurted out, "How many people live here?"

He laughed. *"Sempre una famiglia,"* he replied, adding, "but with Yudda always bringing in all her friends from the forest, we sometimes have many more."

"Hey! Anyone for some coffee?" shouted a woman's voice that I swore sounded as if it had a Tennessee accent.

My eyes whipped to my left, to catch a smiling blond-haired bundle of energy waving at us from an open window.

"That's my wife, Francesca," said Romeo, Giuseppe's father. "She will talk your head off. She loves to practice her English, I must warn you."

To someone who had thought he was going to spend his most important birthday as a recluse, that sounded even better than the coffee.

In a kitchen of microwaves and fireplaces, my three hosts and I shared a pot of delicious coffee poured into fine china cups with warm milk and sugar—which were complemented by glasses of wine. And over sweet, hard sausage slices and springy cheese blocks, I found out that Romeo was simply a prudent man who had used wisely his income as both an architect and a farmer of grapes, sugar beets, and corn. The house was an inheritance that went back further even than Christopher Columbus.

Time passed unnoticed in the midst of all our kitchen-table chatter, and soon enough the walk's stories had captured yet another audience of crossed legs and chins on palms. Eventually, though, someone remembered to yawn. Francesca poked her bright head out into the night, only to come back with a *tsk* and the offer of a spare bedroom. It was beginning to rain, she said, in that peculiar melancholy tone all Italian women use whenever the world about them is not in perfect order.

Flashlight in hands, Giuseppe and I dashed to retrieve my notes and gear. Yudda raced ahead, as if eager to surprise and flush out any lingering spirits. Francesca hailed our return with more hot milk and a plate of thick crusty bread buried in still more succulent meat slices.

"We've a surprise for you," she teased me, glancing first at Giuseppe and then at Romeo, who was keeping a fireplace hearth occupied.

Taking some candles from a drawer, she directed me across the front antechamber, past the grand piano, and through a long room of chandeliers and marble to a low, crudely constructed, shedlike door, in a wall of otherwise lightly flowered wallpaper. Into my left hand was slipped a large candle, which Francesca lighted with a match. The others, too, got lighted candles. Yudda tilted her head with the same bafflement that I felt.

With a key like that of a dungeon warder, the lady of the house clicked open a padlock that looked older than any of those trees in the yard. Gingerly, she gave the door a nudge. It creaked ajar, then yawned wider against the groaning of arthritic hinges. A breath of dust tickled my nostrils. I bent and peered into a dark cavity that hinted not of size or place.

"Do not use your flashlight until we tell you," cautioned Francesca, as if sleeping robbers might lurk in the secret cave. "Steven, you go first, with your candle."

I stepped into a room that I could sense right away was very small. While the wings of the small fires from the others' candles danced around mine, I heard Francesca command me to turn to the wall behind me.

What I beheld were the creations of a painter's brush in a past when buskins and togas were in fashion. The painted scenes on the walls revealed maidens harvesting grain, a Neptune guarding his watery home, an armless Grecian statue thinking perhaps of her fading youth, and some benignly smiling cherubs.

More than just my muscles and nerves tingled. I knew I was gazing at the kind of treasure people traveled to distant corners of the world to see in museums. Yet so often the closest they ever came was a glass case and a HANDS OFF sign, while here I was touching, and even smelling, the frescoes as I might flowers in a vase.

The room we were in was the original home, Romeo informed me. Around it had grown the rest.

Back in the antechamber, Romeo showed me bits and pieces of Roman-statue anatomy he had plowed back into the world. The past, particularly so close to a place like Venice, was never far away, from all the evidence he showed me.

That night I lay in my bed in an otherwise empty wing of the house, and wondered whether a thousand years from now anyone would have even the slightest inkling there had once been a Steven Newman from some little village named Bethel. Or that he had awakened one morning in a field in Italy, to find that the last sands of his youth had spilled away in the night.

As far as I was concerned, the gifts of Giuseppe's family, the audience with the cherubs downstairs, and finally this warm bed on a rainy night were more than mere coincidence. Someone or something *up there* had known today was a special day to me. Maybe none of the other 5 billion persons on this speck in the universe did, but *He,* or *It,* had. I knew because so many times already on the walk I had been cared for when I had least expected help. In some ways, it was almost scary at times: All I had to do was think about what I was needing most, and mysteriously it came, without my even having to ask.

I smiled and rolled over on the bed. I had to admit it had been a heck of a surprise-filled birthday after all.

Perhaps one of the best ever.

June 9, 1984 to October 12, 1984   2,254 miles

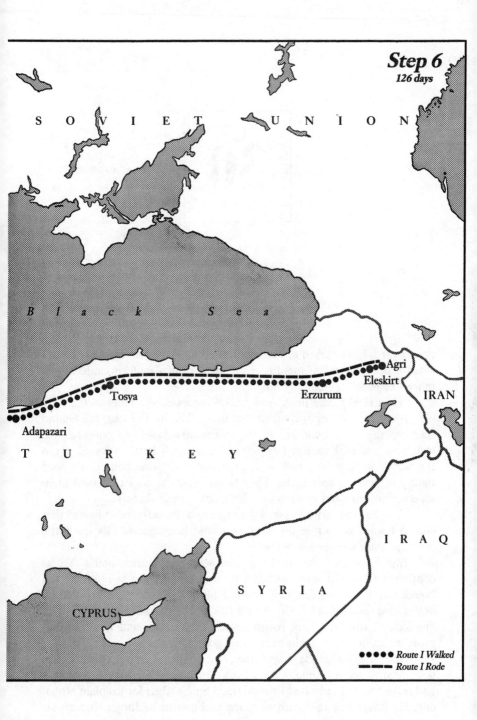

Step 6
126 days

SOVIET UNION

Black Sea

Agri
Eleskirt
Tosya
Erzurum
IRAN
Adapazari
T U R K E Y

I R A Q

S Y R I A

CYPRUS

●●●●● Route I Walked
━ ━ ━ Route I Rode

30

From my side of the tall metal link fence, the two young Yugoslavian army privates looked like POWs in a prison yard. Both reeked of cheap wine and looked as though they hadn't eaten a decent meal in months. Even their brown uniforms fitted them more like pajamas than anything else.

"Hey! Hey! Come here, American," requested the taller of the two.

I looked first one way, then the other, then up the long hill behind them to the brick buildings of the campuslike base. No one else was watching, and so I ventured as close as the fence's lattice allowed. From the weeds at their feet, both men produced their wine bottles, wrapped tightly in brown paper sacks. They slipped out the corks, clunked them together, and poured more than a little down their throats.

"You have my wine?" asked the taller one. Proudly, he indicated that should I want a drink of his wine, he would immediately toss the bottle over the fence's barbed-wire top.

Thank you . . . but no, I indicated with my face and hands. Yet he continued to persist, until at last I gave in and tried a swig of the red liquid, too. It left me coughing like a dying man. They got a good laugh out of that, and so did I. On the oil rigs, I had shared many a bottle of "medicine" with similarly rough-looking characters, and now our impromptu gathering brought back those good memories.

When I saw that the shorter man was admiring an old alligator-skin belt given to me a couple of days before by a rich Yugoslav-American I had stayed with, I indicated I would trade him my belt for his plain brown one. He jumped at that with so much enthusiasm he forgot to grab his pants when he pulled his belt out of the loops. The pants, which were at least three sizes too wide at the waist, flopped to his knees. Through the links in the fence we poked the belts, as quickly and nervously as spies exchanging secrets.

Their English was poor at best, and my Slavic was destitute. But with the help of the wine, some snapshots they had in their pockets, and my maps and Witness Book, which I dug out of the resting Clinger, we somehow managed to carry on a conversation that made sense every so often. I told them where I was from in America ("near Chicago"), and that I was walking not just through the surrounding Croatian countryside and the nearby town of Benkovac, but down through all of Yugoslavia. Which they followed up by telling me of the close friendship the two of them had enjoyed since being young schoolboys.

The taller and slightly more serious of the two was named Papich Milovan, the shorter and heavier, Sabur Zlatan. Both were in their early twenties and originally from Sarajevo. They were something of free spirits and rebels, as was plain to see in the snapshots they had of themselves together over the years. In one, they could be seen up to their knees in snow in the mountains around Sarajevo, their brown hair hanging to their shoulders.

"Hippies!" I kidded with a poke through the wire mesh at the snapshots in their hands.

Instantly, both broke into smiles. "Rolling Stones!" blurted Sabur, excited that he'd finally been able to speak some English, too. "Deep Purple!" added Papich with an excited slap on his friend's back.

Again we all laughed, and the bottles went merrily flying back and forth over the barbed wire, like wooden clubs in a weird juggling act.

We may have been separated by miles of fences and walls, but I felt as close to those two renegade privates as I had to anyone in a long time. Looking at them reminded me in a way of my years in high school with my best friend, Greg Abell; I could easily imagine them plaguing the teachers in Sarajevo with the same sort of mischief Greg and I had been noted for.

I asked them why they were in army clothes. The sour look on their pale faces told me it was not voluntarily.

"Ah . . . we, we in Yugoslavia go, go two—two?—two year in meeleetearee . . . uhmmm . . . regulation," Papich struggled to explain.

He needn't have said another word; I knew exactly his situation. It was very much a carbon copy of most of the rest of the world I'd explored so far.

Sabur held up his almost empty wine bottle and looked at Papich. Said his understanding friend:

"He, he say wine make him forget. He, I . . . we want go home."

I tipped my right hand toward my lips. Sabur's bottle took one last trip through the air. I knew how he felt. I drained the wine into my own homesickness, and turned to toss the empty bottle into the ditch between my back and the road.

It was then that I saw something that caused me to freeze with terror. A white sedan was bearing down on our clandestine picnic. Staring angrily from behind the steering wheel was a crisply uniformed officer of some high rank. I looked desperately at my two friends. They didn't see the car, or the column of armed soldiers marching at us from the nearby hill. They were too busy deciding which photos to give me.

We were caught, ambushed. There was absolutely no getting out of it now. We might as well have had a cage come down on us. I pulled Clinger off the grass with one hand, and with the other gave the fence a good rattle. My thoughts spun like a shot bird crashing to the ground. How many times had the Italian *carabinieri* warned me that the Yugoslavian police or military would arrest me as a spy? And now look at me!

All I could think to say to warn the others to flee was "Captain! Captain! The wine bot—"

The screeching of brakes and their wide frightened eyes told me it was all over.

The officer who leaped from the car had enough stars and medals and crosses to qualify for a general. His stern eyes said it all: We were in *big* trouble. I knew better than to try to decline when he motioned me to get inside the car at once. As we pulled away, with me in the backseat like a criminal and Clinger in the front beside the tight-lipped driver, I saw Papich and Sabur being pushed to the ground by the other soldiers.

"Where are we going?" I asked the driver.

The silence answered me. To jail. And probably for a long time, too. Near the end of my walk in Italy, the newspapers there had been filled with the results of a trial just completed in Yugoslavia, in which a young Italian free-lance journalist and his girlfriend had been caught photographing the perimeter of a Yugoslavian military base. Two years' imprisonment had been meted out to them, even though there was no evidence that they were anything other than careless tourists.

Through the solid metal gates at the base's entrance we lurched. I stepped out into a squad of stiff-footed soldiers and gun-muzzle thorns. With five on each side of me, I was goose-stepped to a bunker that looked like the pit of an ulcerated stomach. There I was left to stew and simmer in my own worry juices.

For two hours, no one came to speak to me, to ask my name or who the heck I was. It chilled me to realize that if no one *ever* came to speak to me again, I would disappear from existence as effectively as if I had been vaporized. There wasn't anyone back in America, not even my family, who had any idea where exactly I was from day to day, or even from one week to the next. By the time my newspaper stories reached Kansas or Ohio, I was usually well on my way again. And it would not be until I missed the next deadline that anyone might start worrying, by which time I might be hundreds of miles away from the previous story's dateline. And given my habit of wandering off onto the less crowded and more scenic back roads and trails, it would be a wild guess at best as to which direction I had taken. If I met my death, *no one* would ever know where it happened.

A junior-grade officer, perhaps a lieutenant, strolled into the room. He couldn't have been over twenty-four, a guess that was confirmed when he told me he was a university student who had interrupted his studies to serve his military obligation. He was to be my interpreter, he explained, and I was to consider him my friend in the upcoming interrogation. He put a blindfold over my eyes, and, along with the always silent, always armed sentries, led me carefully to another building.

With the yank of the blindfold from my eyes, I found myself in a large, curtained room. A massive wood table stretched the length of the room, and on the tall, dark wall opposite where I was seated, there hung a giant portrait of some bushy-browed, thick-jowled hero of the Communist revolution. Presently, the other chairs at the table were occupied by various officers, and even some policemen from the town. And the interrogation began.

"No tourists come through here. Why are you walking in this area?" asked my interpreter.

I explained I was walking around the world, to learn and see it more closely. As I expected, they didn't believe that for a second. So I showed my log books, maps, and even the *Washington Post* interview. Excitedly, they crowded around the exhibits. Said the interpreter after a few minutes:

"They want to know why you walk only by the military bases in Yugoslavia."

I assured him that if I had, it was purely coincidental. What I didn't tell him was that no matter where I went in their country, I never seemed to be far from a troop convoy or military installation. I could take no back roads for a full day without the dust and roar of yet another convoy passing me.

They were especially intrigued by all the dots and dates on the map of Yugoslavia that showed where I had slept or camped. Each one, the interpreter warned me, was near a military installation of some kind. "You cannot walk in this part of the country—there are things you are not to see," he cautioned me on his own. "You must go where tourists go." He pointed to the national highway that ran along the coastline.

"What are all these numbers?" he asked, pointing to my daily log book in which I recorded all my mileage and hours.

I explained, but I could tell that the masses of numbers and maps, along with all the camera gear, the tape recorder (which they did not know was recording the interrogation), the many film cartridges, recording tapes, books, and writing gear were surely condemning me as much as they had in Africa.

Suddenly, I cringed. One of the policemen had found my Witness Book. Inside it was the name and address of the rich Yugoslav-American whose belt I had traded to Sabur. If they recognized his name and saw that I had stayed with him for several days, I knew I was as good as convicted. He was not just any Yugoslav-American: He was also a former Central Intelligence Agency worker. And the Yugoslavians knew it.

He normally lived in Beverly Hills, California, but when I had met him along the coastal road a few days back, he was visiting his sick widowed mother at his boyhood home on Pag Island. It wasn't until later, when I was seated over one of his mom's delicious meals, that I learned he had flown airplanes for over two years for the CIA in Laos during the Vietnam War. His connection to the CIA, he explained, was known to the Yugoslavian secret police. They had even tried to recruit him years ago, in the hope he might help them train their own agents. But he had declined. It wasn't until recently that he had been allowed back to visit his mother, and so I had promised not to publicize his name lest he lose his visiting privileges again.

"You must tell us the names and addresses of everyone you have spoken to since you entered Yugoslavia," commanded the interpreter.

I wet my lips. Everything they wanted was right in the Witness Book.

"Tell your commander I can't remember any of their names," I told the interpreter.

He translated, and it created more commotion than I'd counted on. I had directly disobeyed an order. No one was fooled, least of all the policeman who was still leafing slowly through the Witness Book. Out of the corner of my eye, I saw he was almost to the Yugoslav names and addresses. Once he came upon those, they would know for sure I had been lying to them. And if I'd lied about the names and addresses of those I had met, it didn't take much to figure that I'd probably lied about everything else, too. I had to do something.

Northeastern Turkey, near Iran. Woman with load of fodder for the livestock back at her mountain home.

One of my favorite shots. A Gypsy family in Turkey, along with their horse and loaded cart.

Daughter of a village chieftain in Turkey. She is standing beside a communal oven that is little different from those of a thousand years ago. A basket of freshly baked bread is at her feet.

Close-up of camels in Lala Musa marketplace in Pakistan. Many farmers still use camels to bring goods to the market.

Pakistani farmer and sons acting as weights on oxen-pulled tiller.

Spice vendor in central Pakistan, his spices in dazzling mounds of orange, brown, red and yellow.

A grandfather in Jhattipur, India, enjoys his morning smoke.

Varanasi, one of the four Hindu holy cities in India. Streetcorner barber shaving a customer.

Indian woman with goat in eastern Uttar Pradesh. On her head is a large pile of kindling sticks.

Indian mother and children standing among the cow-dung patties they have made for cooking and heating fuel. Those on the ground are still drying; those in the stack in the background are ready to use. Note the identifying handprint on every patty.

The most beautiful smile on the worldwalk. A poor village boy on the G. T. Road in northern India

Thailand. Burial stupas decorate the site of cremated remains.

Thai Buddhist monks painting the gates of their wat (temple ground).

Western Malaysia. Hindu deities along a beach.

Simpang Lima, Malaysia. Firewalker performing as I watched with his little brother.

State of Victoria, Australia. Unusual rock formations silhouetted against sky of the setting sun. I huddled in their shade during the hot day to keep form being burned.

Victor Harbor, South Australia. Seagulls take over a picnic.

On the left, a regular-size bottle of Australian beer; on the right, the popular size in the Northern Territory.

In the middle of the Australian outback, I get to hold a baby kangaroo.

On the Track in South Australia with Roo, my golf cart loaded down with spare tires, journalism gear, food, Clinger and water.
Jean-michel Brault

Northwest Washington,
U.S.A. Rainforest stream
and rocks.

Odd Nebraska custom of putting old
cowboy boots on fence posts. Very
strange and delightful to pass miles
of such upside-down boots in all
sizes.

A very happy worldwalker coming
into Bethel on that final morning of
April 1, 1987. Behind me are the
flags of every country I walked,
handmade by the Bethel-Tate High
School home-economics class.

My tearful reunion with my mother on the front porch of our home in Bethel, Ohio. Looking on are Charles Fambry, police chief of Bethel, and my youngest sister, Sandy.

Aaah. Slipping out of my walking boots for the last time on the worldwalk.

"The book! I need to show my book!" I suddenly shouted at the interpreter.

That confused all of them. Even the policeman lifted his eyes from the Witness Book. No one knew what I was shouting about.

"What?" asked the interpreter.

"I need that book, to show something to the commander. Please, it is important."

He told the military officers. They directed the policeman to hand the book over. I gripped it as if it was made of gold. Then I waved the book in front of their eyes, babbling that I loved to collect autographs from schoolchildren and their schools around the world. But in Yugoslavia I could not have any autographs, because it was the summer break. I thought I sounded very convincing, till the interpreter spoke again.

"The policeman says that is not true. He says you have police autographs in the book."

"Yes, that's true. I know. He's right. It, ah—it is necessary sometimes for me to get permission from the police to walk in their areas in those countries that aren't as free as yours."

Still, that infernal policeman tried to take the book back. I reacted like a cornered bobcat. A shouting match ensued. He grabbed the book. I grabbed it back. He grabbed it again. I pulled it away from him once more, the final time quickly stuffing it down the front of my shirt. The temper of every Irish ancestor I ever had reared up loudly and clearly.

"I *refuse* to have you going and kicking down the doors of innocent people and scaring them, just because they were kind to me!" I screamed at every face there. "If you want this book, you'll have to *kill* me!"

Thankfully, no one thought the matter of my "hobby book" was worth risking their life over. The matter was dropped, at the stern command of the highest officer.

"In Yugoslavia, everyone is a policeman," the interpreter whispered to me near the end of the interrogation, as the others were busily scribbling their notes. I looked at him, surprised. His words had sounded like a quote from Alexander Solzhenitsyn's *Gulag Archipelago*. I asked him to repeat himself, unsure I'd heard correctly.

"In Yugoslavia, we are all policemen. You cannot talk about anything you want with everyone you meet. It will be best for you to remember that —believe me."

I hoped the slight smile on my lips let him know how thankful I was for his concern.

Around midnight I was brought to a hotel in the town and let off in front. I was told by my police driver to stay there overnight. They might have some more questions to ask me in the morning, he indicated.

But, of course, I walked on. There was still too much of the planet to cross to be dealing with such fools.

As I progressed deeper into the only Communist country on my worldwalk, down through the huge mountains of Croatia into the area along the Albanian border, I continued to be astounded at the great difference between this European society and the others I had walked. Just comparing it with Italy, where I had spent three months, demonstrated that.

Along with the beauties and history of Italy, there was its frivolousness. Venice was an excellent microcosm of that country's character. There I found a breathtakingly beautiful city, with culture and history and splendid, richly adorned religious architecture. Yet Venice was also a carnival, an "historic Disneyland."

But in the Socialist Federal Republic of Yugoslavia, it was definitely back to basics. For the typical Yugoslav rural family, for instance, a major home improvement was a fresh coat of paint on a pair of old wood shutters, whereas in Italy it would have been new brass-ringed storm windows and aluminum shutters.

There were far fewer trucks in Yugoslavia, and those that there were groaned under loads of fuel, firewood, cement, and chemicals, rather than stocks of potato chips and pantyhose, as in Italy.

The Slavs themselves, men and women, were as rugged, weathered, and strongly built as the mountains that towered over their farms of potatoes, corn, wheat, and, of course, grapes. Their daily lives were hard, physical, tedious, with few luxuries such as leisure time. Every day at sunrise the villagers went, many in horse-drawn wagons, to the fields to stay bent over for much of the day. For most, I observed, a long-handled sickle or a simple hoe was their primary work tool. The same horse that pulled them to and from the fields also pulled its share of plows across the rocky soil. What farm machinery I did see was not more advanced than small tractors or hand-pushed gasoline-powered tillers.

The grocery stores in the areas outside the cities were pathetically barren. Fresh produce in those stores was as lacking as any meat and cheese. What few rural stores I came across usually had less than half the shelf space stocked. Apparently, liquor and army rations were the big sellers.

I bought a tinned army meal just to see what their soldiers marched on. The contents left me wondering if maybe the poor fellows didn't do more crawling than high-stepping. What I found was a strip of virtual lard one inch thick and five inches long packed in very bitter sauerkraut.

Such things as nightclubs, cinemas, and libraries were found only in the largest cities and towns, and they were of such rundown condition that it was amazing anyone attended them. The music in nightclubs supposedly for the young was a mixture of Frank Sinatra, old Motown, Bavarian polka, and post-Woodstock acid rock!

The one thing I did not find a shortage of, did not have to stand in line to get, was politics. Be it "the party" or "the people," the arguments and counterarguments, pro-communism and anticommunism debates, were as frequent as the boulders in the fields. I knew Yugoslavia was the freest of the Communist nations, having broken away from the Soviet style of communism in 1948, after only three years of it, but I had not expected such a lively sense of independence in discussions. It seemed the Slavs loved to talk politics almost as much as the Irish, and were not at all afraid to do so—away from their bosses' ears.

To the man and woman on the street, communism was something they could just as well do without.

"Communism is brute!" spat one old Slovenian farmer, while sharing a large white tin cup of homemade wine with me. "We are not like the damned Russians. We are socialist . . . I think."

"Socialism? Hah! Only on the front page of the newspaper every morning," a village merchant scoffed. His wife, who, like him, had worked most of her adult life outside of the country, nodded firmly.

When I met the merchant and his wife, it was late evening. After a long, hard day working in their tiny store, they were on their way to work their small farm plots until it was too dark. It was what they had to do, they said, if they expected a decent standard of life.

"In Yugoslavia, the people work only to pay taxes, social security, and hopefully have enough left over to get drunk," the merchant joked with a touch of seriousness.

Their combined take-home wages each month totaled around four hundred dollars, which actually wasn't bad compared to those of the lawyer, who told me his state-controlled wage was two hundred dollars a month, and almost as much as that of the doctor, who revealed his salary was five thousand dollars a year.

"It's a Mafioso that controls everything," a senior construction engineer said sadly, as we walked back to his small inner-city apartment after a swim in the cold Adriatic near Split. "The best of everything goes to a few families who run each of the region's governments. What is left, which is very little in such a poor country, goes first to their friends, and then to the people."

An example of the above, he said, was in the availability of apartments. Those who knew the right people could get one within a couple years' time. Others, such as himself, had to bide their time on lengthy waiting lists. In his case, he'd had his firm assist him in getting the clearance for a place for himself, his wife, and three daughters to live. After ten years, he finally got one.

On the other hand, though Yugoslavia's government was Communist, there were few state or collective farms. Agriculture was mostly small, private holdings. Individuals could own their businesses, though they couldn't have more than five employees. And, most surprising of all to me, the borders were open to all citizens. They were completely free to come and go as they pleased.

"After all," remarked one Yugoslavian waiting for spare parts being smuggled in from Italy for his fishing boat, "encouraging the people to work abroad eliminates what would certainly be much unemployment here."

Much to the chagrin of the present Communist collective leadership, nearly every Yugoslavian home, business, and public building I was inside had a framed photo of Marshal Tito on one of its walls, even though the former president had been dead for over four years.

According to a journalist I spoke with, the present leaders wanted to phase out Tito's influence and get the country moving forward, but they were meeting much resistance from a populace that still adored the "old ways."

But while those habits and beliefs of the past might have been a headache to some, they provided me with a wealth of tradition.

I *loved* being immersed in such Old Worldliness. There was a cragginess and rawness about life there that the plastic and chrome of the wealthy and more advanced societies had somehow chased away. There was, in other words, *character* in the people of Yugoslavia, just as in the Irish and the French farmers and the Spaniards. And where there were such people of the soil and stone and winds, I knew I would always be taken care of. For those old-fashioned people could still relate to a man being hungry and thirsty and sweaty from a heavy load on his back.

Hardly a day passed that I was not invited to join in a hot meal

around a kitchen table. Though the diet of the average family was simple
—oftentimes only potatoes, pork, watered-down wine, and coarse brown
bread with nothing to put on it—they knew what a feast it was to my lean,
leathery body.

Summer was at its blazing height. It was hot enough to sear a man on
the outside in the early afternoon and have him roasted medium-well on
the inside by dinnertime. I would never have guessed mountains as large
as those in Yugoslavia could be as hot and steamy as a Louisiana bayou.
So many afternoons I could be found soundly napping under a cherry tree,
not able to stir until the coolness of the setting sun finally nudged my skin.
It was not so much that I was hiding from the sun, as from the effects of
too much wine. If there was one "bad" habit the farm families of northern
and central Yugoslavia had, it was that they always gave my thirsty
tongue wine to drink, rather than water. In the heat, the alcohol only
made me thirstier.

Persons my age were an uncommon sight in the countryside. There
just wasn't any work for them there, other than on the land for a meager
subsistence. So once out of high school, off to the cities they went, hopefully to find a factory or construction job, or if necessary to go back to
school, as long as the government would pay for their room and board.
Each village I passed through was heavily populated with black-garbed
elders, most still as strong as ever.

I found this especially true as I worked my way around the edges of
the mysterious Communist police state called Albania. On the outskirts of
that country I wove and wound my way through the enormous mountains
and canyons of two of eastern Europe's poorest and most orthodox regions—the Republic of Montenegro and the Serbian Muslim province of
Kosovo.

Herders of goats or sure-footed cattle, rather than farmers, the
Montenegrans were tall, lean, and fine-featured, not short and thick like
the Croatians. With the dark skin and dark eyes of the Ottoman Turks
who had ruled their area for over seven centuries, the people were as eye-
catchingly beautiful as the land.

For the first time since I had left America, I found homes built of
lumber, but these had tall, steep roofs, wood-slab exteriors, and tiny, shuttered windows. Sometimes, as I came upon their stick-fenced dirt yards
with farm animals, wood piles, open wells, and women cooking over an
open fire, I thought of Africa.

In Montenegro, thick forests of pine, beech, and cool shade replaced
the harsh sun, occasional cherry tree, and semi-arid rockiness of Croatia.
Time after time, I came through a mountain pass to find spread all before
me the glory of more mountains. It was July, and so I savored the cooler

temperatures of the peaks and forests. As in Slovenia, I found myself zigzagging down dirt lanes along leftover snowfields and steep, lush meadows of white-petaled daisies to distant ribbons of silver. Bathing in those brightly bouldered rivers of liquid snow left me wondering if I would ever again be warm. To drink their coldness was almost painful to the throat.

In Kosovo, the very old and poor villages, with their mosques, open-air markets, and horse-drawn carts, were similar to those of North Africa. Only instead of Arabs and Berbers passing me, I had a swirling mixture of Turks, Albanians, Slavs, and Gypsies.

Kosovo had been the most troublesome region for the Yugoslav federation. After Tito's death in January 1980, the Muslims, partly inspired by the Ayatollah Khomeini's actions in Iran, had begun to demand more independence from the central government. Two years of harsh police action and much interracial violence followed. One man around my age told me there had been a massacre near his town in which two hundred Muslims were killed, a fact that was kept secret from the outside world. And there were many Albanians who felt that part of Yugoslavia belonged to Albania.

Kosovo was, I was warned, too lawless and unsettled for someone as foreign and vulnerable as I to be walking through. But that turned out to be just more of the usual silly fearfulness that mankind seemed so intent on scaring itself with.

Apparently, the dark-skinned Muslim men with their white skull-caps, their shaven-headed sons, and their thickly clothed subservient women were still too unusual for most Slavs, even after all those centuries.

Person to person, the people of Kosovo weren't any less loving or kind than any other people. But I could see how others would be concerned, because living conditions in the towns were extremely primitive and dirty. The men were totally unused to the idea of privacy, and so, in a repeat of Africa, I had large groups of ragged boys and men crowding about me and rudely grabbing at me for attention.

The littered and crumbling streets of the cities or villages of this mountainous region knew more hooves and bare feet than tires. In the shadows of the dilapidated shops were always the staring eyes. In public, good manners seemed to be mostly nonexistent. Yet whenever I was brought into a home, I inevitably found myself receiving the best of the family's food and attentions. While the children and wife quietly attended to any need, the men and I sat in our stocking feet on low cushions around a table set with thimble cups of ferociously hot Turkish coffee and plates of goat's milk curds, cheese, and rough, dark bread smeared with honey and plum butter. Overhead would be tapestries of Arab desert scenes and the holy shrine in Mecca, or even portraits of America's most famous athlete and Muslim, the boxer Muhammad Ali.

I was beginning to be a veteran of the Muslim brand of hospitality. A male-oriented religion, its people treated me with honor and high respect more because of my gender than because of the fact that I was a visitor from a faraway land. As our manly laughter and excited conversations, usually in broken English or French, continued through the long afternoons and evenings, I felt a strong sense of my "place." Among the Muslims, I was always distinct and "above" any "mere" kids and women. My place in the home and on the streets was secure: I was Man, Boss, Lord, Honored Guest; Woman was my servant, my comforter—nothing more, nothing less. Coming from a background where such thinking was likely to get one a frying pan on the head should have made me uneasy. Yes . . . it *should* have.

The notion that "country folk are a gentle folk" proved as true in Yugoslavia as in any other country I'd visited. More and more, it was striking me how much kinder and more peaceful the human race was than I had grown up to believe. We really didn't give ourselves enough credit as a race. Sure, some things looked downright scary, particularly in the cities, but now that I understood mankind better, I realized much of the fear and defensiveness I'd exhibited in places like North Africa were largely my own making. The more I learned to trust, the more blessings seemed to come my way.

In the cities I had watched Gypsies scrounge through garbage for food to eat and for cloth to make clothes with, but in the mountains I had seen them hold their jeweled heads as high as any man's.

In both Montenegro and Kosovo, the Gypsies had been as poor materially as their peers in the cities. Indeed, for many a week the pounding of their horses' hooves and the rattle of the wooden wheels on their buckboard wagons were my alarm clock each morning. Yet each time I lifted Clinger to my back and emerged from the trees to greet them, I saw them riding as haughtily on those plank seats as anyone back home would have on the leather cushions of a Cadillac. Those Gypsies had a lot to teach all of us.

Not the least of which was that we need to appreciate what we have, rather than fret about what we don't have.

31

reece. If any country conjured up images of gods, monsters, bronzed adventurers, and voluptuous women, it was certainly this one. And so as I crossed on July 21 into what I had been told was the birthplace of Western civilization, I half expected to see Odysseus or the Trojan Horse waiting to greet me. What I didn't expect was a stubbly faced old farmer on a hand-painted red wagon being pulled by a mare nearly as swaybacked as a loose hammock over bright wheat stubble that could have been straight out of Kansas.

"Whoaaaa," the farmer grumbled to the sleepy-eyed horse when they were just a few yards from me. Obediently, she stopped everything but her tail, which she used to keep the flies honest.

"Hi!" I said to my first Greek.

He slowly pulled his straw from his mouth and scrutinized me from head to toe.

"Have you America?" he asked.

"Yes, I am American," I replied, shading my eyes from the glaring sun. I'd lost my latest ball cap, an ugly thing of orange and white, and as a result the sun was really having a field day with my face.

He put the harness straps on the buckboard's seat and eased himself to the ground. Slowly, methodically, he pulled a long-stemmed black pipe from his bib and poked a pinch of tobacco into it.

"Christian you?"

"Yes. I am Catholic." I made the sign of the cross on myself so he would understand.

He nodded gravely, then stared down at his boots very sadly, almost

as if he might cry. Maybe I was getting sunstroke, but I could have sworn
the strange man was feeling terrible about something I had done. I shifted
uneasily beneath Clinger, the way I always do when I'm uncomfortable,
and felt the sweat on my back run wild.

He waved a shy finger at Clinger and moaned, "For sin?"

I didn't understand. "What sin?"

Again, his low, deep voice snatched at my ear. "How many penance
kilo?"

That one I thought over carefully, especially the word *penance,* until
finally it hit me what was going on. I had to laugh, even though the cactus
in my mouth rubbed my throat raw. He thought that I had done some
terrible sin and was having to walk everywhere with a huge weight on my
back as penance to atone for my act.

"No. I am good man!" I said happily. I smiled extra broadly to show
him I really was not doing penance.

He was like a new person after that. The revelation that I only *looked*
as if I were suffering, but really wasn't (at least not for penance) made him
so happy he wanted to celebrate. Which he did at once by reaching into
the back of the wagon to fetch me a big ripe watermelon. My tongue
dropped a foot. It was the answer to all my prayers, hopes, and dreams.
For six miles, I had been going stark crazy smelling distant ripe watermelon patches. With not a town or house in all that time to ask for
anything to drink, I was as dried as the tobacco in the man's pipe. The
fruit weighed a lot, but I didn't care in the least, because I had no intention of looking at its gorgeous smooth husk for any longer than it took me
to cut it open.

"Ef-fa-lay-sto!" I said happily. For several years in Casper, Wyoming,
I had lived with a Greek family, and the only word I'd ever been able to
memorize was "thank you." I couldn't think of a better time to use it than
now.

The old farmer and his nag rode off, and I strode away to a tree to
gorge myself. But I had hardly slipped into the shade, when along came
another farmer, also high atop a wagon of watermelons. He, too, gave me
an odd looking over, then glanced at the departing farmer and motioned
me to come to his side. I sighed but went anyhow, absently cradling the
melon in my arms. To my surprise, he jumped down from his seat,
grabbed my melon, and immediately smashed it on the lane.

"Wha—!" Was the man insane? I glared at him with more than just
confusion in my eyes, only to break as quickly into a long smile. For into
my arms he slipped *two* of his watermelons.

I thought the strange "feud of the watermelons" was ended right
then and there. But it had one more chapter. Amazingly, a third farmer

was to come along seconds later to repeat the whole scenario. Then leave me hugging *three* of his melons.

People suddenly coming out of nowhere to give me presents was certainly nothing new to me. In Algeria, for example, I had had many strangers come running up to me to put very large (for them) sums of money into my hands, including little children who did not even stay around long enough for me to thank them. The mystery of their generosity was cleared up for me by a friendly policeman in Annaba, who explained the people felt sorry for me: They had heard there were *some* poor Americans, but until meeting me, they had never actually quite believed it. How terrible, they had thought, that I should have to walk everywhere, while all my other countrymen could ride in cars and planes.

While I doubted the Greek farmers had been thinking along the same lines, I was thankful all the same for those sweet, juicy treasures.

Needless to say, all my thoughts of raiding those farmers' watermelon patches were forgotten completely.

It was the second of August, circus time in Kaválla, a popular vacation town along Greece's northeast shoreline. I set aside this night to visit the striped Hoffman London Circus tent on the edge of town.

Like most of the audience, I was to spend a good bit of time gripping seat edges and applauding. Then, when all that remained in the ring was sawdust, I found myself wishing for still more bedazzlements. So, while the others in the Big Top filed out the front entrance, I ventured, instead, to the back curtains to find out if I could see what it would be like to live with a circus.

Behind those curtains I found total strangers who thought life too full of wonderment not to share it with others. Brenda Hani, a fifty-three-year-old English widow with a circus career dating back forty years, and her son, Mario, twenty-four years old and as handsome and thickly muscled as his Swiss father had been, invited me to stay with them in their little trailer. And so, for the last five days and nights the circus was in Kaválla, I became one of its company, my job to shovel after Mario's four trained elephants between acts.

The world I became a part of was every bit as thrilling as I had always imagined it would be. And so were the private lives of the performers. The Great Karah and his monstrous alligators were a perfect example.

In the arena, the reptiles were totally obedient to their giant German master's "hypnotic" commands. To the thrilling roll of a drum, he would stride majestically into the one ring's center and put his wide face right up to the blood-red eyes of those ten-foot-long lumpy alligators—and then have the audience bouncing with laughter at the sight of him dropping off to sleep nose-to-snout with the reptiles. Or else have them screaming for their lives, when his "leetle dawling," Claus von Chomper, did its terrifying act of escaping into the front-row seats, where it always—thank God!—stopped just inches from the petrified spectators.

"Karah, why *doesn't* that old 'gator just take a chomp out of those people?" I finally had to ask one afternoon, while we were in his mobile trailer home.

"Ach! I feeed him goot, so he vant only to tees dos peeple—show dem *hees* number vun!"

"And if you ever forgot to feed him before the act?" I asked.

He rolled his big, glistening eyes back into his head, slapped his large palms against his bald scalp, and dropped into a fake faint.

For practical jokers, Karah was the king of the troupe, if only because he had the meanest gags to use. Once, while I was sleeping after a particularly tiring afternoon of shoveling (didn't they *ever* stop?), I sensed someone jumping onto the straw pile I had snuggled into. Scared out of my wits, I bolted upright to find it was an *it* I had for company. And not just any it, either.

If I had grabbed a fifty-million-volt wire, my hair couldn't have stood any straighter. For virtually kissing me on my lips was none other than von Chomper! I was sure he had escaped from the trailer he was always kept caged in. It wasn't until I heard the laughter coming from behind the lion cages that I knew I'd been duped. But even then I didn't dare crack a smile until dear Mr. von Chomper stepped off me and swaggered on back to his bed.

But my favorite insights into the daily world of the Big Top were those shared with me by the least visible person of the entire troupe—Brenda.

A brightly blond, petite lady on the edge of sixty, with an endless reservoir of energy and kindness, she had, for a long time, been a star herself in the English circus world, first with her now-deceased husband's Wild West act; then, years later, with her own performing horses and her son's trained elephants. Now, though, she was considered too old for the ring. Still, every night she was able for a few moments to don a feathered cap and a bright gown to assist Mario in the ring with his elephants.

But her main "act" now was to do all the side chores—sewing costumes, selling refreshments, grooming animals—that someone had to do to keep the circus's costs down, as well as to give her and Mario some grocery money, since the circus was going broke and no one had been paid in two months. It was a schedule that kept her going full tilt from early morning till past midnight. After which, she would drop to sleep on one of the bench seats in the kitchen area of her tiny trailer home.

I thought her workload way too much for someone her age. And very late one night, after Mario had literally passed out in the trailer's only bedroom from his equally grueling chores, I let her know my feelings. We were in the kitchen, and I was still savoring another of the big meals she said I needed to put some weight on me. She had become still another of my journey's special moms, and so it wasn't easy for me to suggest she should put behind her the only life she'd ever really known, that of a circus mother.

When I was finished with my plea, she smiled softly, but her eyes were tired and drained. She rose from her bench seat and took from a cupboard overhead some thick photo albums. And while I studied the snapshots, she proceeded to tell one of the most beautiful love stories I'd ever heard.

Most of the snapshots showed an extremely cheerful man with huge sideburns, who was dressed in a fancy cowboy outfit complete with pearl-handled pistols and a large, wide-brimmed hat. Usually at his side was one of the most beautiful tan-colored stallions I'd ever seen.

The man, of course, was her husband. The horse was his lead show animal, Trigger, a rogue that all the other trainers had dismissed as being too dumb to be trainable.

"Because of the circus, I had me husband and Trigger," she said softly. "And they showed me for so many years how happy life can be when you don't think only of yourself but are always wanting to make others feel good."

She became lost in thought for a few seconds. I sat still, aware of how big the emptiness in her heart must have been. It was as if the night air had become almost too thick to breathe.

"He was such a kind man. He used only patience and gentleness in teaching his horses," she said. "Oh, I tell you, the man who had Trigger before us was so mean and cruel to that horse. He would flog it mercilessly with a whip, and kick it, and say it was the dumbest animal that ever be. The poor baby was so scared of that mean man. Wouldn't you be?"

"You better believe it," I said, anxious to hear more.

"Finally, me husband, it wasn't in his heart to take no more of watching the poor creature suffer. When he heard the other man was going to take the old horse and have it made to dog food, he paid the other man to let us have it, even though we had no money to be sparing for any more feed. You see, it was the winter at Blackpool. All the circuses in England go to rest there that time of year, and so we had no money coming in from our acts.

"But a circus is a family, Steven," she added very proudly. "We take care of each other, make sure no one is without the necessities. If we didn't, it'd be too hard for most to last long. The wages when you are just starting are so little, and yet a person has to somehow survive to be strong for the next show. So the other trainers helped us. They'd slip us their own animals' straw and feed each day. And in the meantime, me husband kept going to Trigger with always an apple or a carrot and his soft voice saying only the nicest of praise in the scared creature's ears.

"As a result, Trigger learned to trust me husband. Where the others had said the animal was too dumb to train, me husband said it warn't that at all. It was only scared, not dumb. And he was right. Showed them all he did, till they come to think it were a sight indeed. Everyone else had needed whips, or loud voice commands, or a swift kick to get that horse to obey, but me husband by the spring had it doing every trick there was with him only moving a hand or whispering in its ear."

By the end of that first season, her husband and Trigger seemed as one, she told me. And they became enormously popular, both in and out of the ring.

But then, in 1971, in the middle of a Wild West performance, Trigger, as always, reared high and with nobility. Her husband's hand, however, never made it as far as his big cowboy hat. Instead, it went to his heart. At the young age of forty-five, he was dead of a heart attack. As swiftly as lightning strikes a tree, Brenda's life went from being a romance to being a tragedy. The most loving man she knew was suddenly a memory. Broken-hearted, alone with only Mario, she had her husband buried in his cowboy suit.

Overcome with grief, Brenda retired to her home. But not for more than a few years. Coaxed back into the ring by her wish to help Mario realize his own ambitions in the circus world, she returned to become a big star in her own right. For ten years more, the spotlights were her nightly companions, as she and Mario's elephants captured the audiences' hearts.

"I know, Steven, you don't approve of me working so hard. But I don't mind. Yes, it isn't easy, for sure, making all those hot dogs and onion rings to sell every night. But if the money we make means Mario can realize his dreams, like I did, then that means a lot to me. I had me dream. I have no regrets."

On the morning I was to continue on my way across northern Greece to Turkey (while the circus went to the other side of Greece and eventually back to England), Brenda went into Mario's bedroom and came back out with something very big wrapped in a dark plastic sack. She handed the bag to me, and what I pulled out of it left me speechless for several minutes. It was her husband's cowboy hat. The same big straw one I'd seen in the photographs of him on Trigger.

"Brenda, I can't take this," I protested. "It means too much to you."

She brushed aside my words and insisted I try it on. It fit perfectly.

"I'd be proud knowing his hat went around the world with you," she said with an approving look. "For thirteen years, it's only been catching dust."

She looked away, almost as if she'd heard a voice on the sea breezes gently rocking the trailer. "How nice it'd be to think me husband is still helping others in some way," she said.

I gave her a hug and thought how hard it was to say good-bye. She'd scolded me from day one of seeing my sunburned face for not having any cap or hat. I wondered if she hadn't been thinking about making that hat a present to me all along.

When it came time to leave, I was wearing the hat. I might not have fooled anyone at the Alamo, but to the rest of the world now I would be a real cowboy. And so I strutted off to the east, away from the setting sun, with perhaps a bit more bounce in my boots than when I'd come strolling along five days before.

After a minute or so of walking, I turned and gave Brenda and Mario my customary big final wave. As I'd seen John Wayne do once, I gripped the hat firmly in my right hand and swung it as wide and high and grandly as I possibly could.

From her trailer door Brenda waved back, then wiped something from her eye.

32

As the geographical and cultural meeting point of West and East, I felt Turkey would provide some of the best adventures yet on the walk. My only concern was that they not be of the deadly kind.

The nation of 45 million inhabitants was not on my walk route originally. It was only with the greatest reluctance and anxiety that I decided to cross its high, dry plains and rugged mountain ranges. As far back as Morocco, I had realized I would be reaching Greece in the hottest part of the year, and I would thus have to forfeit my original plan of walking south from Yugoslavia to Athens, then going by boat to Alexandria, Egypt, and walking down to the Great Pyramids, which I planned to call the walk's halfway mark.

Instead, I decided to cut across northern Greece and then continue eastward across the northern, cooler land mass of Turkish Asia Minor.

At the time of my decision I felt as if I were trading a diamond for a dull, filthy dagger. Egypt was well known internationally for its warmth and kindness to visitors, while all I'd ever heard about Turkey was of its police and military brutality, corruption, and poverty. The fact that over 3 million Turkish men worked in West Germany, doing the same kind of menial work that many Mexican laborers do in the United States, convinced me that in Turkey I'd again find the terrible poverty I'd seen in North Africa. Any nation that had such a large percentage of its males going so far to find work must be a desperate place indeed, I worried.

I felt very uneasy about being alone and American in some of the more rugged and backward areas I would have to cross. This was largely the result of the memories I still had of a terrifying movie I had seen eight years before, while I was at Ohio University. The movie, *Midnight Express*, was a true account of a young American man's nightmare in the Turkish jails, after he was arrested on drug charges. For many of us of that generation, it had become "proof" that Turkey, like most Muslim countries, was filled with brutal, perverted, ugly, hairy policemen looking for any reason to lock up young men in dungeons and beat and rape us.

A bad incident I had at the Turkish embassy in Washington, D.C., back in the spring of 1983, when I was clearing up a lot of last-minute red tape concerning my crossing of many countries, only scared me all the more. Though at that time I was still set on crossing Egypt, and had just had a wonderfully cordial meeting at the Egyptian embassy that same day, I had gone to the Turkish embassy at the last minute, just in case I needed an alternate route later.

It was very late in the afternoon, around the four o'clock closing time. When I rushed up to the big old embassy's front door, it was already locked and being guarded by a large security guard. I told him I was looking for the consulate office, and he said the entrance was in the back of the building. I rushed to the building's rear courtyard and found the thick steel door to the consulate office. It was locked, and from what I could see through the tiny bulletproof peep window, everyone inside had already left for home. A sign on the door below the window said it was open only during morning hours.

I set my briefcase down beside the door to fish out a pen and notebook. I figured I'd copy down the office hours and come back the next day, before returning to Ohio.

I had started to put my pen back into my dress jacket's pocket when a gruff voice from behind commanded me to raise my arms, or else!

"Make any kind of move, mister, and you're dead," a woman's deep voice growled.

I didn't need to hear any more. My hands were reaching so high, they could have been used as utility poles.

"Turn around, slowly," the voice snapped.

I turned around to find one of the biggest, meanest-looking D.C. law officers I'd ever seen. Gripped in her hands was a submachine gun poking halfway out of a cloth bag.

"Hey, Bob," she called to someone just out of sight around the building's corner, "he's alone."

"Of course I am. I'm here to see the consulate. Why—"

"Did I tell you to say something, mister?" she snarled.

She had gone too far. I put my hands down and demanded to know why I was being treated that way.

"We couldn't be sure you weren't sent here to bomb the embassy," explained her much-kinder partner. "We were sitting in our squad car, and when we saw you rushing back here with that briefcase, and we knew the offices were all closed, we thought you might be an Armenian. You've got to admit, it looks mighty suspicious when you put that briefcase down next to the door."

I had to admit that maybe they had done the right thing after all. I knew that only a few days before, a Turkish diplomat had been killed in California by an Armenian assassin.

"But you know it wouldn't hurt your personality to try being a little nice," I recommended to the still-glaring, silent policewoman.

"I don't get paid to be nice," she snarled.

That evening I had decided I would most definitely go to Egypt after Greece. I was going around the world to learn, not to fight a war.

The yellow-orange flames licking at the horizon from the burning wheat stubble looked eerie in the dusk. The rocky land about me stretched forever, and there seemed no life, save for the dancing flames of the far-away fields and the many Gypsies bedding down for the night.

I held my breath and walked quietly, not sure that I wanted these latest bands of vagabonds to know that I existed. It was August 11, and only hours ago I had crossed into Turkey, across the bridge over the river Meric, and I did not quite know what to make of this rough-looking country whose gruff and arrogant border troops had reminded me too much of the Algerians in the Sahara.

A horse neighed somewhere close by, and I became as still as a tree. The smells of smoking twigs and boiling mint tea wafted over me. The jangle of leather and metal on a restless horse's neck came out of the lowlands along a nearby creek. Voices of men . . . a baby crying . . . the clatter of dishes . . . I had never before come upon such a huge gathering of Gypsies. The white peaks of their teepee-like tents seemed to have multiplied tenfold in just the past minute.

Then my mouth dropped open, as from the depths of the earth there arose a huge, round moon. A violin screeched—and as I watched, the families alongside the road began to dance. I took a deep breath, picked out a campfire, and joined in.

The head of the family who took me into their care was built like a stoker in a steel mill, and had a moustache so black and bushy it could

have been hired out as a broom. His wife was short and jolly, a motherly
figure whose peasant clothes were all that kept her from resembling a
butcher's wife in Kearney, Nebraska. Their two young sons bore the
smudges of growing gladiators. Their horses were tired, their wagons
caked with the mud and dust of a million miles. They were Gypsies pure
and true. And I—I was the stranger who seemed to have given them all,
young and old alike, all the more reason to dance even more enthusiastically.

Till the fires melted, we danced and sang like fairies reborn, though
not a step did I know nor a word could I say. Round and not-so-round, a
fiddle there, a harmonica here, such laughter we gave and received, till at
last the children were yawning and into our beds we reluctantly crawled,
the earth our mattress.

I awoke on the edge of a dream, an edge so narrow and rickety that I
knew the second my eyes swallowed the dawn's light I could not go back
to find it. I arched my back and stretched for the North and South Poles,
for something more powerful than an August morning's chill had just
kissed me—the perfume of cooking vittles. I peered out onto a landscape
and a scene Genghis Khan would have smiled upon.

"*Gel! Gel!* [Come here!]," my Gypsy family ordered me. They were
gathered around the "kitchen table," a metal serving tray on a blanket
beside a campfire that was adding more clouds to the sky and more black
to their pots.

I emerged from my down hideout in my only pajamas—my walking
clothes. I quickly snuggled into the fire's heat, grateful for the cup of hot
mint tea and the buttered rough bread they put in my hands. And as I
warmed myself, the children rushed off to a nearby farm field to snitch a
couple armloads of corn, which were roasted over the open flames till they
were black and then eaten by all of us.

They knew no English, and I hardly knew any Turkish. With our
musicians of last night gone (Had that *really* happened?), we were forced
to smile at each other and pretend that we understood the gabble spilling
out of the other's throat. It was at times like that when I felt my most
frustrated. No doubt my host had as many stories to enchant and enthrall
me with as I did for him and his family. So many tales stored away inside
of ourselves, and still so much room in our hearts and minds to be filled
with more. But not a thing could we do to cure our awkward mumbling.

If ever there was a curse on the intelligence of man, it was that malady known as "language differences." I was one up on most of the world, because English was the "international language," and I had known it from childhood. But what use was that to any Gypsy who knew only the language of his own kind? How did one tell about tears and fears and love and dreams with only ten fingers and a squinnying face for a vocabulary?

I told myself that when I reached Istanbul—still over a hundred miles to the east at the very threshold to Asia—I would search for a book that would help me to learn some Turkish. But for now, I had only sensations to bring away from the Gypsies, not songs or legends, or even their family history.

Thank God for the smile. I knew, they knew, that we had met as strangers and gone away as friends and family. Still . . . if only we could have *said* so.

33

Like an endless procession of rectangular angry elephants, the trucks rumbled past me on their way to Istanbul. With air horns trumpeting loudly and their insides fuming, the eighteen-wheelers of Europe charged to and from the ancient heart of Asia Minor with a recklessness that had me scared for my life. Many, if not most, of the trucks were said to be hauling supplies to the warring, material-starved Iran and Iraq. Whatever, their numbers seemed insane.

As they have since the time of Alexander the Great, Allah's Turks held the overland keys to the Near and Middle East from the commercial centers of Europe. And like the banner-draped caravans of long ago, today's cargo haulers still wore the distinctive colors of their places of origin upon their canvas coverings.

The covered semitrailers of the Communist regimes, for example, were always uniformly sharp, taut, of spotless military gray or blue, and marked with efficiently stenciled block letters spelling the nation's name. But those of the capitalist societies, such as the very rich West Germany, boldly flew the colorful medieval-looking badges of their entrepreneur lords.

The most exciting members of the parade of growling, gnashing work beasts were the much smaller Dodge, Fargo, and DeSoto vehicles of the Turks themselves. Gaily adorned with silk tassels, rainbow-colored beads, tinsel, flowers, and hand-painted panels of mountain homes and big-eyed children, their vehicles were wonderfully wacky misfits in the conservative world of commerce and trade.

By my third day inside Turkey, I was wondering if there might not be a better—quieter—route to Istanbul than the one I was on. When, around five in the afternoon, I saw a village nestled in a small valley off to my right, I made for it in the hope that someone there would know a back road that my highway map of Asia Minor didn't.

Down a long dirt road I ambled, my mind playing over and over again the manner in which I would get the villagers to understand what I wanted. However, all that was quickly forgotten when I turned the corner onto the main street and found a lot of bushy moustaches and large, crooked noses scrambling out of teahouses and shops to meet me.

I slipped out of Clinger, shook the many rough strong farm hands thrust at me, and pointed to the little American flag still pinned to Clinger's backside. As was common in such rural settings, it wasn't until I said "America" that anyone recognized the flag. Then, of course, everyone was all the more amazed to know I was walking.

From my experiences in the other countries, I knew what many of them were asking me, simply by the way they cocked their eyebrows or held their hands. For example, when someone hunched his shoulders and swept his right hand through the air, that usually meant, "Where are you going?" Or when they tilted their heads sharply to the left and placed the palm of their left hands against the cheek, that certainly meant "Where do you sleep?" And, of course, the throwing up of both open hands into the air with a quizzical look always meant, "Why?"

I went into my usual routine of drawing a circle in the dust, pointing to my feet, lifting my legs in a walking motion, then walking my fingers across the circle in the dust while saying very slowly and clearly: "I . . . walk . . . around . . . world." When they went, "Aaaahhh . . ." I knew they had understood. Which meant the next question was probably, "How did you get across the water?" So, as always, I pointed to the sky, stuck out my arms, made a whooshing noise with my mouth, and pretended I was a jet.

Still, it was a lot more enjoyable when we *did* speak the same language. So, when after a few minutes a boy came hurrying along with a man friend who spoke English, I relaxed considerably.

The strongly built man introduced himself as Dr. Hasan Ali Uslu. He said he was twenty-five and the only doctor in the clinic in Inecik.

"When I hear you are American who walks around the world, I come fast," he said. "I think this man he must be brave to do such thing."

For at least a half hour he fielded questions from the others, translated them to me, then in turn told them what I had answered. And so it might have gone on for another hour, had not someone asked the ever-popular question about how I took my baths and washed my clothes.

When the doctor told them that I normally took care of those matters in the creeks and rivers I crossed, there was a sudden clamor. Several of the men spoke at the same time, tugging at the doctor's arms.

"Come, Mr. Steven!" the doctor said, grabbing my hand and pulling me back down the street in the direction I had come from.

"What is it?" I asked, slinging Clinger back onto my shoulders.

"You have been to Turkish bath?"

I hadn't. I described the public bathhouses in France; they had been little more than private shower stalls in cement-block houses with an attendant who took your money and watched your belongings. Was that like a Turkish bath?

"No, Turkish bath is best," he assured me.

I glanced nervously at the wall of moustaches and beards tagging along. I envisioned a long indoor pool surrounded by marble columns and all sorts of hairy men in various stages of undress.

"Here Turkish bath!" he said at last.

I looked to our left, to a low, round stone building about twenty feet wide sitting half-sunken into a weedy field on the edge of the village. It reminded me of a very large crypt in some swampy cemetery.

"How *old* is that?" I asked.

The doctor consulted the others. Some said five hundred years, some said seven hundred, he told me. "I think it is oldest in Turkey," he joked.

I was very impressed. I had thought the public laundry-washing troughs from the Middle Ages still being used by many of the rural house-wives in France had been amazing. But they were nothing compared to this ancient, windowless structure.

"You like Turkish bath?" he asked.

"Yes," I replied, thinking it did look very interesting.

He told the others I liked it, and they pulled me to the other side of the building with such exuberance I nearly tripped over my own feet. Half a dozen hands pounded on the rotten planks of a low door. From inside came a grunt. The door creaked open, and a large, dark hand waved us in.

I bent over and followed the doctor inside. The stench of sulfur flat-tened my nostrils like a heavyweight's fists.

A toothless giant of long, wild whiskers and even longer teeth watched the doctor, me, and about half a dozen of the others stumble into the bathhouse's damp, dungeonlike entrance room.

A bare electric bulb in the crumbling cement ceiling cast a yellowish glow that made the wisps of steam rising from the slimy stone floor seem alive. What a perfect entryway to hell, I thought with a smile at the man-beast.

Dr. Uslu squatted and looked into one of three low, crooked round holes in a concrete wall. I took off Clinger, leaned him against the runny green wall, and did the same as the doctor. At the far end of a passageway that looked as if it had been dug by a two-hundred-pound mole was a gurgling, burping claustrophobic dark chamber of yet thicker steam and odors.

"There you take hot bath, wash clothes," he said.

"I go alone—one? Yes?" I asked hopefully.

He swept his hand toward the others. "No, Mr. Steven. All go! Is Turkish custom."

What! He was expecting me to go crawling *naked* into some dark pit with the descendants of the likes of Gengis Khan? I wondered how I might back out of this communal bath gracefully. But then the giant thrust what looked to be large red towels into our hands. I watched as the others wrapped theirs around their waists like a skirt, and slipped out of their trousers beneath it.

In seconds all were milling around me with their clothes in their arms. As they disappeared one by one into the hole, I struggled for the longest time with the task of slipping out of my boots and pants without losing my grip on the skirt.

To my amazement, the men never once uncovered themselves the whole time we washed and chatted in the volcanic stream that was our bathtub. I eased myself into their midst, no longer worried about being molested but only feeling great pity for every lobster I had ever eaten. So hot was that water and so suffocating the steam that I would have loved to get rid of that heavy towel around my waist. But the others didn't seem the least inclined to think about that. So I suffered in silence, even as I was filled once again with a tremendous awe at the strict morality of the Muslims—a people that so many Americans were eager to label as being immoral and uncivilized.

Back out in the entrance room, I tugged my pants back onto my legs beneath the clinging skirt—not at all an easy thing to do. Once that was over, I gladly handed the soggy covering to the giant and retreated barefooted into the outside world. There I gulped in the cool evening air as if it were the sweetest perfume in all of the world. It made me feel mighty good in no time at all.

Dr. Uslu joined me outside and insisted I be his guest for as many days as I wanted. I went back into the bathhouse and retrieved Clinger, then followed the doctor to a small, one-story, two-room white cement building that was both the government-sponsored medical clinic and his residence. Over a dinner of raw potatoes, a tomato, and some goat kidneys fried over the same tiny bottled-gas burner on which he sterilized his scalpels, he shared with me late into the night his deep desire to turn his attentions to something more adventurous than being a village doctor.

There were just too many days in Inecik in which nothing more challenging than a cut finger came his way, he lamented.

The son of a judge in one of the mountainous regions along the Black Sea, he had been able to get the government to pay for his medical schooling. But now he owed his government six years of service at minimum pay for the money they had spent on his education—plus the obligatory two years of military service every man in Turkey had to do.

He talked wistfully of traveling to places like Nepal and South America while he was still young, but he also admitted with much frustration that he knew he could never visit those places before he was middle-aged.

He had me sleep on his cot, and just before he fell asleep on the examination table around 2:00 A.M., he propped himself up on his elbow one last time and said he would write to my mother to let her know we had met.

"Maybe when my government does not own me, I go to see you in Ohio. Okay with you, Mr. Steven?"

I looked into the darkness in his direction. "You bet. Sounds pretty good to me right now."

Just as Venice had captured my heart as no other city before it, Istanbul, with its fabulous gold markets and centuries-old mosques, was to captivate my imagination.

Built like Rome on seven gently sloping hills, along one of the most beautiful waterways anywhere, the Bosporus Strait, Istanbul was a striking mix of architectural contrasts that resulted from its being located on several of the world's oldest and most important trade routes—and from having been invaded so often. Built by the Romans in A.D. 328, and assailed over the centuries by the armies of the Arabs, the Bulgarians, the Christian Crusades, the Ottoman Turks, and lastly the Allied forces in World War I, the city contained every kind of culture I had visited so far. Plus many that were still ahead.

When, on the warm and sunny afternoon of September 23, I stepped into a little wooden rowboat and paid the fisherman the equivalent of a quarter to take me across the half-mile-wide Bosporus Strait, I took with me thrilling memories of my two days in Istanbul; vivid among them the clamor of the Great Bazaar, with its miles of covered avenues lined with counters and stalls selling everything from priceless antique Persian silk rugs to gold and jewels to Chinese jade to the ever-present posters of American movie stars like James Dean and Marilyn Monroe.

Yesterday, I had been waved into an old mosque by its janitor, who had reverently showed me the inside of its tall, domed prayer chamber. It was the first time I had been inside a mosque, since those in Africa had been off-limits to me, and I would never forget how peaceful it had been in its stark simplicity. No chairs, pulpits, statues, paintings, pews, or even a musical instrument in that thousand-year-old building still used by the many faithful each and every day. Like all mosques, its sole function was for prayer to God. Its only furnishings—the straw mats on the floor, the ceramic-tiled columns holding up the domed roof, and the spindly candle chandelier hanging from a long chain that disappeared into the dome's recess—were permeated with so many prayers and cries of *Aaaallaaahhh Bekar!* (God is great!) that I had felt it would be sacrilegious of me to leave there without having spoken to Him.

And so I had spoken; asking that He please ease my parents' worries, that He bless all those who had helped me get this far, and that He continue to direct me safely back to home. When at the doorway I slipped my boots back onto my stocking feet, I felt strangely more powerful and sure of my future than when I had entered.

I had had only one disappointment in Istanbul, and that had not been any Turk's fault. With the assistance of three Iranian students at the university in Istanbul, I had visited the Iranian consulate to try to get permission to cross that nation—the next country directly east of Turkey. The students, who had been soldiers on the Iraq battlefront, kept telling me that Iranians welcomed American visitors now. The consul, however, quickly righted that misconception.

Very coldly, he informed me that I *might* get a visa after eight weeks of waiting (whereas other nationalities waited only one day). They would need that time to check on my background. Furthermore, my visa would be good only for vehicular transit straight through to Pakistan, would not be renewable, and would not permit me to stray off the highway. Walking was out of the question.

So Iran would be the first missing link in my walk's chain. At least I wouldn't have to worry about becoming a casualty of the escalating Iran-Iraq war.

34

His face was ugly enough to scare away the meanest grizzly, his hands thick enough to be the roots of the mountains guarding his golden rice paddies. To the one hundred or so inhabitants of Güney Köyü, most of whom worked in his rice fields in the valley far below, or were related to him through his four previous wives, Aydi Bekir, age seventy-three, was the boss, grandfather, or father.

My path had taken me across north-central Turkey to the hidden river valley where I spied his mud-walled domain resting high atop a mountain's steep shoulder. I had climbed a dirt footpath to photograph some of the womenfolk baking bread in an outdoor stone oven.

At first I was tempted to refuse Aydi's offer of tea. Already that long day I'd consumed twenty-two teas and two colas in the previous village of Hacihamza. But when the smiling giant quickly added a bed and dinner to the tea, I motioned him to lead on.

The hospitality ritual that followed was typical of the treatment I had received in many of the Turkish rural homes east of Istanbul—now two-and-one-half weeks and 327 miles behind me. In many ways it was still largely unchanged from that described in Marco Polo's own journals.

At the bottom of the stairs leading up to Aydis's home above a grain-storage barn, my shoes joined at least ten pairs of thin rubber sandals. Atop the wooden steps was a veranda of bamboo shades, intricately pat-terned wool rugs, rough wooden benches and one low, hard sofa piled with long and heavy flowery pillows, upon which I was made to recline. Though I would rather have sat upright like the rest of the men, I knew that they were trying to make me feel all the more rested and honored.

A large, round silver tray of mint tea and hot food prepared that very hour, undoubtedly by one of Aydi's several wives or many daughters, was set before me by his youngest sons. In the long courtyard below gathered the curious of the village—the men on benches or thin prayer rugs in the center, the boys squatting along the sides of the walls. Word had spread fast that Aydi had a special guest from some faraway land, and so they had rushed to put forth their own questions, and to let Aydi know that whom he cared for, they cared for, too. Well into the night they were to stay, riveted to my words as translated to them by a schoolteacher.

No women and hardly a girl above the age of ten was to be found among those around me. In a remote setting like Güney Köyü, the law of Allah still ruled strongly. And Allah said Woman was to be baking and cooking somewhere unseen when so many of His men were together in one place. The female presence was to be made known only through the food and tea being obediently served by the sons. Or by the faint sounds of their laughter and chatter. And, too, from the occasional shy maiden's eyes stealing a peek through an open door.

It happened to be the first, and most important, day of the four-day-long *Bayram Kurban* holiday, or "Feast of the Sacrifice." All through the Islamic world, according to my host, those who could afford to do so had killed and butchered a ram for Allah. One-third of the meat was to go to the ram's owner, one-third to his neighbors, and the remainder to the poor. Thus, besides the normal bowls of yogurt, spicy vegetable soup, and freshly picked tomatoes and peppers, there was a generous heap of the sacrificial animal, diced and covered in its simmering greases, on my tray.

Five times, once every hour, one of the young boys sitting silently off to the sides rose to his feet, gripped in his small dark hands a hand-made small hydria, stepped up to each of the grown men and older boys, and poured into our cupped hands a strongly perfumed water. For several seconds the air would be suffocating with the fragrance of lemon, as work-toughened palms vigorously rubbed the perfume into the stubbles of fore-arms and face.

In Istanbul, I had found an English-Turkish translation book to study while continuing to cross the nation. It was a most peculiar book—only one inch square and published in Germany, with the title *Langenscheidt's Lilliput Dictionary*. But with it, I quickly mastered a large amount of the Turkish vocabulary, including the counting from one to a million, in less than an hour's memorizing. Indeed, the Turkish language was one of the easiest I'd ever tried to learn. And so I was able, even if only in the usual broken fashion, to add my fair share of manly chatter during the evening.

At last very late that night, after the village's men had returned to what must be some of the world's most patient wives, I was buried beneath a ton of blankets on that same sofa. A beaming Aydi sat down beside me, his lumpy stout figure dressed in striped pajamas and stocking cap, and looked as if he wanted to do one more bit of goodness for me before he retired. I smiled from beneath my own mountain.

Since I knew from my times in North Africa how much being hospitable meant to a Muslim, I hinted to Aydi that a glass of water might be nice. He jumped from his chair and dashed into the house, then proudly strode back to my side several minutes later, with the water *and* a plate of more kurban. Not until I'd finished every morsel and he'd had the pleasure of fetching me still another glass of water did my gap-toothed and bearded guardian angel finally tiptoe off to be with the wife I never did meet.

Sleep remained as elusive as the stars that were shining between the mountain peaks around the veranda. It was the end of the first week of September. Another autumn on the road was nearly upon me. The last one had been in Normandy and Brittany. After one-and-one-half years of my greatest dream, I was but a whisper from its halfway point. Already I had experienced so much more love than I could ever have hoped for, and yet I was only on the other side of the globe from my own little village, and home. . . .

The closer I drew to the Iranian border, the more desolate the land became. Dirt turned into restless dust, then into rock, then finally into mountains and lifeless fields of lava, cooled and battered into grotesque forms by centuries of chilly winds bred just a hundred miles away to the northeast, on the steppes of Russia's Armenia.

There were many in America who said that the Devil himself now reigned in Iran. As I looked uneasily upon the rough faces and the bleak scenery of the no-man's-land there at the confluence of the borders of Iran, Turkey, and Russia, and saw the amount of war-related material moving to Iran each day, I wondered if perhaps there wasn't more truth to that than the rational mind was willing to admit.

I moved cautiously through each canyon and over every high lonesome mountain pass with the expectancy of death pulling at the roots of my hair. But I was learning to use fear as craftily as it had once used me.

One dusky evening, while entering the folds of some high barren mountains east of Erzurum, I noticed many pairs of eyes staring down at me from dwellings in the cliffs above. Ragged figures of men huddling around fires on those ledges made me feel as though I were an insect trying to sneak through a cave of bats. When several of them silently detached from the others and swooped down the steep side of the mountain, I hurried along . . . only to realize they meant to follow me into the darker recesses of the mountains. I had to attack before they could.

Throwing Clinger to the ground, I charged madly with my knife, screaming as loudly as if I would kill any and all I could get my blade into. They fled back up to the cliffs, where I went also. There I demanded to see the tiny settlement's chieftain, and when he emerged from a door in the cliff I had raced to, I drew my weapon's blade across my throat in a way that said such would befall anyone who followed me into the mountains that night. No one did.

But I was not foolish enough to think I was immune from danger. And I knew that each step I took toward the base of Ararat Mountain was bringing me closer to the danger of robbery. So I stopped in the military town of Eleşkirt, twenty miles from the end of the Turkey trek, to mail home all the exposed film I was carrying in Clinger. If something should happen to me in the unstable area just ahead, at least the record of my thousand miles across Turkey would be salvaged. What I didn't know, as I sat sorting the film in a dark teahouse on a side street, was that danger was approaching that very minute.

It came in the form of a group of four, their jackboots, long brown wool coats, wide black belts, and heavy old carbines reminding me of the Gestapo of my history books. While the others in the packed room slunk out quickly to escape the look of hatred in the policemen's eyes and joined the growing crowd outside on the street, I was forced to stay cornered and seated while they formed a curtain of gun muzzles about my cluttered table. A man I had talked with earlier and to whom I had admitted that I was a journalist now revealed himself to be of the secret police. In a show of intimidation, they shouted at me, pushed me to the floor, and kicked at me when I dared to raise my voice.

My explanation that I was walking around the world and that their town was simply on my route fell onto deaf ears. Even my journals and the signature book failed to make any impression.

I was led from the teahouse like a captured criminal. While one policeman mashed all my film and notes into Clinger and went on ahead with the backpack, the others jostled me out onto the street and practically dragged me past long lines of shouting faces and pointing fingers. My worst fears had been realized: Those who had been inside the teahouse, especially the children, had fanned down the street saying some sort of spy had been captured. I hung my head, not so much from shame as to protect it from rocks. The policemen prodded me along by giving me sharp kicks on the backs of my calves.

Nothing was making any sense anymore. What had happened to the kind Turkey I had known almost everywhere up to now? Why were so many Turks now spitting and shouting at me? From somewhere the shout of *"Yahudi!"* stung my ears. *Yahudi* meant "Jew" in Turkish. It was considered one of the most insulting things they could call another person. I'd heard more than one truck driver use it derogatorily during our conversations at the roadside tea shacks.

At the police post, the commander, a handsome, well-groomed, and well-dressed man in his thirties or early forties who spoke excellent English, made it quite clear why I was being treated like a pariah.

"You Americans think you are first-class world citizens, don't you?" he asked in a mocking way.

"Yes . . . I suppose," I answered hesitantly.

He flung my passport at me and spat at my face. "I think you are fourth class!"

I started to sit down in a stiff-backed wooden chair. A punch on my spine from one of his subordinates made me decide otherwise. I glared at the laughing commander with more hate than I'd known for anyone since that night in Tangier, while he continued to speak to me.

"Every day I read in the newspapers how your country is all homosexuals and drug addicts. You people are perverts! You Americans are so sick. You think only of money and sex." His wide chest shook with laughter as he put his face just inches from mine, and sneered, "And I think your President Reagan is the biggest pervert of them all."

The others in the small, clean office had a good long laugh at the last remark, which the commander translated to them. Perhaps because I didn't seem amused, I was slammed into the chair by one of the policemen. Trying not to show the pain clawing at my back and stomach, I sat there stone-faced for the next half hour as the commander ranted on about the vices of America and the greatness of the Ayatollah Khomeini.

Americans were greedy, living solely to see how much money they could make. Americans were the laughingstock of the world. Americans thought about, and cared for, only themselves. They were the most selfish race ever. Americans were diseased, ugly, stupid, and clowns in the rest of the world's eyes. They were even turning their own children into drug users. They were almost too disgusting to talk about.

"You are just like the dogs on the streets."

A glimmer came into his black eyes. He looked into my passport, then leaned forward onto his elbows. "Have you ever married?"

I knew better than to answer that one. All the Turkish men I had met had been amazed that I was thirty years old and not married. To most of them, who had had several children by that age, it was a sad and baffling situation to be so old and without a woman and children.

"You must be a homosexual, too. Yes?" the commander leered.

I remained silent. To deny it would only make me, in his eyes, one of those dogs on the streets. I was scum any way they looked at it.

His hatred for Americans was such that he relished the chance fate had presented him to torment one. In all likelihood, I was the only American he'd ever had the pleasure of arresting. The facts that I was in a highly sensitive-military area away from any tourist spots, loaded down with codelike notes and an abnormal amount of film and maps, spoke several languages, and had been to several other Muslim countries, made him certain I was a prize catch.

"Show us your international journalist's card!" he commanded.

"I don't have any such card. There is no such card," I replied truthfully.

"You are a journalist. Do not lie! You must have the international card, or else you are a spy. Give it here!" he fired back, directing one of the uniformed men to empty everything from Clinger onto his desk.

I knew I would be searched next, and I tried to delay that by volunteering my wallet from my back pocket. He snatched it and dumped its meager contents onto the table. Meanwhile, other policemen arrived to say there was a crowd gathering out front in the dusk.

Whatever card he was looking for, it was not among the business cards and scraps of paper in the wallet. That only incensed him more.

"Where is your permission from our government to write about us and take photographs?" he asked.

Of course I had no such papers. I hadn't even been aware such permission was needed. I could see the charges against me piling deeper and deeper.

"Why are you doing this to me?" I practically pleaded. "America and Turkey are friends, allies. We both belong to NATO. We give your government so much money—" Immediately, I knew I'd made a serious mistake.

"Ha-ha-ha! You are fools. You think you can *buy* everyone else's friendship, because you are so rich. Do you really think we care? You give, give, give money to buy our loyalty, but we don't care about who gives us money. We'll take American dollars *or* Russian rubles, and laugh at you both!"

Finally, he banged his fist on the desk top and said, "I think you are spying. I think I will lock you up for a few weeks. I will put you in the jail, and we will tell no one. Then"—he nodded his head sarcastically—"then we will contact your embassy to see if you are who you say."

I was jolted. "You can't do that. I've done nothing wrong, and you have no proof of anything wrong."

"I can kill you if I want. You are not the boss here. This is not America." Then, laughing his loudest yet: "If I want, I'll lock you in prison for years and tell no one. I'll tell my men to throw away the key. You are in Turkey."

For the first time in the two or three hours he'd had me there, I was certain I was going to be imprisoned. And I knew that if he really wanted to kill me, it would be very easy once I was in jail.

I racked my brain for how to escape from that jail cell, and saw the answer resting right at his elbows—the *Washington Post* interview done with me in Atlantic City. I leaped for it, before the policemen had a chance to knock me back into the seat.

I waved it in the air, saying in a confessional tone, "I write for the *Washington Post*—here's one of my stories. They know where I am. If they don't hear from me in two days, they'll send someone from Ankara to find me. And many people in this town know I was brought here."

I had noticed during the evening that he had a gold cigarette lighter, a gold bracelet, and a gold chain on his neck. Those, his stylish clothes, and his boasts earlier of being a womanizer told me he was living well beyond what a man in his position made a month in Turkey. In a country as wretchedly poor as Turkey, being a border-post commander, with its many chances for making money on the side, had to be a most desirable position. I decided to threaten his job.

"If anything happened to one of their reporters, it would be front-page news, and your embassy in Washington would see it. What you are going to do to me will embarrass both your country and you. And . . . that could cost your job."

I tossed the *Washington Post* article onto his desk, as if to dare him to look at it. To my relief, he pushed it aside as if he were above such garbage.

"Every day people write bad things about Turkey. What is one more bad story?" he said angrily. He carried on as if the whole matter were unimportant, irrelevant. But I knew I had scared him. I had seen the look in his eyes.

Sure enough, after about ten minutes, he suddenly softened his voice, and said politely, as if nothing had been wrong all along, "I do not want you to think I am a bad man. I will have you stay tonight in a house, instead of the jail. That will be safer for you. I care for you, I do not want to see anything happen to you."

I could hardly believe my ears. There had to be some sort of catch. There was.

He sent one of his officers to a small room across the narrow hallway. For several minutes I heard the sound of typewriter keys clacking. The officer returned and handed a one-page typewritten sheet to his superior, who placed it before me.

"Sign this, and you will not have to go to the jail," the commander said.

I looked at it carefully. It was in Turkish. For all I knew, it was a confession that I had spied or done something even worse. I protested that I wasn't about to sign something I couldn't read.

"All it says is that you were not forced to come to the police station. That we did not take anything from you, and that no one hurt you physically."

He was asking me, in effect, to deny that anything wrong had happened that day in Eleskirt. That I had volunteered (!) to come to his station, and had been treated like a real gentleman. The very thought of signing that paper was against everything I'd been taught about law and justice. But what was the alternative?

I asked the French-speaking plainsclothesman about the document's contents. He, too, said it was basically a release. I asked for a pen: I had no choice. But first there was one more gambit to be played. If I lost it, I would not be leaving Turkey for many years.

"This says you did not take anything from me. But you have all my gear and my camera," I pointed out. "I refuse to sign this until you give me my things back."

He did not like that at all. He insisted his men, and he, were honest. That everything was perfectly safe in his office overnight. I threw the paper, my only salvation, on the floor. I was bluffing for my life. He had no way of knowing it, but just inches from his arms was all the proof he would ever need to convict me of spying. In my camera, on a roll of black-and-white film (which could easily be developed right there in the town overnight), was a photo of what I had been sure was an American tank being hauled by truck to Iran.

But I held out, sweating the entire time that I was blowing my only ticket to freedom.

Till at last he relented, saying:

"Okay. You can have all your things, but you must promise not to change or destroy anything. Right? We agree as gentlemen. I must have your word."

I gave it to him. I signed the paper, and I was allowed to repack everything into Clinger. Even my passport was returned. When my hand clasped the heavy Minolta's clunky body, I thought I could almost feel my feet rise off the floor.

I was being released, he said. But only to the house. I was to stay there overnight, in case they had more questioning to do in the morning. To "protect" me (as he put it), but more likely to make sure I wasn't up before the roosters, I was accompanied by an armed guard. After what seemed an unnecessarily long time of walking from side street to side street in the freezing wind, I was shown into an old house that was little more than an empty shell. There was no plumbing, no electricity, no furniture, not a bit of warmth. I didn't know who had it worse: the guard sitting outside in his long coat, or me inside with all the rats and smells.

I sat on the cold cement floor, feeling as low as a person could. I was away from that mad police commander, but for how long? Tomorrow could bring more of the same abuse, and beatings. He was as likely to decide overnight that I had to be punished as anything else.

I shook with cold and the urge to cry. Drawing my knees up to my chest, I let my head rest against a wall. I looked unhappily at the stars blinking through a back window: I felt like an alien lost a billion light years from my family.

The window . . . my God—the window! *No,* I told myself, *it's too crazy. You can't even think about crawling out that window.* But that was all I *did* think about. Less than ten feet away from me was an open window. I looked to the guard out front. He was smoking and seemed unconcerned about me. I eased myself to my feet and tiptoed to the window. Not a soul behind it, just an open lot. I tried again to talk myself out of it, but there just wasn't much to say *against* going out that window while I had a chance.

I thought the pounding of my heart was going to wake the entire town as I eased Clinger onto my back and snapped the buckles tightly. He hugged me as tightly as a cub would a momma bear. If there was any running to be done, I wanted him clinging like my own clothes.

First one leg, then the other I placed out the window. I sat unsteadily on the sill, holding my breath as if I were about to plunge into a bottomless lake. When at last I shoved and dropped away to the ground, I knew I was free again, that the roads and the skies were mine to keep for a while longer. It could have been a trap, I realized, a ploy to trick me into being killed while "escaping." But it wasn't.

Under the cover of the darkness and with the dark rows of the town's houses watching me like jumbled tombstones, I crawled on my hands and knees to the fields on the edge of the town and made my way along the mountain peaks all night to Agri. When I arrived there the next morning, I was shaking and exhausted with the symptoms of a bad head cold. The grayest clouds I'd seen in my fifty-five days of walking the entire length of Turkey were shrouding that ancient outpost, but still I was very, very happy.

For, at last, I was halfway home.

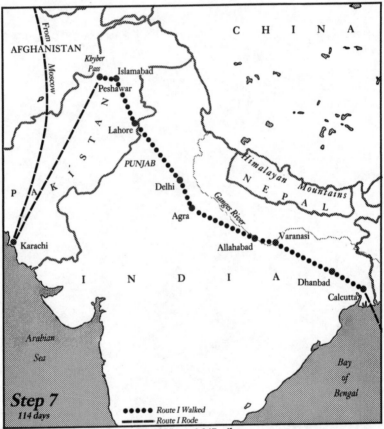

Step 7
114 days

●●●●● *Route I Walked*
━ ━ ━ *Route I Rode*

November 2, 1984 to February 23, 1985   1,347 miles

35

"**H**ey, mista! You going to the airport?"

"Yes! Listen, I'm running late. Get me there on time to catch my flight at twelve-thirty, and fifty dollars is yours."

"Heeeey! You bet—get in!"

"Great!" I flung Clinger into the backseat, and then flung myself into the front seat beside the Greek-American driver. He jammed the stick on the steering column into gear, and I dug my fingernails into the dash and door handle; naturally there was no seat belt.

He pressed the gas pedal to the floor, we lurched into warp speed whatever, and like a demented Captain Kirk, he kept looking everywhere but directly ahead. The other cars and trucks and scooters on the highway to the Athens International Airport became mere pinpoints of color and rust that whizzed past the windshield like swarms of splatter-proof insects.

"Hey, by the way, my name's Nickie." He took his hand off the wheel to offer it for a shake. I lunged at it and shook it quickly, before it could get more than six inches from the madly vibrating steering wheel.

"I was born in Brooklyn. Came over on vacation to visit my uncle. Loved the weather over here so much, I decided to stay—HEY!" He flipped off a scooter rider who nearly didn't move into the ditch quickly enough. "Sure is great here. Not crazy like in New York, ya know—" SCREEEEECH!

He'd just missed starting a chain reaction of bumper collisions. About the thickness of a credit card was all that separated his front bumper from the back end of a monstrous traffic jam. It took several tries, but I focused my stretched and dried retinas onto my watch's hands. The watch's second hand looked as if it were moving through glue.

Twelve-twenty one. It was impossible. The airport had to be at least another five miles, and the highway was packed solid with the stalled traffic. I was going to lose the three hundred dollars I'd paid for the ticket to Pakistan, but at least I would get to keep my life, and the fifty dollars.

"Well, we tried," I said.

"Oh, it ain't over yet, Bud," he said, his eyes roaming every which way.

I didn't like the way he was eyeing the very narrow shoulder along the median strip. Sure enough, that was his idea. He asked to see the fifty dollars. It might as well have been fifty thousand, the way his eyes gleamed. Off we roared, half on the median, half on the grass. This time, I closed my eyes and kept them closed.

All I knew next was he was shouting for me to run ahead to the Aeroflot ticket counter. He would grab the backpack, he said, and be right behind me. I ran as if an assassin were hot on my heels. Twelve twenty-nine, and rapidly counting down. Incredibly, the little cabbie stayed right behind in the maddening crowd. At the Aeroflot counter a Russian man and a policewoman, both with walkie-talkies in their hands, were waiting and poised, as if they had known all along I was coming.

"I'm late! My flight's leaving now!" I gasped to the man.

He said they had asked the pilot to delay as long as possible. Gee, now *that* was service, I thought. It seemed this was my day for miracles. I gave Nickie his money. He wished me good luck. I did the same to him, figuring I was more likely to live to see fifty than he.

Both the backpack and I were rushed through the checkpoints with clockwork precision—the policewoman calling ahead on the walkie-talkie and the security people whisking me past the metal detectors and X-ray machines. If I had been a terrorist or a drug smuggler, I'd have been home safe.

Waiting at the end of the sprinting was a police car, its lights flashing. Into the backseat went the pack and me. The Russian climbed into the front. All the way to the jet he let me know I was not his idea of a model citizen. The pack and I were let out at the bottom of the portable stairs pushed up against the white and red jet's fuselage. I hurried up expecting to come face-to-face with a couple hundred irritable expressions.

Instead, I found only long rows of empty blue seats. The jet had no passengers on this leg of its flight. I looked at the attendants closing the door. This couldn't be right.

"Moscow?" I asked.

"Yes. Moscow."

I thought she had to be wrong. But I settled in anyhow. I gave myself one whole side of the plane. Clinger had the other. In no time at all, we were off and away. I leaned back and unabashedly imagined I was on my own private jet.

Heaven only knew what Clinger was thinking.

On that long flight aboard the Aeroflot jet, first to a gray Sofia, Bulgaria, where we picked up a dozen military officers and an equal number of regular passengers, then to a freezing Moscow where, because I didn't have a visa, I was forced to stay alone all night in a nearly empty terminal, and finally to a steaming Karachi, in southernmost Pakistan, I had plenty of time to think about what had happened in the week I had spent going back across Turkey to Greece for this flight.

I had stayed hidden in Agri for three days in a seedy little closet of a room in a place called the Hotel Divan, fearful that the police from Eleskirt were looking for me. The janitor, a man about my age who had thirteen children and made about ten dollars a month, was kind enough to bring me soup and bread each day from the stalls outside. He was fascinated to be with his first American, and every morning he'd take an hour to squeeze into my cubbyhole to ask about the absolutely unimaginably fantastic wages our millionaire janitors made. To him, paradise would have been being the janitor at Bethel-Tate High School for one year. Why, with that kind of money, he could have retired in wealthy bliss forever more.

When I felt it was safe to move on again, I put myself nearly through bankruptcy to give the janitor a present of a couple months' wages. He thought I was an angel straight from heaven. I assured him I wasn't even close.

I had hitchhiked back to Istanbul, since I had walked from there already, riding mostly with Turkish truck drivers returning from inside Iran. Ironically, the last part, from Istanbul to the Greek border, was in a plush passenger bus that was stopped by a policeman who liked me, and who told my driver to take me anywhere I wanted to go for free.

Of course, that didn't include Iran. But from what the truck drivers told me they had seen inside that country, that wasn't so bad. Anti-American slogans and posters were everywhere, they said. One driver told me of posters depicting bloody American soldiers piled high onto a bayonet.

Another described a "freedom monument" in Tehran covered with such particularly Orwellian slogans as GOD—KORAN—KHOMEINI and ISRAEL MUST BE DESTROYED.

Every driver told of frequent police checkpoints on the roads inside Iran and of the bribes necessary to prevent any "delays."

On my walk across northern Turkey, I had seen trucks rushing war supplies to Iran and had had an up-close look at the gluttonous appetite of a nation at war. I had also seen something that hit me, as an American, particularly hard. I had peeked under the canvas tarpaulins covering the trucks' loads, whenever I came across trucks parked along the roadside. Mostly the materials going into Iran were basic things like truck tires, electrical wiring, diesel-engine components, and sheet metal—almost all of it imported from Japan (sent via Turkey to save it from interception and possible damage by Iraq). But a load I saw one afternoon had stamped on the very large, solidly built wooden crate the words *Communication Equipment:* MADE IN U.S.A.

Apparently, there really weren't many scruples in the business of war. The memory of the hostage taking at the American embassy in Tehran, the recent killings of over two hundred U.S. Marines by an Iran-backed car bomber in Beirut, and the president's pledge to the American people that America would do no business with the fanatical Iranian government evidently had meant nothing to the American firm selling that equipment to the Ayatollah's regime.

In the south Pakistan port city of Karachi, I bid the hefty stewardesses of the world's largest airline good-bye and descended onto the opposite side of the world from my home. In my first three days in Pakistan's largest city, I saw commotion I'd never experienced. So many people dressed in baggy pants, saris, and rags, and bare feet rushing and buzzing with mindless energy. As I looked about me, especially at the hundreds of beggars, it seemed that man had lost all control of his society.

Pakistan was where many had warned me I would be taking my final steps. Right from the start there had been stern warnings from officials, even those at Pakistan's own embassy in Washington:

"You will *not* walk there!" the vice-consul had shouted, flinging his eyeglasses to his desk. "There are too many bandits. You will be killed, that I'm certain of. You must take a train or a bus."

Even Philip, the adventurer at the port in Spain who had instructed me how to handle the Moroccan street gangs, had cringed when I'd said I was going to walk across Pakistan, too.

"In Africa, you stand a chance, because the bandits have only knives. But in Pakistan they carry rifles," he pointed out. "Life there has no value. They'll kill you for your shirt."

And just before my departure from Athens, I received a frightening computer printout from the American embassy:

". . . A high incidence of night-time robbery by bandits. Visitors should be certain to reach their destinations before dark. Bandits have been engaged in robbery, abductions, and shootings directed against road travelers in daylight hours. . . ."

After much thought, I had decided to go to Pakistan's northern region on the Afghanistan border and cross its width from Peshawar, near the famous Khyber Pass, to Lahore. I knew Peshawar was in a frontier area populated mostly by Pathans, the largest tribal society in the world, and that that fiercely independent tribe had never been conquered by any of the armies—from Alexander the Great's to those of the British colonizers—that had intruded into their mountains and valleys.

It had been my experience on the walk that those people of whom others spoke with awe and reverence were from societies where law and order dominated. And certainly the word *Pathan* was always said to me with a trace of awe.

Much of the train ride north from Karachi was over desert and bleak, sweltering plains. The land rushing past the window of my dusty sleeper carriage was, for the most part, flat and hazy, the dust continually disturbed by the hooves of camels and oxen and the sandaled feet of what seemed a million brown-skinned figures.

And when my feet joined theirs, I found that the road exploded into dust with each step. Above me, every trembling aspen leaf was thirsty. Around me, every child's face needed a bath. My new *Rocky* boots—sent to me in Athens by my mom and only the second pair on the walk—were thickly frosted in brown.

As long ago as the fourteenth century B.C., the road along which I was walking from Peshawar to Calcutta, India, was known as the Royal Route. It was one of the oldest, if not *the* oldest, roads in the world. For thousands of years, the principal route over which many of the Indian subcontinent's dynasty-makers had directed their armies, and their worshipers, it was now known simply as the G. T. (Grand Trunk) Road.

Rudyard Kipling had once described the route I was following, from northwestern Pakistan's cool mountain ranges to the steamy low deltas of Calcutta, as "a river of moving life, such as does not exist in any part of the world." But in the eighty years since he had seen that route, the Royal

Route had changed from a river to a flood of humanity. Never would I have thought the air able to bear the weight of so many smells and noises. From Peshawar to where I was now, near Rawalpindi, western Pakistan had struck me as a land bound by the ugliest of poverty, and yet filled with the color of a thousand springtime mountain meadows. All across it had been what I liked to think of as the singers, wailing the Koran from lotus-shaped mosque towers, chanting their lessons in overcrowded classrooms, and hawking their gold, silk, or rotting fruit from inside seedy, closet-sized shops. And there were the dancers: As numerous as atoms they twisted, rolled, squirmed, bobbed, and side-stepped from one spot to an-other. Most were dressed in turbans and had moustaches. Many were young. The women peered over veils with eyes as seductively beautiful as those with which earlier civilizations graced their goddesses. Nearly all seemed so happy to be swirling with life's forces.

Everywhere here was a throbbing, a dashing, and clashing and mash-ing of man and beast that wouldn't allow my heart to slow. Even time had to race to stay ahead.

The warm smiles, the limp handshakes, the humble bowing of heads, left no doubt I was among friends—perhaps the gentlest yet. Still, my eyes darted about like caged animals. With so much energy loosed one had to be constantly attentive, or suffer the inevitable collisions with everything from bicycles to hand-pushed carts to arrogant camels. Five minutes in the market district of any town or city brought with it more speeding objects than a *Star Wars* battle scene. Man, beast, and machine were continually challenging one another for the right-of-way.

Historically, this land was one of the most ancient cradles of society. Cities had thrived here before Babylon's first bricks were laid. The inhab-itants of those cities were supposedly practicing citizenship before the Greeks knew of such principles.

"Love is life." So went a popular saying in that region. Certainly, there was no doubting their love of life. Nearly three out of four people still farmed the land. Even in the cities, the streets were more like farm-yards than roadways.

Though the present culture was Muslim, the vestiges of the prior one of the Hindus were everywhere. Not only was there the love of nature in general, but also a love of color that bordered on obsession. Even the most ordinary buses and trucks, with their skirts of wind chimes and their streamers and hand-painted panels of peacocks, jet planes, roses, tigers, and nature scenes, made me think that everyone was rushing off to a Mardi Gras parade. Indeed, I kept expecting to be served my first bowl of rainbow rice!

Eastward from Islamabad I entered into a fertile plains region known as "the Land of Five Rivers." There I found the truth of the words of the many who'd told me that everything I saw and experienced would greatly multiply the deeper I progressed toward India.

It was in that same area of east Pakistan that the Chinese pilgrim Hsüan-tsang wrote in A.D. 630 of one of the rivers: "The Sin-Tu [Indus] is extremely clear and rapid. Poisonous dragons and evil spirits dwell beneath this river in great numbers. Those who embark carrying rare gems or celebrated flowers find their boats suddenly overwhelmed by waves."

On Hsüan-tsang's return journey, the Indus claimed fifty of his manuscripts and all the seeds of exotic flowers he had hoped to grow in China. The pilgrim, however, was spared. He crossed over on an elephant.

Toward the end of the thirty days I spent crossing Pakistan, I wished often that I, too, had had some sort of indomitable beast to ride upon, to keep me from the deepening poverty I was traveling through. Walking brought me much too close to a life-style that was totally contrary to what my American mind considered civilized, or even sane.

Accepted practices like having the homeless old and the crippled begging on the streets for their survival, the flagrant corruption among the police and civil servants, the lack of such basics as garbage collection and sewage facilities, the right of men to have several wives at the same time (resulting in incredibly enormous households), the division of persons into caste rankings (though supposedly outlawed), and the marrying of one's cousins to keep the family's holding intact made absolutely no sense to me. Yet they were as much a part of daily life as the crows scavenging through the garbage dumped upon the streets and walks.

As I stared at the uncontrolled pollution, the animal corpses, the millions of flies swarming over uncovered food and people, I worried terribly, indeed had nightmares, about my own health.

Before I had left America, I had had an image of Pakistan that was fairly modern, and sanitary. What I saw as I neared the India border was often the opposite. And that scared me, because I thought it meant India would be worse. What good was it that the people were kind to me if I caught any of the diseases prolific in such filth?

Soldiers, their rumbling convoys, and their weapons were everywhere. Many mornings I awoke to the pounding of drums and soldiers' boots marching crisply, while singsong voices drifted to my ears from the nearby compound. For much of the day I would be choked by the dust from trucks and jeeps piled high with the battle-ready. It struck me that there were a lot of people in Pakistan roaming about in search of a war.

One of the unmistakable characteristics of any advanced, mature nation I had walked was that its people, from the common man to the government, thought ahead, not so much for themselves as for their children and the unborn. But in Pakistan, men told me that if they practiced restraint, purposefully had fewer babies, Allah would be greatly displeased, might even deny them entry into paradise. These men were of the opinion that any changes in their lives were totally dependent on fate. As I looked about, I wondered if perhaps Allah hadn't already passed judgment.

Surely, part of the cause of their fear was a lack of education. In Pakistan, the illiteracy rate was a shocking 70 percent. Yet the government, which was dependent on the military for its existence, allocated less than a handful of percentage points of the national budget to education, while over half of the budget went to armaments.

In the city of Lahore, I waited for almost a week to cross the border into India. I knew it was a nation seething with bitterness and violence because of the assassination of its longtime prime minister, Indira Gandhi, by Sikh radicals only a few weeks before, an assassination blamed by some of their newspapers on our CIA. And to add to their woes, there had been a poisonous-gas accident at the American-owned Union Carbide plant in Bhopal, in which three thousand persons had been left dead and tens of thousands ill, many permanently. So I felt I would be walking into a riotous mob once people found out where I was from.

As I lay on the bed each night in my cold room at the YMCA, all I could think of were the many, many depressing pictures I had seen in my youth of starvation and beggars in India. Was it still like that? Or worse? And what of all those news accounts of the bloody race riots there?

I had about exhausted my patience and my wits trying to get permission to cross the border. Every day I was told that the border was open to overland travelers three days each month, but the guards had no idea when the next day for December might be. Why not give up on India, fly around it to my next country, Thailand? I asked myself.

I had walked 8,127 miles across fourteen nations so far. When would my luck run out? How naive of me to keep supposing that my stupid smile and easy laughter would see me safely through. I could only keep bucking the odds so long.

36

The temple stood in a slight patch of eucalyptus and mango trees. Beside it was a small lake that reflected a blue sky and several white humpbacked sacred cows. Squattish, peeling, made of cement blocks and with a small naked veranda wrapped around its circular center, it certainly was not a remarkable temple in any sense.

Yet its utter simplicity drew me away from the slow-motion bicycle riders, hopelessly lazy buffalo, and the shade of the G. T. Road. Places of worship, I'd discovered, were very much like cities and towns: Enormous cathedrals, like big cities, usually held people rushing about with an air of great significance, their minds seemingly preoccupied more with tasks than with other people, while the simpler homes of God, like little towns and villages, usually had someone nearby who was willing to sit down to a cup of hot liquid and an earful of questions.

In the small courtyard around the temple, I kept my distance while I observed intently. Several beautiful young village women, barefoot and in plain cotton pants and dresses, were taking turns pouring water over the small statue of a resting cow at the temple's entrance. As they poured, they bowed three or four times to the statue, then circled the temple, sprinkling water on its sides and on the floor of the veranda. All the while, a frail old man sat nearby on the temple's steps, in the warmth of the morning sun, deeply absorbed in a book.

I shed my pack, sat beside it, and thought about the India I'd spent the past week crossing. I had envisioned so much squalor just across the Indian border from Lahore that I had determined to walk India's width as quickly as possible, and to avoid close contact with the people. Never, I promised myself, would I risk my health by eating food any of the poor might offer me.

My planned route over the country, along the G. T. Road, was through the most populated region on earth—the Ganges Plains. So I was fully resigned to facing thirteen hundred miles of continuous obstacles. And certainly the manner in which I had to enter the Punjab did little to soothe my nerves. More than a dozen heavily armed soldiers had escorted our convoy through all the "nonsociable elements" said to be out there in the dark.

Foot travel was forbidden. Or so warned our convoy's "sheriff," as he tossed back a pair of star-studded shoulders. Thus it was that my driver, a meek missionary from New Jersey whom I had somehow convinced to take me in as a fellow "missionary," had to deposit me "inadvertently" into the blackness of the Punjab just past midnight. When the convoy's vehicles were stretched too far apart along the narrow, potholed road to see one another, the missionary had slipped his old Land Rover into a side lane and let me out.

The next morning's cautious sunlight had found me without my cowboy hat from Brenda in Greece. I had given it to the missionary to thank him for breaking the law and risking arrest so that I could walk through at least the eastern half of the forbidden Punjab. I hated to give up that hat, but its size made it difficult to handle in the constant roughness of the journey. Besides, the missionary had promised to take good care of it.

My first sunrise in India found me centuries back in time. I crawled out of my hidden nest in the forest onto a road that was like a giant sidewalk. Its oxen-pulled carts and slow-motion bicycle riders eased their way past me as though Henry Ford and Albert Einstein had not been born yet.

Right away I noticed that the people here depended upon nature to a degree that I hadn't seen elsewhere. Nothing went to waste. The forests were totally clean of dead brush: Buffalo dung, which was dried and used for cooking fuel, never lay untouched for more than a few minutes. The resulting cleanliness was very different from the image I'd always had of India. The air of peace and harmony I felt that very first morning made much of the rest of the world seem hopelessly noisy by comparison. I'd always wondered what the world had sounded like before the engine, and now I knew. To see people going off to work with only the tinkling of bells on oxen necks and the low, slow creaking of wooden cart wheels as their "traffic noises" was as sweet as anything this side of heaven.

There was a sense of peace about me. It was especially strong on the farms where I stopped for water and directions. For the first time since rural France, I felt a deep and real sense of spiritualism, of being in a world in which people lived in harmony with each other, the land, and the wild and domestic animals they believed contained the reincarnated souls of former persons.

Clang . . . Clang . . . Clang.

The dull ringing of a small bell inside the temple snapped me from my memories. From the temple's dark interior emerged an older woman walking slowly backward as she bowed to the temple's open door. On the side of her nose facing me gleamed a tiny gold pendant connected by a gold chain to a hairpin of gold shaped like a fan. Around her ankles thick bangles in the shape of snakes crowded together. Fine steel and brass or copper bracelets covered much of her forearm.

After a final bow to the cow statue, she turned and approached me. Her cupped hands extended out and down to my surprised figure. Nestled inside them were tiny white sugar lumps. I was at a loss for what to do. Part of me wanted nothing to do with the sticky candy she was offering me.

"Please to accept her *prasada*?" came a kindly voice from my right.

I turned to face a wrinkled, very thin person wrapped in coarse cloth and propped up by an ancient walking stick. It was the old man who had been reading the book on the temple steps. I hadn't seen him move from his spot in the sunlight.

"She has offered the treats to our God. And now she kindly wishes to share them with all she meets. Such food blessed by God we call *prasada*," he explained softly, but a look in his eyes hinted that it would be most unkind of me to turn down such an offering.

I tried my best to look honored and let her push several of the things onto my right palm. She grinned broadly and gave the rest to the old man, who promptly passed them on to me.

"Please, you drink tea," he asked me in a way we would make a statement.

I followed him to a two-room cinder-block hut that was his home. On the way he paused long enough to show me the inside of the temple. All that the windowless, closetlike room contained was a plain pedestal in the center of its concrete floor. On top of the pedestal was a paint-streaked rock in a large bowl of flower petals and smoking incense. On the mildew-stained, unpainted walls of the temple were several calendars from as far back as fifteen years. They offered a little color to the room's barrenness. On the calendars' posters were the brightly colored images of Hindu deities, some of them sprouting enough arms to make an octopus jealous and one with an elephant trunk where his nose should have been. Resting peacefully at their sides were many of the animals familiar to India, particularly the cobra, the tiger, and the Brahman cow. Suspended from the

ceiling, at the end of a long rope, was a small, plain bell. The old man gave
it a nudge; it made the same dull *clang* I'd heard earlier.

"It is for calling down God," he said, with what sounded like a touch
of jest.

He told me he was a monk, the religious caretaker of the temple.
Hunched on the dirt floor of his hut over a tin pan of boiling tea, he
shared with me the details of his quiet and lonely duty in this world. His
knowledge of English came from the thirty-seven years he'd served in the
army, from which he received a small, almost negligible pension.

He was paid nothing to be a holy man, he said, adjusting the twigs
flaming beneath the tea. He subsisted entirely on the charity of the temple's worshipers. Like the monks of thousands of years ago, he still spent
each morning wandering from village home to village home knocking on
doors and asking for food with which to prepare that day's meals.

"You please stay for lunch?" he asked. "It is our duty to feed and
give rest for free to any monks who pass our temples."

"But I'm not a monk," I replied.

He rose and placed a cup of the sweet tea mixed with water-buffalo
milk on the bench beside me.

"Ah, but I think you are," he replied with an odd grin.

He sounded as if he'd read a part of my inner soul. I stole a glance
over the rim of the teacup. He was smiling more than ever.

"You can throw them into the fields if you want," he said with a nod
toward my right hand, which was still clenched tightly.

The *prasada*. I stared down at the sweaty lump stuck to my fingers.
Now it was my turn to smile.

"What's for lunch?" I asked quickly. "Maybe more *prasada*?"

He laughed. "The families today had much buffalo milk to give
away." He paused, as if to think that over, then added with a sigh, "As
usual . . ."

The thought of so much raw buffalo milk made me a bit hesitant, too.
But just then, as if an omen, the bell inside the temple rang unusually loud
and sharp. Involuntarily, I sat straighter.

"When do we eat?" I asked without further delay.

And I cast aside all my foolish worries and sat back to enjoy the
sweetness of the meal's first entrée—the woman's sugar candy.

Someone struck a match. An oil lamp's wick flickered to life. Monstrous shadows leaped with the unsteady flame. I hugged myself as hideous shapes seemed to close in about me. The cold air was thick with dampness and must that settled deep into the lungs.

I stared, as if mesmerized, through the diffused glow at the darkly stained mud-brick walls and the dirt floor—and the humpbacked horned beasts tethered to iron rings set in the wall upon which the lamp glowed.

A tall, narrow figure wrapped in a ragged blanket pointed a long finger at me, then at several hempcord cots lined against a far wall of the stable. A dozen other similarly shaped and clothed figures clustered beside the cots, seeming to be waiting for my shivering body to join their company. I sat down slowly on the middle cot. The others closed around me like the fingers of a giant hand.

"It is a great problem for us these days," murmured the one named Ajad.

I leaned forward to study his angular face. His voice suddenly sounded much older, hardly like that of the young farmer who had talked me away from the G. T. Road two nights before.

"The electricity going off, you mean?" I asked.

As we were weaving down the dirt road to his village of Jhattipur on his old bicycle, Ajad had seemed especially proud that the village of fifteen hundred had four street lamps and four televisions.

Ajad nodded. He lamented that the village received electrical power only two or three hours each day. Still, power failures or not, life in Jhattipur was not going to be affected that much. In a place like Jhattipurr, where meals were cooked over smoking buffalo dung or twigs on the ground outside, electricity was much more of a luxury than a necessity.

I had spent that January day with Ajad and his excited friends, touring their farm fields, their homes, and the separate schools for boys and girls. Almost all of the farming was still done by oxen-pulled plows. Water for the homes was pumped up from wells by hand, or pulled up in buckets by the sinewy arms of the women. Animals, from pigs to buffalo, wandered freely about the streets, followed oftentimes by small girls who gathered the fresh dung with their bare hands for their mothers to make into fuel patties. The schoolchildren did their work on hand-held slate boards, using coal for pencils and rags for erasers. Like the homes, the schools were virtually unfurnished, unheated, badly overcrowded, unlit, and with almost no windows. The children sat on the floors of the schoolrooms, just as they did in their homes. Many, however, had their classes outside in the dirt, where at least the weak winter sun provided a semblance of warmth.

Though I had passed through what seemed a thousand similar villages on the walk to Jhattipur, the primitiveness of each still left me astonished. I found it hard to believe the hordes of loin-clothed laborers I'd seen using primitive wooden tools and just their bare hands to construct high-rise housing projects and streets. At one road-paving project, I'd stared amazed at the sight of at least two hundred men and women in virtual rags squatting in the thick, powdery dust, hammering by hand every single rock into gravel.

And the gap between the technological haves and have-nots seemed to be growing more profound each day. I couldn't even begin to see how it might be narrowed or its growth arrested.

Furthermore, while those I had seen in the countryside of the Punjab and now in the state of Harayana oftentimes bore the calm contentment of monks, those I was meeting in the towns were a different story. In the towns, I met many educated young men with no work. They told me they faced a daily situation in which money under the table and/or the right friends—not skills—determined who worked and who continued hoping.

One intelligent, well-mannered man in the Punjab told me that he had been unable to find work since receiving his bachelor's degree from the university in 1977. Yet to give up hoping would be to condemn himself to permanent unemployment, he said.

He had traveled in the past year to New Delhi to apply for a bookkeeping job that had been advertised in the newspaper. All the money he had saved from working in the fields on his father's farm had gone into the purchase of the train ticket. He had prayed that his time was at hand.

But it wasn't to be. Neither for him nor for seventeen thousand other anxious, hoping, praying young men who had read that same advertisement.

"Do you know what my work will be when I get my doctor's degree?" a tall man had shouted from the crowd of another town. "*Looking* for work!" he answered himself.

A shivering Ajad roused me now from the depths of my sleeping bag. It was dawn. In his hands were a tin cup and a large pot of buffalo milk his mom had heated for my breakfast. I drank all of it, hoping it might keep some of the morning chill away when I left the stable to continue my journey eastward. I sat up on the hemp-rope cot and smiled at his father and grandfather, who had also slept in the stable, the men's bedroom of the house. They grinned back broadly with more gum than tooth showing.

While I drank the turnipy-tasting milk, dozens of village boys who had been waiting since first light to have *their* chance to be friends with the village's first American visitor spilled through the stable door. In no time at all, there was hardly space for a field mouse to fit in among all the blanket-wrapped figures, cots, and cud-chewing oxen.

I searched out the face of Ajad among the steamy breaths and shivering smiles. As was my custom, I asked my latest host for an address to which I could send him a postcard. One of the littlest boys won the race to honor the American with something to write on, and Ajad told me his name and address in a voice trembling with hope.

Then he reached under the old brown blanket he had slept in last night and now wore as a coat, and brought out from his pants pocket twenty rupees. To my surprise, he slipped the money into my hand that was holding his address. I started to hand it back; I knew that for him that was a week's wages.

"What's the money for?" I asked.

"Please send a gift of your country to us, when you can. We want something from America we can show our friends," he explained.

"And," he added quickly, "I will pay any duty."

I smiled. Twenty rupees was worth just under two dollars. Nothing it could buy would fetch a duty fee.

"Sure . . . I'll send a gift," I said softly, but I had to look away for a second before I shoved the money into my jacket.

My ears were struck by the shrill of a single cicada—brilliant, eerie. Gingerly, I pushed a hand-stitched blanket of jute from my puffy eyes. A farmyard silvered with moonlight and shadowed by statuesque oxen, still tethered to their clay feeding bin, came into my view.

The largest of the bulls, Zebus, a veritable giant with a floppy hump as thick as a fat monkey, turned his long neck ever so slightly, and the small bell secured to his fleshy throat tinkled.

Beside me, on another blanket spread on the straw-covered dirt, a black-skinned boy stirred uneasily in his sleep. He was of the lowest caste, a *shudra,* and would soon be at work draining the udders.

The gentlest of breezes kissed my forehead, as scenes of the farm I had explored that day beneath a pink January sky drifted into my mind: a bent and toothless ancient grandmother squatting barefoot on the cold dirt churning milk in a broken clay pot as she sang; a shy young mother plucking ripe guavas from branches as her baby clung papoose-style to her rainbow-colored dress.

For the past ten days, in no haste and without any gainful destination, I had walked this land where it was said the Hindu god Krishna played with and teased his lovestruck human friends over five thousand years ago.

In many of the meticulously cared-for fields, the time-darkened ruins of formerly graceful temples stood. Many of the keepers of those temples had invited me behind their walls to be fed and sheltered from the foggy nights. And with them I found heaven and its God to be of many forms.

The people of the various religions were as different and colorful as the tropical birds swarming through the forests. They ranged from a group dressed entirely in burlap sacks to one that was heavily financed by American money, whose cologned disciples lived in spacious, sterile apartments and danced wildly before sequin-covered deities in an enormous palace built of the finest marble and decorated with crystal chandeliers.

I even had an audience with my first "saint," but after I humbly raised my eyes from my bare feet to his gleaming white beard and gown, I could not bear to gaze upon him for very long. For all I could think of were his six automobiles and the immense property he had lately felt in need of acquiring.

India, it is said, is a religious experience. That I can certainly vouch for. Self-serving saints and monied statue-worshipers aside, there was unquestionably *something* in the air. The people for the most part were happy, laughed so naturally, so effortlessly, and Nature reflected that joy.

What a pleasure to see again man and woman as equals, not women cowering and hidden away, as in the male-controlled Muslim societies. In the serene domesticity of rural India, there was a common pulse of being. Even the animals and their masters seemed to work well together.

My eyelids closed again, heavily . . . slowly. Other sounds of a world not quite asleep trailed across my fading thoughts: the soft rhythm of a baby swaying in a wicker basket, the dogs' paws scampering to—or maybe from—a suspicious moon shadow, a field mouse scratching curiously inside Clinger, a housewife in one of the mud huts chanting prayers before a simple altar.

The sounds, as much as all the glories and all the love I'd experienced in the eighty-three-hundred miles I'd walked, assured me there was much more to life than what seemed obvious.

And yet my tears fell . . . again. For my spirit was still numb from the news I had received ten days before, on Christmas night: Dad was dead. After all those years of struggling, his heart had finally surrendered on Thanksgiving night, Mom's voice had told me softly when I called home to say Merry Christmas.

Not wanting to talk, yet not wanting to be alone either, I had walked from that telephone call in New Delhi to this farm near Agra and the Taj Mahal in shocked and painful silence. More than anything, I had wanted to end what suddenly seemed a silly, stupid journey. But Mom had said again and again that there was nothing my going home would accomplish. The funeral was over, and Dad had been buried in Bethel Cemetery. And Mom reminded me I was not walking just for myself but for hundreds of thousands of other Americans who were reading my stories each week. I had to realize I was in many, many thousands of people's daily prayers. To quit was not only to let myself down, but them, too. Dozens of people from all over America, none of whom she knew, had called and even written to her in the past two years with just "Steven's Mom, Bethel, Ohio" on the envelope. Those people loved me, she said, were walking in spirit with me, were counting on me to continue sharing with them the rest of a world they would otherwise never know as intimately.

But none of that could take away the fact that Dad would not be waiting for me to come back up our long driveway.

I thought I'd never make that first mile out of New Delhi after the phone call home. Yet, on that sad morning, I came to the only Christian church I had seen on my path across India. And so I had a chance to escape the huge crowds and go where there was peace and quiet, where I could speak to God, and Dad.

For what seemed forever, I knelt in a hard wooden pew, my head bent as I sobbed uncontrollably. I hoped that God would forgive me for not being there with Dad and Mom in the end. But even more, I asked Dad please to know how much I had missed him, not just then, but in all those years I had been away from home in Wyoming and on the walk. I cried because I loved him, and because in spite of all the miles between me and home, I could feel the void his death had brought to my life.

Though it hurt so much, I made myself remember the last time I had spoken to my father. It had been in September, in a little town in faraway north-central Turkey.

On that wet and cold day, a van full of excited telephone linemen had pulled alongside me and asked if I was the man walking around the world who had shared a cup of tea with their friend the postmaster. When I said I was, they had hopped out into the downpour to ask if I would like a free, though probably illegal, telephone call to my mother and father in America. Of course I wanted nothing more.

While lightning crackled and the cold northerly blew even harder, the bravest of the group scrambled up a pole in a back alley and somehow connected an ancient field phone to the mess of wires overhead. After dialing and redialing for what seemed an eternity, he finally got a distant ringing tone.

Concentrating so hard that I forgot all about the water dribbling down my moustache, I prayed silently that through some miracle the fragile connection might hold. When at long last the distant ringing finally stopped, there came from another world a teeny voice, like that of a child.

". . . Hello?" It was Dad.

"Hello?" he repeated.

"Dad! It's Steve! Can you hear me—I'm calling from Turkey. Hello, Dad! Dad? . . ."

"Hello, who is this?"

I screamed. I shouted. I ranted into the hard black handset gripped in my fingers. But it was no use . . . for some reason, he couldn't hear me.

Then . . . then something happened that I knew would haunt me to my own deathbed. There was another very weak hello? . . . a long pause, then . . . *crying* . . . so soft, yet so clear over all those thousands of miles.

". . . Steve?" his trembling little voice asked.

"Steve? . . . Is that you, son?"

Then he was *gone*. Blown away by the howling wind. How could I have known that would be our last contact in this world? Or that those gaunt eyes I had seen watching me from that upstairs bedroom as I walked away from home would be my last picture of him?

Mom had told me not long before I left that she'd seen Dad on his knees beside the bed, praying silently with folded hands, the way children sometimes do. He was a religious man, but in a very quiet way—much as his life had been. And now . . . he was on a journey of his own—to his spiritual home. Maybe he was already there. I hoped so, I thought now, as another tear mingled with the straw of my pillow.

For, God willing, we might embrace each other yet one more time.

37

I would never forget the roses. So large and regal as to be from the pages of a tale, each flower seemed a perfect sculpture of Nature.

Nor would the kindly Baba—the elder—be easily dismissed from my mind. He had guided me to those roses. And to the special gift of love they watched over.

It was in a jungle that I first encountered him. At the time I was over seven hundred miles into India and should have been advancing toward my final destination of Calcutta, almost an equal number of miles to the east. Instead, I was hopelessly lost.

Foolishly, I had left the G. T. Road to follow the banks of a small river channel that seemed to parallel the road. The crowds of people along the road had become thicker with each day since my departure from New Delhi, and I wanted to follow a path that was more quiet and private. Those in the towns had a frightening habit of massing around me in unruly crowds of hundreds and even thousands. They would crush against me from all sides and scream for my attention: Twice I had almost fainted from the heat and jostling. I had not realized how overwhelming the reaction to my sudden appearance in those towns and villages would be. Sometimes in the rural villages so many yelling schoolboys and young men swept over any shop I entered that the outside sunlight was blocked out, and the badly shaken shop owner would have to strike up his oil lamps. They even climbed onto each other's backs to get their faces closer to the doorway or the window bars. More than once, a squad of police charged into the crowds to find the cause of the sudden mass "riot," then led me to the edge of the town and made me leave. My presence was causing too much danger, they said. It didn't matter that no one knew who I was, what I was doing, or even where I was from (most didn't have the faintest idea what country the flag on Clinger was from). I had a feeling that as many were drawn to me by the hope of finding out what the unusual contraption of metal and straps and slick cloth was as they were by my red hair.

So simply for my physical safety, I needed to find more peace of mind, and quickly. Furthermore, with Dad's death still weighing heavily on my mind, the need to be alone and with my own thoughts was very strong.

Yet even during the earliest moments of the mornings, when I was wavering between sleep and waking in the chilliness of my tent, I knew little peace. Many mornings I was abruptly awakened by some big-eyed brown head poking unannounced through the tent's flaps. Even more common was having the entire populace of a village crowd around me while I shaved and bathed at the local well. Slowly and surely, the constant stares began to wear me down, and in one farm village, when I cut myself shaving and could not get the blood to stop pouring out of my wound, I felt something snap in my brain. Screaming and cursing furiously, my blood running down my front and soap lather all over my face, I chased my visitors with my disposable razor, threatening death a million times over to anyone who should be so unlucky as to be caught.

By following the river, I was sure there would be far fewer people seeing me, since the river meandered almost out of sight through the farm fields and behind the road's towns. But after a few hours of following the almost empty foot trails along the river, I sensed that I was no longer paralleling the distant roadway. The sun, my only compass, was not setting behind me, where it should have been. By all indications I was heading south, rather than east, as I should.

Though it was nearly dusk, I had little choice but to plunge into a thick forest of bamboo shoots and banyan tentacles and head in the direction I hoped the road still lay. Soon I was stumbling among the vine and root cords of the leafy net draped around me, worried by the approaching night and the unseen wild cries. I was in the state of India known as Uttar Pradesh, the home of deadly cobras and man-eating tigers. Just the day before, I had read of a veteran British guide being killed in the bush of "U.P." by one of those fearsome striped cats. And as dusk grew thicker and every trail led only to more fleeting shadows and deeper swamps, I began to wonder if this maze might be my last vision of the world.

Then, suddenly, as composed as a monk and looking as if he'd been patiently awaiting me, there stood the little, wiry, baldheaded man of about fifty I would later know as Baba. To my relief, a glint of recognition shone in his peaceful eyes at my mention of the elusive G. T. Road. Uttering not a single word, he turned and glided away down the footpath, having simply nodded that I should follow.

I raced toward his fading back. Teetering from my pack's weight, tripping over the roots of trees, and slipping along in the greasy mud, I kept my eyes on the steady form always just ahead and out of reach.

Finally, we were out of the jungle. Before us stretched an enormous checkerboard of inlaid sky mirrors and squares of golden rice speckled with snow-feathered herons. We splashed our way over the paddies to a distant vine of asphalt and broad shade trees—the missing G. T. Road. There a divine scent reached me—and I looked across the still road to see magnificent red roses hanging over a front wall.

Leading me past the roses, through a tall double gate, and under an inconspicuous hand-painted wood sign that read THE INTERNATIONAL GUEST HOUSE, Baba guided me up onto the columned veranda of a beautiful yellow brick home that could have been on a seaside cliff in the south of Europe. I stared at it, then at Baba. How could someone as poor as he be living in such a modern home—probably the quietest and cleanest one I'd seen in all of India?

With a key that he seemed to have picked right out of the air, he opened the front door and waved me to continue following him. I did so, filled with all sorts of expectations about how the dark inside would be decorated. What I saw, when he lit a candle, left me more puzzled than ever. The house's three rooms were nearly empty. The only furniture was a bed, a writing desk, and a wicker chair. Even on the wall shelves, there was little more than a speck or two of dust. The rich, fresh smell of newness still clung stubbornly to the shut-in air.

My host set the candle in a small holder and placed it on the desk. Its light was soaked up by his white shirt, white turban, and white sheetlike wrappings covering his thighs. In the darkness, the white cloths gave off a supernatural glow.

"Your house?" I asked, trying to induce an answer by keeping my question as simple as possible. I even pointed to the smooth plaster walls and then at him with a telltale shrug and arched eyebrows.

He did not answer, just set the key on the desk by the candle holder and turned and left. I was all alone for the first time in weeks. I sat on the edge of the bed, feeling a thousand pounds of frustration slip from my shoulders like a dead weight. I'd almost forgotten how refreshing lonesomeness could be. I wanted to explore the house more intimately, but I was just too worn out. All the hiking on the narrow, demanding footpaths along the river, then being lost in the middle of tiger country, and then trying to make sense out of this house and its owner had been too much for one day. I leaned back to rest for a minute, and promptly fell asleep. When I awoke again, the morning was slipping sunbeams through the slats on the windows, and what seemed a million birdsong notes. The candle had burned down to a wax puddle.

I propped myself on my elbow and glanced at the desk. The key was still there. My situation was just too good to be true. I had needed just this very sort of refuge more than anything. It couldn't have come at a better time.

The sixteen days since I had learned of Dad's death had been some of the hardest in all my life. I didn't know if I was more tired physically or emotionally. Never had I experienced such a mixture of beauty, fascination, and mystery with ugliness, brutality, and banality. I felt that I was on a constant roller coaster that one day had me screaming, the next laughing, then shocked, then inspired. . . .

The Taj Mahal, sitting on the banks of the Yamuna River like an enormous pearl, had given me a glimpse of heaven itself. But only a few days before I saw it, I had searched for a forgotten old palace I had been told by a Hindu priest was high above a village in the jungle far from the G. T. Road, and there I had been as close to hell as I ever cared to be again. My heart had almost pounded itself right out of my chest.

For inside the crumbling ruins of that hilltop fortress of some former Muslim warlord, I had discovered enough homeless poor to fill a town. With a stormy late-afternoon sky rumbling overhead and vultures silhouetted along its ramparts, all that was needed to make it some scene from a demented novel were some skewered heads.

After perhaps an hour, the hundreds of ragged poor, who had crowded about me tightly, began suddenly to scream at each other for some strange reason, and I knew it was time to dash for safety. But it was too late. Turning upon me like dogs on the flank of a fleeing deer, they grabbed at my gear, trying to rip it away. Some threw stones that hit me on the legs and head. Then, inexplicably, and just as suddenly as their frenzy had started, they became silent after chasing me only perhaps a hundred yards and retreated back to the hill with its circling vultures. It was as if something deep in the bowels of that fortress had commanded them not to venture out of sight of its walls. Even when I was back at the G. T. Road, my nightmare wasn't over. For the first person I encountered was a totally naked man, striding past me as if I weren't there.

Now, I rose from my bed feeling more refreshed and alive than I had in weeks, but still not without some trepidation. I was sure that when I opened the house's door, I would find the walled grounds filled with waiting people. But I didn't—only sunshine and the perfume of those roses again. There was a pail beside the well outside, and I gleefully took a bath in the same manner I had all across India—by emptying pails of icy water over my loudly protesting bones. Still, I had good reason to celebrate. It was the very first time I had no large crowds of gawking villagers for bath mates.

It was the first bath in a long time that I came away from feeling totally cleansed. Awash in perfumed mist, warmed by the sun's rays, and with the sparkle of watery diamonds dripping from petals all around me, I set out to see who was responsible for the secret little paradise I had been led to. My answer lay but three strides away, around the nearest corner of that house in a little garden of gold roses.

Beneath the sheltering branches of an old mango tree stood two head-stones. The one on the left was etched in the flowing script of Hindi, the one on the right in the stoic characters of English. I read its special message:

> The divine souls of an extremely simple couple of this area, who symbolized the ideal of love, compassion, and self-less service to mankind are resting here in peace.
>
> This place has been constructed by their son in the memory of his most ideal parents, as an expression of his extreme devotion and love towards them. Having founded this memorial he has made a meek effort to give concrete form to his parents' feelings of 'welfare of all.'

What an honor to have been invited into a home built entirely from love and devotion! And what a strange coincidence that the one man who held its keys had been there in the jungle when I'd needed shelter the most. I picked two wildflowers and gently placed one on each grave.

That day stretched into three, and never a single rupee of payment was wanted, or even accepted. To the Hindus, one of the saddest tragedies anyone can suffer is to be separated from one's family, particularly one's parents. And so it was that many farmers and villagers, some with small gifts of fruit or vegetables, visited me at the guest house to let me know in their own subtle way that I was still among a family of sorts. Some stopped by just long enough to ask where I was from and where I was going (as if they didn't already know), while they puffed on their crude and bitter-tasting *bitas*—cigarettes. Others stayed for hours and took their turn trouncing me at chess, deftly capturing all the pebbles we had standing in for pawns and rooks. Usually, in the background there were children, playing their unusual badminton games in which marigolds were substituted for shuttlecocks and hands became rackets.

Eventually, I learned about the man who had built the guest house. He lived in West Germany, having gone there many years before as a young man from a nearby village, and had been fortunate enough to land a good job with the government. But though he had found the material riches he'd hoped for, he was still plagued by homesickness. Acutely aware of how it felt to be alone and in a strange culture, he'd had the home built to shelter and provide comfort to any foreigner who should need it.

The night before my departure, I sat up late reading the messages of gratitude contained in the house's guest book, which Baba had brought to me from his own bamboo hut in the woods. Since the house was but three years old, and unknown to any except the occasional foot or bicycle traveler who chanced upon it, there had been only a few guests inside its walls. I was the thirteenth, a very lucky number in India, where many associated with it the meaning "giving to all." I was also the first American.

38

Thunder boomed. Water drummed relentlessly against water.

Rushing bodies and weaving bicycles, their movement intensified by the pitch-blackness and angry horns, surged against and past me. It was all I could do not to become another piece of human driftwood. How tempting to let myself be swept back down the G. T. Road to the quiet little side pools of mud huts and banana trees where most of this throng was undoubtedly heading.

Over two million people, all Hindu and mostly very poor, had made the pilgrimage to the holy city of Allahabad in the past week to celebrate the festival of Mankar Sankranti. From all over India they had come, most with babies in both arms and pots and blankets on their heads.

Mother Ganga, the Ganges River, had called their souls. It was almost the end of January, the time of the new year to bathe body and spirit in her oily muddy flow, to wash away sins and give the gods reason to smile once again.

Krishna, Rama, Shiva, Ganesh, Durga—all the countless lords and goddesses of a Vedic past, dating back thousands of years, danced in the brown eyes tumbling by me. Even in many of the lifeless white eyes, so common in India, there glinted a hope of new energy.

In the darkness following each flash of lightning, the vermillion *tikka* dots and candy-colored stripes on the foreheads of the pilgrims glowed with eerie vividness. They wore their beacons proudly, as outward proof that they had journeyed somewhere to be among the gods themselves.

Tired and weary of being caught in shoulder-to-shoulder humanity, I slogged through flooded streets in search of a place to rest my head from the noise and wetness. But there was none. None at all. The image of a pretty child leaped at me in the lightning before another crack of thunder —the image of a broken stick doll. For she dragged her bent, useless legs behind her. But the lack of bitterness in her eyes, the smile on her face, testified to the blessing she had received.

It was after midnight when a kind, bearded stranger rescued me from wandering the roads and took me to a Sikh temple, where I slept on the floor of an upstairs room.

The next day, I reached the Ganges. On the mud flats alongside the roiling river was the largest number of tents I had ever seen. There were no gaps between the patched angled canvases of Mother Ganga's brood. The notes of flutes and the voices of playing children floated up to me along with the smoke of campfires. Those squatting around the fires reminded me of the Gypsies of Turkey—but Allah's nomads had never traveled as lightly as these Hindu Indians. The Gypsies' camps had smelled of horses, wool, and leather. The camp below me reeked of body oil and incense.

I continued east, contented to leave such places to explorers less bothered by crowds and noise. Four days later, at dusk on the twenty-fifth of January, eighty-three miles downriver from Allahabad, I came to Varanasi (or Benares, as most still called it). Whereas Allahabad was a place to renew the soul, in a sense to be reborn, Varanasi was reserved for the dead. That was where the Hindu faithful had their bodies consumed by fire and then tossed into Mother Ganga. It was a returning of themselves to the All.

Yet, ironically, the business of death had attracted to Varanasi a greater bustle of life than was found even in cities several times its size. Swept along by the tide, I nearly forgot the pyres burning nonstop along the river, the many lepers and dying cripples just outside the railroad station. The wistful shouts of the religious-paraphernalia vendor, the streets choked with rickshaws, the children charging from everywhere to practice their school English, made death go almost unnoticed.

Even down at the river, at the smoky gate to death, there was a great display of life. Curly-tailed monkeys screeched from temple walls, children raked embers from spent pyres for their mothers to prepare dinner on, cows savored marigold garlands that had decorated the deceased, and brightly dressed old women cackled delightfully at each other's stories. And as if to show that death was not to be taken seriously, the people splashed merrily in the same spot where the ashes and charred remains of the dead were raked into the river.

In the evenings in Varanasi, the sun became a perfectly round orange dot of great beauty, a sort of celestial *tikka* dot. When it set, it left behind a flaming world and a din that did not soften until just before the sun rose again.

On my sixth and final day in Varanasi, I stepped into the early morning fog from my back-alley hotel to take one more good look at a city that was too lively ever to know completely. I had not gone two steps when the bewitching smile and large eyes of an old man in saffron-colored robes stopped me in midstep.

Politely, the monk told me in halting English that he was a Tibetan lama. With him were two of his much younger Buddhist devotees. On all three backs were crude packs of board and cloth. They had journeyed from the hidden reaches of the Himalayas in Nepal to learn more of the world below their solitary monastery. During the night they had slept on their blankets, on the porch of a house directly across the alley from the hotel entrance.

"What is your name?" the holy man asked softly, as the three bowed toward their tattered sneakers.

My voice rang out like an excited schoolboy's. "Sir! My name is Steven!"

He smiled. He liked that.

And I liked him. I wondered if I could have the honor of buying breakfast for others who had also walked a fantastic and difficult distance. They didn't see why not. After all, who were they to question the direction of fate?

We went out of the alley, and the four of us with our backpacks paraded down the already-crowded street to an open milk bar. Anywhere else in the world, we would have looked a strange procession indeed: me with my long, fluid strides, they shuffling behind in perfect step; my body as tall as most of the stalls and as thin as a pole, theirs stumpy and lump-headed and bent under pack-animal loads.

But in a place like Varanasi, we were merely four of many, many strange pilgrims from every part of the world.

The milk bar was an open-fronted hut with old planks for walls, palm branches for a roof, wooden benches with no tables, a huge cast-iron wok bubbling with buffalo milk above a bed of coals, and a cigar box for a cash register. Our glasses were filled by a man squatting beside the wok, and we sat in a corner to enjoy the milk and a piece of plain cake the lama unwrapped from a piece of cloth.

I could have asked that lama a million questions, but the English in his head was, alas, as limited as the milk now left in his glass. I had to be content to have met him and shared with him a few smiles and warm words. But that was okay, too. For it seemed that each such meeting, no matter how short, always left me knowing something new. And, after all, that was what traveling was all about—learning.

The slow waters of the Ganges cast back the sun's last light like an old dirty mirror. This was probably the last time our meandering paths would ever cross. For behind me on this mid-February day's dusk was the entire width of the Indian subcontinent, fifteen hundred miles of the G. T. Road.

I was done, or nearly so. Calcutta, the Royal Route's easternmost anchor, was at the end of the bridge on which I'd paused.

I laughed aloud, causing a rainbow of parrots to stretch out over the river. How utterly absurd to think that all I had seen, learned, and felt those past months could ever be put into ordinary words! No words existed that were extraordinary enough to describe my time in that region at the base of the Himalayas.

"Life is a song!" India had seemed to be saying. "Sing it!"

A rumble to my right caused me to turn. There, its smokestack horns flaring and its dark labyrinth snarling, lay the "Black Hole"—Calcutta. I knew it would be covered with the grime of never-ending poverty, but that no longer scared me. If I was sure of anything now, it was that fear is an unnecessary part of life.

Nevertheless, I had learned that India had its share of the ugly side of mankind. And particularly ugly were the widespread corruption and brutality of the police. The way the Hindu policemen demanded money from the more ambitious and prosperous Sikhs was nothing less than shocking to me.

Nearly every day, I saw long lines of trucks driven by Sikhs parked along the road. The drivers were patiently but angrily waiting out the patience of some bribe-seeking Hindu police commander who had a crude stone or wood barrier thrown across the road. Once I was but a few feet from where a Sikh driver was run off the road by a police jeep for having tried to crash through one of the illegal barriers. As the police commander sat in his jeep and laughed at the shock on my face, his cronies beat both the pleading driver and the co-driver unconscious. Frantically, I tried to save the men's lives by digging out my camera from inside Clinger and pretending I was taking photos (the batteries were dead!). But the commander simply told his men to hold up the bloodied faces of the drivers and pose smiling for my useless camera!

One day I actually witnessed, from behind a tree on the G. T. Road, a prisoner being murdered by the police. With his hands bound behind his back, the man was taken from a jeep at a lonely police post in the countryside and clubbed to the ground from behind. The beating started with a simple nod from the police commander to his men, as soon as the prisoner's feet touched the ground. Long after his body was lying lifeless on the ground, the men were still clubbing his head. I not only became physically ill, but was so frightened at being discovered as a witness that I walked late into the night, until I was out of the area.

Fortunately, most Indians I met were not like those policemen, but, instead, had the philosophy of Mahatma Gandhi, a simple villager who had become a dominant figure in India's war for independence from the British. As America's Martin Luther King, Jr., did later, Gandhi stressed nonviolence and peaceful co-existence. Because I was from the nuclear superpower America, I found myself continually having to answer for the current nuclear-arms buildup by the United States and the Soviet Union. I was forced into being a sort of back-roads diplomat more times than I cared for.

Unquestionably, the United States' support of the Pakistan military had plunged the image of the U.S. government to its lowest level in a decade in India. And it made the average Indian all the more willing to believe that America wanted to see India divided and weakened.

"We want only to live in peace. We don't want any more wars with Pakistan," said a postmaster I stayed with. "But if you make it so, we will defeat Pakistan."

"Why is your government forcing us into an arms race with Pakistan?" asked a teacher bitterly. "We don't even have enough money to educate our children!"

All across the world, even in some of the most isolated spots, I had found the vision of a dead planet, charred by nuclear war, to be on most people's minds. In India, that sense of doom was the strongest yet.

Unfortunately, I had no answers for their worried faces. I had no clear understanding of why the superpowers keep building so many nuclear weapons. I could, however, understand the words of a village sage I shared tea with one night:

"My friend," he said slowly, staring into a campfire, "if you want peace, look not to others' faults, but to your own. You and I and all *must* learn to understand that no one is a stranger, that the world belongs to all. When we seek only for goodness and the beauty God has placed in every single man and woman, then will evil lose its hold. Then we will know peace."

His name was Awadhesh. To the men of Police Station Nirsa, he was the officer-in-charge. To hear such words coming from a man who lived and worked in the middle of the coal fields of India's most dangerous and violent state, Bihar, struck me as a marvel. If only more would have the boldness to live those words!

I took one long look at what would be the last Indian sunset I would see outside of Calcutta. Then, glancing down at my tiny image swirling in the dull mirror of the Ganges, I lifted a very tired-looking Clinger onto my back.

"Don't give up now, kid," I said with a laugh, pulling his nylon arms tighter around my shoulders.

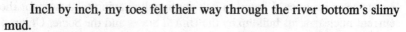

Inch by inch, my toes felt their way through the river bottom's slimy mud.

Along with an entire neighborhood of kids and young men, I waded into the Ganges, wearing only the loincloth given to me by my host, Madan Mohan Bhattacharyya.

In all my meandering along the Ganges River, I had seen enough sewage, corpses, and pollution in it to convince me it was the dirtiest waterway in the world. Yet here I was—in it to my chest, feeling as strangely elated as I was concerned that any minute everything from leprosy to leeches would be covering my skin.

I looked at my Calcutta host merrily brushing his teeth with the river water, then over at his friends dunking themselves into the strong current. How was it that they did this every day and yet never caught any diseases? Was the Ganges indeed so holy that it couldn't be polluted, as many Hindus claimed?

I hoped so. In fact, I was *praying* so!

With the others looking on anxiously, I inhaled deeply, covered my mouth, pinched my nostrils so tightly a gnat couldn't have found them, noted once more a bloated cow bobbing to our left, and plunged myself into the water. Furiously, I swished my sudsy head beneath the water to let every germ know I wasn't the tolerant sort, then exploded back into the chilly morning air—happy that I was alive and terrified that enough creepy crawlers had bored their way into my ears to turn me into a carnival sideshow.

The others cheered. This was something they'd been waiting a long time for me to do.

Five days ago, when I had walked across that bridge into Calcutta, I had met Madan at a jute warehouse where I'd stopped to ask for water. He had asked me to be his guest at his mother's big brick house on Sanak Para Lane in the old neighborhood of Ariadaha, and I had accepted, not knowing that he and most of the rest of the neighborhood liked to go to the Ganges each day to do their bathing. They had their own shallow little wells out beside the back door, but Mahan and the others, like many Hindus, believed that the more one was washed with the river's holy water, the more one would be blessed and pleasing to the gods.

More times in my walk across India than I could remember, Indians had invited me—usually with much pride in their voices—to splash in the Ganges and be imbued with its blessings. Every time I had declined . . . until this morning, when I had admitted to myself that I wouldn't experience India to the fullest until I had been "baptized" in the holiness of Mother Ganga.

"Now Kali smile on you all the way to America, Mr. Steeben!" Madan shouted gleefully, pointing to the cloudy domain of his favorite goddess.

I laughed, then gave him a good dunking. Why, even *I* knew that Kali had been smiling down on me since my first step in the Punjab.

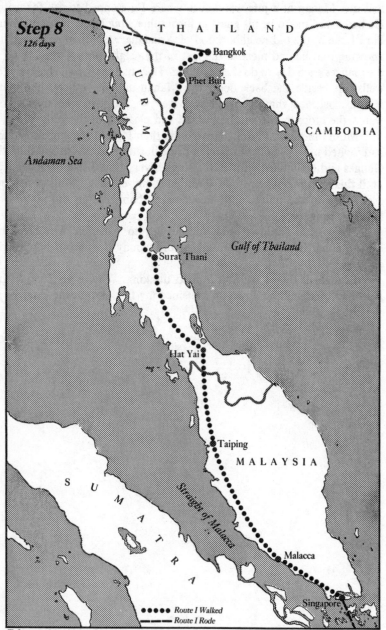

Step 8
126 days

THAILAND

Bangkok

Phet Buri

BURMA

CAMBODIA

Andaman Sea

Gulf of Thailand

Surat Thani

Hat Yai

SUMATRA

Taiping

MALAYSIA

Straights of Malacca

Malacca

Singapore

•••• Route I Walked
— — Route I Rode

February 24, 1985 to June 29, 1985   1,231 miles.

39

The thick Bangkok traffic rolled up to the red light. Engines roared impatiently. Drivers stared intently through swirling fumes like racers on some colossal drag strip.

Along the edges of the six lanes of asphalt was another jam of humanity. Dressed mostly in jeans and T-shirts, the mob pulsated to overamplified American rock music. Though hardly a lip knew a word of English, many a chest displayed such messages as PITTSBURGH STEELERS, LAUREL HIGH SCHOOL WILDCATS or—as one unknowing boy's did—such faddish clichés as CUTE GIRL.

Red—

Yellow—

Green—*Vroom!* The race was on again!

Lurching and darting, the racers zipped along their tracks of concrete or asphalt to wherever it was crowds were always scurrying. Some would peel away from the pack to replenish their tanks with Big Macs, Kentucky Fried Chicken, A&W root beers, Dairy Queen banana splits, Shakey's pizzas, or, as one pit crew's sign simply put it, AMERICAN FAST FOOD, HOT HAMBURGERS, SERVED WITH NO WAITING.

Designer jeans, knobby cassette players, wide-striped running shoes —anything and everything in a department-store manager's wildest dreams—rushed past me at dizzying speeds. I stumbled backward, as feverish from culture shock as from the Thai summer heat. From the open door of a fancy discotheque came Hank Williams's "Cheatin Heart," while the giant figures of Clint Eastwood and Burt Reynolds stared down at me from a massive multiscreen movie theater's marquee.

Dumbfounded and soaked, I collapsed onto a lawn chair beneath an umbrella of Civil War flags. Why hadn't anyone told me America now had fifty-one states? Was this what the travel posters had meant when they had said, "Thailand—Asia's most exotic country"?

"Drink, sir?" purred a waitress straight off the cover of *Cosmopolitan* magazine.

On her tray, glaring at me like some haunting specter of a long forgotten past, was a can of Budweiser beer.

"Maybe you like watch American football?" she asked. Then, pausing as if to wait for my eyes to fall out entirely, she added, "Today inside on big screen we have Super Bowl."

Super . . . Bowl—*the* Super Bowl? In Pakistan and India, hardly anyone had heard of the thing. But now, in a land I had expected to be the most primitive yet, I was being offered in the middle of March the most sacred of all American spectacles.

"Ma'am, is this really Thailand?" I wanted so much to ask.

What I had forgotten to take into account were the effects on Thai society of the Vietnam War. Thailand had been a major part of our military's logistics in that protracted conflict. Separated from Vietnam by Laos in the north and Cambodia in the south, the ancient Buddhist kingdom formerly known as Siam had become a strategic place to put bomber bases, supply depots, and battle-weary soldiers looking for rest and recreation.

And Thailand was still an extremely popular "R&R" spot for the U.S. naval fleet. As such, the Thais had been subjected to a continuous influx of Western culture. And unlike India and most of the Muslim countries I'd visited, the Thai monarchy had not tried to stem Western materialism or influence. To the contrary, the Thais had taken both the good and the bad of American culture with fervor.

Unquestionably, the Thais' willingness to take Americans to their hearts and tills had brought them wealth that otherwise would have been unimaginable. Instead of the largely poor, chaotic, and backward society I had expected, this was perhaps the most modern, efficiently run, and monied society I'd seen outside of Europe.

With prices for luxury and electronic items reputedly some of the lowest in the world, Bangkok was filled with Europeans and Americans scurrying about exercising their credit cards. Their arms loaded down with everything from fake Rolex watches to alligator-emblemed polo shirts to gaudily carved elephant tusks, those red-faced shoppers seemed to have an awful lot of "friends" back home. At the main post office, which conveniently had an entire department set aside solely for the rapid packaging and mailing of tourist purchases, the Western shoppers barely

took the time to scribble down their mailing addresses before rushing off
again to load up on more handmade silk suits and whatever.

For the serious shopper, Bangkok was a dream come true. From
sapphires to Mercedes, they were there—and cheap, very cheap. To many
Germans and Americans I talked with, a trip to Bangkok for several days
of shopping and bargaining (an accepted and expected part of any purchase) was as ordinary as a car ride to the closest shopping center near
Bethel would be for me.

While the rest of the world went shopping, I went off to do letter-
writing. Waiting for me at the American Express office in Calcutta had
been four hundred more letters from my readers. Now, I wanted to answer them.

It was a task that took the better part of thirty-eight days.

The visa stamp I had received at the airport was, another American
traveler pointed out, good only for two weeks, not the two months I had
thought. Because I learned this the day before the visa was set to expire, it
was all I could do to catch the new express train out of the country.

By one of those bizarre quirks of foreign bureaucracy, it seemed one
could not obtain a visa extension in Thailand. Rather, one had to go clear
to another country to obtain a new visa at one of Thailand's foreign
consulates.

On the thirty-six-hour train ride to the quite un-Malaysian-sounding
town of Butterworth (a vestige of Malaysia's days as a British colony), I
discovered, to my pride's relief, that a large part of the packed train was
made up of other foreigners likewise hurrying off to Malaysia for Thailand
visa extensions. Indeed, I learned that the same train was *always* rushing
off dozens of new visa aspirants. Any Westerner who stepped into the
Bangkok train station was automatically directed to the ticket window for
the southbound express.

I certainly couldn't help wondering if the Thai king's treasury hadn't
come up with a way to make the railroads and foreign consulates pay for
themselves.

Still, I felt His Majesty's treasurers were mere amateurs compared to others, like the Italians, who could make you smile broadly no matter how many traveler's checks fell prey to your signature. So I decided to let the others do the huffing. I would settle down and make a point of enjoying what seemed to be a very special sort of journey.

Sitting in the only real air-conditioning of my "air-conditioned coach," the breeze blowing over the outside steps at the coach's end, I watched with growing pleasure the tropical scenery passing by. Though it was the hottest time of the year in Thailand, a dark rainstorm swept off the seas to cool things down. As if trapped inside a demonic cyclone, the train sliced through winds that howled in my ears.

Where did that wonderful scent come from? Perhaps from the bright orchids waving at us from the edges of bamboo-hut villages.

How beautiful and proud the tall lone palms seemed, aloof from the tangle far below. And yet there could be pirates plotting on the beaches under those arched trunks. After all, the seven-hundred-mile-long isthmuslike arm of south Thailand, between Bangkok and the Malaysian border, was considered one of the most bandit-infested areas of the world.

The train ride through the villages and towns reminded me that if I hoped to discover the exotic Thailand I had always dreamed of, I was going to have to start looking for it and stop worrying.

I learned that though the rural people, too, might wear surplus U.S. Army gear or bright T-shirts, they still spoke only Thai, and still prayed reverently each day before the highly elaborate little "spirit houses" they had in their shops and homes.

"They are the hardest people to convert. We've had the least success with them," a Christian missionary from Wichita told me on the train. "Always so polite. Always listening so well to all you have to teach. But inevitably . . . always going away with that strange smile on their lips to pray to Buddha," he sighed wearily.

And when I was back in Bangkok, I discovered, particularly on the quieter side streets and in the less hectic hours of the dawn and late night, that even the modern society was threaded with fantasy.

As beautiful as they were in the sunlight, the graceful and intricately adorned spires and columns of the more elaborate temples, or "wats," took on a true fairy-tale quality in the late hours of night. Their brightly colored porcelain, ceramic, and gold reflected the lights of both the city and the moon as if they had been dusted by a magical wand.

In the earliest gray of the dawn, as I stepped noiselessly, almost furtively, along the empty sidewalks, I saw on every block the orange-robed Buddhist monks performing the ancient custom of *bintabat,* the taking around of a bowl in which to collect the day's food from the faithful.

At one market stall, I saw cockroaches on sale for use in cooking, while another offered monkey brains.

But of all the new experiences that opened up to me, perhaps the most meaningful occurred in a park by the Grand Palace. Tired, soaked, and resigned to the idea that I would never get back on the correct bus, I slumped onto a bench in the shade of a small tree. Leaning back to rest, I saw right above my head a special bit of exotica—kites!

There were hundreds of them. All fluttering about on the sky's currents like graceful, long-tailed tropical fish struggling on the ends of fishermen's lines.

I wondered if there were any kites to be purchased in the park. There were. So many I could hardly decide what manner of shape and size I wanted my air pet to be. At last I settled on a pink fish.

Timidly, I released my striking little paper fish into the currents, then marveled at how strongly such a delicate creature could struggle for its freedom. Memories of a windy spring I spent as a child on an old farm in upper Pennsylvania came back to me. That had been twenty years ago. Could I really have gone so long without knowing again the thrill of coaxing a kite into the clouds?

Abruptly, I was again in Bangkok. My fish was escaping! My kite's string had snapped.

Frantically, I zigzagged through a maze of fruit and soda-pop vendors in a futile effort to keep up with my fleeing fish. Breathing heavily in the thick air, I dashed onto the grounds of an enormous wat where I felt sure the kite had come to rest. I looked high, low—and then I started laughing. Cradled in the lap of a golden meditative Buddha statue was the little kite, as if to say to those who cared:

"This, my friend, is the *real* Thailand."

The eyes of the two young men narrowed like those of hateful tomcats. The men's arms cocked, and their fists challenged each other to advance. Bare feet danced nervously over straw-covered dirt.

The light from a bulb hanging from an overhead tree limb made the thick sweat on the men's dark, farm-hardened bodies shine like grease. Their chests heaved, and their heads moved from side to side with wariness. They seemed totally oblivious to the deafening shrill of the cicadas in the jungle surrounding the crude boxing ring's ropes and fence-post corners.

The cumulus of moths and bats around the bulb exploded. A roar erupted from the crowd around the little battlefield. Raw muscle charged, collided, pounded. Guttural cries burst from bruised lips. In the background, tom-toms and a raspy Java flute tried frantically to mimic the battle's tempo. Feet slapped against ribs, elbows thudded against skulls, knees pushed into stomachs. It was Thai boxing, where every limb and joint is a part of the fighter's arsenal.

At last a straw-hatted scarecrow leaped onto a horse cart and wildly beat a spoon against a metal dinner plate. *Clang! Clang! Clang!* End of round four!

Their nostrils gasping desperately at the steamy midnight air, the boxers sank backward into their corners. One more round to go in this gypsy camp ring.

Neither man had refused a punch or kick. What stamina! What courage!

And yet . . . there it was, glazing their eyes as surely as the veins bulged from their necks—fear.

Fear . . . Of what? Of losing? No. Each hurt too much to be thinking of anything other than surviving. Nor was there any actual prize to be won or lost, other than perhaps boasting rights. And that, too, meant nothing anymore, for each had long ago proven his courage and fighting skills.

What a strange thing fear could be, I thought yet again. We could laugh in the face of death a million times, and still have fear with us when the toughest challenge came.

I closed out the excited crowd of spectators and listened to my own inner trembling, to the fear that had been growing inside me for over eight days, since my own battle with death on an empty stretch of road seventy miles south of Bangkok.

It was the height of the Thai summer, and every step I had taken south from Bangkok seemed to be edging me closer to the fires of hell. Beneath the large striped golfing umbrella I held over my head, I felt as if I were inside a sauna. By each midmorning, my clothes were soaked; by midday, I barely had enough energy left to find some tepid shade to collapse into.

By the time I had reached the city of Phet Buri on April 6, I was so sapped of strength by the unyielding humidity that I had no choice but to spend four days recovering beneath a cheap hotel room's wobbly ceiling fan. I had gone only sixty miles, but my poor body felt it had suffered through sixty thousand. My worst fears about the effects of tropical heat on my Ohio-raised body were being realized, I thought uneasily. And, worse, since every step took me closer to the equator, I knew the battle to keep my strength would get tougher each day. I had never taken well to heat and humidity, and here I was trying to plod my way through the worst of it with fifty pounds of dead weight on my back and the monsoon season coming. The chance of my reaching Singapore, the end of the thirteen-hundred-mile-long walk through Southeast Asia, seemed remote.

I decided that I was going to have to do more of my walking at night, when it was cooler. Yet I knew that if I did, I was brazenly inviting death. Ever since I had left Bangkok, cars or trucks had pulled over to the side of the road to tell me that bandits were everywhere. As the drivers drew their forefingers across their throats and let their eyes grow larger with their warnings of sure death ahead, it was all I could do not to laugh at their animations. But there had been frequent news articles about packed buses being held up in broad daylight by bands of armed robbers along the same highway I'd be following. If they were reckless enough to rob an entire busload of people in the daylight, then what chance did *I* stand, alone and totally exposed? Behind my seeming calmness there took root a nervousness that I hadn't known since North Africa.

Still, I hated the heat so much, I was willing to risk walking at night. Even a police officer who rode up to me on his little motorcycle the evening I left Phet Buri and forbade me to go any farther on foot was not enough to make me change my mind. I tried to justify my foolishness by reminding myself of all the hundreds of times on the walk I had heard people cry wolf before.

And so, deeper into the dusk and then into the night of that mid-April day I pushed myself, hoping that the same guardian angel who had helped me make it unscathed through so many of the world's other danger spots would not abandon me for at least one more night.

It was around eleven-thirty on a moonless stretch of empty road thirteen miles south of Phet Buri when I found out just how far I could go on insulting common sense. This time it *was* the wolf—or rather, the wolves. And, worse, there was no one to hear my screams. Nothing but empty pineapple fields, jungle, and the thickly muscled men behind the machetes.

Then I looked down the tall bank on which the road had been built to keep it out of the quicksand and soggy peat of the jungle, and saw two men crouching in the tall weeds between me and a fire-blackened pineapple field. Quickly, deftly, they came at me with their long, thick machetes poised.

I stood frozen with fear and shock that my life was to end in some snake-infested jungle. Why or how I even thought to do it I will never know, but at the last split-second something caused me to raise my folded umbrella to my right shoulder, take aim at the bandits' faces, and yell through my mouth in a ferocious voice:

"HALT! OR I'LL SHOOT!"

It was the craziest, most insane deception I'd ever tried, but it worked. It bought me that extra second I needed to think about how I might escape. For the slightest of moments, the men paused in their advance and looked confusedly at the long, metal-tipped object in my arms. Meanwhile, in my own head the voices of reason were running amok.

Steve! What are you doing?! They're going to see it's only an umbrella. No rifle has red, blue, and yellow stripes running up and down it, for crying out loud! scolded one side of my brain.

Well, what'll I do? I don't have any tanks or bazookas! pleaded a higher-pitched voice from the other side.

Run! came the chorus.

If I'd waited just a second more, I would never have made it away. The bigger and uglier of the bandits had already decided he was being made a fool of. Even as my body was turning to run, the machete in his thick right arm was swooshing past my face close enough to guarantee I would not blink again the rest of the night.

Running for all my long, skinny legs and flailing arms were worth, I struck back out in the direction of Bangkok as though the entire Russian Army were on my heels. Desperately, I willed any car, truck, scooter, or policeman in Asia to come roaring down the road just then. But the long, dark ribbon of asphalt ahead of me stretched emptily on and on.

Since my legs were probably nearly as long as the bandits were tall, I was able to get quite a jump at first. But that was soon dissipated by the awkward weight of Clinger causing my rubbery limbs to go everywhere, it seemed, but straight ahead. As the patter of the bandits' own shoes drew nearer and nearer to my back, I was like a marathon runner at the halfway mark of the race, before he has caught his second wind. Yet the big bandit passing me on my left looked strangely serene and refreshed, as if he were out for a casual jog. He was carrying his machete in his raised right hand, as though he were a torchbearer in an Olympiad.

"Hey! Stay away with that! I'm a nice guy, I never hurt anyone! You don't want to rob me!" I said over and over, as he passed me as effortlessly as if I were standing still.

But he stopped before me and waited. He knew he had me, that I was dead. And I had to agree, when I heard his partner's shoes pounding closer from somewhere just behind.

Then, with a howl, I did the only thing I could think of: I charged madly at the bandit in front, trying my very best to get him to eat my umbrella. He slashed away at the heavy umbrella stabbing and pounding at his face. Crying, screaming, cursing, spitting, yelling, barking, pleading a thousand words a minute, I whirled and jumped and dived and dodged like a man who has half a dozen cobras and a couple hundred fire ants down his pants. And so it might have continued until one of us dropped from exhaustion, or my umbrella fell apart.

But then the other bandit caught up with our strange sword fight. Grabbing my pack, he pulled me backward, away from his hapless partner, and let fly with his own machete. From the corner of my right eye, I could see his machete's blade sweep toward my neck. My mind went blank, as if refusing to feel the blade slice through my skull and neck, but was jarred back when the blade hit Clinger's exterior frame, an inch from my jugular vein.

Not for a second did my wild gyrations stop. If only to stay alive for another few seconds, I fought on with a new surge of fury. And suddenly the bandit in front looked as if he were seeing a ghost and ran off into the jungle.

I whirled to confront the other—only to see headlights bearing down on me like two runaway comets.

Waving my arms frantically, I charged the lights and screamed at the Datsun pickup truck as it passed me.

The truck's brake lights flashed on.

I rushed to its back end, but it was piled so high with loose pineapples that I doubted even a monkey could have found a handhold. Wasting not a second, for I knew the bandits would come as soon as they saw the driver was not the police, I scrambled to the passenger door's window. The front seat was crowded with a farmer, his wife, and two young girls. Even without Clinger, I couldn't have fitted a leg in alongside them. But I had to make the truck's passengers realize I was inches from literally losing my head.

With the ragged umbrella flailing in my right hand, my left one demonstrating my plight by slicing and stabbing me silly with an invisible knife, I ranted and raved outside their door, as the eyes in the truck expanded in terror.

When I saw the shaking farmer's hand fly to the gearshift on the floor, my skin leaped a mile. If they drove off without me, I was a dead man. Throwing all caution to the stars, I tore open the door and jammed my arms, shoulders, head, and what I could of Clinger inside. Onto and across the girls' legs I wriggled madly, my hands groping blindly for anything to hold onto.

Over the next several minutes, as the truck sped down the road with my legs flopping out the side, it was a scene even a nightmare would have had difficulty matching for sheer confusion: Everyone was screaming; my

348 Steven M. Newman

heart was pounding against my eardrums; and in my mind I saw the bandits sprinting alongside the truck trying to grab my legs so they could chop them off.

Though I had no idea what it was I had grabbed to keep myself in the truck, I was aware that it was soft, and screaming something frightful.

Only when the truck eased to a stop in what was a tiny police shack's dirt yard did I finally loosen my eagle grip. Then I found to my embarrassment that for two miles I had been hanging entirely by the poor farmer's wife's breasts. Though I had grabbed her in her stomach area, I had latched onto her bra-less breasts because they hung low.

And it seemed I wasn't finished tormenting her yet. While trying to act out for the two policemen at the post that I had just been attacked by bandits, I kept pointing frantically down the road, putting an imaginary rifle to my shoulder, and shouting, "Bandits! Go kill! SHOOT!"

Only instead of putting some clothes on—they were in their underwear—and hopping onto their little Honda scooter to go after the bandits, they kept giving me the meanest looks. Because standing in the direction I was pointing was the bent-over old woman beside the truck, still trying to coax her chest back into shape. The policemen thought I was telling them to blast the poor innocent woman.

Eventually, everyone came to understand what I was jabbering about. The policemen put on some pants and boots and puttered away with a rifle in the direction of the ambush. But of course they were too late. All they found was a silent road, and my crippled umbrella.

Later that night, as I was lying on the floor in the back room of the wooden post, listening uneasily to splashing sounds in the swamp outside and watching the gecko lizards chase each other across the dingy ceiling, a familiar voice I'd struggled with so often the past years spoke to me again:

There is nothing to be ashamed of in quitting, Steve. You have gone far enough. Everyone will understand. Why risk your life anymore? You can't expect to continue to be so lucky in escaping from death.

But I knew that quitting anything because of fear somehow did not seem "right." To give up now would have been proof of how terrible the world is to those so eager to condemn it.

I had to keep going, if only to show there were not as many bandits as some were trying to make us believe.

Some things in life couldn't be explained in words. And certainly one of those was fear, that mysterious cloud on the human spirit. Why some were so willing to be its slaves, while others chose to challenge it to the last round would probably be something I could spend a lifetime seeking an answer to. . . .

The spoon pounding the plate brought me back to the present. The

faces screamed. The fighters charged and staggered, charged and staggered. Until, in the end, there was a winner, and a loser. And no more
need for showing fear.

For a while, at least.

40

The frail, saffron-cloaked monk paused at the cave's dark entrance. Slowly, he slipped his callused feet from their sandals. Then he feebly tugged at his togalike garments, as if to chase away a few of their innumerable wrinkles. In the pale glow of an evening sun shrouded in rain forest, it was hard to see what message his tiny dark eyes might be flashing. But there was no mistaking the inviting nod of his shaved head.

Like beacons on a distant shore, the flames of several candles beckoned us from the other end of the large, still interior. A sweet fog of incense smoke wafted across the small sea of darkness. At our sides were large, squat Buddha statues, some with heads and arms long eroded into dust.

At the far end of the cave the monk lit another candle on the altar. With the agility of a much younger man, he eased himself to a straw mat on the packed dirt floor. Four other monks, who had been silently awaiting the elder's arrival, acknowledged his presence by nodding their shaved heads slightly.

Respectfully, I eased myself onto the cold earth behind the five men, just outside the globe of the candles' glows. And with much inner groaning, I tried to coerce my stiff legs into the lotus position favored by the monks.

From atop a low altar in front of them, a golden Buddha with feline eyes, long ears, and a benign smile gazed down upon the disciples. Mountains of candle wax lay at its feet, a yellowing stratum of ancient prayers and long sultry nights spent in silent meditation.

While the monks' attention retreated inside themselves, my own flitted about the temple, darting from shadow to shadow to see what surprises their holy grotto held. There were many: a pair of long deer antlers protruding from a skull like gnarled stalagmites; enormous hand-sized spiders resting on their webs; a dozen moldy and stained paintings of the Buddha's mortal life in India over twenty-five hundred years ago; short blank paper prayer slips, and squares of gold-colored foil stuck onto the statues like freckles run amok; portraits of the present-day king and queen dressed in the costumes of their ancestors.

A rustle of rough cloth brought my eyes back to the monks. They were bowing low, as if in response to an unspoken command. I bowed, too, lest some misfortune fall upon my head for not being attentive. Deep chanting filled the cave:

"Araham samma sambuddho bhagava. Buddham bhagavatam abivademi . . ." The Lord Buddha, the perfectly enlightened and blessed one. I bow before the Buddha, the exalted one . . .

I had not expected to have any close contact with the religious community of this nearly totally Buddhist society. But because of the attack by the two bandits near Phet Buri, and the stories I heard of thieves who liked to slit their victims' throats while they were sleeping, I knew I could no longer walk at night. And so I had decided to seek refuge in the wats whenever I did not have a family to take me into a home.

While a few of the wats I had stayed in since that frightful night were large and centerpieced with a tall and glittering temple, most were a tiny cluster of stilt-legged plank huts deep inside a forest or at the base of some half-wild mountain. Gardens of tranquillity, those little wats were normally occupied by a handful of elderly monks who wanted a place to spend their final years undisturbed. Occasionally, there might also be a lone *maichee* (nun), humbly dressed, her head also shaved. Always there were the stray animals and chickens, dashing about in search of food scraps.

Though rarely visited by anyone other than the village children and the farm wives bringing food and idle conversation, the monks did not shy away from my unexpected appearance. They always showed me the bathing well or stream, then waved me up rickety steps to their one-room bungalows for some hot Ovaltine and a meal of rice, fish, and boiled bamboo. Furnished with little more than a straw sleeping mat, a mosquito net, a kerosene lamp, a small altar, and perhaps shelves crowded with old prayer books and a few chipped teacups, their dwellings reflected their humble views of man's existence.

At most of the wats, my stay was no longer than one night. I stayed at one, though—Wat Suan Moke—near the city of Surat Thani, for over two weeks. Its head monk, the Venerable Buddhadasa, was said to be one of the world's greatest living masters of the Buddha's teachings, but it was from the monk just under him, the Venerable Poh, that I received an invitation to pause and rest my body and soul.

I decided to try the life of a monk while I was there, both the mental and the physical aspects. To do so meant I had to dissociate myself from all my normal habits and, most important, from my own ego. Like the monks, I was to live a life filled with inner meditation and learning to achieve harmony with the forces of nature. It was a demanding and—contrary to popular image—a very grueling life-style. I had to learn to go every day without doing anything that might distract me from concentrating on my inner "light" or peace. I could not speak to anyone other than my teacher (Poh), could not make eye contact, write, read, listen to the radio, make music, eat meat, leave the wat's secluded compound, or kill any living creatures, including ants and mosquitoes.

In the end, my mind proved too restless. Nor were all the scorpions and snakes that surprised me on the paths of that forest monastery helpful to my concentration.

The monsoon rains had caught up with me at Wat Suan Moke, and with them had come hordes of what I hated more than snakes—mosquitoes. It was bad enough trying to take a bath in a creek where I had to dance around leeches and scoop up the water in a droopy plastic pail. But to have to fight off a million frenzied bloodsuckers at the same time was more than I thought even Buddha could have endured.

Maybe, just maybe, my inner searching might have led me to something inspirational, if there had not been a hundred other beings taking advantage of my stilled hands to nibble, crawl, bite, and sting me everywhere I had feeling. I knew the other monks were all as still as statues, and that I was supposed to have my eyes shut. But I didn't like being whittled away by things that had more eyes than I had fingers, and that first night left me with a distinct impression that I was the new meat in the wat.

But that wasn't the half of it, for next came the one sound I wished to God had been created on Mars or Venus, or anywhere else but Earth. I had just about got back to concentrating on something other than the rain and thunder, when it whined in my ear like a dirt trail motorcycle at the other end of a mile-long canyon. And it seemed the harder I concentrated on what was inside me, the louder that noise grew, till after a few minutes I was alive with capillaries going through fits of panic.

A master torturer couldn't have made me squirm and whimper inside more than that mosquito did when it landed just below my right eyeball. But I had promised myself I would not kill anything, and I aimed to keep that promise. For how else could I ever find Truth and be a real monk? So I brushed the pesky little vampire away.

Quickly, I returned to collapsing into myself, and just as quickly the enemy jabbed at my other eye. I brushed it off again. And again. And again. Then finally decided that *tomorrow* would be my first day of being a serious monk.

"You must see that this 'I' and 'mine' is the main cause of all forms of pain and unhappiness. Whenever there is a clinging to anything, then there is the darkness of ignorance. There is no clarity, because the mind is not empty," Poh said in a very low voice the last night I was there, as the glow from a ring of kerosene lamps played off his impassive eyes.

"And what of my dread of another attack by bandits?" I asked.

"One does not look on anything as ever having been, as currently being, or as having the potential to be self or belong to self. There is no self in the present and no basis for anxiety regarding self in the past or future," he replied in his usual serious, indecipherable way.

One thing of Poh's I did decipher, though, was *his* worry for me, on the morning he came to see me off. It was at the same huge front gate where we'd met two weeks ago that he said, "I wish you would consider taking a bus. Otherwise, I will worry so much."

"But I am walking. You know that," I replied.

"I know . . . I know," was all he said, letting his eyes say the rest.

When I walked through the monastery's tall front gate to continue on my way to Malaysia, I told myself I was unquestionably a much calmer person . . . even if poor Poh was still fretting.

Wandering through the hilly rubber "estates" that seemed to cover all of northern Malaysia was like being in a giant park. To come upon something as wild and bizarre as a firewalking ritual in such a quiet and conservative setting was a shock, but also a delight for my curiosity, for here was a firsthand chance to study an ancient penance ritual.

It was near the rubber-plantation village of Simpang Lima that I spent a long and humid afternoon watching as the Hindu temple whirled with energy. Young women, figures of grace with flirting eyes, their handmade saris shimmering like patterned rainbows, promenaded across the colorfully decorated temple's grounds while in the background a sweat-soaked, three-man ensemble played flutes and tom-toms. With the sudden and gleeful *pop! pop!* of hundreds of coconuts being smashed against the temple's cement floor came the parading of the lei-draped goddess statue around the village streets and the temple compound.

In the first of the two penance rituals to be done by the bravest of the villagers, several women, one with her baby in her arms, all of them with long and wicked metal pins stuck through their cheeks and lips and noses, were led around the glowing firewalking pit. They looked to be heavily drugged as they were guided by their friends. As they passed me, one by one, I couldn't bear the look of pain and daze in their faces.

Fortunately for me, every so often the spell of the preparations was broken. Once, dark men in white *dhotis* came to invite me to the festival's feast in an adjoining field. There small mountains of rice and string beans were being ladled onto banana leaf "plates." At other times, the shrill of a celebrant's flute caused my eyes to dart, or I would be distracted by the jingle of loose jewelry on a mother and daughter, bowing to the black stone Mariamman and symbolically washing their faces in the flames of her holy fire.

As the only outsider at the festival, I was surrounded by others eager for me to share their joy. Once, a young man dipped his thumb into a bowl held by a bare-chested priest and smudged gray ashes onto my forehead. Delighted, his friends danced around this *orang puteh* (white man) who was now like them. In that instant, I was swept back in memory to a street parade in Varanasi, celebrating the Hindu goddess Shiva. There I had been pulled into a crowd of young men with wildly shrilling clarinets and blaring trumpets. As their brightly splashed faces and swirling torsos did circles about me and a papier-mâché Shiva, they'd shouted happily, "Disco! Show us disco!"

And why not? Throwing every care I'd ever had to the chattering monkeys on the parapets, I'd dived into the orgy. I'd wriggled, bumped, bopped, and hopped till their instruments could get no funkier. When Shiva's harem and I had finally gone our separate ways, I had felt ten years younger and twice as alive.

And wasn't that very same lust for *feeling* life, for *feeling* their god inside their very own flesh and blood and soul what this sticking of pins and hot coals into their flesh was maybe all about?

But when it came time for the actual firewalking, my muscles and nerves were as tense as if I were about to go myself. I had read somewhere that the heat on the coals of such firewalking pits was usually around a thousand degrees. And all afternoon I had watched closely the preparations of the seven men taking part in the ritual. I knew without any doubt that there was no trickery of any sort being used. The flesh of their bare soles, much softer than mine, would be pressed against red-hot wood coals that I could not stand to get within five feet of—coals that would have set a pan of water to boiling in no time.

As the large crowd of Indian plantation workers watched in hushed expectation, the first bare-chested villager, his eyes wide and unfocused, was led by two friends to the far end of the twenty-foot-long, three-foot-wide pit. Around them, the air was filled with the sounds of chanting. Fierce heat waves undulated from the coals at the man's feet.

Crouching on the ground beside me was a teenage Indian boy, a descendant of the thousands of Tamils (South Indian people) shipped here in the 1800's by the British to work their rubber plantations. Excitedly, he nudged me: It was his older brother about to walk across the pit of fire.

A year ago, that brother had promised the Hindu temple's goddess, Mariamman, that if she would protect his poor family, he would walk over fire to thank her. She had done well; now it was his turn to repay the favor.

I bit my lower lip, dug my nails into my thighs, and cringed when the walker threw his head back, let out a deep cry, thrust his clenched fists into the air, and broke loose from his companions' grips. In that first plunge of his lead foot into the glowing coals, I felt my own feet shrivel involuntarily inside my boots; when I was seventeen, I'd accidentally reached my hand into a vat of boiling oil at a restaurant where I worked, and now that sharp, almost indescribable, feeling of heat clawing at my every sinew and nerve came rushing back.

The crowd cheered loudly for the man to succeed, to make a mockery of that thing called pain and reaffirm our hopes that the spirit is indeed stronger than the body. Every plunge of his toes into that pit was as the sword of a warrior ripping into the guts of something we all wished the world could be rid of forever.

Though he was from one end of the pit to the other in less than five seconds, the suspense had made his walk seem endless.

The look of pain on his face had been almost unbearable, and from the way he collapsed into the arms of his family at the end, I was sure he would release any second a scream heard to the furthest reaches of the heavens. But not a sound was there other than joyous laughter. Amazingly, within seconds of his finish he was joking with all at his side.

To the pride and joy of the young boy beside me, his heroic brother was okay. And to the relief of the man who had spent the past three months coaching them not to fear the heat, the others followed suit with flying colors.

I examined each man's feet very carefully. Some had soles as soft as an office worker's. Yet, mysteriously, there was not a single scar or blister.

Not even a speck of redness. And all smilingly swore there hadn't been the slightest bit of pain.

Was it all extraordinary? The priests and walkers told me it was possible only because of the intervention of the heavens.

The morning sun rose slowly through the long fingers of the coconut leaves. The one-lane road to Malacca was still lacquered from a midnight shower.

Beside the road were flimsy family-run stalls filled with freshly picked fruits—purple mangosteens, heavy, succulent papayas, tart star fruit, hairy red and yellow rambutans, and spiked durians, with their rotten odors.

As it dropped into a marshy swamp, the road was surrounded by mangrove roots and high branches rustling with fleeing monkeys. Stepping around a freshly killed snake the width of my arm (How many was that now? One hundred? Two hundred?), I caught my breath at the sight of a crocodile sliding off a stream bank. Then it was back to the rice paddies and buffalo, including one slumbering in a mudhole, his swept-back horns being used as perches by several large birds.

At noon I came upon a fishing village on the banks of a chocolate river. Wooden shacks leaned crazily upon stilts stuck into the water. Planks pungent with fish smells formed the sidewalks.

My pack suddenly felt too heavy, and my stomach very empty. Ducking into an Indian coffeehouse shaded by bamboo porch screens, I ordered lunch as wobbly ceiling fans swooshed overhead. The *chapatis* (flat Indian bread) were sizzled on an oil drum stove by the shop's open front. A tart soft drink with the delightful-sounding brand name Kickapoo was placed on my table.

As I sat there, the village's inhabitants spilled in and out of their narrow homes and shops. They were a study in contrasts: bustling Chinese matrons in flowered pajama suits, demure Indian girls in shiny saris, Muslim Malay men in long cotton tunics and new *kopiahs* (small black felt hats).

A Chinese man who knew fewer than ten words of English paid for my meal without telling me.

I continued along the empty beaches toward the south, as the call to Allah came from a distant golden bronze dome. As I had done ever since leaving Bangkok, I shaded myself from the harsh tropical sun with an umbrella. Several young children peered at me from behind a group of coconut tree trunks. With a quick twirl of my umbrella and a crossing of my eyes, I soon had them laughing—a *mistake*.

"Hello, mister! Hello, mister! Hello, mister!" sang out their voices for what seemed an eternity.

That evening my host, John Fernandez, near the town of Sentosa, filled me with *sirap* (rose-colored sugar water) and all sorts of dainty Hari Raya cookies and cakes. Hari Raya was the Muslim equivalent of our Christmas. It marked the end of a month of fasting, during which no food or water could pass the lips between sunrise and sunset. Fortunately for me, my Muslim hosts during that period had not felt I needed to go hungry, too. Observed during the ninth month of the Muslim calendar, the fasting before Hari Raya was meant to remind the faithful how the poor often feel. At its end, gifts were given.

Dinner was rice and spicy mutton. Mmmmmmm! Afterward, I retired to the high wooden front steps to listen to the crickets. Far, far away, a crescent moon smiled through a starry night.

"It's been a nice thirty-first birthday, hasn't it?" I whispered to the Old Man in the Sky.

He just kept smiling.

During the remaining 470 miles to Singapore, I thought often not only of the mystery of the firewalking ritual, but also of the Phet Buri nightmare and the calming teachings of the Buddhist monks.

Just being here this very second was, I now realized, a wonderful thing. And as the kindly old monks had been trying to show me, I could use that precious gift of life to bring others as well as myself more freedom and joy. By simply accepting what life offered, and seeking to learn from it instead of judging it, I could begin to experience life with a far greater energy and boldness.

My reaction to the firewalking scene told me how much I had changed since leaving Bethel. Before the walk, my Western mind would have kept me a respectable distance from all such superstition. But not anymore. I had gladly let those plantation workers smear their paints upon my face and sweep me up into their songs and dances.

Yes, that singing and dancing had been silly, and wild, and "sinfully" primitive. But it was a part of life, I was finding out on my long journey.

And it had been magical for those few laugh-filled hours to forget that we were supposed to be different and better than anyone else.

It had been a year, or nearly so, since that afternoon in Istanbul when I'd handed a boatman a lira and told him to take me across the strait to Asia. And now I was prepared to leave that continent for my final foreign one, aboard a jet from Singapore.

I had walked just under eleven thousand miles. It was June 29, 1985, and I felt I was a very lucky man.

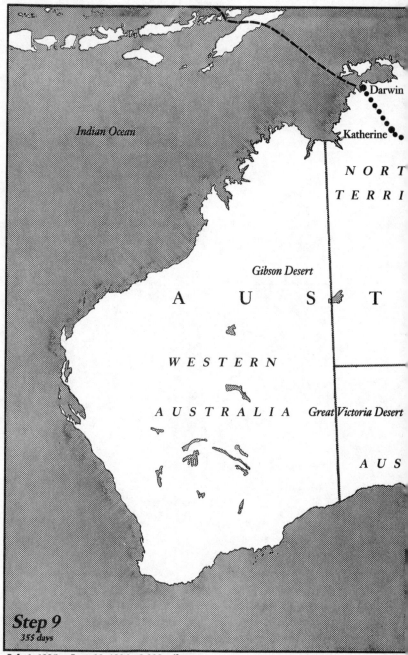

Indian Ocean

Darwin

Katherine

N O R T

T E R R I

Gibson Desert

A U S T

W E S T E R N

A U S T R A L I A   Great Victoria Desert

A U S

Step 9
355 days

July 1, 1985 to June 20, 1986   2,338 miles.

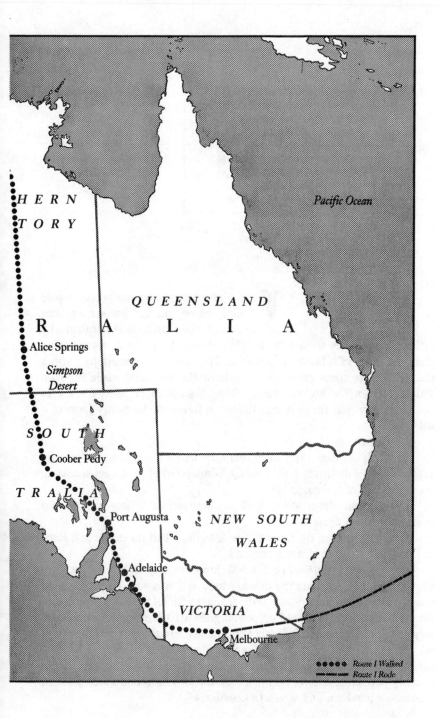

HERN
TORY

Pacific Ocean

QUEENSLAND

R   A   L   I   A

Alice Springs

Simpson
Desert

S   O   U   T   H

Coober Pedy

T R A L I A

Port Augusta   *NEW SOUTH*

WALES

Adelaide

VICTORIA

Melbourne

●●●●● Route I Walked
━━━ ━━━ Route I Rode

41

Like an egg yolk oozing across a pale blue china plate, the setting sun stained the northern Australian sky yellow. Then, ever so slowly, its glow dimmed against a never-ending plain the color of a brown paper sack. The crackle of something parting the tall, brittle spear grass on the side of the still road made me stop walking. From the broken reeds, a long head with curiosity-filled eyes poked its way into the clearing. Behind it followed the tawny form of a wild dog.

I held my breath—a dingo!

Startled, the dingo sprang in one leap across the roadway, then zig-zagged effortlessly through the ghostly, white-trunked gum trees speckling the other half of the road.

I was again alone, left to inch my way across a hot vastness that smelled of brush fires.

Five days earlier, on August 5, in Darwin, I had taken the first steps in this latest chapter of my worldwalk.

For the first time since I'd left home twenty-eight months ago, Clinger was not weighing me down. Much as I was sure he felt insulted about it all, he was ingloriously lashed, along with all the extra supplies, to the creaking frame of an old borrowed golf cart I had rigged with BMX bicycle tires. Nicknamed Roo (short for kangaroo), the cart was for carrying the ten gallons of water and up to fifty pounds of canned beans I figured I would need to get me from one settlement to the next in the sparsely populated deserts that made up the two thousand miles between Australia's northern and southern coastlines.

I had walked away from Darwin very hopeful and happy. The thirty-five days I had spent there preparing for the Australia walk had given me much to smile about. For starters, for the first time since leaving Ohio, I had met some familiar faces. While in Darwin, I had stayed with big bush-hatted, thickly moustachioed Don Zoellner and his lovely petite wife, Ardys. Both had graduated from Bethel-Tate High School just a couple of years before me, and had grown up only blocks from my parents' home.

Don had been lured to Australia in the early 1970's to teach. Later, he'd convinced Ardys to give up her highly successful television advertising career, marry him, and emigrate to the Land Down Under to settle down with him in the huge country's most isolated city. Now a biology teacher at the Darwin High School, he had taken wholeheartedly to the rough and tumble life of the Northern Territory's crocodile-infested jungles and harsh desert outback.

When not with the Zoellners, planning and preparing for the walk down through Australia's "Dead Center," a trek that everyone told me could not be done alone and on foot, I was usually with a former long-distance trucker named Leon Roberts. Like most of north Australia's "Territorians," Leon knew the few water holes out there along the road I would be walking on. He schooled me on how to survive the desert, and what I should pack onto Roo—and gave me a black umbrella to use against the fierce sunlight.

Those in Darwin with the most wrinkled faces had referred to it as "the Track." Others, much younger and a little more domesticated, had preferred calling the road I would be following "the Stuart Highway." All I knew from what I could see on my maps was that the mostly one-lane road, five hundred miles of which was still sand ruts, would be leading me into my greatest challenge yet.

The loneliest highway in the world, the Stuart Highway was the only overland lifeline from Australia's populated South to the still largely undeveloped North. Along its twenty-two-hundred-mile length, it held, according to my maps, fewer inhabitants than many Main Streets in the United States. I could count on just three fingers the number of *real* towns (those with over two thousand inhabitants) along its whole length. And on one finger the only city—Alice Springs, with just over twenty thousand residents. And that was eleven hundred miles south of Darwin, and just as far to the north of the next city, Adelaide!

I figured that if I didn't die from thirst by the time I reached Alice Springs, then I would probably die from loneliness. The Northern Territory region covered one-sixth of the Australian continent, yet fewer than 140,000 people inhabited it.

Of the twelve hundred miles I'd be walking in the Territory, some one thousand would be in the torrid, semi-arid zone between the equator and the Tropic of Capricorn. The remainder, with its large sand dunes and claypan deserts, was even harsher: the "Dead Heart" of what was reputed to be earth's driest, flattest, and oldest continent.

Who would choose to live in that cruel region, with its creeks that flooded fifty miles wide, its monstrous tidal waves of dust, its immense wastelands where poisonous spiders crept around in temperatures of 150 degrees? Surely, I had decided long ago, only a courageous fool struggling to tame that unsympathetic brown giant.

Yet it was that very pervasiveness of nature in the outback that attracted me to go down the center of Australia, rather than the populated "Gold Coast" in the East. Though everyone said I was as mad as a kookaburra, I wanted to try the deadly center route, because, more than anything, I needed a break from the masses of humanity. After two-and-one-half years of walking through mankind, I wanted to take the looking glass off Man and turn it to something I hoped might be more predictable—Nature.

Almost from the start, however, Nature, Australian-style, didn't seem to take kindly to my brazen intrusion. The more ornery residents in the outback let me know that the privacy I was seeking wouldn't be all that private—or peaceful. In no time, I was introduced to an insect world that seemed straight out of a science-fiction novel.

The most frightening, and painful, encounter was with a monstrosity appropriately called the bull ant. Half as long as my thumb, absolutely fearless, and nastier than anything Hollywood has yet to dream up, the huge, evil-looking insects attacked my gear and my skin and left no doubt that, should I be so unfortunate as to fall lame in their midst, they would soon reduce me to little more than a skeleton.

I had been napping in the middle of the afternoon under a scraggly gum tree when suddenly a piercing, burning pain on my jugular vein caused me to jump up screaming. Instantly, I reached up and ripped from my flesh several large reddish lumps that moved when I tossed them to the hot sand. Rubbing the sleep from my eyes, I looked closer and saw that there were hundreds of similarly red things coming at me from every direction. To my horror, my bare feet became red with ants that immediately tore into the skin as if it were made of paper.

Into the sun and far away from the tree I ran, yelling every curse known to man and then some more. Once out of the red tide of wriggling antennae and clicking jaws, I ripped each of the little killers off me. I was so scared, I didn't notice at first how dehydrated I was quickly becoming in the 120-degree temperature. All I could do was sit there in the sand and rub the dozens of welts on feet that felt as if they had just been salvaged from a meat grinder.

But then I began to feel weak, and the whole of me was suddenly as hot as my neck and feet. Not only were my boots and the cart and its gear being swarmed over by hundreds of the insects, but so were my baseball cap and the umbrella. It didn't look as though I could rescue anything.

I knew many a person had died in the outback in just one day from lack of water and from being stuck in the direct sun. I had to get something over my head soon and some water in my throat.

I grabbed a fallen branch that the winds had tumbled away from the tree and set it on fire with a lighter I had in my shirt pocket. If anything would make the ants flee, I figured it would be fire. After all, it worked in the movies with other monsters.

Incredibly, the ants not only weren't afraid of the flaming branch, they savagely attacked it! I dropped the branch and jumped back as if I had seen something from another planet. I'd never heard of anything in *this* world that wasn't afraid of fire.

Somehow I got enough nerve to go back and retrieve the stick. I had to stop them from gnawing at the Cordura nylon in the boots and Clinger. When I lifted the smoldering limb, the blackened remains of dozens of ants dangled from it.

Nearly at my wits' end, I decided my only course of action was to run into the angry horde and swish a path through it with the limb. With another small branch I would then try to spear my boots and throw them far away from the main body of ants, hopefully before they had a chance to swarm too thickly over my feet. I straightened, gripped the two branches as a knight would a lance, took a deep breath, and charged.

The swiftness with which those ants regrouped from my mad sweeping and dashing and hopping about like a Mexican jumping bean was nothing short of admirable. Madder than ever, they swarmed at my screaming toes.

"Aw!—ooh!—eek!—aaah!—ouch!—haa!—hoo! . . ." If ever I had any ideas of trying firewalking, they were cast aside in those few hectic seconds of retrieving the boots. The ants that were able to hang onto my toes set me tumbling crazily back through the air. They were worse than any coals, because they were too darn ornery to drop away. I hopped around like a one-legged grasshopper, tearing ants off one set of throbbing toes while stomping those on the other foot.

It would be almost two hours before I picked every living and dead ant off myself, my boots, and my gear, and could finally be back on my way. I wanted so much to pour every drop of water I had over my feverish forehead and the throbbing bites, but I knew I just didn't have that luxury. So I had to content myself with dabbing myself with a damp sock and a cup of water that felt as if it were soaked up immediately by my tongue.

For a week afterward, I was as jumpy as a minnow in a bass pond at feeding time. There were bull ants everywhere on Roo, including in places I never did find. And hardly a mile went by that I didn't think I felt one of them sneaking up the back of my shirt to butcher my jugular vein again. It took nothing more than a fly or a loose hair brushing against my sun-burned skin to make me holler out loud, drop the handle to Roo, and whirl around slapping my poor tortured skin like a man possessed with the meanest demons God ever did make.

Bull ants, though, were like friends when compared to snakes. Ever since the time I'd had a copperhead mistake me for a piece of driftwood while I was skinny-dipping at the old dam on Clover Creek, I'd taken to anything legless and with scales about the way a rabbit does to a hound.

Needless to say, it was not with the best of humor that I found out in Darwin that the Australia I'd always, for some reason, thought was free of such slithering vermin had 140 (!) of such breeds. And that eleven kinds of those snakes had a venom more toxic than the cobra, which killed more than ten thousand people each year in India.

"Best you don't hesitate a second to git yourself running, mate, if you see any of them two-step snakes," warned one old-timer thirty-three kilometers south of Darwin, near the turnoff to Humpty Doo.

When I admitted I hadn't heard of that particular snake, he stared at me through his ketchup-covered whiskers as if I were the most uninformed person that ever did live.

"Hell, more than one cockie [farmer] I've heard of that stepped within three or four meters of a two-step and never lived to tell 'bout it. Aye, there aren't much more horrible a way to go than to have one of them brown killers go leaping at you, all straight and swift as a fanged spear."

Normally, I might have had good cause for doubt, but I knew he wasn't joking. The whole time, he never once touched his can of beer. For a man in the Northern Territory to go more than two breaths without some "grog" passing his lips meant he had something pretty awfully serious on his mind. The average Aussie in the outback was said to drink more beer in a day than most of the world drank in a year.

"How long do you live, if one gets its venom in you?" I asked naively.

I thought he was going to slug me. "Crikey, if'n you Yanks haven't the learnin' of an Abo!" he hollered. "Why, mate, one bite and you got only *two steps* till you go crook, you bloomin' know?"

As if man-eating crocs, two-steps, Hollywood-sized ants, wild boars, thirst, drunkards, loneliness, wildfires, and heat stroke weren't enough to keep me from reaching my first watering hole—an obscenely misnamed clearing in the dust called the Emerald Springs Roadhouse—one hundred miles south of Darwin, there was something a hundred times worse: the flies. All the meanest bull ants and two-steps in the world put together could never have matched the outback's flies in their ability to drive a man insane.

Forever the curse of the bush country, those ordinary-looking little pests had probably sent more persons scurrying back to civilization than anything else in the outback. A daily plague that thickened with each jump in the mercury, they never pounced upon my face **and** arms in numbers less than the hundreds. More than once, something very definite snapped inside me, as I felt yet another one dash up my nose to buzz somewhere between my eyebrows.

In a setting drained of almost all moisture by several years of drought, where anything still alive seemed teetering on the brink of self-combustion, the flies fought endlessly for the taste of the moisture in my mouth, nostrils, eyes, and ears, as well as any moisture my seared flesh still managed to ooze out to the thermals. Sometimes when the wind was still and I was at the mercy of every fly within a hundred miles, I could not help but think of an eighteenth-century explorer named Matthew Flinders. The first person to sail the entire coast of Australia, and thus prove it was an island, he had written in his journals of a northern Australia that was a ". . . poor dried-up land afflicted by fever and flies, fit only for a college of monks whose religious zeal might cope with suffocating heat and musketos which admitted no minute of repose."

There was a saying in Australia that a person living there wasn't truly an Aussie until he had accidentally swallowed a fly. Well, by the end of my introduction to the outback, it could safely be said that I had become an Australian many times over.

The tall, dark Irish publican leaned his angular frame over the cluttered bar counter. A devilish grin pulled back the corners of his big eyes. His thin fingers rose to eye level. Pinched between them was a golden stone the size of a blacksmith's thumb.

"Now maybe, mate, you be thinkin' this rock a wee bit bonza, eh?" his voice crooned.

I was mesmerized by the shiny nugget.

Six other motley-looking men and one short, sinewy woman crowded about the lonesome little roadhouse's counter.

"Ya . . . nice!" a stocky bundle of syntactical eccentricities known as "Joe the Bouncing Czech" whistled.

"And what you thinking now?" the bartender asked me, plunking the rock into my hands.

It felt as if it weighed a small ton.

"The boys say there's likely four ounce in that thing," the woman, Carolyn, said.

My brows worked their way closer to my hairline. At five hundred dollars an ounce, that was . . .

"You say there's heaps of gold on top of the ground around here?" I heard myself wondering aloud.

"Fair dinkum! Mobs of it!" a twenty-eight-year-old prospector of lanky height and giant energy named Greg Germon exclaimed.

Nearly forgotten memories of enormous gold-leafed murals in the cathedrals of Venice, of a covered market in Istanbul with every shop dealing in breathtaking gold jewelry, and golden Buddhas in the Grand Palace of the king and queen of Thailand whirled in my mind's eye. *Gold!*

A raucous roar erupted from a crusty creature four stools down. It was Dickerson, the orneriest, most bush-blooded of the lot. And the most successful. He thumped a tin of baked beans wrong side upon the counter. Gold nuggets, not beans, spilled everywhere.

When I'd pushed on the screen door of Emerald Springs, caked in about as much dust and odor as one of the many wild camels in that area, and timidly asked about taking a shower, neither the bartender and his wife nor any of the gold prospectors were about to let me leave without a lot of spoiling and resting. They not only were amazed that I had *walked* there from Darwin, but they *liked* the fact. After all, every one of the gold prospectors spent as much of his day walking as I did. If I had driven into Emerald Springs, I doubt that I would have been invited to join in their search, for if there was one thing gold prospectors were particular about, it was keeping their "lucky turf" a secret from all but their partners.

But being as unusual a sight as any of them had ever given up a pool game to know better, and having made it in one piece around pretty near the whole world, I was, they figured, reeking of good luck and fate. And if there was one thing a gold prospector never had enough of, it was good luck. Three of them scrambled to get Roo into the back of their old brown pickup truck and take me to their camp. And the way we all hit it off immediately had everyone, even gruff Dickerson, feeling that when the sun rose again, it'd practically be dripping gold on our heads.

With Greg Wickham, who was the same age as I and about thirty pounds heavier, wrestling the truck's steering wheel all the way, we bounced and rattled through a dark, roadless world that literally sprang alive with each jar of the truck's lights. So many kangaroos and wallabies were bounding every which way that D-for-Dog, Wickham's mongrel gray-speckled sheepdog in the back of the truck, was practically having a heart attack. The only thing that kept him from doing a triple somersault was that Greg had him tied to the back toolbox.

"You'd think after his millionth roo, D-for would get it into his head that maybe this isn't his territory after all," Wickham said. "Dumb dog, but ya gotta love him for being so faithful."

Camp was a large blue tent for Joe and Germon, a tin lean-to for the rest. The lean-to belonged to another prospector named Clive, a white-haired, pot-bellied, scholarly sort, who had had about as much luck with gold as he had with sore backs. Though it was way past the normal ten o'clock bedtime of the prospectors—for they took their work as seriously as a corporate executive—they couldn't resist an hour around the campfire telling me what I might be expecting the next several days.

With a skillet of snags (sausages) and onions sizzling away on the flames, the billy can bubbling with tea, and my ears burning with prospectors' lore, I could have stayed around that campfire a hundred years.

"There's hundreds of other prospectors in Australia right now blipping all over the old gold fields with metal detectors, like we're doing," explained Clive, our self-appointed cook.

"It's another gold rush, what with Pommies [Englishmen] and rubbernecks [tourists] joinin' the fray!" blasted Dickerson. "Why—why there's thousands lookin' fer the lode."

"Fair dinkum!" came the chorus, above an orchestra of mosquitoes.

Clive adjusted his glasses on his large face and continued, "Australia is the only place in the world where much of the gold is in nuggets, right on top of the ground and spread throughout every part. The detectors have made it possible for anyone to be a prospector. New patches are being discovered all the time. Although most of the finds are in old gold-mining areas, where they go back over the old diggings."

"A find of one to two ounces a week is doin' darn good. Why, there's

many the times when several weeks pass without any cries of 'Gold!' "
Dickerson explained.

Smiles flickered on the faces showing in the light of the fire. It was no
secret that while the others were on a dry spell, Dickerson had added
three thousand dollars in nuggets to his hoard in the past two days.

"There's tens of thousands of square miles of gold country which
hasn't been gone over with a detector. There's more than enough gold to
support thousands of full-time prospectors," Clive concluded with a stab
at one of the snags.

Germon leaped into the rare pause in the conversation.

"My girlfriend and I prospected for two months in the Western Australia deserts and came back with ninety-six thousand dollars in gold
nuggets. And that was after my dad and brother came back with a hundred thousand dollars' worth from the same area, after spending five
months looking," he related with a twist of pride.

Altogether, Germon had over $400,000 worth of gold nuggets to his
credit, since he'd started prospecting with a detector at the age of seventeen.

However, perhaps in keeping with his life-style, that huge fortune
had been sunk into the search for more gold.

"If you're willin' to stand the heat and the loneliness, you can pick up
fifty thousand dollars within a few months," Germon talked on confidently.

"It was a four-day ride to any sort of settlement, and I was bitten by a
scorpion while digging a hole, but I just got a bit sick and recovered. The
whole area was alive with wildlife, including emus and kangaroos, as well
as pythons and lizards galore slithering around the workings. And during
that time we didn't meet one person who hadn't found gold."

Charlie, a sixty-nine-year-old retiree from Ohio, heaved an enormous
wild buffalo-dung patty on the fire to smoke away the mozzies droning
just outside the lean-to, patiently awaiting their meal of blood. He explained that he had been wanting to come to Australia to prospect for
many years, and had finally decided to do it, even though most of his peers
were doing everything they could to avoid any kind of discomfort or risk.
He showed me his hoard from the past month, about three thousand
dollars' worth of gold lumps, with the kind of pride and joy I would have
shown Indian arrowheads to my parents years ago.

"Got my air fare all paid for," he said happily. "Even if I don't find
any more, at least I got a free vacation and a whole lot of memories out of
coming over here."

Long after we'd settled down into our sleeping bags, or swags, my
mind was dreaming only in gold colors. I was so excited about how I was

going to spend all the millions I'd be stumbling onto the next day that I even forgot entirely about the giant python Clive said liked to check out the campsite every other night.

"Don't mind it none, if you see it," he'd said. "It's just like a pet to us."

Long before the sun was up and baking the earth, our band of fortune-seekers was already fed and gone its separate ways to where each one felt the gold would be. Greg Wickham had me for a partner, and proceeded to lead me and D-for-Dog on a hike far into the hills that had me panting like an old man in one hour flat. By the time we'd slipped and slid our way across all the loose rocks between the camp and the ridge that Wickham wanted to explore, the water in my canteen was already half drunk and the old detector they'd lent me felt as heavy as a log.

Wickham showed me how to use the detector and then gave me one side of the hill to probe, while he did the other. I thought I "smelled" gold everywhere, and went about my task with such eagerness I almost forgot to put on my earphones. I hadn't gone two meters when my earphones beeped so loudly I let out a yell. Wickham came running, scarcely able to believe my good luck. Using a geologist's pick hammer, he knocked away the rocks below the detector's disk to uncover the large gold nugget I had obviously found.

What he found, instead, was a very old can. I felt robbed, as well as confused: What was a can doing out in the middle of nowhere?

"Remember, this whole area has already been picked over once before. Back in the last century, the gold-mining companies had probably over ten thousand imported Chinese picking over every inch of this area for the gold. Of course, they only had their eyes to use, so we can find with the detectors what they missed," he said confidently.

All I came away with from that day were some rusted nails, corroded corned-beef cans, and complaining vertebrae. I might have added sunstroke, too, if I hadn't found a shade tree to nap away most of that hellishly hot afternoon.

By the end of the second day, I was still no closer to a mansion in Beverly Hills or a penthouse in Manhattan. By the third night, the amount of gold I had found wouldn't have covered the point of a sewing needle, let alone paid for a wardrobe. Except for Dickerson, Joe, and

Germon, who were taking turns using a bulldozer to scrape beneath the rocks in their areas, the same could be said of the rest, too.

Come the fourth day of 100-degree heat and no gold, I was mighty glad I had a college degree and knew how to use a word processor. On the fifth day, I thought of at least a hundred reasons why being poor and just living a simple life was about as enviable an existence as there was. And then, on the sixth day, I decided it was time to let the gold come looking for me.

By midmorning of the seventh day of my one big shot at being rich, I was where I planned to spend the rest of my gold-searching days—the local shaded waterhole.

My golden nuggets were the swarms of rainbow-colored cockatiels that moved in such beautiful sweeps against the blue sky, the large white and pink cockatoos with their red or yellow crests sprinkled throughout the gray gum-tree leaves, and the other animals—the large red kangaroos, little gray wallabies, and giant water buffalo with their long curved horns —that came to drink during the day and evening. I thought for sure that I'd gotten the idea of looking for yellow stones out of my system permanently. But then on the tenth night, Wickham returned to camp with something decent to show for all that walking and sweating. It was a nugget the size of my big toe—big enough, in other words, to make me fidgety all over again.

So I took a detector and went back to prospecting the next morning, right on Wickham's and D-for's tails. And when the three of us stumbled upon the dark opening to an old abandoned mine shaft on the backside of a rugged hill, I thought my palms would never stop sweating. Anyone who'd read any adventure books could tell you that an old abandoned mine shaft meant treasures and robbers and secrets of the kind to be talked about in whispers.

When Wickham spoke to me in a real low and slow voice, I knew he must have been thinking the same thing.

"What do you think 'bout going in it?" he asked.

"How we gonna see anything?"

"Oh . . . hey! I got a lighter."

We gathered some twigs, scrunched them into a crude sort of torch that we fastened together with some strips from my rotted shirt, and eased ourselves into the tunnel with the torch spitting ashes and flames everywhere. D-for would have none of it. He stayed at the entrance looking at us as if we were leaving him for good.

To our surprise, the passage was taller than our heads and as dry as outside. Our shadows played off the dirt walls. Wickham led the way, while I held back slightly to try not to lose sight of the entrance. Both of

us had ears like radar, from all our time spent outside, and at a strange
sound, like that of something scuffling in sand way up ahead of us, we
froze in our tracks.

"What do you think it is?" I asked.

"Maybe just our footsteps echoing."

We pushed on, more slowly than ever. Then something to the right of
our feet made me jump half out of my socks.

"What's *that*?" I asked. It looked like a small porcupine without any
head or legs or tail.

"It's a spiny anteater," he said.

"Where's its head and legs?"

He handed me the torch and grabbed at the thing. I waited for him to
scream with pain and come up with hands like pincushions. Instead, he
sank his hands into the long, pointed quills as if they were made of silk
and pulled with all his might. Try as he might, he could not get the animal
to relinquish its grip on the ground. I thought I could see the small head
and legs of the animal tucked under its hunched back. I handed him the
torch and gave it a try. The quills were so rubbery and flexible they didn't
seem real to me.

We continued deeper into the earth, and again I heard something
stirring ahead. I tried to ignore the sound, but goose bumps were starting
to populate my skin. Even my ears were humming, and my face suddenly
felt as if it were breaking into a rash.

"Bloody mozzies!" shouted Wickham, flailing the torch crazily.
"Mobs of 'em! Run for it!"

I wanted to, but I was being swarmed over. There were so many
mosquitoes they were spilling from the earth's bowels like a massive tidal
wave of needles. They were in my hair, in my eyes, in my ears, in my nose,
even between my teeth. I was breathing the things. I scrambled and yelled,
bumping into the walls and throwing my arms about as wildly as someone
drowning.

I looked back at Wickham to see if he needed help, and yelled out
again: Coming right at my scalp were some red eyes and fangs on black
wings the length of my arms. Fruit bats! I dived to the ground and crawled
madly back to the entrance along a floor that I was sure was seething with
snakes, rats, scorpions, and spiny anteaters. Every bat that zipped past
was taking a swipe at my ears. Every rock or lump of dirt my hands
landed on made me want to cry out. All I needed was something to bite
me, and I would have dropped dead on the spot.

Back in the light at the entrance, the mosquitoes retreated into the
darkness like vampires. It was several minutes more, however, before the
bats stopped pouring out the entrance. Both Wickham and I just lay there

374   Steven M. Newman

looking at each other's red arms and faces. Meanwhile, D-for was loving every minute. He was yelping and leaping at each furry squeaky "bird" escaping from the hill as though he thought he could catch it. By the time Wickham and I finally emerged from that hole, it was hard to tell who was the more tired, we or D-for.

Thus ended my one shot at being a millionaire. The only actual gold I took away was a nugget Wickham gave me to remember those days by. But that motley group of gougers had given me memories and stories more to be cherished than any yellow rock.

42

Bright red dust billowed from behind the pickup truck in which I was riding. On my right there was a thin line of gum trees, their droopy branches silhouetted against a darkening horizon purpled by the smoke of uncontrolled grass fires. To the south, on my left, a "willy-nilly" was churning, the small but powerful twister seemingly unable to decide in which direction to head.

It was, for me, for Tiny, the Aborigine cowboy in the back of the truck, and for the truck's driver, Bruce Rose, the winding down of another cloudless September day spent repairing miles of barbed-wire fences on Bruce's elderly parents' Western Creek Station, fences damaged over the years by such natural vandals as rust, wild steers, and trees toppled by grass fires or termites.

I glanced at the fingers I was resting atop a black cowboy hat on my lap. Bloody, blistered, and as encrusted with dirt as nearly everything else in this thirsty land, those hands suddenly seemed too abused to be my own.

I gazed back out at the wild land that showed no sign of ever being tamed, and I shook my head for the umpteenth time in awe of those like the Roses who called it their home. If walking around the world had taught me anything about human nature, it was that the part of us called the spirit was a mixture of versatility, persistence, and durability. Certainly, the Roses lived in a land that promised little more than continuous physical and emotional turmoil. And yet, somehow, in the past three years since they had acquired the Rhode Island–sized spread in a bankruptcy auction, they'd learned to accept gladly the near-impossible odds of ever turning a profit, because this period of their lives had become a magical chapter.

Time in such a wilderness was figured by the sands of red dunes, the dazzle of bruised skies and strange, unscented flowers, and an electrifying sensation of freedom. And in the cool black sea of each night, the gods themselves came, all asplendor in the brightest diamond stars imaginable. It was only in the Southern Hemisphere that the whole of the Milky Way's robe could be seen. I had never known a night sky like that of the outback —and always with just me and it, one on one. If every person could spend just one night in such an immense heaven, perhaps all of us might realize what a miracle each second of life is.

Like a well-salted sailor on a vast outback sea, I could now sense beneath the flapping cloth of my umbrella any breaking of the weather, long before any change in the wind. Whether it was a boiling heat wave from the equator to my stern, or a titanic cloud pack drifting toward me from the Antarctic's stormy wastes in the south, my body sensed its approach long before my eyes could discern it. It was like being able to see the future from a hundred miles away. Most of the time I saw peace. Sometimes I had to tremble, watching great hateful forces approaching. At those times I wanted to scuttle away, like some puny hermit crab on the floor of a deep and dark ocean.

"What are you thinking?" Bruce's deep, pleasant voice asked me.

"Oh . . . I guess mostly about how much I'm going to miss you and your mom and dad. It's hard to believe that it's time to be moving on again," I said.

The two weeks since I'd first ambled into the Larrimah roadhouse, some thirty miles away, and met Bruce's seventy-year-old white-haired dad pumping gasoline in his pickup truck, had flown by.

"How would you like to make some spending money?" he'd said to me almost as soon as he'd seen me.

"Sure. What have you got in mind?" I'd fired back, figuring the tall, strong old man just needed some help changing a tire or unloading a battery.

"Picking watermelons," he'd said.

"Oh, sorry. I'm heading to the south." I assumed he had a farm somewhere back up by Katherine, 118 miles to the north. There were several large melon farms around that small town, because of irrigation from the Daly River.

"I live east of here," he'd said, holding out his thick hand and glancing at my American flag hanging from Roo's side. "My name's Gerry Rose. You must be a Yank, too."

When I said I was about as American as you could get, he'd laughed so heartily that I knew then and there I had to get to know that man better. He arranged for the roadhouse's owner to store Roo in a safe place, and off we went to see the watermelon patch he insisted he was growing out there in the outback, despite the fact that there wasn't enough water for a hundred miles around to fill a cup.

Sure enough, after about twenty miles of dirt roads, there were the watermelons right out where he'd said they'd be—the thickest and heaviest watermelons I'd ever seen.

The secret, he had explained, was that he was running the water from an old cattle bore through a drip form of irrigation that had been developed by the Israelis for their similar desert conditions. The water from the well was pumped through thin plastic tubing containing many little holes that allowed the water to drip out into the soil around the plants' roots. Since the ground around the plants was covered in plastic sheeting, hardly a drop of water was ever wasted to evaporation.

"This soil is incredible. Give it water, and plants grow in it like you would never believe," he said firmly.

It was at that two-acre patch of melons that I'd met his wife, Darlene. She had been dressed in a wide-brimmed flowered bonnet and was reading the Bible in a net-draped lean-to, with an ice chest of water and sandwiches to her left and a shotgun to her right. The shotgun was for the big crows and the occasional wild-born cattle ("clean skins") that came too close. Water was such a treat in that area at that time of the dry season that the cattle could smell it from miles away and would do anything to get at it.

Gerry and Darlene were standing in the little yard of their tin-roofed home when Bruce and I drove up now. They were watching the swirling clouds of smoke from a giant grass fire in the distance. Fires in the outback were allowed to burn at will, since there were so few people to be in any danger. The one they were watching had been burning uncontrolled for weeks, and had spread to about two thousand square miles in size. They knew it would take only one good strong wind from the west to push it quickly toward their station's thousand square miles of brittle brush. As the fence lines showed, it had happened many times in the past.

I jumped out of the truck, and stared uneasily at the enormous bank of smoke blackening almost all of the western horizon. To me, it looked a lot closer than it had that morning. I didn't like the idea of being trapped in the center of a grass fire that enormous. Even if the fire didn't touch the house, which was in the middle of a large clearing, the whirlwinds and lightning that sometimes accompanied such heat could be deadly.

Tiny glanced more than a few seconds at it before he left to go join his wife and little daughter in their shack. Having spent the last three days walking the fences with Tiny, I'd learned to respect greatly his knowledge of the outdoors. I knew that if he showed any concern, there really was something wrong.

"Now don't you be worrying about that fire," said Darlene, who was the last one through the kitchen door. "I've always one eye on it, and the Lord has both of His. We're going to sit down and enjoy this last supper with Steven. I don't want *none* of you men jumping up and letting your food get cold. I spent all afternoon making this one special."

She took off her bonnet and marched back to the propane-gas stove to check the lamb roast.

While I went to wash at least a couple pounds of dust off me, Gerry went out and started up the diesel-powered generator from which they got their electricity. That was all the excuse Bruce needed to give the radio knobs a twist. As usual, all he found was static. The only station they ever picked up that far from civilization was the Voice of America for a couple of hours some mornings.

The ranch was isolated even from something as rudimentary as the telephone. All that linked Bruce and his parents to the outside was a small shortwave transmitter wired to some car batteries on the house's front veranda. The week before, I'd watched in amazement as Gerry made three trips to Katherine to get a telephone call through to the States. That was a total of nine hundred miles for one telephone call!

I came back to the kitchen to find Darlene practically skipping back and forth across the kitchen. For a woman who'd been through as many hardships and heartbreaks as she had, she was still as full of life as a young girl. In more ways than one, she reminded me of Rina Jaquith in Morocco. They were both strong, older, optimistic women who looked a lot younger than they were.

Before her marriage to Gerry, right after World War II, Darlene had survived—*barely*—several years as a POW of the Japanese on a jungle island. Though managing to avoid the beheading her first husband (a missionary) had suffered, she had been decimated by hunger and illness by the time she was rescued. Then, for most of the following four decades, she and Gerry, also a Protestant missionary, called the largely unexplored interior of New Guinea their home. There, living and preaching among cannibals who had never before seen white men and who knew nothing of metal or alphabets, Gerry put his medical background to use treating horrid tropical diseases and spear or arrow wounds.

And still they had somehow managed to find the energy to raise a family and to run two highly bountiful coffee plantations, both of which were taken from them, with little more compensation than a ticket out of the country, by corrupt governments.

Instead of returning to America's security and an easy retirement, they had repacked their few belongings, rekindled their magical flame of energy and courage, and gone off to conquer yet another part of the world.

Meanwhile, their two sons, who were attending colleges in Casper and Seattle, felt the same itch as the parents. So it was not long before they, too, hurried back to the challenging life-style of less civilized lands: Bruce to his parents' outback ranch, the other son to a small fruit plantation in eastern Australia.

"Do you ever wish you had just stayed in America and lived a nice, easy, comfortable life?" I asked no one in particular and everyone in general, as we sat around the table piling steaming veggies and mutton and gravy and potatoes on our plates.

Gerry answered me. "I tried to settle down and retire with Darlene in the States, after the Papua New Guinea government took our plantations. But after all those years of working and living in such exotic settings, of helping those people who were sick and wounded, I just couldn't sit around and wait for the years to pass. America seemed too ordinary."

Bruce broke in. "I could see the big change from the Dad I grew up with in the jungles of New Guinea, and the one in America who was supposed to be going to bridge parties and watching television, like a good retiree."

"Oh, I'd thought so many times about how nice it would be to just have a hot bath whenever I wanted one, and someone else to do my hair, and to wear makeup," Darlene confessed. "But, well . . . those things just aren't as important as following the Lord's calling."

"I might be American on paper, but not in here, in my heart," said Bruce. "This is where I want to live. Here I feel so much more alive and free. I grew up with native kids and cannibals with skins and bones in their noses. We explored jungle cliffs where they piled their ancestors' bones and skulls in the caves. My life was sunshine and flowers and color. And fresh air and lots of nature and happy people. The people really cared about me, and loved me like one of their own children.

"But then I go to America, and no one hardly says hello to you. So many are afraid of strangers there. I just couldn't feel free there like I do here."

"But it seems to me that you're putting yourself through so many worries," I said to Gerry and Darlene. In our drives out to the fences each day, Bruce had told me all his parents had gone through in trying to generate income: cattle rustling, equipment breakdowns, theft, the damage and the spread of disease from the wild cattle among their own few stragglers, fire, duststorms, the broken promises of financial assistance from the banks.

Even the watermelon experiment had been a huge loss to them. Last year they had not been able to find anyone, even in the unemployment lines in the cities on the eastern coast, to come and harvest their melons. Consequently, the three acres they had went to waste—tons of perfectly good fruit abandoned to the sun and ants. And this year it looked as though the shortage of any labor would again be the crop's undoing.

The curtains on the windows flapped in a sudden breeze, and I thought I smelled something burning. I took a long drink of the lemonade Darlene had made from a couple of the huge yellow lemons on a tree out in the side yard and smelled it again. I was about to say something when Tiny poked his head through the door and muttered about fire. Gerry got up and looked out the door's screen. The look on his face, when he turned around, wasn't optimistic.

Bruce, Tiny, and I quickly returned to the Toyota truck. The wind had shifted toward our position. Gerry asked Bruce to drive the fifteen miles to the ranch's boundary to try to determine just how far away the fire was. The black wall of smoke looked close, but anything that huge would, even from a hundred miles away.

I stood in the back of the truck and held on tightly to the roof of the cab, while Bruce and Tiny rode inside. The smoke-scented wind blew my hair back and made the pastels of the dried land seem much more alive. Large white clouds of cockatoos exploded from the gum trees and scolded us for scaring them. A few kangaroos raced alongside, their long, clumsy-looking tails hanging behind their rumps like useless rudders.

When we reached the boundary, the fire looked so close I almost wanted to get into the truck and flee back to the east. But Tiny assured us it was many days away. The Aborigines said they could feel the spirits of the dream world in the winds, and when Tiny stood there staring at the smoke that looked pale in comparison to his own black flesh, I noticed he was as still as a rock. It was as if each brush of the wind through his eyelashes and fuzzy hair and against his skin was talking to him. He seemed to understand that you can only listen to the wind, never speak back to it.

I tried to listen, too—*really* listen, for once. What I heard made my heart slow down to almost nothing. Very faintly, yet clearly, I could hear the popping and crackling of dry vegetation being consumed by flames. That moment, more than any, told me just how empty the outback was.

That I could hear a fire from dozens of miles away said that I was in the purest and wildest piece of land outside of the poles.

As we were returning to the station house to give the good news to Bruce's parents that the fire wouldn't reach them for at least a few more days, I had taken a final look at the smoke and seen a sight I would never forget. The sun, which had been but a hazy orange ball for days, had turned a brilliant red that made my own blood seem dull by comparison. It had been as if the eye of all creation, for that brief moment, had stared at me.

"What will happen when the fire reaches your land?" I asked Bruce.

"Oh, the same thing that's been happening every year for thousands of years. All the dried grasses will quickly burn off, the rains will come, and through all the smoldering ashes and blackness so many green plants will suddenly sprout that you wouldn't even know this was the outback. It's just Nature's way of redressing herself, I guess you could say."

"What about the house, though? And your mom and dad?"

He looked at me as if I were being silly, and laughed in a friendly way. "We'll survive. Some people got plugged drains or stray dogs to give them fits, we've got fires the size of states and wild bulls mean enough to take on a semitruck. But either way, it doesn't matter. You always find a way to fix the problem and get on to the next one. We've just learned to live with a different set of headaches, you might say. The fire might burn all the ranch, but I guarantee you the house, and Mom and Dad, will still be there after it's all done and gone.

"They're survivors through and through. Or else they wouldn't be calling this their home."

43

I lowered my book. My heart was pounding. Something wasn't quite right in the misty dawn outside the four-foot-wide storm pipe into which I had retreated during a frightening lightning storm during the night.

I concentrated all my attention on the increasingly louder sound of gravel or rocks tumbling against one another.

That's not any car on the road! screamed a voice in my head, when I realized that the rocks were making an awful lot of splashing sounds.

My guts twisting, I bolted from my sleeping bag. Bent double in the low, long pipe, I scrambled to the far end and stared out wide-eyed into the dawn light. Churning around the last bend in the dry ravine I was in was a two-foot-high wall of brown water and foam pushing dead limbs and rocks before it.

Flash flood!

"Oh, my—" My reflexes didn't give my mouth a chance to finish the sentence. In less than a second, I was all the way back to the sleeping bag. I grabbed madly for any gear lying loose around Roo and flung it onto the dirty bag. Already a foamy brown flow was swirling around my ankles.

Everything was happening so quickly that it was as if I were trapped in a revved-up movie reel. My escape route out the near end of the cement pipe was filled with the jumbled hulk of the cart I had squeezed into the pipe behind me last night. Gear was sweeping past, and with a rapidity that had me screaming, the flood had climbed from my ankles to my calves to my knees.

Wild with fear, with images of my body entangled in the cart in that dark and roaring hole, I bulled toward Roo and pushed on it with all my strength. Both it and I popped from the little round opening like party streamers. Arms, legs, books, gear, bicycle tires, limbs, and a dirty foam went tumbling. Roo swirled out toward the rapids, which were fed from the floodwaters gushing from six adjacent storm pipes.

I heaved the sleeping bag and its bundle of loose gear, including my camera, onto the rocks of the nearest bank, and plunged after Roo. All my log books and notes were in Clinger, who was latched to Roo's spindly metal frame and BMX wheels. If I didn't save those books, there was no way my journey could ever be verified.

The roar was deafening. I couldn't tell if the lightning and thunder exploding in my head were for real, or from the waters ripping and battering at me.

Where was Roo? I couldn't find it!

There! *Let it go, Steve! You'll drown! You're slipping—GET IT NOW, OR GET OUT!*

My hands lunged. Fingers latched tightly onto something slippery, something hard and smooth. Legs strained, strained, *strained.* The wheels were caught on the limbs!

Without a second thought, I dived under the water and tore at the unseen trolls, my adrenaline pumping a gallon a minute. I just *wouldn't* let the flood win. All those years and miles *had* to be saved.

The cart loosened. I exploded from beneath the swirling with my lungs screaming for air. Falling, splashing, lunging, I reached the bank with the cart in tow. Like a pair of muddy beasts after some great struggle, we tumbled awkwardly onto the rocks.

I lay there sobbing with fright and pain, and the realization that I had almost died. It would be many minutes before I even felt the thick rain washing me into the mud. All I could think, over and over and over, was how incredibly lucky I had been that I did not camp in the middle culverts. It was into them that the majority of the flood waters had gone. I would have been drowned for sure.

Not enough rain had fallen overnight around me to soak a decent-sized sponge, let alone drown me. As I gathered what was left of my gear into the cart and tried not to notice how much I was shaking from the cold wind cutting through my soaked clothes, I looked from time to time at the purple misty hills of the Macdonnell Range to the east of me. They looked as barren as a scene from the moon, yet it must have been there that the rains fell during the night, there that the flash flood was born.

Many Australians had told me stories of the sudden and deep outback flash floods. It was not unusual, they said, for the Stuart Highway to be completely cut off for weeks in spots where normally not a drop of water would be found.

With the rainy season approaching, I would now have more than just heat to worry about. With the ground too hard and baked to soak up the water, even the lightest of rains in the outback could conceivably cause flooding.

Water was such a cruel joke in the outback. You either had too much or too little. I estimated I was sweating a pint an hour, which meant that my ten gallons were good only for three days, if I was careful. Luckily, though, I had always somehow, some way, found more water within a day of running out. A few times it had been in an Aborigine camp, other times at a distant windmill on the horizon, and many times from a passing rancher who let me refill from the supply he never drove anywhere without. It wasn't easy going weeks without a bath, or having to eat only a can of beans a day, or having to swallow the same water I rinsed my teeth with, but it was better than the alternative.

I pulled Roo back onto the empty road and continued south into a howling wind. At least tonight I would not be drowning or thirsty: My first city in almost twelve hundred miles of walking—Alice Springs—was only twelve miles farther. I was ready for a little civilization again. And a shower!

Both of which I got plenty of in the eleven days that I stayed in beautiful green Alice Springs on Kurrasong Drive with wild Bob Strickland, "Stricko," the city's lone street sweeper.

I accompanied Stricko on his rounds more than once, and got to see not only the city's curbs and parking lots, but also camel-crossing signs on some of the main streets, wallabies raiding flower gardens, a fairly large "Abo" camp in the park, and lots of pub "yabberin' " (small talk) between the bush-hatted patrons and Stricko that usually started out:

"Howagoin', Stricko! Where ya been? Orright?"

"Not worth a bloody zac, ya know. Dusty as 'ell out there. Got me feelin' all knocked up [tired]."

"Who's yer mate wi' the bloody big conk [nose]?"

"This is Steven, from America."

"Fair dinkum! Bloody Yank, eh?"

"Don't be thinkin' I'm blowin' me trumpet [bragging], but Steven here's been humpin' the bluey [walking the roads] with a swag [pack] all's the way from his home in America to here—three years, he sez!"

"Hooly-dooly! Now that's a bloody walkabout! Shout [order] yer a grog, mate?"

On my way out of Alice Springs on October 24, I paused long enough to read on the pointed white directional slats of a twelve-foot-high kilometer post:

DARWIN 1535

RUM JUNGLE 1451

KATHERINE 1182

MOUNT ISA 1156

AYERS ROCK 270

TENNENT CREEK 507

ADELAIDE 1648

Only in Australia could the distances to the nearest towns or points of interest—such as Ayers Rock—have been so far away from each other, I thought. It scared me to think that the next city, Adelaide, was still 1,648 kilometers to the south—with perhaps the meanest desert terrain in the world and only a couple of little towns in between!

When on October 30 I crossed from the Northern Territory into South Australia's even harsher and less populated Great Victoria Desert —the deadest of Australia's Dead Heart, or Never-Never—the land was virtually devoid of mankind's traces. There was not even a speck of asphalt upon the sand-drifted ruts of the much feared, and avoided, "South Road" of the Stuart Highway. Nothing but lizards, snakes, grotesquely gnarled scrub, and unhindered spaces.

During the day, I became a prisoner of the sun, hiding under my umbrella or in the shade of large boulders carved by the sandstorms into surrealistic forms. With weakened body and with thirst tormenting my throat, I tried to stay still and motionless in the day, prepared to move swiftly and cautiously in the more merciful nights.

The land was cruel, grabbing endlessly at the cart's knobby tires and offering me only my own shadow in which to hide. Yet night after night, I found myself elevated to the company of the gods, dressed in a wide velvet robe of more diamonds than any king or queen had ever known.

I was almost three hundred miles south of Alice Springs but still two hundred miles north of my next planned rest stop when Johnny B. Coolie's clunky old Holden auto roared at me from out of the damp blood-red dunes. I was sitting in the sand with about ten Aborigine cowboys, all of us savoring the fleshy, sweet tail meat of a five-foot-long goanna they'd shot about twenty minutes before.

Putting his big-bellied, wide-hatted Aborigine body through the missing windshield, Johnny shoved the usual beer into my hand, strode cockily to the campfire, tore off a hunk of the white lizard meat for himself, then sat down at my side to dare me to go with him to an isolated little camp of opal miners situated far to the west of the Stuart Highway.

There, in the Great Victoria Desert, was a "Wild West" camp of around 250 prospectors sitting on the richest opal claims in the world, he boasted. Mintabie was its name, and as sure as the sun was hot in those parts, it was a perfect refuge from all that was civilized and tame.

I was more than a little bit hesitant to load myself and my cart into Johnny's battered tank. For starters, I didn't know Johnny from the man in the moon. Could he be trusted?

Still, Johnny insisted it would be unlike anything I'd seen yet in all my wandering. And so I gave my curiosity permission and succumbed once more to the adventure of living with prospectors.

A thousand missed heartbeats and several spilt cans of Foster's beer later, I came racing on a cloud of dust and smoke into Mintabie's unusual gathering, where it turned out I was meant to be, anyway.

Right away Johnny introduced me to his best mate, Ron. I was quite taken aback when the short, wiry man of about forty stroked his black beard calmly, looked up at me closely out of one eye, and asked if I might, by any chance, be walking around the world?

"Why, yes," I replied, astounded. How could he have possibly known what I was doing?

"Well, I don't know if you remember or not, but you wrote to a lady in Melbourne, a few years back from Africa. Her name's Peg Matthews," he said.

"Sure! I know Peg well. She reads my stories in *Capper's Weekly.* A pen pal of hers in Kansas City, Missouri, sends them to her. She's been following me ever since I left home. Heck, she even writes to me every six months or so at the addresses the editor puts in with my stories. By golly, you wouldn't be Ron *Elliot,* would you?"

He leaned back real proudly and stuck a thumb under his suspender. "That's who you're looking at for sure, mate."

I could have dropped dead. Now *that* was just too much of a coincidence to be a coincidence. Peg had told me in the last letter I got from her, in Darwin, to ask for a person named Ron Elliot when I got to the Marla Bore roadhouse south of the Northern Territory border. Peg, who was retired, was related to Ron's ex-wife in some distant manner, and she was sure he'd look after me and put me up in his trailer for a spell. But if I had gone to Marla Bore, I'd never have met Ron, since he was out here in the sand dunes at Mintabie.

Ron had already been told by a letter from Peg Matthews that I was coming through his area. He simply put one and one together when he heard my American accent.

"This calls for a celebration, don't you think?" shouted the ever-happy and thirsty Johnny, who was a sort of free-lance bulldozer driver for some of the claim owners in the boom camp.

The two men swaggered ahead of me to a neat little tin-sided shed called Luka's Goanna Grill. Inside we found a scene of poker and beer and grizzled faces and torn coveralls and cowboy hats and piles of money and raucous merriment that needed only a couple of cancan girls high-kicking it on a stage to a tinny-sounding piano to make me feel I had gone back in time. The smell of success was as thick as the smell of dust and steaks.

Two large bearded men, one of whom was an absolute giant, rose and came to meet us with smiles as huge as their banded bush hats. They were the other two partners on the claim Ron was working.

"Good on yer, mate! Me name's Ian McClellan!" boomed the giant, giving my hand a shake that would have sent California crumbling into the sea.

"And my name's Ron Gregory," the other said with only a whisker less enthusiasm.

A double order of "camp pizza" and grog was ordered from Rosie, the camp's only female and cook, by Ian for me, and soon Ron, Ron, Ian, and I were shooting the bull as if there were no limit to a swaggie's common sense.

Although they did not look it by Madison Avenue standards, those three forty-year-old-plus adventurers, who had given up secure jobs in the big cities to chance opal prospecting, were millionaires. They had come to Mintabie together to look for the area's highly prized opals in a place where everyone else had said there'd be none—and had been known as the Three Silly Gooses ever since. They had encouraged even more ridicule by using a divining rod and the directions of a white witch Ian's wife knew— only to strike the El Dorado that all the others were still looking for, and become the boom camp's most celebrated heroes.

Six days I stayed at Mintabie, with these perpetual boys of summer.

With millionaires in grimy overalls, tens of thousands of dollars changing hands in games of poker and two-up, Chinese gem buyers in small rented Cessna planes dropping onto the dirt air strip with as much as a million dollars to buy opals dug during the past month, and with dollar-an-egg prices at "Nobie's General Store," Mintabie was M*A*S*H and Jack London and Mark Twain all rolled into one—an outpost of derring-do and foolishness that still let the occasional lucky penniless and hard-working immigrant become a rich man without the tax man having to know.

A breed quite unlike any other pick-carrying soldiers of fortune I knew, the Mintabie prospectors were strangely open and easygoing. No one seemed to bother keeping any secrets of his claim intact from the others. There were no threats, no NO TRESPASSING signs, no raised voices. And yet, and in spite of the varied backgrounds and temperaments of the prospectors, an almost uncanny order prevailed—from the merry, free-spending beer guzzlers in Luka's Goanna Grill to the human moles in the cool, narrow tunnels who hadn't seen that magical glint of blue or red or yellow or pink in many, many years.

"It was the life-style that drew me here," remarked Ian, a former bus driver from Adelaide.

He scruffed his rich dark beard, then pointed at several others in the noisy pub. Just around us, he said were twelve Yugoslavians, mostly Croatians, and several other nationalities. He himself was originally from Liverpool, England.

"It's amazing, but we're like a family here. Everyone's so different, and still you rarely see trouble. We don't even have police of any kind," he continued.

"Some of those you see came here penniless and hungry, but not for long. We do things our own way here, mate, and no good man is going to go wanting. We're proud to be our own bosses. It gives us a good feeling to know we could come to a place like this to try and make our own fortune. It shows in how we look after each other."

"And if you do happen to get someone who is a natural trouble-maker, or worse?" I asked with a quick glance at our pile of empty Swan Lager cans.

"Let's just put it *this* way, mate. There's more than one of them shafts out there with something other than cuttings down it. You know what I mean?" He said it with so much drama and relish in his voice, I could almost hear the body bouncing against the curved sandstone walls.

Certainly I knew what he meant. In fact, I knew too well. Two days earlier, Ian and the two Rons had invited me down into their subterranean treasure chest. The vertical round shaft to it had been barely wider than Ian's shoulders and as straight as an arrow to the hollow at the bottom, 180 feet below. And as if all that weren't bad enough for a worldwalker who still was uneasy with heights, the only way down was a free-hanging rickety metal ladder the width of two hands and no thicker anywhere than a pencil.

I had gotten no more than ten feet down, when the ladder began swinging away from the wall like a rope over the side of a ship in a roiling sea. Everyone else had scrambled down it like monkeys in a circus and set it to rattling. When my hands went to trembling and my feet slipping, it was all I could do to hold on for dear life. For a good ten minutes, I could convince neither my toes nor my fingers to take me one way or the other. I knew that each ten-foot section of the ladder was connected only by two open hooks, and that all of it was connected to a single metal bar at the top. With each link moving in a different direction from the one above, I was like a flea on a rosary in a worried woman's hands. Eventually, I made it by convincing my nerves that the farther I went, the less I had to fall.

Just as Ian's wife and children lived thousands of kilometers away, along the coastline of the continent, so did the families of the other miners who were married. Mintabie was, plain and simple, just not a place for being domestic. It had none of the trappings of a town, or even of a trailer court—no television, no radio, no power except by individual generators or kerosene lamp, no newspapers, no shops, no school, not even a medical clinic. Mail sometimes came in twice a week in the back of someone's pickup truck. The same was true for the produce for Nobie's General Store shack. Even vice had a hard time finding such an out-of-the-way place: Everyone wagered on the biggest event of the year in Australia, the Melbourne Cup horse race, using the names of the horses listed in a newspaper article, then had to wait three days after the event to find out who had won.

Once a month, the plane of the Flying Doctor Service dropped in on the dirt airstrip. And every great once in a while, someone came snooping around from the government to see that there weren't more claims staked than seemed possible, as well as to try to catch someone drunk enough to let slip that he'd found something taxable.

For most, the only time with the family was during the hellishly hot summer months of December, January, and February. Then the heat forced a halt to all the diggings, and everyone retreated to the sea's breezes, redynamiting their shafts and bulldozer scrapings to make it worthwhile only to the Devil to take their fortunes and misfortunes.

On my last evening in Mintabie, in the crude though comfortable stone hut of one the camp's millionaires, a young man my age named Tom, I was allowed to look over the happy opal prospector's private collection, which he'd dug and polished himself in the past few months and which was not for sale. Reputedly, he had several fifty-five gallon drums of the striking gems still stashed away in a secret place in Adelaide. Those he was hoarding till the time when the increasingly rarer gem would be easily worth ten times as much.

This was my first close encounter with opal in its finished state. I picked one small tear-shaped piece up and was at a loss to describe it. Australia produced most of the world's supply of this mysterious and little-known gem.

In each of Tom's prized velvet-mounted stones I saw not only the colors of other precious stones, rubies, amethysts, emeralds, but something even more special—memories of the outback: the red of the snake-like lightning that had left me clinging to the earth at times in terror, the blue of the endless morning skies, the gold of those few minutes at the end of the day when the sun set, the brown of the giant sandstorms that rolled over the very sun in the sky, and the white of the salt flats whose glare seared even through my sunglasses. All that was the outback concentrated into one stone.

Sadly, slowly, I started to place the stone back into its black mount.

Suddenly, an enormous hand closed the stone's case while my fingers still held the gorgeous milky tear-shaped opal. I looked up, startled. Ian was crumpling several fifty-dollar notes into the hands of a smiling Tom— who just as promptly forced those same wrinkled bills back into Ian's pocket.

"I appreciate what you are doing—but I can't accept such an expensive thing," I protested. I tried to hand the opal back to its rightful owner. But Tom only pushed it back.

Ian seemed almost as embarrassed as I was. But he was not about to let me lose out to my pride.

"You got a mother?" he asked defiantly.

"Yes, but—"

"No buts, mate! You give that to her, you hear?" he ordered.

"Ian, I can't take some—"

"Oh, yes, you can! This is Mintabie, and that's the way we do it here." Then Ian let loose with one of his giant laughs.

So I smiled and tucked away, safely inside my shirt pocket, my little wishing stone.

I had known that the opal is considered bad luck, had borne that label since the late eighteenth century, when it was blamed for famine, pestilence, and even the fall of a Spanish monarchy. I had not known that it was to cause both my saddest and happiest moments in the outback.

A day after leaving Mintabie, I found myself at a small collection of sunbaked buildings labeled on my maps as Marla. As is usual in the outback, there was not any actual town, but merely a roadhouse with a pub and café, an attached motel of sorts, a tiny police post, some neglected petrol pumps, a sleeping dog coated with dust, and a house or two.

About the only thing that differentiated Marla from the rest was that intersecting it were *two* Stuart Highways—the dirt one I had been struggling to pull Roo over since crossing into South Australia, and the future paved one that was still another year from being done.

It was down the paved one I ventured the next morning. Though it meant I would be largely on my own, and out of sight of the old Stuart Highway's traffic for most of the remaining 180 miles to the two highways' next intersection, at Coober Pedy, I looked forward to having something other than sand dunes to pull Roo over. It had been such a struggle at times to get anywhere with the cart's tires sinking up to their axle in the powdery sand.

What I did not know was that the pavement on the new road existed for only thirty-seven miles, after which I would be back to the dreaded sand for the remaining long haul to Coober Pedy.

The heat and sun that first day out of Marla were some of the fiercest yet. By noon I had no choice but to retreat from the thermals and a screeching dust storm that blocked out the sun entirely. I sweated half to death in a storm pipe under the roadway until the sun set and I could continue southward again.

Then came monstrous thunderclouds with high winds and more wild and savage bolts of snake lightning that made me—the tallest thing for a million miles around—want to crawl into my boots. And just an hour shy of midnight came something even more dangerous.

The drunkenness of the road-construction workers in the truck that pulled alongside me was obvious from the start. No sooner had I opened my mouth to answer their questions about what I was doing in the middle of nowhere in the middle of the night on foot than the massive driver began cursing me in a slurred voice for being some "lying Yank greenie" (conservationist). The man couldn't seem to spit out enough obscenities, criticism of Americans, and hatred of journalists in general.

It was his belittling of America—something that seemed to be quite fashionable with Australians lately—that got my hackles rising. I laid into the idiot verbally and let him know just how ignorant he struck me as being.

Suddenly, he got out of the truck and confronted me, then lifted me and threatened to snap every rib in my body. Each of his arms weighed more than I did, and I had no choice but to let loose a well-placed punch to his eyes. What followed was a frightening cat-and-mouse game, in which he tried to make true his vow to kill me.

In the pouring rain and the glare of the truck's headlights, he looked bigger than ever, and it was all I could do to dodge his lunges and land punch after punch on a face that probably felt them as much as a wall does a mosquito. I'd dropped Roo's handle when he first came after me. Now I wanted to flee, but there was no way I was going to abandon Roo. I was doing everything I could think of to make him forget the little cart, including drawing him away from that side of the truck. But it was no use. Frustrated at not being able to kill me, he went directly to the cart, lifted all two hundred pounds of it above his head as if it were nothing, and heaved it into the cactus and rocks beside the road.

"Load my shotgun! Load my shotgun!" he screamed at the other scared man in the truck. Then, to me, he snarled:

"I'm going to kill you! I'm going to KILL you!"

I knew he meant it. I had no choice but to turn and run as fast and furiously as gravity allowed. BOOM! BOOM! The buckshot *ziiiinged* past my ears, like swarms of killer bees trying out for the Olympics. For once, the night couldn't be dark enough. Luckily, the rain was probably throwing that drunken galoot off as much as it was me.

With the rain pouring and stinging, my clothes in tatters, thunder rumbling, lightning exploding, and my shins tripping and scraping and banging against all sorts of invisible rocks and sage bushes, I ran. Patiently, he waited for me to return to the cart. Instead, I ran to the road-construction camp, thirteen miles to the south, where it just so happened he worked. Around one-thirty that morning, I was on the camp's radio telephone, speaking to the Marla police sergeant. The sergeant promised to be out around daybreak. In the meantime, the camp's foreman brought me back to the shattered cart, and I spent a restless, drenched night beside it.

The assailant escaped. All the policeman and I found of his truck and trailer at the construction camp was an empty space. Very conveniently, he had, in the early morning hours, been "transferred" to another work site at Port Lincoln, nearly one thousand miles to the south, on the coastline.

"He didn't even pick his tomatoes in his little garden," the young policeman noted with a touch of wryness.

Everyone at the camp was sure that I was a lucky fellow, indeed, to be alive, after having tangled with the orneriest man in the outback. They told me I was especially lucky because he was on parole for killing another man with a shotgun five years before. No one would give out his name. It was not until I was back on the road, and the policeman had finished helping me put Roo back together, that he asked to see my address book and wrote in the back of it the killer's name.

"Don't tell anyone I gave you that," he said. "I really shouldn't do that, but I got to admit I hope he gets his due some day. I never liked the guy, he's made too many people miserable."

Two days and one hundred miles down the road from where I had been attacked, I was resting in the meager shade of a sage bush when a pack of wild horses stampeded by. Their many colors and the way their manes streaked out behind their necks made me think of the opal gemstone. But when I looked for it in the upper left side pouch of Clinger where I usually kept it, I couldn't find it. Desperately, and with a broken heart, I searched everywhere on the cart, in Clinger, and on myself, only to realize it was gone. It had either been stolen by my assailant or had fallen when the cart was thrown through the air.

I was more heartbroken than I'd been at any time since Dad's death. I wanted to use that stone in a pendant for Mom. It was to be a special way of thanking her for her work on my behalf the past two-and-one-half years. Dad's death and worrying about me had been hard enough on her, but she'd also had to deal with the hundreds of letters and phone calls from my readers.

So it was far more than just an opal that had been lost to that lonely stretch of dust, rocks, and wind. And in such a senseless and cruel manner, too, I screamed out to the sky.

There could be no going back to search for it. It was too far to walk: My water supply was down to critical, with Coober Pedy still days away and I on a road with no traffic.

Two days later came the luck . . . or the magic.

Two opal prospectors on an old mine site twenty-three miles north of Coober Pedy had sighted me in the shimmering distance and come after me. Soon I was enjoying their ice-cold grog in the shade of a road-culvert pipe. As the forty-two-year-old Ralph Martin put it, "I looked at Paul [Wundersitz] and said, 'There are *three* people crazy enough to be out in this heat today—you, me . . . and whatever *that* is, way down there with that cart and umbrella.' "

When they heard about my attack by the drunkard and my discovery that my mother's opal was missing, Ralph immediately offered to drive me back to where the attack had occurred. And Paul agreed without hesitation.

It was the darn foolhardiest offer I'd heard in a long time. I wasn't about to have them wasting all their time and gasoline on me, for a stone that might well be riding around in a killer's pockets in the other direction. It was just too great a distance, the roads were extremely poor, and the chances of finding the tiny opal were a million to one—maybe a billion to one!

Yet there was absolutely no talking them out of this bit of sudden adventure. And in no time at all, we and Ralph's old blue-gray dog, Sally, were racing off to the north in his battleship-sized old Holden car.

The petrol and the beer grew low. The bumps and the ruts stayed ever constant. But never did those two men's enthusiasm for finding the opal waver.

Ralph, an independent bulldozer operator and former professional kangaroo hunter, and Paul, an engineer on oil rigs, were hardly demonstrating the tough-guy image normally associated with such occupations. Indeed, at one point they stopped to observe some finches through binoculars, and left a bowl of water along the road for a thirsty-looking lizard! There was certainly not a nicer pair of men to be found anywhere.

When we reached the site of the attack, there was no trace of the lost opal. We sifted endlessly the sands around where the cart had been flung. Back and forth, back and forth, we wandered, probing carefully with our eyes, kicking here and there with our shoe tips. *Nothing.* Not a single glint of green or blue. Only more sand and dust.

I was the first to surrender to the obvious: The attacker had stolen it from my pack while waiting for me to return. That such a thing of love and friendship was in the hands of someone so vile brought my spirit even lower. All I wanted to do was to leave that scene of bad memories as fast as possible, and get Australia over and done with, too. For me, the memory of the Australia walk had become tainted.

I was irritated now that Ralph and Paul persisted in searching, even long after I had gone back to the car. And especially when Ralph went far out into the desert on the wrong side of the road. He was just being silly. I wanted to scream at the men to take me as far from the outback as possible.

Then, incredibly, Ralph was holding something small and black in his hand, and shouting to me. I rushed to his side.

"Is this what you lost?" he asked. It was the tiny plastic box in which I had put the opal. Amazing! But where was the opal? Had the attacker taken it out and flung the box on the other side of the road? I felt as if I were being slowly tortured into insanity.

But then something barely poking out from under the toe of Ralph's left shoe made my eyes pop wider. The opal!

"Magic . . . *real* magic," Ralph mused aloud over and over on the joyful, though still bumpy, drive back to their camp at the old mine they'd been exploring.

Each time he repeated those words, I would nod in agreement in the backseat, and look down at the gem clutched in my hand. My heart was still beating fast. And my mind wasn't too far behind. Considering how slim our chances had been of finding that stone, which was no bigger than the nail on my little finger, its recovery seemed a miracle. To find such a little stone in such a vast area—and on the wrong side of the road!

"When I got out of the car, I noticed right away the direction the wind was blowin'," Ralph explained. "I figured it would've blown the opal into the opposite paddock, if it had been blowin' that direction when you had your trouble."

No one but an experienced bushman would have thought of that. Certainly Paul and I hadn't. Such a stroke of luck—to have had Ralph's experience along on the search. Without him, that opal would have stayed there to be buried for all of eternity, never to be worn someday by Mom.

"You know, finding your opal really made our day. It makes me feel good to know you got it back," Paul said by their campfire that night.

Ralph nodded his agreement and poked another stick in the blaze before adding, "I always like to look at every little thing in nature and not always be in a hurry and thinkin' only of myself. I don't get much free time in my work, but still I figure I always got time to help anythin' or anybody that needs it."

Looking up at the gorgeous night sky arching over their tent, and the ghostly white hills of old mining tailings around us, I thought of all the love those two rugged men had shown me. And from somewhere deep inside a big smile grew all over my face. For, just then, it came to me that I had been gifted with not just one gem that day . . .

. . . but three.

44

On December 9, I gazed down from a treeless ridge at the thin seashore marking the boundary of the continent I had finally crossed.

I was about to lose, perhaps forever, a tremendous freedom. It was a freedom very few knew anymore, that of being alone for a long period with only the sky and the land for companionship. That feeling was perhaps the greatest memory I would take with me from the outback.

Freedom, I knew now, was what had drawn those men and women to the outback's open spaces, despite the hardships of life there. The freedom to live as they pleased, to have no other man as their master. Only the sky, the land . . . and the young child still in their soul.

As I boarded a bus in Port Augusta later that same gray, drizzling day to go on to Melbourne for a much-needed rest, and, hopefully, to get a six months' extension on my visa (due to expire in less than two weeks), I had a strong suspicion I would not return to finish walking the remaining 670 miles to Melbourne as originally planned. Quite honestly, I was ready to call it quits for the Australian phase of the worldwalk.

For the last four hundred miles, the wind had tried its best to push my tired, skinny frame back into those empty deserts and endless salt flats. As a result of the incessant battering, I was more tired physically and mentally than I had been during any other part of my journey. The vast deserts over which I had been struggling for more than four months were the most arduous terrain I had ever experienced.

Was it really necessary to do any more walking in Australia? I asked myself. Had I not crossed the entire continent? Surely, there was nothing to be ashamed of in not coming back after Christmas.

I was bothered in part by the worry that the remainder of the Australia journey would seem a letdown in comparison to the mysteries of the outback. Even after all that I had heard about the dazzle and energy of the large cities of Adelaide and Melbourne, and the beautiful colonial architecture of the far South's well-preserved towns, I did not see how a region of mostly sheep and wheat farms could keep me interested, especially with the images of cowboys, lizards, and red dunes still strong in my mind.

I found waiting for me in Melbourne some two hundred letters along with hundreds of cards and cheers from what must have been the world's greatest American schoolchildren and teachers.

And ready to wrap me in her warmth and love was my pen pal Peg Matthews, the woman who knew me through my *Capper's* stories and who was now eager to share her home with me. I had expected to meet also her husband of almost fifty years, Bert, a disabled World War II veteran, but he had died from multiple organ failure just two days before I arrived.

Nevertheless, she tried her hardest to make me feel welcome in her simple little brick home on Rotorua Street, with its big shade trees and flowers, just like back home. And I did my best to help her with the funeral and her loss. Because she was a tremendously positive and optimistic person, Bert's death was not as hard on her spirit as it might have been on someone less strong. Bert had been too ill and his army pension too small to be much help in the raising of their four children, so Peg had learned long ago to handle life's challenges entirely on her own.

She used her marvelous cooking skills to make me such totally un-Aussie dishes as southern fried chicken and pumpkin pie, getting the recipes from books she checked out of the local library.

Comfortably surrounded by family kindness, fed heaping plates of home-cooked meals beneath the world map on Peg's kitchen wall that she had used to follow my progress from Bethel, and constantly being whisked "live" via commercial television to America to watch everything from presidential news conferences tc the Super Bowl, I felt it was only sensible that my next steps should be back on the native soil for which I was acutely homesick, not at the unsympathetic fringe of the outback.

Yet on January 28—the letters mostly answered, my frame heavier by a "stone" (14 pounds) and my spirit well rested—I returned by bus to the little port on the northern point of Spencer Gulf. It was not because I had conquered my homesickness, but rather because I couldn't face leaving this nation without having fully tried to learn about it and its people.

I knew that to have left others, let alone myself, with the impression that Australia was mostly deserts, cowboys, and kangaroos would have been wrong. What remained to be explored might perhaps be much tamer, but that did not mean it had to be any less inspiring. To rush off so soon would only leave me all the poorer.

As with any relationship to which we give our heart and mind, haste deserved no place in it.

My knuckles rapped against the old farmhouse's wood door. No answer came forth, save for the sounds of honking geese and a creaking windmill. I rapped again, more rapidly and more sharply. Still silence from within.

A month had passed since I had resumed my walk from Port Augusta, and by this morning Adelaide's meticulously cared-for boulevards and Mediterranean weather were two days behind me to the west.

Roo was also a memory. I had decided the cart was no longer necessary, since the deadly outback was behind. A social worker at the community center in Port Augusta had offered to haul Roo in his pickup to Melbourne for me, while I struck on down through the rest of Australia, through the wheat-farm country, with only a backpack once again.

And it had become time to retire Clinger. Poor Clinger had simply become too old and worn to be usable, and I had realized I had to replace him. Having served me so faithfully across thirteen thousand miles and nineteen countries, he had undoubtedly set more than a few world records himself.

Along with my boots, Clinger had been the most important part of my gear. He had been through everything with me, had even saved my neck from that Thai bandit's machete blade. I knew I was going to miss my buddy as much as if he had been a real person. Maybe some people would have thought I was silly, but when I sealed the box that Clinger would be shipped back to Bethel in, I felt somewhere between a traitor and a crybaby.

I'd returned to Port Augusta with a new backpack rushed to me by air as a gift by JanSport and with my third pair of *Rocky* boots, also sent to me for free. When I'd asked the William Brooks Shoe Company in

Nelsonville, Ohio, back in 1982 if I could have a couple pairs of boots for walking around the world in, they hadn't thought I stood a chance of making it. So those first two pairs I'd had to buy. Now, though, that I had made it four-fifths of the way to home, I guess they had got to thinking maybe I wasn't so crazy after all. And they wanted their boots to contribute to my success.

Ever since first light, I had been following an abandoned dirt lane into the depths and onto the summits of an increasingly rugged land. To my surprise, the path had ended abruptly at this farmhouse's open veranda.

My canteen, as well as my lips, begged for water. It was late February, the hottest part of the Australian summer. It felt every bit as hot and itchy-dry as the outback had. So, with little hesitation, I followed the veranda's floorboards to the rear of the bluestone home. Just as I expected, there stood the welcome trademark of every rural Aussie home—the rainwater-holding tank.

I slipped out of my backpack, only to be surprised by a man stepping from the side door of a patchwork shearing shed. Dressed in coveralls, and with a red beard and ruddy cheeks, he waved and shouted the Aussie trademark "G'day!" Dashing from between his short, thick legs came his black work dog.

Gary MacDonald was the man's name, Mandi the dog's. And as so often was the case in this country of instant strong handshakes, an invitation to stay on for tea (dinner) with him, his wife, and their small baby boy, as well as an offer of the spare bedroom, was soon forthcoming. And I accepted.

While leading me on foot to the back reaches of his property during the afternoon, Gary revealed that it had been in search of some purpose to his life that he had moved from the confines of Adelaide to the open country. He might have become a factory worker like his father and grandfathers, except for the horrors he had watched others commit while serving in the Vietnam War. Unable to put those scenes in Asia's jungles out of his mind, he had returned home to a nervous breakdown. Confined to a hospital bed for three weeks, he knew he somehow had to find a reason to keep living. It was then that he decided to try raising sheep—felt in his heart that even though he knew nothing of such a life, it was the answer to his survival spiritually.

To some, the cast-off property he ended up buying would have been discouraging. Hilly, rocky, and able to support only 500 sheep, its 350 acres held far more promise of hard work than of wealth or comfort. Still, to Gary, it offered the possibility of a way of life that had purpose. Rather than slaving to others' whims, he now had only himself and his small family to consider.

To stand atop one of those broad hills in the strong, cool wind and watch Gary and the two-year-old Mandi herd the sheep from one pasture to another was thrilling. That dog lived to obey her master's voice and hand commands, and, after a day's work, to race across the flock's backs and leap high into Gary's arms for a hug and a bit of well-earned praise.

Toward dusk, with Gary and Mandi sitting on the rocks beside me, I spied two large foxes fleeing up the side of a hill opposite us. Zigzagging from cover to cover, the beautiful creatures went unnoticed by a nearby group of sheep. I asked Gary if those same foxes might harm a newborn lamb we had found beside one of the fence lines a few hours earlier.

Yes, they might, he answered. Still, that did not mean he would shoot the foxes. Killing no longer seemed the right thing to him. Instead of hunting the foxes, we gathered up the lamb and its mother to put them into a pen near the house, where they would be safe and better fed.

As I held in my arms the quiet softness of the lamb and waited for Gary and Mandi to steer the ewe to the holding pen, I couldn't help feeling a tremendous surge of my own spirit.

That tiny lamb's heartbeat was the rhythm of Nature. Somehow I understood why those who lived by Nature's clock seemed so much happier and kinder. Theirs was a life of sharing.

The night after I left Gary and Mandi, I was sound asleep on the ground on a bald hill when, for some unknown reason, I woke after midnight. The air was very chilly, and I didn't want to budge from the warmth of the sleeping bag. But still I eased a hand up to the open end of the bag and pulled a corner down so I could peer out. Perhaps it was just my imagination, but I felt I was not alone on that exposed hill of sagebrush and rocks. It seemed there was something or someone looking at me from right above my head.

I glanced with one eye at the clear fall sky above me, noted about a million stars keeping me company, then quickly retreated back inside the bag to find some more sleep. But the sleep disappeared when I suddenly realized there *was* something up there in that sky right above my head.

I tugged the sleeping bag off my entire face this time and looked again at the heavens right above. Yes! At long, long last, I had found it— Halley's comet. And, oh, what a beautiful sight it was!

It was just as I had seen it pictured. From a small, fuzzy, immobile star there tailed a long and faint plume of light that looked like a painter's stroke on a velvet canvas. It was so delicate, so wispy, that I dared not blink for fear I wouldn't find it again.

All across the outback I had looked for that homeless traveler of our solar system in the flawless night sky. Always I had been unsuccessful. And I could not understand why, for it was common knowledge that the outback was the best place on earth from which to view the comet. But now I was happy. Since Halley's comet only came once every seventy-five years to visit our little planet, I knew this was my only chance to see it.

Funny, I thought while drifting back to sleep, *I had spent all those months searching so hard for the comet—only to meet it when I wasn't thinking about it at all.*

On March 3, I followed a dirt secondary road lined with massive red gums into my third and final state in Australia, Victoria. Autumn now was giving me some relief from the harsh, never-ending sun. There were a few more clouds, a drop or two more rain from time to time, and maybe a couple of minutes' less daylight than before. So I was willing to believe it was fall, though I would have much preferred the blazing colors of the maples lining our driveway back in Bethel, and the fuzzy squirrels running around the big sycamore in the backyard.

And soon the nights were so chilly I had to start taking shelter in the many haystacks to keep halfway warm.

Because I made it my habit to walk as much as possible away from the main highways, following instead the railroad tracks, water pipelines, and back roads, the majority of those who befriended me were farmers. And they were always surprised to see a lone Yank with just a pack on his back, strolling miles from anywhere past their vast acreages of wheat stubble. Consequently, I continued to be invited to far more dinner tables and spare beds than I suppose any everyday normal swaggie would have been offered.

Rain—or, rather, the lack of it—dominated every kitchen-table chat. So long had the rains been absent from northwestern Victoria that to talk aloud about when they might return was almost considered bad luck. In the last four years, there had been but one good wheat harvest.

Some blamed Halley's comet for the record cold (!) Victoria summer and its hint of a coming dry winter. There was even talk of another Great

Depression, of all the small farmers going under and only giant subsidized "farm corporations" being left to grow the grains. Hundreds of family farms had folded in the past five years, many said, with worried glances at their own horizons. Most of the failed farmers, I was told, had gone to the streets of Melbourne to join the record ranks of the unemployed.

"I wish I could be here just long enough to see who will be left to do the farming," said a seventy-seven-year-old tall, lanky retired wheat farmer near Stawell named William Nitschke.

He and his petite wife, Edith, had served me an array of goodies when I came knocking on their back screen door for some water for my canteen. Ice cream on peaches, ham sandwiches, cups of sweet tea, iced fruit cake . . . like so many who ran the world's farm homes, Edith would never have allowed me to go away with just a drink of water.

The Nitschkes came from backgrounds rich in farming, hers from Germany and his from Poland. Farming had seemed to them one of the few things that would always be secure. The farm was not only their income and their love, but also their gift to the future.

Said William, sitting a little straighter on his side of the linoleum-topped kitchen table, "Edith and I cleared the land, built the house, and always saved what money we could spare to buy more land. We didn't borrow money unless we needed more land. And then we made sure it was quickly paid off."

In time, all three of their sons followed in their footsteps, settling onto the lands that belonged not to any banks but to the family. But even owning the farm offered no real security anymore, thanks to the high expenses of planting and harvesting, and the low prices coming in for grain from an international market already choking on surplus food.

"It's a mistake for the government to let the family farms die off," William reflected. "Everyone in power says everything has to be on a big scale and run like some factory. But I ask you, who's going to pay for all those high union wages, and all their time off, and coffee breaks, and all the sloppiness?

"It costs too much for an ordinary bloke to go into farming anymore. Only the big businesses can get the money and afford those ridiculously priced machines. Why, a Ford tractor's going for over a hundred thousand dollars. And that's a simple one, too. Yet do you think those big conglomerates will be watching every expense and always be putting something away for the bad years, like Edith and I did?"

That evening, as I continued toward the east along the railroad tracks that had taken me by William and Edith's white frame house, I thought more than once about the little present from them tucked away in my backpack. It was an intricate doll-sized rocking chair William had fashioned out of an empty Coca-Cola can. That handmade gift seemed to me to represent the Nitschkes' lives. They had taken something others had not wanted—a piece of litter—and with patience, imagination, and work had transformed it into an object of beauty—just as they had transformed several hundred acres of arid scrub land.

It was said by many that the honest hard worker was a disappearing breed. If that was so, then it was a sad day, indeed, for everyone.

I hope that there will never cease to be in each person's life at least one screen door like the Nitschkes' waiting to be knocked upon.

Melbourne's skyscrapered lines and old-fashioned electric streetcars greeted me for the second time just after dawn on March 27—and marked the end of my walking on the Australia continent.

Originally, I had planned to go either to New Zealand or Japan after finishing Australia, after first spending the last three months of my visa catching up on my writing chores and resting at Peg's, where she had given me the use of a bungalow at the rear of her small backyard. But on April 1, the worldwalk entered its fourth year, and, try as I might to ignore its power, I knew there was a voice more powerful than adventure now calling me: the voice of Home.

But there was still one more important thing I had to do in Australia. Two months before, Frank Ward, the publisher of the newspaper in War-racknabeal, Victoria, had asked if I would come to that hub of the wheat-farming country to help run his family-owned newspaper. His twenty-seven-year-old married son, David, the editor of the newspaper that came out twice a week, hadn't had a vacation in over two years. Since experienced journalists were in short supply in the countryside, particularly ones who could take over the photography duties as well, Frank had wondered if I would return from Melbourne and be the editor while David went away for a month.

So I went, by train, to help run the paper during May. I was not at all sure what to expect, because I had not even walked through War-racknabeal. I *had* gone through the town of Horsham, fifty miles to the south, and it was there that I had met Frank's brother, Ian, the photographer at the *Mail-Times* newspaper, who had subsequently hooked me up by telephone to Frank.

As the train rumbled across the low brown fields already harvested of their wheat, I was very excited, but also a bit worried. It had been eight years since I had been a newspaper man. I wasn't sure I even remembered how to poke at a typewriter or word processor. All my stories back to America during my walk so far had been done longhand, usually on little more than scrap paper and in "offices" that varied from haylofts to tents to caves to teahouse tables to beneath bridges and atop cliffs.

Still, I saw in the approaching task not only a different sort of challenge but also a wonderful chance to observe closely the daily life of an Australian small town. And, after all, that was what I was doing here in the first place.

And that was exactly what I got.

Warracknabeal would have seemed the end of the world to some of my city-slicker friends. Two hundred miles northwest of Melbourne, in the center of the Wimmera Plain, that old-fashioned town of thirty-two hundred purely Aussie folks was a perfect antithesis to "life in the fast lane."

There was one main street, no traffic lights, not even a stop sign. Quite simply "Warrack" was the sort of place where one needn't look down the street more than once before crossing it. The two rows of one-story shops were all tidy and modest, their square façades still mostly big planes of old, hand-stenciled glass dated 1883 or 1904, and their flat, horizontal roof lines from those same years.

A reporter could cover most any day's news by simply taking a stroll from the cemetery at one end of Scott Street to the Lions Club Park at the other end. But if I had any notions that I would be hard-pressed to find a sufficient amount of copy and photo material to fill the sixteen pages of *The Herald* twice each week, I was quickly put in my proper place— behind a hopelessly cluttered desk, a constantly ringing telephone, and under a persistent cloud of deadlines. Ah, yes, back to the confusion of newspaper work. And in a foreign land, to boot! Though my chief responsibilities were photography and editing, I was barely able to keep up with them.

The amount of energy behind the quiet exterior of a small town was nothing short of amazing.

If it wasn't some historical celebration or someone's fiftieth-wedding anniversary, then it was some farmers' group meeting or maybe bingo at the local golf clubhouse.

I spent one day riding across miles of sunbaked, wheat stubble in a hundred-year-old steam train that left me looking like a walking coal bin; what seemed another whole day melting through an interview at an over-heated old folks' home with a prolific-tongued ninety-nine-year-old man who read me five hundred beautiful and lengthy poems about his stint at Gallipoli; froze half to death in the old courthouse on some mornings trying to make sense of the monthly court session before the traveling judge, the major disputes usually concerning fence lines and rustling; made myself hoarse at the rough-and-tumble "footy" (Aussie Rules Football) clashes at the car-ringed sporting oval; sympathized with the worried faces of both man and animal at the midweek sheep sales; and hung around with the elderly white-dressed ladies at the country club's lawn bowls courts, because they *insisted* on making me sit down every time and eat through another couple tons of strawberry cream pie and cheesecake.

Once again I was having to learn, with not a minute to spare, how to compose articles with a telephone stuck in my ear, a doughnut in my mouth, strawberry jam on my fingers, and cups of coffee balanced on my notes. And always there was a stack of film to be developed, which meant I would be up till midnight. The darkroom was a tin shed in back of the Ward's big old clapboard home that had more holes in it than Swiss cheese. To develop any film in the daytime, even with every towel in the house stuffed in the holes and cracks, was like playing Russian roulette. I never knew where the next light beam would zip from.

A phone call from the schools, alone, was enough to make me look for a white flag. Surely, all the Maori tribal dancers and field-hockey games and field trips they needed someone to come out and write about was part of a plot to keep the newspaper from being published on time.

As I stared idly out the window of the train that carried me back to Melbourne for the final days of my stay in "the lucky country," the train's whistle blew to signal the next stop. I smiled, and tried hard at the same time not to cry, too much.

I'm coming home, Mom . . . finally.

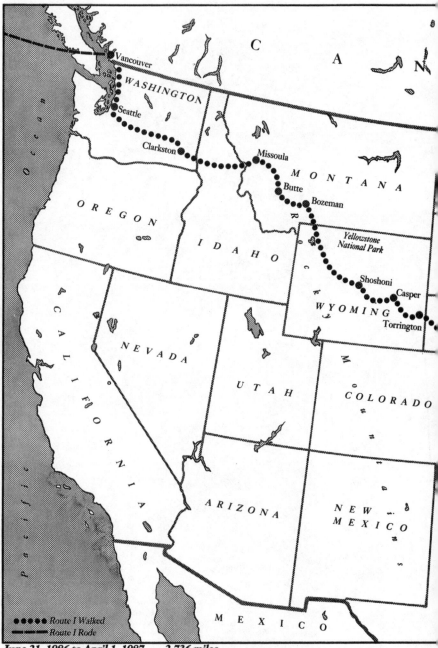

Vancouver

WASHINGTON

Seattle

Clarkston

Missoula

MONTANA

Butte

Bozeman

R

OREGON

IDAHO

Yellowstone
National Park

Shoshoni

Casper

WYOMING

Torrington

NEVADA

M

UTAH

COLORADO

CALIFORNIA

M
o
u
n
t
a
i
n
s

ARIZONA

NEW
MEXICO

MEXICO

C A N A D N

Ocean

Pacific

●●●●● *Route I Walked*
───── *Route I Rode*

June 21, 1986 to April 1, 1987   2,736 miles

Step 10
285 days

A   D   A

NORTH DAKOTA

MINNESOTA

L. Superior

SOUTH DAKOTA

WISCONSIN

M I C H I G A N

L. Michigan

L. Huron

NEBRASKA

I O W A

North Platte

Cozad   Lincoln

Kansas City

ILLINOIS

INDIANA

Indianapolis

OHIO

L. Erie

Bethel

St. Louis

K A N S A S

MISSOURI

KENTUCKY

OKLAHOMA

ARKANSAS

TENNESSEE

MISSISSIPPI

ALABAMA   GEORGIA

T E X A S   LOUISIANA

45

On June 29, exactly at noon, I walked beneath the striking white Peace Arch on the U.S.A.–Canada border between Vancouver and Seattle. For the first time since July 1983, my shoes had American soil stuck to their soles.

None of the burly customs officers at the border checkpoint knew me, but when I introduced myself, they were quick to gather around and give my hand a hearty shake. They were the vanguard of what I was sure would be a very friendly last leg of my journey.

However, in the week that I spent getting to Seattle, I was rudely reminded that the American brand of friendliness is sometimes not all that easy to experience. The only person in the entire world to refuse me a glass of water was the first person I asked during that rainy stretch. It happened on the edge of a teeny community called Big Lake. The person shooing me back to the road at the end of a shotgun was a drunken geezer who didn't want "no dang strangers on my land."

In a society where the auto is so incredibly pervasive, there just simply weren't many people on the streets and sidewalks with whom to strike up a chat. Indeed, in the rural areas, between the towns, to see anyone else freely strolling along the roads was almost a shock. And even those I did meet walking in the towns and cities were always in such a rush that I felt guilty asking them for a minute of their time.

Much of American life was spent behind doors—car, home, business, and otherwise. And when people weren't behind a steering wheel or busily working, then most likely they were glued to a television set.

Gone were the crowds of the curious who flocked to me. Gone, too, were the religious who constantly told me it was their "duty" to help me in some way: the teachers, shopkeepers, and village headmen who did not hesitate to spend days at a time, away from their work, as my personal guide.

In many ways, I had been spoiled by the overeagerness of so much of the rest of the world to help this novel visitor to their towns, villages, and farms. Now, I was back to being just another American, not *the* American. And probably not a very desirable American at that, since I was evidently too poor to own a car.

The sun was too hot and the land too dry for a journey on foot. More than one of the sunburned wheat farmers looked at my big pack and told me somberly of steep hills up ahead on the road I was following into southeastern Washington's Tucannon River Canyon. Too difficult, too lonely, too long . . . Take the highway, they cautioned.

Still, I took the way they shunned. My road map said it was the shortest way out of the frying pan that was eastern Washington State in August. And besides, since when was there a canyon whose walls did not hold a certain mystique, and lots of shade?

Cooled by the premature dusk of that very deep wrinkle in the earth and lulled by the murmur of the crystal-clear river coursing through its bottom, I decided to stay and make the canyon my home for the night.

Dinner was a fresh trout, caught by luck and a pair of surprisingly swift hands. Bed was the same patchy sleeping bag Rina had given me in Morocco. I spread it on the worn floorboards of an old, forgotten schoolhouse.

The whitewashed shell of the two-room schoolhouse had drawn me to it, even though I knew I should have been ascending the canyon's opposite wall to someplace warmer and more open. To my surprise, the door was not locked. It was almost as if I had been expected.

Inside I found an amazingly well-preserved time capsule of candy-colored globes, long and narrow blackboards with chalked letters like *Aa Bb Cc,* pint-sized desks, dozens of neatly shelved textbooks from decades ago, with titles like *The New Basic Reader, The Follett Picture Story of the Tale of a Trailer, Rico the Young Rancher—New World Neighbors, Ten Snappy Plays for Girls and Women,* and an old Remington piano whose ivory keys still spoke beautifully. In the smaller front classroom a basket-ball hoop and backboard hung above the blackboard, while in one corner a pair of simple, metal-wheeled roller skates with rough leather straps shared space with a box of Crayolas and gummed gold stars.

The next morning I learned from the Norwegian farmer next door that the old school had, at the turn of the century, been surrounded by a town of three hundred people. Having spent almost all of his eighty-two years in that canyon, the widower remembered the bustling flour mill, the post office, the two saloons, the stores, and the other homes that had stood in the now-empty fields beside the school. Now, he said, only an occasional hunter or fisherman stepped through the invisible streets of the town once known as Marengo.

The gravel road I had followed into the canyon went "two miles up, one mile across the top, and then one mile down" till it reached the new highway again, Emil Hourud told me, with a look of sympathy in his one good eye. I thanked him and walked on, feeling a tinge of guilt at leaving behind in such an empty canyon someone so fragile and alone.

Butte, Montana, was once one of the greatest of mining camps. Founded on the "richest hill in the world" under which were billions of dollars worth of gold, silver, copper, and zinc, the mile-high settlement on the western slope of the Continental Divide had been, in its time, unrivaled for bold, unashamed, rootin' tootin' hell-raisin'.

Its inhabitants came from the four corners of the world, but mostly from Ireland. Their number swelled from around four thousand in the 1880's to over one hundred thousand by the Great Depression.

But then came poorer ore finds, and finally the dreaded layoffs. By the 1970's, the talk was that Butte was finished. Only just under twenty-five thousand residents were left to call what is said to be America's ugliest city their home.

Then, while Butte was on its way to what seemed its last dying gasp, something very strange happened. Butte, the abandoned beast, stirred and actually started to grow! And now, as I came back to it for the first time since my years on the drilling rigs, the city I remembered as so hopelessly lethargic was looking much healthier.

The reason, I decided in the four days that I rested there during early September, was its people. The long spell of bad fortune had slowly weeded out the weakest and the least committed and left mainly those who loved that place the most. People, for instance, like my host, thirty-seven-year-old Ray McMillan, who claimed proudly, "I was born here and will die here." There was, he pointed out to me as he took me one cold afternoon to the old leaning house where he was born, a strong sense of brotherhood and faith among the Butte people.

Ray and his wife, Marlene, told of such community projects as bake sales for financing cancer treatment for a town resident. But mostly they liked to tell about "the Lady of the Rockies," a classic true tale of faith that was one of the most special I had heard anywhere in the world.

The beloved wife of one of Butte's older residents, Bob O'Bill, had become seriously ill with cancer. Bob had prayed fervently for Mrs. O'Bill to be cured. And he had made a promise that should she be cured, he would put a small statue of the Virgin Mary atop the Continental Divide that Butte is huddled against.

Incredibly, in 1981, several years after the cancer had been detected, Mrs. O'Bill was pronounced fully cured. So grateful was Bob that he decided to enlarge his promised statue. He set out to have one erected that would be taller even than the Statue of Liberty, one that everyone who passed through Butte would see. It was a task that seemed impossible, given his own meager resources and the immense natural obstacles. There was not even a road to the top of the seven-thousand-foot-high mountain on which he wanted the Madonna built.

But the people of Butte rose to the challenge from a collective sense of pride. From every religion and social class came volunteers, donations, and offers of the construction gear and raw materials that would be needed. So great was the community effort that the National Guard stepped in and used one of their huge Huey helicopters to lift the finished pieces to the top of the mountain.

And so, on December 20, 1985, the "impossible" promise was fulfilled. With the golden rays of a setting sun gleaming in her eyes, the fifth and final piece of the statue, the fourteen-foot-high head was airlifted by helicopter from the city to the torso waiting on the mountain. Weighing sixty tons and standing *nearly* as tall as the Statue of Liberty, Bob's dream now stood atop one of Nature's own forested steeples. The Lady of the Rockies' white form looked out at every single home and resident of Butte.

When I first noticed the Lady, as she is affectionately called, it was late at night. The big Montana sky was filled with twinkling stars. And gleaming right there in the center of them all was the huge, spotlighted statue.

When I left Butte on my way to the other side of America's backbone, I paused to say a silent prayer that the kind of brotherhood and fortitude it stood for would become a lesson for many, many others in the years to come.

Maybe, as someone told me, it was true that Butte could never be the kind of place in which to mature gracefully. But no matter. For she was strong, she believed, and she was—I was proud to say—part of America. *My* America.

Young schoolchildren have always held a special place in my heart. With their budding imaginations, they seem to appreciate much more than most adults that this world is filled with beauty and enchantment.

By the time I reached Bozeman, Montana, in the third week of September, I had shared my journey with many, many classrooms the world over—from the uniformed, boisterous Catholic schoolboys of Father Clay's in north Philadelphia to the barefooted, big-eyed children in faraway India to the straw-haired and sun-scrubbed faces in the one-room schoolhouses deep in Australia's wheat fields. Yet, as different as these children were on the outside, they showed themselves to be like brothers and sisters inside. If they asked me one question, they asked me ten thousand. They all wanted to know more about their world, our world.

While at Peg Matthews's home in Melbourne, I had received a letter from a third-grade class in Bozeman, Montana. Covered on both front and back with dozens of very intelligent questions about my worldwalk, the huge sheet of paper was a giant Valentine's Day letter from the students of Ms. Robin Morris at Emerson Elementary School. Measuring three feet by three and one-half feet, their letter was so impressive that I rerouted my walk across America through southern Montana. Not at all an easy decision for me to make, since it meant going almost five hundred miles out of my way!

Robin Morris had been using my stories of the worldwalk during that school year to help her third-graders get a better idea of the everyday people in the other countries. By the time I showed up in person in her classroom, her students knew more about the world's geography than most high-schoolers I had spoken to.

Robin had put in ten-hour workdays to come up with new and interesting displays about the world's peoples for her pupils, because teaching was more than just a job to her. A year she had spent recently traveling on her own throughout Europe had taught her just how special we all really are, no matter where we may live. The art-filled walls of her classroom and the open warmth of the children in her care showed me the value of her vision of mankind.

While I was visiting Robin Morris's classroom, I ran into another unique walker. His name was Walkin' Jim Stoltz, and he had bushy whiskers the color of rich farm soil. I sat back, like the other kids, and listened to his songs of his very personal treks across America's countryside.

With his long, sinewy fingers strumming an old guitar, he sang of rainbows and frogs and grizzly bears and untamed horizons he had found in his walking from one side of America to the other.

Later that day, Walkin' Jim and I sat by ourselves on the edge of the school's small stage and shared a few of our adventures.

He told me he had spent several months of nearly every year since 1974 hiking alone through the wild regions of America, after which he would share in song all the great beauty and peace he had experienced. His home was a cabin in a teeny settlement called Big Sky, in the snowy Rockies overlooking Bozeman.

His experiences with Americans had left Walkin' Jim feeling positive about his countrymen, quite a turnaround from his earlier days.

"Time was when I first started walking that I didn't want to be around people at all. But I've really evolved since then. Now, I find that it's the people that make life so special."

And he shared a story with me that I felt summed up the people both of us had come to call our family:

"In Washington State, I was walking down this dirt road, and there was an old farmhouse with the most beautiful flower garden up against the road, with a fence between the flowers and the road. And there was this elderly lady standing in the garden just kind of looking at things and soaking up the beauty," he related in his slow, soft, flowing manner.

"And I stopped and talked across the fence to her. And it turned out her husband had just had a stroke, and they'd been there for forty or fifty years and now had to leave, to move into town, away from her much-loved garden and home.

"It was a very touching story she told me over the fence, and I was really interested in all she had to say. I just sensed, too, that she needed a friend. So I thought it was so important to stop and talk with her for a while.

"As I left, I said, 'Good-bye.' And I started walking down the road. But then she cried out, and said, 'You know what?' And I stopped and turned around, just as she said so sweetly, 'You know, it's kind of nice to meet a friend once in a while . . . isn't it?' "

A big smile parted Walkin' Jim's whiskers. Almost as if he were thinking aloud to himself, he just spoke a real low, long ". . . yeah."

And so did I.

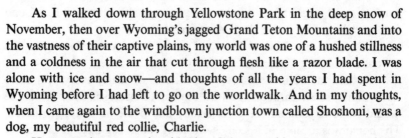

As I walked down through Yellowstone Park in the deep snow of November, then over Wyoming's jagged Grand Teton Mountains and into the vastness of their captive plains, my world was one of a hushed stillness and a coldness in the air that cut through flesh like a razor blade. I was alone with ice and snow—and thoughts of all the years I had spent in Wyoming before I had left to go on the worldwalk. And in my thoughts, when I came again to the windblown junction town called Shoshoni, was a dog, my beautiful red collie, Charlie.

He was only two weeks old when I'd gotten him. It was now eleven years almost to the day since he had been mistaken for a coyote by a steady-eyed rancher, and shot.

Back then, as it was now, the Wyoming sky above Shoshoni had been sullen with early winter, and the sagebrush heavy with snow. I had been a twenty-one-year-old uranium prospector. Charlie, who had not yet known two years in this world, had been right where he belonged—in the freedom of the outdoors, where there was always a jackrabbit to be chased.

Together constantly, and with only one another for company, Charlie and I had spent the summer living one of the most magical times imaginable, camped deep in the interior of the remote Red Desert.

I had been sent there to look for uranium, only to discover that the natural wonders were the far richer treasure.

But then the early winter, so normal to these mile-high plains and granite ranges, blew in. And with its bitter winds came tragedy.

The rancher who pulled the trigger did not know the dog in his rifle's scope was anything but wild. He did not know it was someone's best friend. He didn't realize there *was* anyone else on that remote slope of Copper Mountain. He didn't know—until he came to claim the pelt, and saw my anguished face.

I did not hear the shot that shattered Charlie's spine. But I would never forget the sight of him dragging his shattered body across the virgin snow on the slope, a trail of red following him and his large, baffled brown eyes all the way to my boots. Or the agony in my voice as I knelt in the snow beside my friend for hours and cried out his dear name again, and again, and again, well into the freezing night. From none other had I known such love and faithfulness, or such delight in life. For Charlie, as well as for me, life had held little pain—until that tragic afternoon.

Now, I sat staring at the gray stone of Copper Mountain thinking of Charlie and the Red Desert, because there was more than just a dog buried up there in all that lonesome scrub and rock. There was also a boy buried somewhere up there, too—the boy I had been before my heart began to set into that of a man.

I thought about crossing the fields to climb that mountain, to visit for the first time since that day the barren ledge with the lone yucca plant where I finally buried Charlie. I had, after all, promised on my knees to come back someday to that pile of stones.

But I couldn't. Instead, I walked on in the opposite direction.

For me, the snow on Copper Mountain was still too red to bear.

46

The mellow smells of fresh pine sap, roasted ham, and burning cottonwood logs filled the old farmhouse where I was spending my last Christmas on the road. I leaned forward on the edge of my wooden chair, letting the stout cast-iron stove warm my hands and face.

I had expected to be walking this day, then curling up somewhere at night in a field, with nothing more than cold toes and homesickness for company. But instead I had found myself invited to spend one more holiday in yet another loving and caring home.

Though my hosts, Robert and Vickie Prillman, and their three little children were now asleep in their beds, and their other guests had long since gone home, the signs of a joyful day still lay scattered all about me. Last night, it had been the Christmas tree resplendent in glitter and surprises; tonight, it was the floor. With Cooties, Masters of the Universe, dumbbells, Preppy Bears, moon boots, half-licked candy canes, and evil-eyed robots underfoot, certainly no toe was safe.

The lights on the tree were unplugged, the kitchen had finally cooled down, and a soft bed awaited me. But a part of me persisted in staying awake awhile longer. I was thinking of how much more special and dear America was becoming to me in these last miles and months of the worldwalk. And not just because it *was* my home. But, rather, because it held the most stunning scenery, the most abundant wildlife, and some of the freest people I had met anywhere in the world.

Where else but in an empty Yellowstone Park could I have gone soaking in the buff in an old steamy hot spring, with two feet of snow all around, only to have forty-four wild bison, each probably weighing more than half a ton, come and plop down around my "hot tub" to stare at me with horned amusement. When I had been forced eventually to crawl forth from the thick, swirling volcanic fog and walk, hunchbacked and wide-eyed, between all those snorting dark giants, they had let me be, only making me jump like a bullfrog once, when a particularly curious bull took a quick sniff at my behind with a pair of icy-cold nostrils.

While following the old Lewis and Clark Trail across southern Washington, Idaho, and Montana, my eyes and my soul had feasted on rugged whitewater rivers and thickly forested mountain ranges still virtually unchanged from the time the first trappers and mountain men had passed that way two hundred years before. "Life consists with wilderness," wrote Henry David Thoreau of his beloved outdoors in the early part of the last century. "The most alive is the wildest."

I still got goose bumps when I thought back to that Fourth of July night in Seattle when I'd gazed from high above the harbor at the hundreds of white-hulled sailboats gathering below, then gasped in delight again, and again, and again, as a fantasia of fireworks blossomed above my head, only to be multiplied a thousand times over in the mirrored windows of that futuristic city's skyscrapers. It was two hundred years since the signing of America's Constitution, and she was still the world's major stronghold of personal freedoms and opportunities.

Already on this Christmas night, I was missing people like Barry and Martha Horn in Casper, Wyoming, who had feasted me with my first Thanksgiving dinner on my worldwalk. Even though those around me were saying it was the worst of times economically in Wyoming, that jobs in the uranium mines and on the oil rigs were very few, the table I was seated at that night would have looked to most of the world like a scene from a prince's dream.

People. That was what America was all about. People like Mary Higgins, the "Apple Cider Lady" in Snohomish, Washington, who quenched my thirst at her roadside stall then insisted I go home with her to "put some meat on them bones." People like Mark and Clara Sue in Seattle, who had put me up for ten days in their home because a relative of theirs in Columbus, Ohio, had written and asked them to do so. People like LeRoy Little Bull on the Yakima Indian Reservation in southeast Washington, who had walked with me, sharing his dreams of being a journalist, and then invited me to stay with his family. People like Bill Myers, a policeman in Lewiston, Idaho, who took me to a warm church basement to sleep out of the rain. People like Kirt Miller in Missoula, Montana, a rock singer who took me on the road for four days with his band to show me why he loved entertaining others. People like Quincy

O'Haire, a Kentucky "hillbilly rebel" who lived in a cozy home made from a school bus in the hills outside of Bozeman, Montana, and whose "New York Jewish" wife, Rae, stuffed me royally on their "almost organic" farm eggs and large dinners made with the discards from the local supermarkets. People like Bruce McCormack, the editor of the *Cody Enterprise* newspaper in Wyoming, who drove over two hundred miles so his young daughter, Molly, who had been reading my *Capper's* stories all through elementary school, could finally meet me. And especially people like Mel and Rosalie Eaton, near tiny Linch, Wyoming, because they represented so well the notion that home is where the heart is.

With a pair of hosts who liked to think of visitors as part of the family, I couldn't help but love those days I had spent with Mel and Rosalie, sharing the warmth of their wood-burning potbellied stove, the snugness of their old farmhouse kitchen, their delicious home-cooked meals.

And yet, for all the homey comforts I had known with them, it still had seemed to me that if anyone had a lot to complain about, it would have been those who had to earn their living from the dusty soil of that interminably flat part of America. And so I had asked what it was about the prairie that made them love it so much.

"I love the wind," Rosalie said, almost right away. "Lots of farmers' wives get really depressed by it, but I really love it. It is my friend. It cleans the air, keeps it clear, prunes the trees. Why, I love the way it flaps the laundry on the clothesline, and even how it howls around the chimney —'Listen to that, Mel!' I'll suddenly say when it gets really going."

Making his wiry figure comfortable in his "hibernating spot" at the potbellied stove's side, Mel had explained contentedly, "All those doctors and lawyers in the cities work so hard all their lives so they can move to a little place in the open country and spend their last few years living like I'm doing. So I figured out early on, why not just stay right where I am, since this is what all the others want so much to have in the first place."

So many times, as on this Christmas night, I had paused alone with my memories of all those across the face of the earth who had done their best to make me feel like a son or a brother. Every time I had felt so proud and humble at the same time that I didn't know whether to cry or smile.

I could never again believe that we were a planet without hope and a future. The newspapers might print all they wanted, the leaders might scorn and condemn till their faces were blue, but I knew better. Love—yes, Love—was truly everywhere on this most wondrous globe. And where there was Love, I knew there was God. He was still with us as much as ever, and always would be.

From earlier experience, I knew that if there were two things the prairie could be counted on for, it was dust storms in the summer and blizzards in the winter. And so I had been deeply worried as far back as Australia about crossing that part of America in the months of December, January, and February. I had felt sure that there was no way I could get across America's heartland in those months without being caught in at least one monstrous snowstorm and many weeks of sub-zero weather.

Mother Nature, however, had other ideas. From Christmas on, the weather was more like summer than winter. Never again that winter did the temperatures go below freezing for more than a day or two, and snow was as rare as a farmer who was making money. In early January 1987, in eastern Nebraska, I found myself sweating profusely in temperatures as high as the mid-80's! It was absolutely nuts. The same Gore-Tex jacket that had seen me through minus-25-degree temperatures in Yellowstone Park and served as my ground cloth the three nights in the Teton Mountains when I slept in my sleeping bag on knee-deep snow was now useless baggage.

With my sleeves rolled up and mud on my cuffs, I could have sworn that I had the months turned around, that the days were melting into June, rather than February. There I was with enough bird chatter around me to drive any tomcat to torment! I wanted to throw away my mittens and parka. But fortunately I listened to those farmers like Harold Schippert of Rockport, Missouri, and his ninety-year-old mom, Minnie, who cautioned me that Nature had a tendency to be as confounding as any man alive.

47

The faint, almost inaudible *schhhliffff* of a clump of snow falling to the ground from a tree limb made me stir restlessly in my sleeping bag. The big snow had finally arrived. And so had my last morning on the worldwalk. It was April Fool's Day, 1987—the day I came to the end of the long road around the world that began on my childhood home's front porch, and would end there.

A big, wet, fluffy snowflake landed on the hair sticking out the end of the sleeping bag. It felt sort of like a big feather prodding me to get up and face the truth—that after twenty countries and more than fifteen thousand miles of logged walking time, after what seemed a lifetime's worth of tears and laughter and worry and hopes and discoveries and new friends, I was only eight miles from realizing the dream I had had as a nine-year-old.

I knew I should have been thrilled to have done the "impossible." But instead I was as sad as I was happy. How for the love of God could I expect to settle back into one spot now, with only one set of acquaintances, when I knew that my real home encompassed dozens of nations, and my family inhabited a large part of this planet? Would restlessness be my curse from now on?

The sound of something small stepping clumsily, though lightly, past me pulled me from my thoughts. Slowly, I peered from the warm darkness of the bag into the grayness of a dawn that wasn't quite sure of itself. I blinked from the pure whiteness each spindly limb and fattening bud of the maple forest was coated with. Then, through the wisps of smoke still rising from the ashes of my campfire, I saw it, only a few feet away. It was a wobbly fawn, its beautiful delicate coat speckled in the white of both its youth and the snow of this earth. In its soft brown eyes I could see it was wondering just what sort of strange forest creature *I* might be.

"You be careful, little fella. Okay?" I whispered.

It only looked at me innocently, twitched its little nose, and went on looking for its momma. For it, the world was still without fear.

The sun shone brilliantly that morning from one of the bluest skies I had ever seen. The land that had been so gray and foreboding on the same date four years ago now sparkled as if coated in finely ground diamonds.

By the hundreds, the people of Bethel came to meet me that crisp, fine morning: their smiles and happy voices stretched for a mile behind me. Students, housewives, doctors, clerks, mechanics, farmers, teachers, executives, shopkeepers, babies, grandparents, friends, enemies, neighbors, strangers . . . they kept coming and coming. It was all I could do to keep my tears inside. Never had I imagined that so many cared so deeply about the man who had left a fool four years ago.

It was the middle of the week, and many had had to take off from their jobs or skip out of school. Yet they had poured forth from our little spot in the universe to let me know—*really* know—that my pilgrimage had not been a solitary one.

Those fourteen thousand or so final steps to my front porch added up to the happiest hours of my life. And, I was proud to know, some of Bethel's, too. Behind me was a stream of large and brightly colored flags —those of every nation I had walked across, including the Stars and Stripes of my own. Each had been made by hand by the home-economics classes at the high school, and now their blue, red, white, green, yellow, and gold colors furled and unfurled in the gentle breeze like something in a medieval crusade. The sidewalks were crowded, and there were welcoming signs on all the shop windows along Plane Street. The tears pressed all the harder at the corners of my eyes.

A very, very proud elderly lady stepped timidly from the crowds along the sidewalks and placed a small American flag in my hand. On the marquee of the old theater were the words RETURN OF THE WORLDWALKER, which made me smile all the wider and wave the little flag more proudly. I saw the new mayor, Roger Hardin, who had spent months preparing the homecoming, and I gave him an extra big wave of thanks. I saw so many of my former classmates and neighbors. And then, at last, I saw the one thing I'd wanted for so, so long to see—*home.*

The tears that poured from my soul to my eyes when I stepped onto the porch to embrace my crying mother were not sudden. They had been falling since the red brick walls of my home first caught my eye while I was struggling to get through the crowd that had spilled onto Charity Street.

When I could finally bring myself to turn and look over the mass of humanity jostling to get even closer, I wiped my hand across my blurry eyes and said simply, in a breaking voice, to all those beaming faces:

"I love you. I shall never forget you, the rest of my life."

I squeezed my mother a little tighter, swallowed and continued:

"When I left this same front porch almost to this very minute all those years ago, there were those who warned that only a nightmare could come from such foolishness as walking around the world. To be so trusting of so many people was asking to lose everything, especially my life, they warned. Still, I ventured forth . . . I had to know the truth.

"And what is that truth I have found?

"It is that Love still lives as strongly as ever. Maybe even stronger than ever.

"It is that I am your son and your brother. And you are more than just my neighbors. You are my family.

"It is that goodness reigns over evil. That for all the ugliness and hurt we see each day, there are a million times more acts of compassion and beauty going unnoticed.

"It is that I am lonely without you beside me, sharing in both the sadness and the joy of this magic force we call life. For you are my friends, too.

"Finally"—I looked into my mother's eyes—"it is that home sweet home was where I belonged all along."

Mom kissed me again and turned to lead me back through the front door. And as the cheers and shouts of the crowd rose in one final display of emotion, I knew that it was the acts of love from the people I had met —and the people who had cheered me on—that had enriched my life beyond description.

To me the people all over the world were the true heroes of the worldwalk. They deserved the cheers and tears of my homecoming in Bethel that crisp, snow-covered morning.

I only walked. They did much more. They loved me—again and again. For that, I owed them so much.

And so what I wanted to say was, Thank you, World, for making your home my home. My heart and mind shall never forget you.

I looked at the smiling faces of my brothers and my littlest sister, Sandy, waiting for me just inside the door.

And then I paused for just a second to take a red rose from a bouquet Sandy was cradling in her arms. There was one more trip I wanted to make that morning, one more person to let know I had made it home again, safe and sound.

Index

Abell, Greg, 14, 132, 265
Aborigines, Australian, 378, 382, 384
Adelaide, Australia, 361, 383, 386, 388, 396, 397
Adriatic Sea, 255, 271
Adventures of Huckleberry Finn, The (Twain), 15, 77
Aeroflot, 306–307
Afghanistan, 309
Africa, 169, 176, 199, 206, 211–250, 393
Agra, India, 321
Agri, Turkey, 302, 307
Ajad (Jhattipur friend), 317, 318–319
Alain (Swiss student), 211
Albania, 273
Alcalá de Chisvert, Spain, 194
Alcira, Spain, 200
alcoholism, 113
Alexander the Great, 309
Alexandria, Egypt, 283
Algeciras, Spain, 208, 211
Algemesí, Spain, 197
Algeria, 233–246, 278
    border guards in, 230, 232–233
    customs officials in, 244
    departure from, 244–245
    entry into, 230–231, 232–233
    escape from killer in, 234–235
    hospitality in, 233–234, 239–240, 245–246
    people of, 239–240, 245–246
    police in, 240–245, 278
    ruggedness of, 237–238

scenery in, 238
war of independence of, 240
Algiers, U.S. embassy in, 249
Ali, Muhammad, 275
Alicante, Spain, 201
Alice Springs, Australia, 361–362, 382–383
Allah, 295, 312
Allahabad, India, 329–330
alligators, performing, 278–279
Almería, Spain, 191, 207–208
almond harvesting, 181–183
Almusafes, Spain, 196–197
Americans, conceptions about, 120, 184–185, 220, 222, 239, 242, 245, 278, 298–300, 307, 364–365, 390
Amiot, Alain, 160
Ankara, Turkey, 300
Annaba, Algeria, 278
antinuclear protesters, 149
apathy, English, 144
Ararat Mountain, 297
Argentré-du-Plessis, France, 161–162
Ariadaha, Calcutta, 335
Armenia, 296
Armiñana Sanchez, José Antonio, 201
Athens, Greece, 283, 305–307, 309
    U.S. embassy in, 309
Athens, Ohio, 24–26
Athens International Airport, 305–307
Atlantic City, N.J., 49–52, 300
Australia, 360–404
    "Dead Heart" of, 362

drought in, 400–401
farmers in, 400–402
final stretch in, 396, 397–402
gold prospectors in, 366–370
hospitality in, 400
meals in, 360, 367, 377, 384, 396, 401
newspaper work in, 402–404
sheep farming in, 398–399
see also Northern Territory, Australia; outback, Australian; South Australia
Awadhesh (Nirsa police officer), 333–334
Ayers Rock, Australia, 383
Azzaba, Algeria, 240–241

Baba (Indian host), 323, 325–326, 328
Bainbridge, Ohio, 20–21
Bakewell, England, 145
Baltimore, Md., 46
bandits, 296–297, 308–309, 340, 343–347
Bangkok, Thailand, 337–339, 340, 341, 354
   shoppers in, 338–339
Barcelona, Spain, 172, 175
Barcelona, University of, 179
Barker, Ella and Sandy, 17
bathhouses:
   French, 290
   Turkish, 290–291
Bayram Kurban, 295
Beehive pizza parlor, Coolville, 26
Beirut, U.S. Marines in, 308
Bekir, Aydi, 294–296
Bel Air, Md., 46
Belfast, Northern Ireland, 41, 121–123
Belpre, Ohio, 26–29
Benares, India, 330–332
Ben Franklin Bridge, 46
Benicasim, Spain, 195
Beni Ounif, Algeria, 231
Benkovac, Yugoslavia, 265
Bernard, Eddie, 46
Bethel, Ohio, 7–10, 321, 339, 355, 400, 421–422
Bethel Cemetery, 321
Bethel-Tate High School, 5, 307, 361

Bhattacharyya, Madan Mohan, 334–335
Bhopal, India, 312
Big Lake, Wash., 408
Big Sky, Mont., 413
Bihar, India, 334
bintabat, 340
birds, giant, 128–129, 130–132
bison, 417
blackberry trenches, 112–113
Blackpool, England, 281
boars, 236–237, 238
Bolton, England, 143, 159
Bolton Marathon, 143
Bosporus Strait, 292
Boston, Mass., 80–81, 82, 83–84
Boucher, Marie-Jo, 217–218, 219
Bourg-Madame, France, 165
Bourneville, Ohio, 19
boxing, Thai, 341–342, 347
Boyne, Battle of the, 109
Bozeman, Mont., 412–414, 418
Brahmi, Abdel Ilakim, 239, 240
Breda Park, Mount Oriel, 123
Briquebec, France, 153
Brittain, Parks D., 9
Brittany, 158, 296
Britton, Neal, 54
Buddha, 340, 348–349, 350
Buddhadasa, the Venerable, 350
Buddhism, Buddhists, 331–332, 340, 348–351
Bulgaria, 307
Bulgarians, 292
bull ants, 362–364
Butte, Mont., 410–411
Butterworth, Malaysia, 339

Calcutta, India, 309, 323, 332, 334–335
   American Express office in, 339
Caldecott, England, 146–148
Calders, Spain, 180–186
California, 181, 184
Cambodia, 338
Cambridge, Mass., 83–84
Campbell, Mildred, 120
Campbell, Samuel, 120–121
Canas, Jordi, 176–179
Canas, Muntsa, 176–178

Canet Selva, Alfredo, 197–200
Cantinella, Italy, 253
Capper's Weekly, 15, 19, 122, 125,
    158, 207, 213, 384, 396, 418
caravan people, 103–105
    see also gypsies
Carcagente, Spain, 200–201
Caribre, Aine, 109
Caribre, Caitlin, 108–111
Caribre, Fiacre O., 106–108, 110
Caribre, Roisin, 106
Cartagena, Spain, 205
Casablanca, Morocco, 217
Casper, Wyo, 5, 8, 44, 277, 377, 417
Casper Star-Tribune, 5
castle, forgotten, 326
Castle Douglas, Scotland, 126
Catholic Church, 138–139
CBS Network News, 6, 82
Cecil (Aurora bartender), 33
Chadli, Bendjedid, 233
Charlene (Wyoming girlfriend), 8, 15
Charlie (collie pup), 168–169, 414–
    415
Charlie (gold prospector), 368
Chase, Helen, 69–74
Chase, Reverend James, 70–73
Cherbourg, France, 151, 153, 154,
    159, 166
Cherchell, Algeria, 234
Chevy Chase, Md., 32
children, curious, 196, 201, 239, 412
chapatis, 354
CHiPs, 165
Chomper, Claus von (alligator), 279
Christmas, 320–321, 416–419
churra, 200
CIA (Central Intelligence Agency),
    268, 312
cigarettes, 192–193
Cincinnati, Ohio, 53
Cincinnati Post, 207
circus, in Kaválla, 278–282
Clay, Father, 38–41, 42–46, 412
Clinger (backpack), 13, 23, 35, 151–
    152, 360, 397
    American flag on, 58, 149, 289
Clive (prospector), 367–369
Clover Creek, 364
Cody Enterprise, 418

Cold Spring, N.Y., 58
collie dogs, 120, 256–259
Columbus, Ohio, 417
Columbus Dispatch, 15, 158, 207
communication, nonverbal, 289
Continental Divide, 410, 411
Coober Pedy, Australia, 389, 392
Cooley mountains, 110
Coolie, Johnny B., 384–385
Coolville, Ohio, 26
Copake, N.Y., 68
Copper Mountain, 414–415
Cork, Ireland, 100
corruption, police, 308, 332
Cosette (La Mothe–St. Heray friend),
    160
Cousteau, Jacques, 194
cowboy hat, 280, 282
Croatia, 264–270, 273
crowds, curious, 289, 323–324
Cruell, Imma, 181–186
Cruell, Pep, 180–185
Cruell, Pepit, 182, 183–184
Cruell, Pol, 183–184
Cuesta del Gallo (Rooster Hill), 205
Cumbria Mountain range, 135

Daily Log Book, 15, 18, 34
Daily Worker, 56
Daily World, 55–57
Dallas, 165, 239
Dallas Cowboys, 160
dancers, phone, 77, 78–79
Darwin, Australia, 360, 361, 364, 383,
    385
Darwin High School, 361
Delaware River, 46
Depression, Great, 410
Dew Drop Inn, Cold Spring, 58–62
D-for-Dog (dog), 367, 369, 370, 371–
    372
Dickerson (prospector), 366–368, 369
Djemaa El Fna, Morocco, 222–223
Drogheda, Ireland, 105–111
Dromara, Northern Ireland, 119
    police station in, 119
Dublin, Ireland, 84, 87, 96–102
    departure from, 101–102
    impressions of, 96
Dundalk, Ireland, 113

Dun Laoghaire, Ireland, 95
dust storm, 389
Dynasty, 239

Earl's Court Station, 89, 92
Eaton, Elmer, 58–60, 61
Eaton, Mel and Rosalie, 418
Edna (Manchester hostess), 142
Egypt, 283, 284
El Bahri, Abdelaziz, 246
El Candil, Murcia, 203
Eleskirt, Turkey, 297–303, 307
El Kala, Algeria, 242–244
Elliot, Ron, 384–385
Emerson Elementary School, 412
Engelhardt, Anna Olley, 59–60, 61–62
England, 87–95, 134–149
   anti-Irish sentiment in, 95
   churches in, 136
   economy of, 143–144
   fish and chips in, 94
   India and, 308, 333, 353
   lack of public drinking fountains in, 136
   North vs. South in, 143
   people of, 143, 144
   stone walls in, 134–136
   towns in, 144
Erzurum, Turkey, 296
Estaline (Virginia widow), 30–32
Esteve, Rafael, 198–200
Evans, Jodie, 32–33, 35–36

Fambry, Charles, 9–10, 142, 143
Farmer, Ferdinand, 38
Farmer House, Philadelphia, 38–39, 42
farmers, family vs. corporate, 400–402
fawn, 420–421
Fayetteville, Ohio, 17, 18
fear, 332–333, 342, 346–347
"Feast of the Sacrifice," 295
Fernandez, John, 355
Fez, Morocco, 225
Figuig, Morocco, 231, 232
fires, 373, 375, 378–379
firewalking ritual, 351–354, 355, 363–364
fish and chips, first, 94
Flamingo Road, 165

flash floods, 380–382
flies, in Australia, 365
Flinders, Matthew, 365
Flying Doctor Service, 387
France, 151–166, 178, 192, 198
   Americans in, 164–166
   eating in, 163–164, 192
   language barrier in, 158–160
   laundry in, 290
   music in, 165
   northwestern, 153
   people of, 152, 160, 163, 164–165
   poverty in, 158
   spiritualness of, 314
   television in, 165
   World War II and, 153–158
Francesca (Italian host), 258–259
Franco, Francisco, 179
frescoes, Italian, 259
fruit bats, 371–372

Gallipoli, Turkey, 403
Gandhi, Indira, 312
Gandhi, Mohandas K., 333
Ganges Plains, 314
Ganges River, 329, 330–331, 332, 334, 335
   bathing in, 334–335
   dirtiness of, 334
Gavray, France, 153–157
George (Ohio coal miner), 19
Germany, Federal Republic of, 288, 328
Germon, Greg, 366–368
Giuseppe (Italian host), 256–259
gold, 366–367
   prospecting for, 366–372
Gormanstown, Ireland, 103
Gougeon, Xavier, 160
graffiti, 38, 39, 46
Grand Palace, Bangkok, 341, 366
Grand Teton Mountains, 414, 419
Great Barrington, Mass., 75
Great Bazaar, Istanbul, 292
Great Potato Famine, 104
Great Victoria Desert, 384–395
Greece, 276–282, 283, 285, 307
   circus in, 278–282
   farmers in, 276–278
Gregory, Ron, 385

G. T. (Grand Turk) Road (Royal
    Route), 309, 313, 314, 317,
    323, 326, 329, 332
Guinness, 99
Güney Köyü, Turkey, 294–296
gypsies:
    Irish, 103–105
    Turkish, 285–287, 330
    Yugoslavian, 275

Hacihamza, Turkey, 294
halfway point, 296, 303
Halley's comet, 399–400
Hani, Brenda, 279–282, 314
Hani, Mario, 278, 281, 282
Harayana, India, 318
Hardin, Roger, 421
Hari Raya, 355
Harvard University, 83–84
health, concerns about, 92–93, 311,
    313–314
Heasley, Connie, 123
heat, tropical, 342–343, 354–355
helicopters, 115–121
Hemel Hempstead, England, 148–149
    Police Club of, 149
Higgins, Mary, 417
Hilary (Manchester host), 142–144
Hillsboro, Ohio, 19
Himalayas, 331, 332
Hindus, 310, 329–331, 351–354
    death and, 330–331
    firewalking by, 352–354
    Ganges River revered by, 335–336
Hoagland, Ohio, 17–18
Hoffman London Circus, 278–282
Holyhead, England, 93, 94–95
homecoming, 421–423
homesickness, 119, 148, 151, 199,
    252–253, 397
Horn, Barry and Martha, 417
Horsham, Australia, 402
Horsham, Mail-Times, 402
Hotel Divan, Agri, 307–308
Hourud, Emil, 410
Hsüan-tsang, 311
Hugh Sands Folk Group, 110–111
Humpty Doo, Australia, 364
hunting knife, 22, 214, 215

Iberian Peninsula, 175
Idaho, 417
immunization shots, 92–93
India, 311, 312–335, 338, 349
    approach toward, 311
    attack by homeless in, 326
    curious crowds in, 323–324, 326–
        327
    entry into, 312, 313–314
    peacefulness of, 314–315
    planned route through, 314
    police in, 323, 332–333, 334
    preconceptions about, 311, 312, 314
    primitiveness of, 317–318
    religions in, 320
    soldiers in, 314
    spiritualism in, 314–315
    temples in, 313, 315–316, 320, 330
    unemployment in, 318
    villages in, 317
    war of independence of, 333
    women in, 319–320
Indus River, 311
Inecik, Turkey, 289–292
International Guest House, 325–328
interrogations, police:
    in Algeria, 230, 232, 240–243
    in Morocco, 213–214
    in Turkey, 298–302
    in Washington, D.C., 284–285
    in Yugoslavia, 266–270
IRA (Irish Republican Army), 114
Iran, 274, 288, 293, 296, 307–308
Iran-Iraq war, 293, 307–308
    American business and, 307–308
Iraq, 288–293
Ireland, Republic of, 41, 96–114, 121–
    122
    alcoholism in, 113–114
    blackberry trenches in, 112–113
    gypsies in, 103–105
    people of, 113–114, 143, 144
    poverty in, 103–105
    security dogs in, 114–115
    television in, 165
Irish Sea, 93, 95
irrigation, desert, 374–375
Irving, Father Bryan, 137–141, 143
Islamabad, Pakistan, 311

Istanbul, Turkey, 287, 288, 292–293, 307, 366
  history of, 292
  Iranian consulate in, 293
Italy, 170, 249, 250–260, 270
  impressions of, 251–252, 255, 270
  police in, 251
  route through, 255

James, Jimmy and Mrs., 146–148
James II, king of England, 109
JanSport, 6, 397
Japan, 308, 402
Jaquith, Clifford, 221, 223–225
Jaquith, Rina, 220–222, 223–225, 376
Játiva, Spain, 202
Jerry (Manchester host), 142–144
Jesuit house, Philadelphia, see Farmer House
Jesuits' residence, Dublin, 96–100
Jews, anti-Semitism and, 213, 298
Jhattipur, India, 317–319
Joe the Bouncing Czech, 366, 367, 369
John Paul II, pope, 112, 139
Juan (Spanish soldier), 211

Kaled (Tebaba host), 246
Kali, 335
Kansas City, Mo., 384
Karachi, Pakistan, 307, 308, 309
Karah, The Great, 278–279
Katherine, Australia, 374, 376, 383
Kaválla, Greece, 278–282
Khomeini, Ayatollah Ruhollah, 274, 298
Khyber Pass, 309
Kickapoo, 354
Kiley, Dennis, 17
King, Martin Luther, Jr., 333
Kipling, Rudyard, 309
kite flying, 341
kopiahs, 354
Kosovo, 273–275

La Chapelle-Pontaneyaux, France, 218
Laddie (collie), 120
Lady of the Rockies, 411
Laessle, Wilona, 19
Lahore, Pakistan, 309, 312, 313

Lake District, England, 134–136
Lancaster, England, 136–141
"Land of Five Rivers," 311
Langenscheidt's Lilliput Dictionary, 295
language barriers, 130–131, 158–160, 286–287, 332
Laos, 268, 338
La Ribesa-Cabanes, Spain, 195
Larne, Northern Ireland, 123–125
Larrimah roadhouse, 374
Lassie, 165
Las Tapas, Santo Angel, 206–207
Last Whole Earth Catalog, 185
"Laundry Bomb" (Newman), 125
Lawson, Joan, 117
Lebanon, 245
leeches, 350
Lessay, France, 153
"Letter from Steven," 19
Lewis and Clark Trail, 417
Lewiston, Idaho, 417
Limoges, France, 159, 166, 192
Linch, Wyo., 418
Little Bull, LeRoy, 417
Liverpool, England, 386
Llords, Daniel, 19
London, England, 87–92, 146
  impressions of, 91
Londonderry, Ohio, 22
Lopes, Kevin, 54
Los Castaños, Spain, 207
Lourdes, France, 139
Ludwig, Dean, 46, 96
Luka's Goanna Grill, Mintabie, 385, 386

McAdam, John, 120–121
McClellan, Ian, 385–387, 388
McCormack, Bruce and Molly, 418
McDermott, Kevin, 54–55
MacDonald, Gary, 398–399
Macdonnell Range, 381
McMillan, Marlene and Ray, 410–411
Madrid, Spain, 188
maichee, 349
Malacca, Malaysia, 354
Malaysia, 339–340, 351–356
  firewalking in, 352–354
  fruits in, 354

meals in, 352, 354
Manchester, England, 142–144
Mandi (dog), 398–399
Mankar Sankranti, festival of, 329–330
Manresa, Spain, 177, 179
Maori, 404
Marengo, Wash., 409–410
Mariamman, 352, 353
marines, Algerian, 234–235
marines, U.S., 249, 308
Marla, Australia, 389
Marla Bore, Australia, 385
Marrakech, Morocco, 212–213, 215–216, 217, 219–225
Martin, Ralph, 392–394
Martinez, Angel, 203–207
Martinez, Felipe, 207
Martinez, Vincente, 203–207
Maryland, 32–33, 46
Massachusetts, 68–84
Matera, Italy, 255
Matlock, England, 145
Matthews, Bert, 396
Matthews, Peg, 384–385, 396, 402, 412
Mediterranean Sea, 190, 207, 208
Melbourne, Australia, 384, 395–397, 401, 402, 404, 412
Melbourne Cup, 387
Meric River, 285
Midnight Express, 284
military service, obligatory, 265, 292
milkshakes, Irish, 119
Milky Way, 374
Miller, Kirt, 417
Mills, Tom, 104
Milovan, Papich, 265–266
mine shaft, abandoned, 370–371
Mintabie, Australia, 384–388
missionaries, 314, 340
Missoula, Mont., 417
Mobley, Tammy, 26–27
Mohr, Reverend, 52
Moia, Spain, 176–179
monks, Buddhist, 348–351
  life-style of, 349–350
monsoon rains, 350
Montana, 5, 182, 410–414, 417, 418
Montenegro, 273, 275

Monty Python, 201
Moorhead family, 85, 88
Morocco, 170, 211–232
  beggars in, 218, 221, 226
  bus rides in, 216–219
  departure from, 231–233, 241
  dinner in, 239–240
  entry into, 211–216
  hustlers in, 214–216, 222–223
  Jews and, 213
  knife attack in, 214–215
  people of, 225–226
  police in, 215, 216–217, 232
  poverty in, 216, 218, 221, 226, 249–250
  runaway wagon in, 227–228
  taxi driver in, 214
  terrain of, 225
  theft in, 225
  violence in, 214–215, 221, 226
  warnings about, 211–212, 214
Morris, Robin, 412–413
Morris Nursing Home, 60, 253
Moscow, Soviet Union, 306–307
mosques, 292–293
mosquitoes:
  in Australian outback, 371–372
  at Mount Washington, 69–70
  in Wat Suan Moke, 349–351
Motel Sahara, Morocco, 232
Mother's Day, 253–254
Mount Isa, Australia, 383
Mount Orab, Ohio, 17
Mount Oriel, Northern Ireland, 122–123
Mount Oriel Clinic, 122
Mount Washington forest, 69, 74–75
Mourne mountains, 110
Murcia, Spain, 203–207
Muslims, 273–275, 310, 320, 354
  clothing of, 354
  hospitality of, 274–275, 296
  male-orientation of, 274–275
  morality of, 291
  Western influence on, 338
Myers, Bill, 417

National Geographic, 27, 44
National Guard, Butte, 411
national identification card, 241–242

Nebraska, 419
Nelsonville, Ohio, 398
Nepal, 331
Newark, N.J., 85
New Delhi, India, 318, 321, 323
New Guinea, 376
New Jersey, 46, 49–52, 85
Newman, Edwin, 252–253
Newman, Elliot, 252–253
Newman, Gary, 13, 14, 142, 253
Newman, Mary Ann, 13–14, 253
Newman, Sandra, 253
Newman, Steven:
    attacks on, 214–216, 326, 389–391
    birthdays of, 256–260
    climbing accident of, 204–205
    early life of, 5, 43–45, 140
    father of, 1–2, 4, 5–7, 252–253,
        320–321, 322, 324, 326
    mother of, 1–2, 4, 5, 7, 13, 14–15,
        21, 252–254, 321, 322
    murder witnessed by, 333
    talks given by, 40, 122, 412
Newry, Northern Ireland, 116–117
New York, N.Y., 53–57, 82–83
New York State, 58–68
New Zealand, 402
Ni Caribre, Drogheda, 107–111
Nickie (Athens taxi driver), 305–306
Nicole (French poet), 161–162
Nirsa, India, 333–334
Nitschke, Edith and William, 401–402
Nobie's General Store, Mintabie, 386,
    387
nonverbal communication, 289
Normandy, 151–159, 178, 296
North Egremont, Mass., 72
Northern Ireland, 41, 109, 114–125
    Americans in, 114
    farms in, 118–119
    security in, 116–117, 119, 121
    violence in, 115, 117, 120, 122, 123,
        124
Northern Territory, Australia, 360–
    384
    population of, 361
    see also outback, Australian

O'Bill, Bob and Mrs., 411
O'Haire, Quincey and Rae, 417–418

Ohio, 1–29, 368, 420–423
Ohio University, 5, 27, 284
O'Keefe, Father, 97
opal, search for, 391–394
opal miners, 384–389
Oran, Algeria, 232
Oropesa, Spain, 195
Oujda, Morocco, 231, 232, 233
Our Daily Bread soup line, 46
outback, Australian, 361–395
    beer drinking in, 364
    bull ants in, 362–364
    departure from, 395
    fires in, 373, 375, 378–379
    flash floods in, 380–381
    flies in, 365
    gold prospecting in, 366–369
    hardships in, 364–365, 383–384,
        389
    heat in, 363, 383, 388, 389
    irrigation in, 374–375
    life in, 377–378
    meals in, 360, 367, 377, 384
    night sky of, 374
    opal miners, 384–389, 391–394
    preparations for, 360–361
    route through, 361–362
    shotgun attack in, 389–391
    snakes in, 364–365
    telephoning in, 376
    towns in, 389
    water in, 374–375, 381–382
    wildlife in, 360, 367, 368, 370, 371,
        391
Oxford, England, 92–93

Pag Island, Yugoslavia, 268
Pakistan, 293, 306, 307, 308–312, 338
    beggars in, 308
    colorfulness of, 309, 310
    culture of, 311
    illiteracy in, 312
    land in, 309–310
    people of, 309–310
    poverty in, 310, 311
    route through, 308–309
    soldiers in, 311–312
    U.S. support of, 333
    warnings about, 309–310
Palermo, Italy, 251

Papua New Guinea, 377
Paris, France, 161
Parker Meridien Hotel, N.Y., 82–83
Parkersburg, W.Va., 29
Parkersburg News, 27
Parthenay, France, 158
Pathans, 309
Patrick, Saint, 109, 110, 112
Peace Arch, 408
Pennsylvania, 37–46, 341
People Express, 84–85
Peshawar, Pakistan, 309, 310
Peter (Australian cyclist), 129–133
Phet Buri, Thailand, 342, 343, 349, 355
Philadelphia, Pa., 37–41, 46, 412
Philadelphia Inquirer, 41
Philip (American adventurer), 211–212, 308–309
phome dancers, 77, 78–79
pilgrims, Hindu, 329–330
pineapple farmers, 345–346
Pine Plains, N.Y., 63–67
pit bull, 47–49
Poh, the Venerable, 350–351
Police Station Nirsa, 333
Polo, Marco, 294
Port Augusta, Australia, 395, 397
Port Lincoln, Australia, 391
Portsmouth, England, 149
Portugal, 175
prairie, U.S., 418–419
prasada, 315, 316
Prillman, Robert and Vickie, 416
protesters, antinuclear, 149
Puebla Larga, Spain, 201
Puerto de Tosas pass, 167, 169
Puigcerdá, Spain, 165
Punjab, 314
Pyrenees, 162–163, 165, 167–171

Rabat, Morocco, 217, 225, 226, 231
rabbits, huge, 127
Rafelguarde, Spain, 201–202
Railey, June, 38
Raithfriland, Northern Ireland, 117, 118
rats, 173–174
Rawalpindi, Pakistan, 310
Reading, England, 149

Reagan, Ronald, 179, 298
Red Desert, Wyo., 5, 25, 168, 182, 199, 414–415
Rennes, France, 158
Rescue Mission, Atlantic City, 51–52
Reynolds, Burt, 337
Ricky (Spanish hermit), 190–195
Roberts, Leon, 361
Robinson, Thomas, 123–125
rock climbing, 204–206
Rockport, Mo., 419
Rockwell, Norman, 72–73
Rocky boots, 16, 397
Roisin, Philippe, 192
Rome, Italy, 292
Romeo (Italian host), 258–259
Roo (golf cart), 361, 390, 397
Roos, Grandma, 60–61
Rooster Hill (Cuesta del Gallo), 205
Rose, Bruce, 373–379
Rose, Darlene, 373–379
Rose, Gerry, 373–379
Rose Cottage, Caldecott, 146–148
Rosie (Mintabie cook), 385
Rosie (Victoria Hotel worker), 90
Route 23, Mass., 76
Route 50, Ohio, 17, 22
Route 82, N.Y., 63
Route 344, N.Y. and Mass., 68
Route A6, England, 145
Route C3320, Spain, 196, 202
Route N1, Ireland, 112
Route N340, Spain, 192
Royal Route, *see* G. T. Road
Ruby (Farmer House cook), 38, 46
Rum Jungle, Australia, 383

Sahara Desert, 230–233
St. Georges-des-Gardes, France, 160
St.-Hilaire-du-Harcouet, France, 160
St. James cemetery, Gavray, 156–157
St. Joseph's Prep School, 37, 40
St. Joseph's University, 37
St.-Maixent, France, 160
St. Mary's, Bethel, 140
St. Sauveur-le-Vicomte, France, 153
Salvation Army, Atlantic City, 51
Salvation Army Transient House, 29
sandstorms, 207, 232, 233
Santo Angel, Spain, 206

Sarajevo, Yugoslavia, 265
sardines, 255–256
Saturday Evening Post, 72
Saudi Arabia, 211
Scarface, 233–235
Schippert, Harold and Minnie, 419
schoolhouse, abandoned, 409–410
Scotland, 100, 120–121, 126–133, 138
 giant birds in, 128–132
 huge rabbits in, 127
 peacefulness of, 126
 religion in, 138
Seattle, Wash., 377, 408, 417
security dogs, 114–115
Sentosa, Malaysia, 355
Shap, England, 134
sheep farming, 398–399
Shiva, 352
shoppers, in Bangkok, 338–339
*Short Happy Life of Francis
 Macomber, The* (Hemingway),
 237
Shoshoni, Wyo., 414
Shrewsbury, England, 93
shudra, 319
Siam, 338
Sicily, Italy, 249, 250–252
Sikhs, 312, 332
Simpang Lima, Malaysia, 351–353
Singapore, 343
sirap, 355
Slovenia, 274
Smith, Ivan C., 27–28
snakes, Australian, 364–365
Snohomish, Wash., 417
snowstorms, 167–170
Sofia, Bulgaria, 307
Sorbas, Spain, 207
South Australia, 383–395, 396, 397–
 400, 402–404
South Egremont, Mass., 72
Soviet Union, 296, 306–307, 333
Spain, 165, 167–208
 Americans and, 184, 196–197
 coastline of, 190
 coldness of, 167–170, 176–177
 economy of, 178–179, 198
 interior of, 187–188
 land of, 187, 203, 205

meals in, 178, 181–182, 184, 191–
 192, 200–201
 north of, 167–197
 people of, 172, 187–188, 206–207
 police in, 197–200
 poverty in, 175–176, 187
 prison cells in, 197
 rate through, 175, 188, 208
 rats in, 173–174
 snowstorm in, 167–169
 south of, 197–208
Spanish Communist party, 172
Spencer Gulf, Australia, 397
spiny anteater, 371
Stalder, Mary, 24–26, 32
Stallone, Sylvester, 83
Staten Island, N.Y., 54, 176
Stawell, Australia, 401
Stoltz, Walkin' Jim, 413–414
stone walls, 134–135
Storer, Winona and Melissa, 19
Strait of Gibraltar, 208, 212
Stranraer, Scotland, 126
Strickland, Bob, 382
Strong family, 64–67
Stuart Highway, 361, 381, 389
 kilometer post on, 383
 length of, 361
 population along, 361–362
 South Road of, 383
students, Iranian, 293
Sue, Clara and Mark (Seattle), 417
sunset, Spanish, 182–183
Sunshine, 80
Super Bowl, 338
Surat Thani, Thailand, 349–350
Surber, Dan, 27–28

Taconic State Park, 68–69, 74–75
Taj Mahal, 321, 326
Tamils, 353
Tangier, Morocco, 208, 212–216, 298
 impressions of, 215–216
Tarragona, Spain, 171
Tastee Freeze, Hoagland, 17
Taza, Morocco, 226–227
Tebaba, Tunisia, 245–246
Tehran, Iran, U.S. embassy in, 308
television, 165, 239

temples:
  Indian, 313, 315–316, 320, 330
  Malay, 351–352, 353
  Sikh, 331
  Thai, 340, 349
Tennent Creek, Australia, 383
Thailand, 312, 337–351, 366
  American influence in, 337–339
  bandits in, 340, 343–347
  boxing, 341–342, 346–347
  Buddhism in, 340
  Buddhist monks in, 340, 348–351
  police in, 343, 346
  preconceptions about, 338–339
  rural people of, 340
  temples of, 340, 349
  visa extension for, 339–340
  wats in, 349–350
  wealth in, 338–339
Thames River, 91
Thanksgiving, 417
Thibault, Guy, 163–164
Thibault, Isabelle, 163–164, 168
Thoreau, Henry David, 417
Three Silly Gooses (opal prospectors), 385–386
tikka dots, 329
Time Bandits, 201
Tiny (Aborigine cowboy), 373, 375–376, 378
Tito, Marshal (Josip Broz), 272, 274
Tom (London traveler), 88–93
Tom (opal miner), 388
Topeka, Kan., 15
Torreblanca, Spain, 195
Track, the, see Stuart Highway
Trapani, Italy, 250
Trigger (horse), 280–281, 282
truck drivers, Sikh, 332
trucks:
  Pakistani, 311
  Turkish, 288–289
  war supply, 307–308
Tucannon River Canyon, 409
Tunel de Sant Quirze, 171–173
Tunis, Tunisia, 244–245
Tunisia, 170, 240, 241, 244–246
Turkey, 283–303, 307–308, 321–322
  anti-Semitism in, 297–298
  bathhouse in, 290–291
  border-post commander of, 297–302
  border troops of, 285
  as commercial connection, 288
  departure from, 307–308
  hospitality ritual in, 294–295
  imprisonment in, 301–302
  interrogation in, 297–302
  jails of, 284
  land of, 296–297
  language of, 295
  meals in, 286, 291, 294–295
  police of, 284, 297–303, 307–308
  preconceptions about, 283–284
  robbers in, 296–297
  women in, 295
Turkish bath, 290–291
two-step snakes, 364–365

Ulster, see Northern Ireland
Union Carbide, 312
United States, 1–85, 408–423
  cultural influences of, 337–340
  foreigners' interest in, 99
  lifestyle in, 377, 408–409
  love for, 416–418
  military support of Pakistan by, 333
  nuclear arms in, 333
  prairie of, 418–419
  reentry into, 408
  unfriendliness in, 408–409
uranium prospecting, 5, 25, 182–183, 199
Uslu, Hasan Ali, 289–290, 291–292
Uttar Pradesh, India, 324
Uxbridge, England, 92

Valencia, Spain, 188, 201
Vancouver, Canada, 408
Varanasi, India, 330–332, 352
Venice, Italy, 256, 270, 292, 366
Victoria, Australia, 400–404
Victoria Hotel, London, 90
Victoria Station, London, 89
Vietnam War, 268, 338, 398
Vinton County, Ohio, 22
Virginia, 29–32
Virgin Mary, 411
Voice of America, 376

wagon, runaway, 226–229

Wales, 94
Wall Street Journal, 84
Wamsutter, Wyo., 168
Ward, David, 402
Ward, Frank, 402, 404
Ward, Ian, 402
Warracknabeal, Australia, 402–404
Warracknabeal *Herald,* 402–404
Warren, Flo, 65–67, 103
Washington, D.C., 6, 92
    Pakistani embassy in, 308
    police in, 284–285
    Turkish embassy in, 284–285
Washington Post, 82, 267, 300
Washington State, 408–410, 413, 417
watermelon farmers:
    Australian, 374–379
    Greek, 276–278
wats, 340, 349–351
Wat Suan Moke, 349–351
Weekly Reader, 207
Western Creek Station, 373
West Virginia, 29, 33–34
Whitie's Bar, Aurora, 33
Wichita, Kan., 340
Wickham, Greg, 367, 369–372
William Brooks Shoe Company,
    Nelsonville, 6, 397–398
William III, king of England, 109
Williams, Hank, 337
Wimmera Plain, Australia, 403
Wise, Gerald, 79, 80
Wise, Patricia, 78–80
Witness Book, 15, 28, 34, 154
    incriminating evidence of, 268–269
Worldwalk:
    doubts about, 18–19, 21, 22–23, 26–
        27, 29, 44–45, 188, 215–216,
        320–321, 346–347

halfway point of, 296, 303
lessons learned on, 373, 419, 422
original itinerary for, 3–4, 283, 402
preparing for, 5, 43–45
provisions for, 14–16, 33–36, 53,
    80–81, 168, 360
purpose of, 2–3, 4, 5, 35
World War II, 147–148, 376
    France and, 153–158
Wundersitz, Paul, 391–394
Wyoming, 1, 8, 182, 277, 321
    climbing accident in, 204–205
    Red Desert of, 5, 182, 199
    returning home through, 414–419
    snowstorm in, 168–169
    uranium prospecting in, 5, 25, 182,
        199

Xativa, Spain, 203

Yakima Indian Reservation, 417
Yamuna River, 326
Yellowstone Park, 414, 416, 419
YMCA, Lahore, 312
Yudda (dog), 256–259
Yugoslavia, 255, 264–275, 283
    economy in, 271–272
    military police in, 266–270
    music in, 271
    people of, 270, 271, 273, 274–275
    society in, 270–271

Zebus, 319
Ziama Mansouriah, Algeria, 239–240
Zlatan, Sabur, 265–267, 268
Zoellner, Ardys and Don, 361

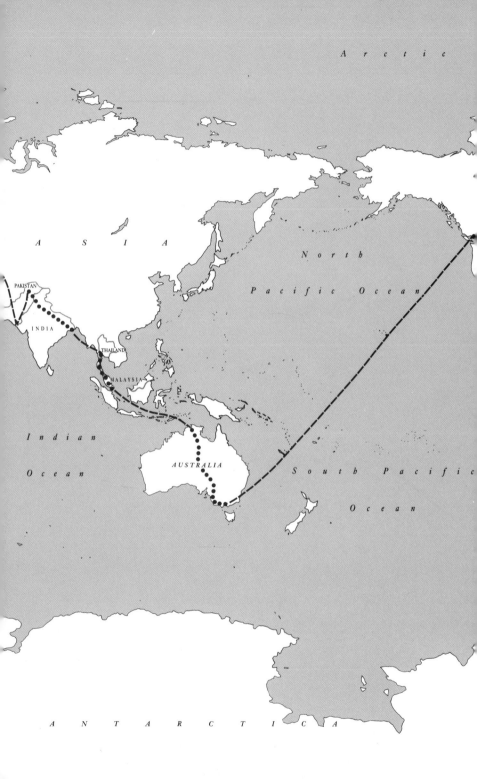